THE OHIO RIVER VALLEY SERIES

Rita Kohn and
William Lynwood Montell
EDITORS

Lion of the Forest

James B. Finley, Frontier Reformer

CHARLES C. COLE, JR.

THE UNIVERSITY PRESS OF KENTUCKY

Frontispiece: James B. Finley, 1781–1857

Copyright © 1994 by The University Press of Kentucky
Paperback edition 2010

Scholarly publisher for the Commonwealth,
serving Bellarmine University, Berea College, Centre
College of Kentucky, Eastern Kentucky University,
The Filson Historical Society, Georgetown College,
Kentucky Historical Society, Kentucky State University,
Morehead State University, Murray State University,
Northern Kentucky University, Transylvania University,
University of Kentucky, University of Louisville,
and Western Kentucky University.
All rights reserved.

Editorial and Sales Offices: The University Press of Kentucky
663 South Limestone Street, Lexington, Kentucky 40508-4008
www.kentuckypress.com

Publication of this book was assisted by a grant from the Indiana Humanities Council.

The Library of Congress has cataloged the hardcover edition as follows:

Cole, Charles Chester, Jr.
    Lion of the forest : James B. Finley, frontier reformer / Charles C. Cole, Jr..
        p.   cm.—(Ohio River Valley series)
    Includes bibliographical references and index.
    ISBN 0-8131-1863-8 (alk. paper)
    1. Finley, James B. (James Bradley), 1781–1857. 2. Pioneers—Ohio River Valley—
History. 3. Missionaries—Ohio River Valley—Biography. 4. Social reformers—Ohio
River Valley—Biography. 5. Ohio River Valley—Biography. I. Title. II. Series.
F518.F55C64 1994
287'.6'092—dc20
[B]   93-47932
ISBN 13- 978-0-8131-2969-3 (pbk. : alk. paper)

This book is printed on acid-free recycled paper meeting
the requirements of the American National Standard
for Permanence in Paper for Printed Library Materials.

Manufactured in the United States of America.

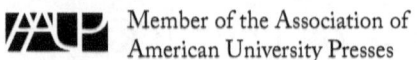

Member of the Association of
American University Presses

In memory of the Reverend Charles C. Cole (1890-1984)
and Kathryn Snyder Cole (1903-1992)

Contents

List of Illustrations	viii
Series Foreword	ix
Editors' Preface	xi
Author's Preface	xii
Chronology of James B. Finley's Life	xiv
1. The New Market Devil	1
2. The Expansion of Methodism in Ohio	14
3. Encounter with the Wyandots	40
4. Fight against the Federal Government	73
5. Power and Struggle	101
6. Crusade for Temperance	116
7. A Hero in Spite of Himself	129
8. The Prison Years	162
9. The Occasional Historian	182
10. The Last Years	213
Notes	220
Bibliographical Essay	249
Index	262

Illustrations

1. James B. Finley, 1781-1857	ii
2. A Page from Finley's Diary	11
3. Camp Meeting	32
4. Between-the-Logs, Wyandot Chief	53
5. Mononcue, Wyandot Chief	63
6. Wyandots at the Mission Church	67
7. The Lord's Prayer in the Wyandot Language	71
8. Ruins of the Wyandot Mission Church	98
9. Wyandot Mission Church after Restoration	99
10. Convicts Attending Church at the Ohio Penitentiary	167

Map

Darby's View of Ohio and Indiana	Endsheet

Tables

1. Population of Ohio	15
2. Membership in the Ohio Conference	15

Series Foreword

The impact of the Ohio River in the context of the larger American story gained widespread public attention as a result of the "Always a River: The Ohio River and the American Experience" project sponsored by the National Endowment for the Humanities and the humanities councils of the states of Illinois, Indiana, Kentucky, Ohio, Pennsylvania, and West Virginia, with a mix of private and public organizations.

The Ohio River Valley Series, conceived and published by the University Press of Kentucky, extends the work of the Always a River project through the publication of an ongoing series of books that examine and illuminate the waterway, the land in its watershed, and the waves of people who made this fertile and desirable area their place of residence, of refuge, of commerce and industry, of cultural development and, ultimately, of engagement with American democracy.

The goal of the Always a River project has been to aid our understanding of the implications of change caused through natural and human interrelationships with the Ohio River. The unifying theme for the Ohio River Valley series carries forward this initial goal as each author contributes to a wider understanding of Ohio River Valley history and folklife. Each title's story is told through people interacting within their particular place and time. Each reveals why records, papers, and oral stories preserved by families and institutions offer rich resources for the history of the Ohio River and of the nation. Each traces the impact the river and its tributaries has had on individuals and cultures, and conversely how these individuals and cultures have made an impact on the valley as we know it.

The components of the Always a River project included:
• A floating exhibition on a specially fabricated barge that stopped at 21 sites along the Ohio River from May 22 to September 8, 1991.
• A book of seven essays and an introductory historical overview,

Always a River: The Ohio River and the American Experience (Indiana University Press, 1991).

• A river-wide newspaper supplement containing seven articles that addressed current issues surrounding life and commerce along the Ohio.

• A "Watercolors of the Ohio" exhibition and catalog of juried paintings by artists associated with watercolor societies in the states along the Ohio.

• A valley-wide library reading/discussion program covering three themes: "Exploration, Encounters, and Change: The Ohio River and the Nation," "Heroes and Heroines of the Ohio River Valley," and "Landings: New Perspectives on Local History in the Ohio River Region."

• A valley-wide conference bringing together scholars and experts to examine the history and folklife of the Ohio River Valley.

• A series of locally developed educational initiatives.

Follow-up activities in addition to this Ohio River Valley series include plans for an Ohio River Heritage Corridor, continuation of library reading/discussion programs, biennial conferences on specific themes relevant to the Ohio River Valley, and a major new Falls of the Ohio Interpretive Center at Clarksville, Indiana.

In the process of being a river, the Ohio (and its tributaries) has touched us individually and collectively. This series celebrates the story of a valley through multiple voices and visions.

Kenneth L. Gladish
President and Executive Director
Indiana Humanities Council

Editors' Preface

The Ohio River Valley has a rich story to tell, in and of itself, as a fascinating geologic, geographic entity and through diverse waves of inhabitants whose known residency spans from the withdrawal of the last great glaciers some fifteen thousand years ago up to the present. Each volume in the Ohio River Valley series illuminates an aspect of life along the Ohio, which stretches 981 miles from the confluence of the Allegheny and Monongahela (at Pittsburgh) to the confluence with the Mississippi (at Cairo) and along the multiple tributaries that together provide an inland waterway system connecting nearly one-third of the present United States. Written by scholars and experts in various disciplines, these books engage readers in discourse about the heritage and the future of the Ohio River Valley as it relates to the nation as a whole.

Lion of the Forest, the first book in the Ohio River Valley series, is a compelling story of a man whose nineteenth-century frontier concerns remain relevant to the approaching twenty-first century. James B. Finley combined unique aspects of intellect and action. His range of work thrust him into the thick of matters as diverse as federal government treatment of Native Americans, in particular, the Wyandot nation, public education, the role of the family, prison reform, temperance, antislavery, racism, sexism, and the role of religion. Extensive use of letters, diaries, and original documents provides a vivid portrait of life in the Ohio River Valley during the time between the American War of Independence and the War Between the States. Finley emerges as someone who has made a more significant contribution to our heritage than has been previously recognized.

Rita Kohn and William Lynwood Montell
Series Editors

Author's Preface

Every reader deserves to know why a particular book has been written. Especially when one thinks of biographies, it is useful to discover why an individual's life and career are worth learning about, are worth the time and energy to capture in print. Why should you read this book when there are so many others that may attract your attention?

James B. Finley is an underrated figure in American history. He was a Methodist minister in Ohio in the early nineteenth century who became a leader in his church and who was active and influential in many aspects of our social and religious history. The fact that he wrote five books was in itself a noteworthy accomplishment. In his seventy-six years he witnessed many changes in the area he covered as a circuit rider and contributed to those changes in reform movements such as temperance, prison reform and antislavery.

Yet few persons today remember much about him. In the last forty years only two doctoral dissertations have dealt with his career. Even the *Dictionary of American Biography* has listed the date of his death incorrectly. I gave inadequate attention to him in my book, *The Social Ideas of the Northern Evangelists, 1826-1860*. In terms of his influence, however, he deserves more recognition than he has been given.

It would not have been possible to write in as much detail about James B. Finley had he not saved so many of his letters and letters to him. Fortunately, he had a great sense of history and preserved diaries, journals, and documents that reveal much about his ideas and personality. Most of his letters are in the James B. Finley Papers in the United Methodist Archives Center in the Ohio Wesleyan University Library. Other letters are in the Finley Papers in the Hayes Presidential Center Library. Still others are scattered through the collections of those with whom he frequently corresponded.

Author's Preface

I have made extensive use of these letters for they reveal much about early nineteenth-century life and times. People then lacked telephones and fax machines, and letter writing was the best way to communicate over distances. Letters, diaries, and journals are, in a sense, pathways to the mind. How better to find out what persons were like, what they thought about, believed in, feared or loved, than by reading what they have written and preserved? Because their own words and phrases reveal so much about their attitudes and perspectives I have quoted extensively from these nineteenth-century letters and articles. To paraphrase them sometimes is to lose much of the flavor and style of the early 1800s.

As I began my research, I must have asked myself, "What was it like to be James B. Finley?" As I discovered more about him, other questions came to the fore. What was it like to be a circuit rider in Ohio in 1809, to be a missionary to Native Americans in the 1820s, to have been in a prison in the 1840s, to have participated in the disastrous division in the Methodist Episcopal Church over the issue of slavery?

Ultimately, no one can ever fully know what another person was like, especially someone who lived in a previous century and whose personality was so complex. I believe it was Paul Nagel who once wrote, "Writing about another person's life is an awesome task." But now I believe I have a better understanding of Finley's life and a greater appreciation of his remarkable career. Nevertheless, anyone seeking to write a biography should ponder Lytton Strachey's words, "it is perhaps as difficult to write a good life as to live one."

Research for this book began on a three-month sabbatical leave when I was Executive Director of the Ohio Humanities Council. I am grateful to the National Endowment for the Humanities and the board members of the Ohio Humanities Council for making the leave possible. It was only after retiring that I was able to devote my full time to this project.

I am indebted to many librarians for their assistance in my research. I am especially grateful to Susan Cohen, curator of the West Ohio United Methodist Archives Center, and Kathleen Weibel, former director of the Beeghly Library at Ohio Wesleyan University, for their generous help. Bruce Bowlis and Nan Card at the Hayes Presidential Center Library were also helpful. I appreciate all the assistance received at the Ohio Historical Society Library, the Library of Congress, the New York Public Library, the State Library of Ohio, Ohioana Library, Capital University Library, and the libraries of The Ohio State University. I must also thank Linda Thornburg, Patricia Williamsen, and Lorie Wolfe for teaching me to write on a computer. I am grateful to Patricia Williamsen for the illustrations.

If there are errors of fact or interpretation, however, only I am responsible.

Chronology of James B. Finley's Life

July 14, 1781	Born in North Carolina
Fall 1791	Robert Finley family moved to Kentucky
Spring 1796	Family moved to Chillicothe area, Ohio
March 3, 1801	James Finley married Hannah Strane
August 1801	First conversion at the Cane Ridge revival
Fall 1808	Second conversion in the Ohio woods, became a Methodist
May 1809	Began preaching
1809-10	Appointed to Wills Creek circuit, Muskingum district
1810-11	Appointed to Knox circuit, Muskingum district
Sept. 29, 1811	Ordained by Bishop Asbury
1811-12	Appointed to Fairfield circuit, Muskingum district
1812-13	Appointed to West Wheeling circuit, Ohio district
1813-14	Appointed to West Wheeling and Barnesville circuits
1814-15	Appointed to Cross Creek circuit, Ohio district
1815-16	Appointed to Steubenville circuit, Ohio district
1816-19	Appointed presiding elder of Ohio district
1819-21	Appointed presiding elder of Lebanon district
May 1, 1820	Attended his first General Conference in Baltimore, Md.
1821-22	Appointed missionary to Wyandot mission, Upper Sandusky
1822-23	Appointed presiding elder of Lebanon district and Superintendent of Wyandot mission
1823-24	Appointed missionary to Wyandot mission
1824-25	Appointed presiding elder of Sandusky district and Superintendent of Wyandot mission
Oct. 14, 1824	Appointed sub-agent for Department of Indian Affairs (until Feb. 20, 1826)

Chronology

1825-27	Appointed missionary to Wyandot mission
1827-29	Appointed presiding elder of Lebanon district
1829-31	Appointed to Cincinnati station
1831-32	Appointed presiding elder of Miami district
1832-33	Appointed presiding elder of Cincinnati district
1833-34	Appointed to Cincinnati station
1834-36	Appointed presiding elder of Chillicothe district
1836-39	Appointed presiding elder of Lebanon district
1839-43	Appointed presiding elder of Dayton district
1840	*History of the Wyandott Mission at Upper Sandusky* published
1843-46	Appointed presiding elder of Zanesville district
May-June 1844	Attended General Conference in New York and submitted resolution that led to the division of the Methodist Episcopal Church between North and South
April 2, 1846	Appointed chaplain of Ohio Penitentiary, Columbus, Ohio
July 1849	Replaced as chaplain because of illness
Sept. 19, 1849	Superannuated because of feeble health
1850	*Memorials of Prison Life* published
1850-51	Appointed to Yellow Springs
Sept. 27, 1851	Superannuated again because of health
1852-55	Appointed to Clinton Street Methodist Church, Cincinnati
1853	*Autobiography, Pioneer Life in the West* published
1854	*Sketches of Western Methodism* published
Oct. 6, 1855	Superannuated again
1856	Attended his last General Conference in Indianapolis
Oct. 6, 1856	Appointed Conference missionary, Dayton district
1857	*Life Among The Indians* published
Sept. 6, 1857	Died

1

The New Market Devil

> From that eventful moment, I set myself to seek the Lord.
> —James B. Finley

In the fall of 1808, at a time when ninety percent of Ohio was covered with trees, two brothers in their mid-twenties set out on their usual hunt. On horseback they followed a narrow trail through the woods near their homes. The one in front carried his gun carelessly on his shoulder. While they were riding through the dense shrubbery, the gun suddenly fired. Feeling an overwhelming burden of suspense, the youth stopped his horse and waited, expecting to hear his brother fall to the ground. After his brother had recovered from the shock, he called out, "Brother James, I am not hurt."[1]

At first, James B. Finley, who had almost killed his brother, felt relieved but soon was overcome by what he later described as "tumultuous ragings of despair." He suddenly realized how sinful his life had become, and he fell into a profound melancholy state.

He became so gloomy that for three weeks he did nothing but brood over his miserable condition and almost committed suicide. He read the Bible, but that only intensified his self-condemnation. Having been converted seven years earlier at the famous Cane Ridge revival, he felt that his backsliding had doomed him forever. He had gained the reputation for being "rough, reckless and irreligious" and was called the "Newmarket Devil." He fled to the woods every day for three weeks and crawled, feet foremost, into a hollow log to "read, and weep, and pray." He finally gained the relief and blessing he yearned for and shouted so loudly with joy that the entire neighborhood heard him.[2]

The incident was so traumatic that he finally decided to devote his life to preaching. As he put it, "From that eventful moment, I set myself to seek the Lord." In a short time, he and his wife became Methodists; he started exhorting at meetings, and nineteen of his neighbors were converted. At about the same time John Collins organized the first Methodist class in the town of West Union in Adams County in the home of Peter Shultz. The first sermon preached to them was by the doubly converted James. The turbulent career of one of Ohio's foremost circuit riders was dramatically launched.[3]

James Finley's ancestors came from Scotland, Wales, England, and Germany. He was particularly fond of his English grandmother, a talented, well-educated woman who operated a hospital for wounded soldiers during the American Revolution. His father, Robert W. Finley, was born in Bucks County, Pennsylvania, and attended Princeton College. After studying theology he became a Presbyterian minister. He volunteered to preach in the Carolinas and Georgia. He fought in the Revolution and married Rebecca Bradley in 1780. James was born the following year. In 1784 Robert Finley joined Daniel Boone's party, which explored parts of what later became Kentucky. At the close of the war the Finley family moved first to Virginia and later to Kentucky. Robert and Rebecca Finley had five sons—James, John, William, Samuel, and Robert, Jr.—three of whom became ministers.

The family's journey down the Ohio River was hazardous. They were part of a powerful movement westward once the new federal government had been established. Over three hundred flatboats carried six thousand settlers down the Ohio River past Marietta in the spring of 1788, the year James gave for the trip in his *Autobiography*. However, it was probably one or two years later. Several times the travelers saw Indians on the shore who sought to capture them. The day before the party was to land at Limestone, James's grandmother died.[4]

Once in Kentucky the Robert Finley family lived in the woods near what became the town of Flemingsburg. In the spring of 1792 the family was subjected to sporadic Indian attacks. According to James, "We all lived in constant danger, and exposed to death . . . the Indians would come in undiscovered, and kill our friends, and steal the horses. We had to depend, for our daily living, on the hunters, and what we could kill ourselves of the wild game. This gave me an early love for the chase."[5]

In 1793 his father moved the family to Cane Ridge in Bourbon County, Kentucky. In addition to preaching to two congregations, Robert Finley opened a high school, the first of its kind in the area. It was there that the young James received his classical education. He readily learned Greek and Latin, memorized sections of the *Iliad* and *Aenid*, and was adept in mathematics.

As early as 1794 Robert Finley wrote General Nathaniel Massie, a land speculator who had a settlement at Manchester, to inquire about land in Ohio along the Scioto and Paint Creek. "I would be pleased to know its qualities . . . for the settlement of two congregations." His letter persuaded the general to seek a settlement north of the Ohio River. He joined Massie and a group of forty in the spring of 1795 to explore the area along the Scioto River. They discovered some Shawnee Indians and attacked them, much to General Wayne's irritation. He wrote Governor St. Clair to complain. He accused the group of trying to prevent an amicable treaty and "plundering the Indians," who, he claimed, were "in a peaceful hunting trip." Governor St. Clair replied to correct the general's information. Part of the Indian raiding party was in Kentucky killing and stealing horses. James described the incident in detail in his *Autobiography*.[6]

"Mad" Anthony Wayne's victory at the Battle of Fallen Timbers in 1794 and the Treaty of Greenville in 1795 reduced the threat of Indian attack and opened Ohio to increased white settlement. Robert Finley and some of his congregation had trouble with unscrupulous speculators and lost their land. After receiving advice from Massie, Robert Finley selected land near Chillicothe for his home. Massie offered a tract fifteen to twenty miles square for Finley and those accompanying him. It was an area called Station Prairie. Robert Finley appears to have been the first white man to plant corn there. James recorded later that it occurred May 10, 1796.[7]

James described the beauty of the place in his *Autobiography*. "The soil itself for richness was not exceeded by any in the world." The land contained many elm, walnut, oak, hickory, cherry, and hackberry trees. "All nature had a voice which spoke most impressively to the soul, and while all the senses were pervaded with an unutterable delight, the solemn stillness seemed to say, God reigns here."[8]

The Finley family were part of the twelve thousand settlers who moved into the Scioto Valley in the late 1790s. As James recalled his neighbors' attitude years later he wrote, "A desire to possess the rich lands overcame all fear of sickness, and the living tide rolled on heedless of death." Both Edward Tiffin and Thomas Worthington arrived before the end of the decade.

The fifteen-year-old James had the responsibility of leading the blacks, whom his father freed upon moving from Kentucky, into Ohio. Twelve of the fourteen who were freed accepted Robert's offer of support in Ohio and rode pack horses up the Scioto Valley that cold December in 1795. As James recalled the incident years later, "We carried with us clothes, bed clothes, provisions and cooking utensils. We were accompanied with parts of three families, with a great drove of hogs, cows and sheep . . . [in Ohio] we were not able to travel more than eight or ten miles per day. . . . After sixteen days of toil and hardship we reached our place of destination. . . . In the Spring my father and the rest of the family moved out."[9]

During 1796 James traveled from Chillicothe to Manchester sixteen times for his family. Once settled in Ohio, he continued his medical studies although his primary interest was hunting. "I became so passionately fond of the gun and the woods, and Indian life," he wrote, "that my parents feared I would go off with the Indians and become connected with them." The youth enjoyed parties, "frolics" as he called them, and shooting matches. He enjoyed "giddy mazes" and the "frenzied whirl" of the dance.[10]

He still had not settled down, nor had he selected a career. He was even contemptuous of religion at times. He and his cronies spent their time "drinking, fighting, carousing," even on Sundays. He felt that he was drifting. As he recalled his circumstances later, "Having attained the age of twenty, I felt considerable uneasiness and indeterminateness in regard to my future course in life. There were many things to divert my mind, and much that was calculated to produce dissipation of thought. An abundance of youthful company, with every variety of diversions, such as huskings, quiltings, dancings, and plays of all descriptions, presented themselves and were urged upon my attention. All these, however possessed not the charm of a hunter's life."[11]

He was already showing signs of leadership, however. In 1797, when a thief stole several articles, the settlers living in the Hillsboro area selected James to carry out justice in the absence of any regular court. He also assisted Thomas Worthington in surveying in the Jackson County area in 1799.[12]

He completed his medical studies under Dr. Edward McAdow in the fall of 1800 and was admitted to practice. He did not enjoy visiting the sick and disliked being a doctor, much to his parents' disappointment. Throughout his life, however, he kept a notebook containing prescriptions for a variety of diseases and must have consulted it from time to time. It took little persuasion to get him to join a group in October who drove some cattle they purchased to Detroit.[13]

In 1801 Robert Finley moved his family to the banks of White Oak Creek in what later became Highland County, Ohio, where he established an academy to teach the classics. He became a Methodist itinerant in 1812. With his brother John's help, James built a cabin on land his father had bought. On March 3, 1801, James married Hannah Strane against her father's wishes. Apparently Mr. Strane thought so little of the young doctor who preferred to hunt in the woods that he gave his daughter nothing for a wedding present and would not even let her take her clothing. Their only child, Eliza, was born December 20, 1801.[14]

Finley's first conversion was at the Cane Ridge revival in August 1801. The story of the famous Cane Ridge revival has been frequently told, most recently by Paul Conkin who has traced the camp meeting format back to the seventeenth-century Scottish three to five day communion service. Its religious, social, and psychological aspects have been analyzed from various perspectives. The revival had several unusual features. The service was planned by Barton W. Stone, Presbyterian minister of the Cane Ridge church, along with others. Methodist preachers were invited to participate, and doctrinal differences were set aside with the formation of a union planning committee. Public interest in the coming event increased through the spring of 1801, for the meeting was well publicized. The site selected was on a gentle shaded slope of a large hill. Crowds began to arrive on Friday, August 6, and the roads leading into the small town were choked with horses, carriages, and wagons, many of which contained provisions as well as people.[15]

The services continued day and night for an entire week. Bonfires were kept blazing from sunset to sunrise. According to Peter Cartwright, who was there, "Ministers of almost all denominations flocked in from far and near. It was not unusual [for many preachers] to be addressing the listening thousands at the same time from the different stands erected for the purpose." Although James did not mention it in his *Autobiography*, according to one report, his father, Robert, was one of the preachers.[16]

The simultaneous sounds of preaching, praying, and singing must have had a hypnotic effect on the assembled crowd. Many fainted while others experienced uncontrollable jerking of their bodies. The physical activities were not as unusual then as they may appear now. (In his study of social movements, Hadley Cantril describes a critical situation in which a person confronts a chaotic environment that he cannot well interpret and that leads to aberrant behavior. Conkin has asserted that physical activities at Cane Ridge resembled those at the protracted communions in Scotland in the 1620s.) Some participants were overcome with fear for their souls; others shouted and praised God for their conversion. Cane Ridge was the largest and probably the most emotional revival in American history.[17]

Estimates of the size of the crowd varied from ten to twenty-five thousand. Finley's estimate was the latter but, given his tendency for exaggeration, a smaller number seems more likely. Even so, while thousands came from Ohio, Tennessee, and elsewhere, the majority were from Kentucky, which in 1800 contained no more than 250,000 persons. Apparently, all segments of the population and many leading citizens participated. According to some accounts ten thousand were converted, although in 1819 Thomas Hinde put the figure at three thousand.[18]

Finley claimed that five hundred were swept down "in a moment." He wrote, "The noise was like the roar of Niagara. The vast sea of human beings seemed to be agitated as if by a storm. I counted seven ministers, all preaching at one time, some on stumps, others in wagons. . . . My heart beat tumultuously, my knees trembled, my lip quivered, and I felt as though I must fall to the ground."

He fought against the feelings that were overwhelming him. He fled through the woods twice to get away from the scene. Later he went to a tavern for one of the few brandies he ever drank, wandered about, slept in a barn. Later he started for home but broke down and wept on the way. The following day he went into the woods and became one of the converts.[19]

When he returned home, however, his doubts and confusion continued for about three years. Some of his friends ridiculed him for his conversion. Because he was a pugnacious youth he had an exhausting fight with one of his hecklers. Years later, when he was reminded of the incident, he replied, "I remember it very well, and I remember another thing about it—I remember I whipped the fellow."[20]

At this time he had acquired about a hundred acres of land and some horses, but he lost it all when he put it up as security bail for a friend who then disappeared. He started over again near the town of New Market. Chillicothe in 1805 was already too large for his taste. It had 150 houses and a weekly newspaper. It was not until his second conversion, following the shooting in the woods, that he and his wife joined the Methodist church.[21]

Earlier he had realized that he could not become a Presbyterian, for he didn't believe in the doctrine of unconditional election and reprobation. He even had arguments with his father over predestination. He visited other sects before embracing Methodism. Two years after he started preaching his father also became a Methodist preacher.

Ohio in 1800 held for its forty-five thousand inhabitants both great attractions and many fears. The area contained miles of forests of walnut, ash, elm, maple, buckeye, hickory, and oak. The new arrivals had to become woodsmen before they could be farmers. The land contained rich game—bear, deer, turkey, ducks, geese, squirrels—and the many streams were filled with fish. But it was a land of terror and loneliness as well as a place of plenty. Families faced hardship and privation. Social contacts were infrequent. There was little evidence of security or stability. One visitor in 1816 commented on the "forests of gigantic growth. We sometimes traveled miles through these woods without seeing a single human dwelling."[22]

It has been called "a region of violent contrasts, attracting as it did the most self-reliant and the most vicious." A diverse group of people purchased land or squatted in the area. Some were educated lawyers, doctors, and merchants. Others were illiterate migrants and outlaws. The Northwest Ordinance of 1787 had ordained a system of rights and laws in order to encourage systematic growth. Yet the distance from eastern civilization created a potential for much violence.

Settlement in Ohio did not quite conform with the Turner frontier thesis, if we think of a frontier as the constantly moving line dividing the farthest settlers from the wilderness. Persons of enterprise and capital founded towns such as Marietta and Cincinnati at the same time as backwoodsmen wandered the forest to flee from the restraints of society. Even in the towns, and certainly in the scattered farms along the streams, there was serious isolation. There were few occasions when organizations or institutions brought people together. It was a lonely as well as a brutish and short life. Daniel Drake described the situation well when he wrote, "None of those who have lived where they saw many persons every hour in the day can fully estimate the feeling of loneliness which comes into the heart when only trees and a few domestic animals can be seen."[23]

The church was almost the only institution to provide social as well as spiritual succor. The religious institutions also served to encourage sobriety and the acceptance of laws and regulations. It was not an accident that the title for the Methodist collection of rules was the *Discipline*.

On May 1, 1809, the first year of James Madison's administration, John Sale, the presiding elder of the Scioto district, asked James to travel on his circuit even though he did not yet have a license to preach. Despite his lack of confidence, he was immediately successful and received his license at the August camp meeting and was recommended to be received on trial. That action was taken at the Western Conference annual meeting Thursday, October 5. During that week of meetings sermons were preached twice a day by some of the leaders in the Church including Bishops Asbury and McKendree, James Quinn, Henry Boehm, and William Burke.[24]

Finley was one of 103 Methodist preachers admitted on trial in the United States in 1809. That year the Methodist Episcopal Church had over 163,000 members and 589 preachers on 324 circuits. He was first assigned to the Wills Creek circuit, which was 475 miles in length. It took him four weeks to traverse it from Zanesville to Cambridge to New Philadelphia to Canton and back. He wrote, "I entered upon this work with great fear and trembling." He couldn't find a place for his wife and daughter to live so he built a cabin, twelve by fourteen feet, fourteen miles west of Barnesville. He was so poor he had to sell his boots to buy food for his family.[25]

The head of the Church, Bishop Asbury, visited his circuit in late August and early September 1810 and must have unnerved the young preacher. Asbury's assessment, however, was very positive. He recorded in his journal, "The prospects are encouraging in Wills Creek." Finley converted 178 persons his first year on the circuit. A revival continued in the area for several years.[26]

Finley's eagerness to save souls, however, got him into trouble early in his preaching career. He and Thomas Hinde were disciplined by their presiding elder, John Collins, for starting an unauthorized service at a camp meeting in 1809. He and Hinde, impatient to see results, went into the woods, started singing hymns and collected a gathering. A crowd, attracted by the disturbance in the woods, left their tents. The service became noisy, and hecklers interrupted the young exhorters. Finley recalled, "We had raised a storm sure enough, but how to guide it was what had not entered into our calculations." Collins called them to the preachers' tent where "he gave us such a trimming for our disorderly proceedings which, though severe, did not break our bones, and proved of great service to us in after life."[27]

His second year of full-time preaching was on the Knox circuit, and his first service in Dillon's Falls had to be in the house of the person who ran the only tavern in town. Finley organized a class of six Methodists, one of whom was a black man. Even this early in his career, he solicited pledges and money to build a log meeting house, which was quickly built.

Finley and nineteen others were ordained by Bishop Asbury Sunday, September 29, 1811, at the Western Annual Conference meeting in Cincinnati. At that time in the Indian Territory, Governor William Henry Harrison was leading a one-thousand-man army northward toward Tippecanoe to stop Tecumseh's plans for an Indian confederacy. And on the Ohio River the first steamboat was sailing from Pittsburgh to New Orleans.[28]

The circuits to which Finley was assigned in his first decade of preaching were all challenging. In 1811 he was appointed to the Fairfield circuit and in 1812 to the West Wheeling circuit. While traveling that year his home was in St. Clairsville. In 1813, the year he was elected to the office of elder, it was the Barnesville and West Wheeling circuit where he became noted both for his spiritual vigor and his eloquent preaching. The Barnesville area was noted in 1800 for producing tobacco. In 1814 he was assigned to the Cross Creek circuit, which included three counties. He preached thirty-two times on every round, which meant an appointment every day and twice on Sunday. That circuit held fifty classes with whom he had to meet.[29]

Not all of his difficulties were related to poverty and hazardous travel. Some services were interrupted by disturbances. Rowdy gangs enjoyed heckling ministers and upsetting the decorum. Finley eagerly and vigorously stopped them. One account described how he would "seize disturbers at his meetings, shake them until their teeth rattled, and pitch them out of a window or door." However, he had his saintly side as well. One contemporary wrote, "his heart was most genial, his discourses full of pathos and his friendships the most tender and lasting."[30]

Finley was of medium build with broad shoulders and muscular arms.

As he matured, he became slightly corpulent. Abel Stevens gave one of the best descriptions of him. He called him "a genuine child of the wilderness, . . . of stalwart frame, features rather coarse, but with large, benovolent eyes, sandy hair, standing erect, a good expressive mouth, a voice like thunder, and a courage that made riotous opposers quail before him."[31]

Many contemporaries spoke of him as fearless, outspoken, and energetic with a sonorous voice that conveyed deep emotions. Another nineteenth-century description of him spoke of "multitudes of hearts . . . thrilled with his weeping narratives of his youthful wickedness, his remarkable conversion, and the labors and triumphs of his itinerant life." John Stewart, another Methodist minister, called him indefatigable and eloquent and declared that "his mightly voice, whether in its plaintive and pathetic wail or in its thunder tones of exhortation, seldom failed to penetrate to every citadel of the soul." He made such an impression on people that his nickname was "Lion of the Forest."[32]

He was described by Daniel Ryan as "of giant form, of belligerent, yet benevolent disposition and of courageous spirit." Many described him as a person with great knowledge of human nature who was able to sway large audiences. One of his younger colleagues wrote that he "accustomed himself to eat anything that was set before him, to sleep anywhere, and to accommodate himself to any inconvenience."[33]

Five years after he started preaching he became very depressed and confided his unhappiness in letters to his colleague, David Young, who was then in Lancaster. Young tried to cheer him. On March 13, 1815, he wrote, "In your family trouble I am afflicted & in your circuit troubles I sympathize with you. . . . Can you remember the years since you traveled that did not produce its difficulties? Do those you now meet exceed the rest?" Despite his occasional depressions, he persevered. In 1815 he was appointed to the Steubenville circuit.[34]

On March 15, 1816, he wrote a long letter to John Sale to criticize the itinerants' conditions. He wrote, "Much, very much depends on the ensuing General Conference to encourage the itinerancy which, in the present situation of things, must in the course of a few years, fail exceedingly if proper measures are not taken to strengthen the things that remain." He pointed out to his mentor that people judged the value of something in terms of the cost and asserted that the cost of itinerant preachers was too low. "In my humble opinion it ought to be at least three hundred dollars for a married man, and one hundred fifty dollars for a single man." He concluded his letter with a dire prediction. "Unless something is done to support the itinerant plan more bountifully, and to destroy that jealousy which exists between the traveling and local ministers, the downfall of Methodism is not far distant."[35]

In early April he wrote his brother John to inform him that he had bought a residence in Steubenville, and he invited his brother to join him. John arrived in May and started teaching in a school. One of his students was William Cooper Howells, who had a high opinion of his teaching abilities. He recorded that John's school was large and that many of his pupils were sons of the leading citizens. Howells did not think as highly of James. He characterized him as "a preacher of great zeal and piety, for which he was more distinguished than for learning." He considered John a better preacher than James.[36]

Once James became a presiding elder, his travels increased even more. A presiding elder had charge of several circuits and stations. He had to visit them each quarter, preach, administer sacraments, and preside at quarterly meetings. In 1816 he was assigned to the Ohio district, which was composed of eight circuits that later became the Erie Conference. His "Memorandum Book for the District of Ohio" begins with characteristic lines:

James B. Finley is my Name
Steubenville is my Station
From Miami I came
And Christ is my Salvation.[37]

Finley found northeastern Ohio somewhat less receptive to Methodism than the rest of the state. There were too many Calvinists from New England there! Nevertheless, during his three years in that area church membership increased over 50 percent and a new circuit, called Huron, was established. Bishop McKendree complimented him on his success in that area. March 21, 1817, he wrote, "The contents [of your recent letter] were truly gratifying. I rejoice to hear of Zion's prosperity."[38]

Some of his doubts and depressions continued, however. He recorded in his diary for April 2, 1818, "Left home under much affliction of Body and Mind but resolved to let nothing hinder my journey. Traveled 23 miles through wind and rain." David Young, who had retired to Zanesville, tried to cheer him and get him to move to that area. On November 28, 1818, he wrote a long letter to assure James of his continued friendship.

Your stay cannot be much longer in that "muddy and melancholy" region. . . . But my dear if you will conclude to make the place near enough for your own convenience I'll vouch for trying to be your social companion & friend, until you be weary of my attention. You have not said whether you wish to live in town or country. But in either case perhaps you might be as well accommodated about here as any where else. . . . This place is fortunately marred with very few preachers. A great many is perhaps the greatest curse. I really wish you would come here to live. I might get to your house to borrow some little thing once in a while. Write me what sort of property you want.[39]

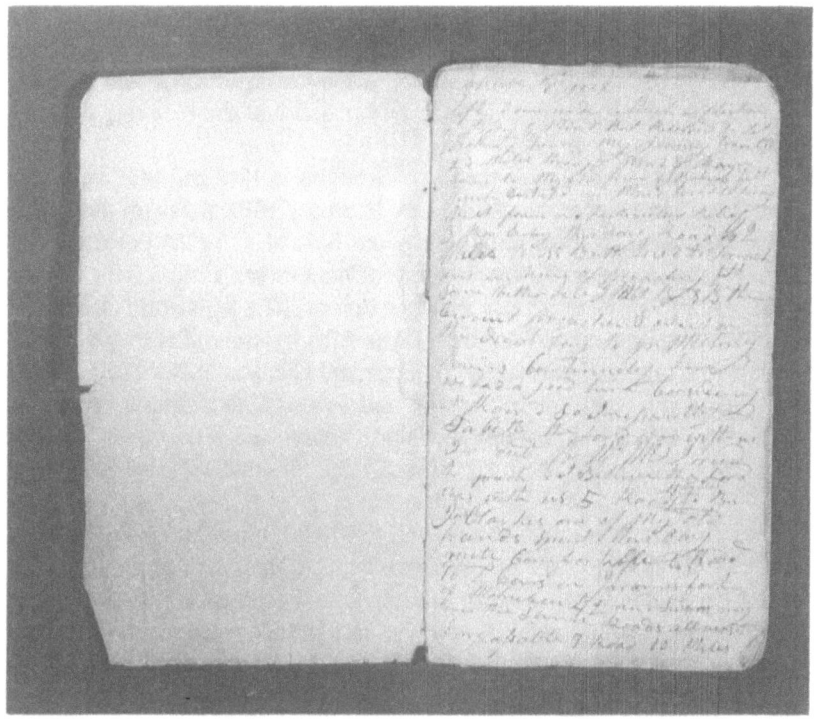

First page of Finley's diary for April 2, 1818, when he lived in Steubenville and was presiding elder of the Ohio district. He records leaving "under much affliction of Body and Mind."

Part of Finley's worries were probably financial. Married Methodist circuit riders at that time were entitled to annual incomes of two hundred dollars, but this amount depended on contributions from church members. His income reached that amount only once in his first decade as a preacher in 1817. In other years the amounts ranged from $95 in 1811 to $189 in 1818.[40]

Economic conditions in 1818 probably contributed to his financial worries. A severe economic depression began that year that eventually affected about one-third of the population. The reduction in loans and a deflation precipitated bankruptcies in the West and South. Commodity prices and real estate fell sharply that winter. Finley reported to his book dealers that banks in his area were in a poor condition. Soule and Mason wrote him on January 23, 1818, to advise him to send notes on Marietta, Steubenville, and Chillicothe banks. They reported that those notes were from 6 to 8 percent below par. "Unchartered notes will not pass at all."

They suggested that he deposit funds in the Cincinnati branch of the United States Bank and take a draft on the branch in New York payable to them. They concluded, "With respect to the damaged stock you have on hand the best thing you can do with it is to sell it at the best rate you can but at all events get it off."[41]

Things got worse during the year. Droughts in 1818 and 1819 made the Ohio River too low for navigation. By February 1819, notes on the banks Finley was using were discounted in the East at 15 to 20 percent. The Ohio legislature made the discounting of bank notes a misdemeanor that could result in a fine up to five hundred dollars. The legislature also voted to tax the two branches of the U.S. Bank fifty thousand dollars a year, an act declared unconstitutional by the Supreme Court in 1824. The panic of 1819 led to five years of depression and severely hurt Ohio's economy. Methodist church membership in Ohio, which had been rising sharply since 1814, suddenly declined from 35,596 in mid-1819 to 34,178 in mid-1820, almost a four percent loss.[42]

His brother John, who had moved to Piqua, wrote James in Steubenville July 12, 1818, to urge him to move west. "There will be a treaty with the Indians held 28 miles from this place to Commence 15th Sept. Our Agts are about to purchase 100 miles square of land from them, if they do our chance for good land will be very good." He wrote again October 17 to urge James to buy land. "I fell very forlorn for the want of your company. I do not know how to live without you. I fully expected you here this fall, but alas! I am sadly disappointed. . . . The treaty is concluded with the Indians, the principles of which you have perhaps seen in some of the papers. Bro Johnston says that it is the greatest purchase that has ever been made. The land is generally good highly situated, and well watered and of course will be healthy."[43]

John continued to seek help and advice from his older brother. On June 3, 1819, he wrote to complain that he had not heard from James for six months. He sought his aid in getting a job in the Land Office in Piqua, although he admitted that he would rather be a circuit rider. On August 29, 1821, when he was teaching, he wrote to say that his situation was desperate, that he could not "command a congregation." He pleaded, "Now do not forget us . . . remember that we are ship wrecked . . . I wonder if you will pay any attention to this when you read it."[44]

James had other family problems. His brother William, who entered Methodist itinerancy in 1814, suffered a fractured skull when he was thrown from a horse in 1820. His mind was affected, and he died shortly thereafter. Later in the 1820s James's nephew, who was named for him, was in serious trouble for "falsehood, calumny and detraction."[45]

The New Market Devil

If James Finley had been contemplating resettling, however, the decisions made at the Annual Conference in Cincinnati in August 1819 changed his mind. At that conference he was appointed presiding elder of the Lebanon district, and the conference took actions that led to his involvement in the Wyandot mission at Upper Sandusky.

2

The Expansion of Methodism in Ohio

> They appear determined to take heaven by storm.
> —Isaac Holmes

The significance of James Finley's role in the early 1800s is more readily appreciated in the light of the development of Ohio and the expansion of Methodism in the state during this period. Ohio's rapid population growth after 1787 resulted from the Northwest Ordinance, which provided for an orderly establishment of law and civil rights in the area, the future admission of states on the basis of equality, and the prohibition of slavery and involuntary servitude northwest of the Ohio River. It also was speeded by Wayne's military victories over Indian tribes that resulted in the Treaty of Greenville in 1795. The fertile soil and abundance of game made the area very attractive to farmers, merchants, lawyers, and others from New England, Pennsylvania, Virginia, and Kentucky.

Ohio's population grew rapidly after 1795 (see table 1). By 1825 Ohio was the fourth most populous state. By 1850 its population was 1.9 million, and almost 10 percent of its inhabitants were members of the Methodist Church.

The increase in the number of Methodists during the early years of the nineteenth century was phenomenal. The rapid expansion of Methodist membership in the nation helped guarantee the permanency of a voluntary system of religious institutions. In 1800, the Western district, which comprised more than the territory of Ohio, contained 1,741 members. By 1808, the Ohio district, created as part of the Western conference, held 16,887 members. In 1812, when the Ohio conference was organized, membership was over 23,000. Increases after that date were dramatic (see table 2).[1]

In the 1850s one-quarter of the inhabitants of seventy-two of Ohio's eighty-seven counties were Methodists; in sixteen counties one-half of

Table 1. Population of Ohio

1790	3,000
1800	45,000
1810	230,000
1820	561,000
1830	937,000
1840	1,500,000

Table 2. Membership in the Ohio Conference

1812	23,000
1820	34,000
1823	36,000
1833	51,000
1843	107,000
1855	121,000

them were Methodists. Forty-four percent of the churches in Ohio in 1850 were Methodist. In the entire nation, Methodist membership grew from fifteen thousand in 1785 to eight hundred fifty thousand in 1840. By 1844, there were over one million members, 3,988 circuit riders and 7,730 local preachers.[2]

The number of Methodist preachers increased in similar fashion, from eight in Ohio in 1804 to 559 in 1853. The itinerant preachers were the primary leaders in the church in that they were the delegates to the general conference that met every four years. James B. Finley became part of a movement that influenced many people in the Ohio River area and that helped alter the direction and development of a vast newly populated region.[3]

The growth of Methodism can be credited to three factors: the organization of the church, which was ideally suited for serving an expanding frontier area; the doctrinal message, which was one that many settlers in Ohio responded to; and the powerful perseverance and inspired activity of the hardy circuit riders whose responsibility was to proselytize. The minister was all the more important in Ohio in the early 1800s because he was a conveyor of culture as well as a spiritual guide. That the frontier was transformed into a civilized area in such a short time was largely the result of the efforts of these remarkable religious men.

Robert Paine, who wrote in the 1860s, may have overstated the case, but the words he used in characterizing Methodism bear repeating: "Its fruit was healing the chronic ulcers of the nation. It introduced order, social and moral, it subdued the vices, restrained the passions and vitiated appetites, refined the taste, enlightened the minds of men, and spread peace and happiness through society. It instituted an unequaled system of propaganda."[4]

Of course, the frontier would not have disappeared so quickly had not the many settlers arrived. The migration into Ohio seemed at times like a flood of humanity. Narrow roads were filled with wagons, sometimes more than two hundred passing westward in a day.

As early as 1785, General Richard Butler, who was removing squatters from Indian territory around Cross Creek, recorded that the people "appear to be much imposed upon by a sect called Methodist, and are becoming great fanatics." Methodism officially first came to Ohio in September 1787 when George Callahan preached at Carpenter's station near Warrenton in Jefferson County. Bishop Asbury and several ministers crossed the river into Ohio June 26, 1786, but apparently no preaching occurred. In 1793, Francis Clark preached at Fort Washington, near Cincinnati, and was struck by the "godlessness" of the troops and the "wickedness" of the settlers. Two Methodist ministers preached in Steubenville in the summer of 1794 and encountered considerable opposition. The first circuit in Ohio was in 1798 when John Kobler was sent to the territory to serve about ninety Methodists. The Western conference was created in 1802 and out of it the Ohio conference in 1812.[5]

Methodism was particularly strong in the Scioto Valley. Henry Smith preached to the faithful living near Chillicothe, and the first society of Methodists started there on July 7, 1800. At about the same time, Robert Finley held services in New Market. By 1805, the Scioto circuit had 472 members. Three years later Bishop Asbury preached to audiences of thousands in that area. He returned in 1810 and again in 1814 when he stayed a week at Senator Worthington's home. John Sale, who gave Finley his first preaching assignment, wrote to Edward Dromgoole February 20, 1807, to say, "I expect this State will be as the Garden of God and it is pleasing to me to live in a Country where there is so much of an Equality and a Man is not thought to be great here because he possesses a little more of the world's rubbish than his neighbor."[6]

Although the message, as we shall see, appealed to the frontier settlers because of its optimistic egalitarianism, it was the organization of the Methodist Church with its combination of centralized control and expansive flexibility that assured numerical success. Under Bishop Asbury the church was governed centrally and autocratically. It expanded through a mechanism of conferences, districts, and circuits, whose borders were constantly changing to reflect the westward movement of settlers.

At the broad base of the pyramid was the class meeting, which met regularly under the leadership of one of the group who was usually not a minister. The class, which was a mechanism created by Wesley, provided a degree of continuity and cohesion between the visits of the circuit riders. The class leader was supposed to see his class members at least once a week and to ask them about their spiritual condition. It was his responsibility to guide, encourage, and even reprove them. It served as an accepted form of social control. According to John Miley, who wrote *A Treatise on Class Meetings*, published in 1851, they were an important part of the Methodist system.[7]

Newly converted persons were admitted to membership on trial. After six months, if they received a good report, they could be made full members. The spiritual guidance was in the form of singing, prayer, Bible study, and individual witness. A good class leader was familiar with the personalities and backgrounds of his group. In a sense, he was able to exercise some degree of social control over them. One of the benefits of being in good standing was receipt of a class ticket that permitted the bearer to take part in the sacrament of the Lord's Supper, or communion. Members in the class meetings developed a responsibility for each other, especially in terms of their spiritual welfare. If one missed a meeting or failed to live up to the standards of conduct, there were friends who would express interest and concern. It was similar to a second family, a devout one that felt free to care for each other's souls. James Finley recorded his first attendance at a class meeting in his *Autobiography*. "It was a time of profound and powerful feeling; every soul seemed to be engaged in the work of salvation. . . . I never heard more plain, simple, Scriptural, common-sense, yet eloquent views of Christian experience in my life."[8]

The classes in an area comprised a local society, and a group of societies made up a circuit that in some cases stretched for hundreds of miles. A preacher or two were assigned to travel the circuit, which took between two and six weeks to traverse. Each day usually involved both traveling and preaching except for Sunday when traveling was not supposed to occur.

Many of the places where the circuit riders preached were cabins. Some services were in schoolhouses; a few were in taverns. David Young recorded that he had preached in a barroom in 1802. There were few meeting houses in the early 1800s. Twenty-one of the twenty-three preaching sites on the Muskingum circuit in 1823 were at settlers' homes. According to one participant, "Our old circuits were the best means devised for the development of every energetic quality; and the acquisition of every practical qualification which could be acquired out of the study. They made our first ministry . . . the thundering legion of Christendom."[9]

The circuits grew as the population increased. As the wilderness receded, the church expanded, growing like an amoeba, creating new districts and transforming old ones. In his memoirs, William Cooper Howells described a circuit in eastern Ohio. "The Methodists had about thirty preaching places on the circuit, each of which contributed something for the support of the two preachers, whose salaries were very small. . . . It was poor pay, and generally it was equally 'poor preach'."[10] One circuit rider described his travels in this fashion: "The way was through dense woods, the tall forest trees, some at least a century old, throwing a dark shadow over all below. Sometimes, after ascending a long hill, I would get a brief glance of a wide, wild extent of country, all as thickly wooded as that in which I was wandering I knew not whither. Then the road would dive down into a deep, somber valley, and steadily onward, but not a human face not a human habitation met my view."[11]

The size of circuits meant that the preachers were frequently in transit. On one circuit Finley had to preach thirty-two times on every round. Some circuit assignments involved looking after the needs of over a thousand members. Some circuits were large even in the 1840s. Uriah Heath wrote Finley January 1, 1845, to report that he had ridden 180 miles in eleven days.[12]

A group of circuits made up a district, which had a presiding elder appointed to it on a yearly basis. His duties included traveling the circuits, preaching, counseling the circuit riders and local preachers, conducting quarterly meetings, and attending other events to advance the cause of the church. There were many meetings. A two-day quarterly meeting was held in every circuit and was attended by circuit riders, local preachers, class leaders, exhorters, and stewards.[13]

A number of districts comprised a conference, and each conference held an annual meeting. These week-long gatherings of the traveling preachers conducted business that included admitting new preachers, scrutinizing the religious purity of the established ones, and were the occasions when a bishop made appointments for the following year. Normally, the preachers had no say in where they were assigned, and they were rarely assigned to the same circuit or station more than two years in a row. All the annual conferences sent delegates to the General Conference, which met every four years and was the supreme governing body.[14]

The hierarchy of ministers consisted of bishops, elders, and deacons. Bishops were elected by the General Conference. The annual conferences admitted persons who had been called to preach. In some cases preachers began as exhorters, who were licensed to speak and evangelize but not to serve as ordained ministers. Exhorters could not base their remarks on the Scriptures. They usually followed a preacher's sermon to appeal to those not yet converted. Local preachers, not as highly regarded as circuit riders, were those who felt they could not enter the permanent ministry or who were too ill or too old to travel. Initially, preachers were admitted on trial for a two-year period. The church preferred single men as circuit riders. The fact that Finley was already married made his rapid success all the more remarkable. Men with families frequently went to stations that required no travel. When a preacher became "settled," he lost some status with those who traveled.[15]

Bishops exercised control through their appointment process and by virtue of presiding at annual and general conferences. One circuit rider described his feelings waiting to hear his assignment in this fashion: "Last Day of Conference—A few hours will decide where I shall go. I wish I could feel no concern. Earnestly did I pray this morning, that I might be endowed with a spirit of resignation. . . . Four o'clock—It is all over. . . . I am appointed to ——— circuit among the mountains, two hundred miles away."[16]

Efforts to democratize the system were for the most part unsuccessful. Finley realized at the 1820 General Conference, which was the first he attended, that the motion to provide for the election of presiding elders was opposed by the bishops and by most of the presiding elders.[17]

The early Methodist preachers had to be vigorous, strong, sturdy persons to withstand their arduous travel schedules. They were notable for their endurance, piety, and willingness to endure poverty. Finley's comments about his colleagues at the close of the 1817 Annual Conference were appropriate. "Great were the toils and hardships they were called to endure. The winter was extremely severe . . . the rides were long and the roads rough, the fare hard and the provisions scarce."[18]

William Burke recalled his early years in the ministry in these words: "We were half our time obliged to put up in taverns and places of entertainment, subject to the disorder and abuse of the unprincipled and half-civilized inmates, suffering with hunger and cold, sleeping in open cabins on the floor, sometimes without bed or covering."[19]

The typical circuit rider's clothes were distinctive. He usually wore a "straight-breached coat, high collar, long waistcoat, sometimes breeches and stockings, long hair, often a wide-brimmed hat. It was a dress coat for all regardless of age. On their horses with their saddle bags, they cut a distinctive picture."[20]

Their day usually began at four in the morning. They were expected to spend several hours praying and reading the Bible. After breakfast, if they were staying in a home, they would lead devotions for the family and possibly counsel them. Then they would ride to their next destination where they would conduct a service or meet with a class at their next host's home. In addition, there would be weddings, baptisms, funerals, or other meetings to require their attention. The evening might be devoted to prayer, meditation, or reading. They had their *Discipline* to remind them, "Be diligent—never be unemployed. Neither spend any more time at any place than is strictly necessary."[21]

Many of the circuit riders and their church members deprecated a learned ministry. The unlettered preachers were often preferred over those who had been to college. Robert Baird, writing in 1845, observed that the Methodist church had a dread of ministers who might be learned but inadequately converted. Peter Cartwright's attitude was typical of his generation. He wrote, "A Methodist preacher in those days, when he felt that God had called him to preach, instead of hunting up a college or Biblical institute, hunted up a hardy pony of a horse, and some traveling apparatus, and with his library always at hand, namely Bible, Hymn Book, and Discipline, he started."[22]

There was another consideration. One Methodist minister wrote in 1821: "We believe it to be an universal principle, that people adhere more to the man who teaches from his own experience and knowledge of things, than he who attempts to teach from books only, or the experience of others. Give me the man for my guide that has traveled the way himself."[23]

James Quinn was representative of the prevalent attitude. "Where and how did the Methodist preachers learn to preach?" he wrote in his journal. "By preaching."[24]

Timothy Flint was a keen observer when he declared in 1827: "The preaching is of a highly popular cast, and its first aim is to excite the feelings. Hence, too, excitements, or in religious parlance, 'awakenings' are common in all the region. Living remote, and consigned the greater part of the time, to the musing loneliness of their condition in the forests, or the prairie where they congregate on these exciting occasions, society itself is to them a novelty, and an excitement. The people naturally are more sensitive and enthusiastic, than in the older countries. . . . This country opens as boundless theatre for strong, earnest and unlettered eloquence."[25]

Scholarly sermons were not what was needed. Indeed, there was some indifference and hostility toward the intellect. Finley reflected this point of view. "The backwoods Christian is shut up to his Bible; and I have wondered if the great multiplication of books has not had a deleterious tendency, in diverting the mind from the Bible." This attitude was carried to the extreme in the often repeated statement: "larnin isn't religion, and eddication don't give man the power of the spirit. . . . St. Peter was a fisherman—do you think he ever went to Yale College?"[26]

It was only after 1830 that there was a serious effort among Methodists to make literacy a requirement for those entering the ministry. When Finley wrote his *Sketches of Western Methodism* in 1854 he expressed a more positive position on the subject. "We do not decry knowledge. God forbid! Let the minister of the present day study all the branches of theological literature, and all collateral sciences, posting himself up thoroughly in all departments."[27]

Although circuit riders gained a reputation for lacking formal education and although some may have been uncultured, they were highly talented in many respects. Finley's knowledge of medicine was an extra skill for him in his work. Circuit riders did spend a lot of time reading mostly religious works. They were shrewd observers of humanity and had a basic understanding of how best to communicate to others. The Ohio political leader and jurist, John McLean, who was a good friend of Finley, justified the circuit riders' lack of polish in these words: "Will Methodist preachers forget their college lessons, and study human nature, by learning the methods of the pioneers of Methodism? This method, pursued by devoted lives and sanctified hearts will subdue the world."[28]

The circuit riders had two images in society. People who were unconverted and untouched by their activities looked down on them as ignorant busybodies preaching up storms. Some of the more orthodox and conservative persons were suspicious of them. Those who were pious church members or who encountered them daily looked upon them as noble members of society, opinion formers and opinion leaders who contributed to the stability and maturing of the area. William Henry Harrison paid circuit riders the compliment of calling them "a body of men who, for zeal and fidelity in the discharge of the duties they undertake, are not exceeded by any others in the world. . . . They are men whom no labor tires, no scenes disgust, no danger frightens in the discharge of their duty." They were indeed influential in helping to maintain law and order.[29]

Their poverty was well known. In 1800, the annual salary for Methodist ministers was increased to eighty dollars. Wives could receive another eighty dollars, and sixteen dollars were allowed for children under seven and twenty-four dollars for those eight to fourteen. The salary increased to one hundred dollars in 1816 with another one hundred dollars for a wife and remained at that level for forty years. But ministers' salaries were not always fully paid. Finley failed to collect the full amount in his early years. In 1812, over one-half of the preachers in the Ohio conference failed to collect their full salaries. When he was assigned to his first circuit, Finley had to build a cabin, twelve by fourteen feet, fourteen miles west of Barnesville, so that his family could live on the circuit. He wrote in his manuscript, "I borrowed a blanket, and wore it instead of a great coat through the winter, and by that means paid my debts. . . . I sold the boots off my feet to purchase provisions." In 1812, he received $151.50, in 1813 only $114.75. He didn't receive the full two hundred dollars until 1817. Twenty years later Andrew Carroll faced similar straits: "The circuit is to give me one hundred dollars, if the people are willing to raise it. . . . This amounts to the sum of eight dollars and thirty-three and a third cents per month, and I furnish my own horse . . . which hardly meets expenses."[30]

The rotation system every two years or so had disadvantages in uprooting families and cutting short a person's influence in one area. However, it had some advantages in broadening the ministers' experience, giving them the opportunity to become known in other parts of the conference, and allowing them to deliver the same messages in other places. The rotation process brought preachers and congregations together who were new to each other and used the attraction of novelty to gain attention. Some circuit riders complained about their assignments. Except for one occasion when he was sent to eastern Ohio against his wishes, Finley defended the system. To a colleague who complained he wrote, "I have gone where I was sent without Murmuring and thought any place in God's vineyard was good enough for me."[31]

The circuit riders were also carriers of popular education in the Ohio forests. One of their tasks was to sell books and pamphlets printed by the Methodist Book Concern that had been established in 1789, although some Methodist books had been printed earlier. The *Discipline* of 1801 read:

It shall be the duty of every Presiding Elder, where no Book Steward is appointed, to see that his district be fully supplied with books. He is to order such books as are wanted and to give direction to us how same are to be sent; and he is to take the oversight of all our books sent into his district, and is to keep an account with each preacher who receives or sells books. . . . It shall be the duty of every preacher who has the charge of a circuit to see that his circuit be duly supplied with books.[32]

Although most of the books sold were religious in orientation, the newspapers, magazines, and tracts they distributed also contained secular information and provided useful links with the rest of the world. In many homes the only literature introduced came by way of the circuit riders. They helped create a love of reading as well as a love for religion.

Some ministers found the circulation of books a burden, but there was a positive value in that they sometimes shared part of the income from sales. The minutes of the Western Annual Conference held in Chillicothe on Monday, September 14, 1807, recorded the following: "The preachers shall be allowed, for their trouble of selling the books, not less than 15 nor more than 25 percent, upon the wholesale price, for all the Books sold by them, but the prices shall be regulated as in the judgment of the Editors the different impressions will best afford. . . . One third of which the Presiding Elder shall have for his trouble. The other two-thirds shall be allowed the preachers, who sell them, in their respective Circuits."[33] The General Conference in 1828 changed the rates and stipulated that "the preacher making such sales shall be allowed $26^2/_3\%$ from the retail prices & presiding elder $13^1/_3\%$."

Later, in 1834, when the *Western Christian Advocate* was founded in Cincinnati, the Methodist Book Concern offered circuit riders a twenty-five-cent commission on subscriptions and sent them the names of current subscribers. After six years the circulation reached fifteen thousand, thanks mostly to the preachers' efforts.[34]

Finley was especially effective selling books and tracts on his circuits. Early in his career he showed vigorous leadership in this regard. Selling books involved ordering them from New York, carrying volumes in saddles, persuading church members and others to buy them, keeping accurate records of purchases and sales, and sending monies to New York at regular intervals. Finley sometimes recorded the amounts of book sales on letters he received and saved.[35]

On October 18, 1815, Daniel Hitt and Thomas Ware, book dealers, wrote, "Your communications of the 5th inst. were received yesterday. We readily thank you always for your hearty attention to our business, but greatly regret that you have not forwarded the money, for we are in pressing want, and made our calculations on the remittance from the Ohio Conference."[36]

He received another long letter from them dated November 18, 1815, urging him to send the money due them. Finley managed to send them payments of $915 and $750 before the end of the year. Their letter of acknowledgment on January 4, 1816, contained not only their thanks but also a lesson in the difficulties of discounting bank notes from the West. "It was wrong information that you received that Kentucky paper was at par. . . . The brokers will not take it at less than fifteen percent discount; and we presume the notes from the western part of Pennsylvania & Ohio will be but little better. . . . Thus the concern is obliged to sustain these great losses in circulating paper of those banks at a distance."[37]

In 1816, Joshua Soule and Thomas Mason became the book dealers for the Methodist operation. In August they sent suggestions for improving the preachers' record keeping. "We recommend that a suitable book be procured to receive the names of Subscribers in each Circuit and Station, and when the preacher in charge leaves . . . let him lodge the book with one of the Stewards for the next preacher. . . . Some such course we conceive to be necessary in order to prevent confusion in the business." They too complained about their losses in cashing bank notes. On December 10, 1816, they wrote: "Your letter containing $1700 came safe and altho there was great loss on it we were greatly relieved by it. On the Kentucky bills we had to give up 19 percent discount and on those of Ohio 20 beside between 3 and 400 dollars which we could not change at any rate in this city . . . by all means avoid sending notes of unincorporated banks or companies as we can do nothing with them here."[38]

In 1817, over twelve hundred books were sent to Finley for sale in his district. In May of that year he ordered $568 worth of books, including five hundred hymn books, one hundred copies of Wesley on original sin, one hundred copies of Sutcliffe's sermon, and four other titles. The May 17, 1817, letter informing him that the three boxes had been shipped ended with thanks for his attention to the agent's financial problems. "We approve of your caution not to sell books for any other than good notes. The contrary conduct has subjected this concern to heavy loss." They wrote him again on December 8 to urge him to send the $173 due from the Ohio Conference.[39] Indicative of his interest in books was the fact that Finley submitted the motion in the 1820 General Conference that established the Cincinnati branch of the Book Concern.

Although the circuit riders were noted for their rhetorical skills, the eloquence itself would not have been effective if it had not been for the message to which their audiences responded so eagerly. Finley described the basic Methodist message of the 1800s: "Repentance, faith, justification, sanctification, the possibility of falling from grace, with the doctrine of atonement as contra-distinguished from the Calvinian view."[40]

Accessibility to all was emphasized. Everyone was equally worthy of salvation. God was real in every sense of the word, not an abstraction or something unreachable. Men and women could discover God through a moving experience in which God's power could save their souls. Methodism called out to persons of all classes, of all levels of education and wealth, of all degrees of sinfulness. Free will and free grace were offered to those who would take the first step and accept individual responsibility for their lives. Even the lowliest persons on the frontier could become masters of their religious fate. The appeal to the poorer economic classes was clear and effective. The message was one of hope and optimism. Typical of the spirit was the action taken at the Western annual conference in 1805: "It is the opinion of this Conference, that we live in an age in which there is great need to cry aloud, and spare not, and show lukewarm professors the danger of resting in a form only, and urge experimental and practical holiness, and teach sinners their utmost peril, and lead them to the Savior of Men."[41]

In its simplest form it was an emotional call of spiritual regeneration. Salvation had to be sought with constant vigilance. The convert had to be faithful in following the word of God. He or she had to have love, joy, peace, goodness, meekness, and temperance. The circuit riders preached a stern morality. The individual was inspired to become pious, to strive toward perfection. The idea of working to reform society came later, perhaps as people realized that not everyone was becoming perfect and that the evil outside threatened the sanctity of the faithful.[42]

Ernest Bormann was correct in calling the circuit riders' style "the rhetoric of romantic pragmatism." The preachers, some of whom liked to speak extemporaneously, used their own experiences as well as Biblical incidents to get across their message. They were adept storytellers. Finley included some of his personal anecdotes in his *Autobiography* and other writings. In mid-century the *Methodist Quarterly Review* evaluated the early Methodist preaching in this fashion: "The naturalness, the colloquial facility . . . were adapted to true oratory. . . . The trait . . . tended to produce . . . direct results. Our fathers expected men awakened and converted under their sermons, and the expectation led to an adaptation of their discourses to this end . . . [use of] the vigorous vernacular of the people."[43]

The message did not always come from study. Sometimes it was something inspired or improvised. Frequently it was loud and vigorous. To one circuit rider, study was of no use: "just get up, and look to God, and fire away." Peter Cartwright preferred "a preacher that could mount a stump, a block or old log, or stand in the bed of a wagon and without note or manuscript, quote, expound, and apply the word of God to the hearts and consciences of the people." Sometimes theological training was considered an impediment.[44]

One of the reasons why the message was accepted by so many was because of the uncertainties, harshness, and lonely drabness of early nineteenth-century life. There was, as Catharine Cleveland described, a consciousness of constant danger, of great, life-threatening insecurity. There was a profound sense of one's weakness in contrast to the immense power of God. Charles Johnson summarized the prevailing attitude aptly when he wrote, "The possibility of sudden extinction must certainly have made the question of one's immortality a matter of great concern." It was mostly the women and the young who were reached by the Methodists' eloquent preaching.[45]

It is also understandable that in a world of adversity with few comforts and many hazards the emphasis would be on the future and on rewards attainable in a life after death. Elizabeth Nottingham was sound in her conclusion that the starvation of the finer aspects of secular life put a premium on religious emotionalism and on the promise of something greater after this life.[46]

The message was normally conveyed at a religious service. Services were held during the week as well as on Sundays. If a service was held during daylight hours, people interested in attending interrupted their work. When a circuit rider arrived in a locality, all the Methodist families would assemble to greet him.

The weekends were ideal times for several services. Fridays were usually fast days. On Saturdays, preaching began at ten or eleven in the morning. A short service might be held in the afternoon. If it was time for one, there might be a quarterly meeting. That night there would be more preaching, or a prayer meeting might be held in the community. Sunday mornings would begin with a love feast followed at eleven by a sermon preached, perhaps, by the circuit's presiding elder. That might be followed by another sermon or by an exhortation given by someone hoping to become a preacher. Baptism and the Lord's Supper would be administered toward the end of the morning service. At night there would be more preaching followed by a prayer meeting. Converts might be won at any of the services.[47]

William Cooper Howells recalled Methodist services unfavorably in his memoirs: "Among the Methodists at that time there was a very steady succession of meetings of one kind or another, and those who belonged to the church found abundant entertainment, if nothing else, in the continued round of preaching, class and prayer meetings. There were then very few public entertainments, and religious meetings took the place of these for nearly all the people. A consequence of this was, that meetings were carried to the extreme, and religious enthusiasm and extravagant experiences were cultivated at the expense of propriety."[48]

A series of religious services designed to intensify church members' religious conviction but primarily to convert people, and originally held out-of-doors in order to accommodate large crowds, became known as camp meetings. Russell Richey has pictured them as evolving from the quarterly and annual conference meetings in Virginia, Maryland, and Delaware in the 1780s. The camp meeting served to carry on the spiritual functions of conference meetings, which focused more and more on business and legislative details. Richey suggests that camp meetings became a way in which Methodism changed over the years while outwardly remaining the same. Henry Boehm recalled that at the 1792 Annual Conference there was a camp meeting at which the preachers "ate and slept in their tents."[49]

The earliest camp meetings could be considered interdenominational in that Methodist, Presbyterian, and Baptist ministers frequently participated. Kenneth Brown has asserted that one of the first Methodist camp meetings on this continent occurred near Terrill, North Carolina, in 1794 when the congregation held a six-day series of services outdoors because of the large crowd. Many slept in wagons and camped on the grounds. Bishop McKendree was one of the preachers. The first camp meeting in the West was claimed to have been held in July 1800 in Logan County, Kentucky. According to some accounts, it occurred almost by chance and was unplanned. A family who had just migrated from the Carolinas wanted to attend one of McGready's Presbyterian services, but it was too far away from where they were to live. A woman in the family suggested that they camp in their wagon near the church in order to attend the service. At the next meeting several other families camped along with them. McGready seized the opportunity and announced a meeting at Gaspar River where people would be expected to camp on the ground. Services continued for days, and forty-five were converted.[50]

The McGee brothers attended McGready's camp meeting. They returned to Tennessee where William McGee held a five-day meeting that attracted a thousand people. On the last day, Bishop Asbury and William McKendree attended and were invited to participate. Asbury was impressed.[51]

At the end of his history of Methodists published in 1810, Jason Lee described the physical arrangements and the schedule followed in camp meetings. The site was usually a wooded area of up to four acres, cleared of undergrowth, surrounded by a row of tents. Wagons and carriages were stationed behind the tents and places for cooking fires in front of them. One or two stages for preaching were erected at opposite ends with seats placed between them. The sexes sat separately. Preachers might preach at both stages simultaneously.

At dawn a person walked in front of the tents blowing a trumpet. Ten minutes later there was a single note of the trumpet at which time the people began to sing and pray. A service was held at sunrise followed by breakfast. Preaching occurred again at ten and at three. People ate at one and at sunset. There was preaching at night by candlelight. Lee counted 120 candles burning at one camp meeting. Meetings usually lasted from Friday until midday Monday, although some continued for up to ten days.[52] Usually a guard of men were assigned to patrol the camp grounds at night to protect persons and property.

A camp meeting manual forty years later reveals how little the schedule had changed:

1. Rise at five, or half-past five in the morning.
2. Family prayer and breakfast from half-past six to half-past seven.

3. General prayer meeting at the altar, led by several ministers appointed by the Presiding Elder, at eight-thirty.
4. Preaching at ten thirty followed by prayer meeting to noon.
5. Dine at twelve-thirty.
6. Preaching at two or two-thirty followed by prayer at the altar till five.
7. Tea at six.
8. Preaching at seven thirty followed by prayer meeting at the altar till nine or ten.
9. All strangers to leave the grounds and the people to retire at ten, or immediately thereafter.[53]

The great Cane Ridge revival in 1801 was a mammoth camp meeting. The camp meeting's utility quickly became apparent to church leaders. Large fields where many wagons could congregate and where tents could be erected were ideal sites for large religious gatherings, especially in areas lacking in meeting houses. The camp meetings became attractive social events that involved families over a wide area. Late summer was the ideal time. They tended to be scheduled in connection with quarterly meetings or annual conferences. Farm families would schedule their work so that they could make the yearly trip to the campground in their area. It was not long before camp meetings became institutionalized, were carefully planned, and were announced weeks in advance.

The first Methodist camp meeting in Ohio was apparently held in 1804 at Deer Creek. One four years later at the same place drew 125 tents and wagons. Twenty-three preachers held services for two thousand persons. Bishop Asbury, who was there, was pleased with the "blessed results."[54]

Peter Cartwright participated in a camp meeting near New Lebanon, Ohio, in 1806. He wrote, "The pulpit in the woods was a large stand; it would hold a dozen people." Finley participated in four camp meetings near Chillicothe between May and August 1809. At the annual conference in 1809, when he was admitted on trial, the minutes recorded satisfaction with the number of camp meetings. The Muskingum district had four with attendance reaching three thousand. Seventeen camp meetings were held in the Miami district that year while four were held in the Scioto district and eleven elsewhere in the Western Conference. Bishop Asbury wrote in his journal that year, "We must attend to camp meetings, they make our harvest time."[55]

Finley quickly saw their utility and frequently scheduled camp meetings at the time of his district's fourth quarterly conferences in order to swell the size of the congregations. He conducted one in Belmont county from Friday, October 12, to Tuesday, October 16, 1810, that resulted in seventy-two conversions. He recorded the events in a seven-page diary.

The diary concluded, "8 o'clock Tuesday. We then proceeded to close our meeting by solemnly walking around the camp ground with the circle formed by the tents the men in front 2 deep the women following in like manner, the preachers standing in front of the stand and as the men and women past by giving the preachers their hand in token of love and connected with a promise through Grace to meet them in heaven, then we parted for a season."[56]

Bishop Asbury attended camp meetings in Ohio the next three years. He spoke at one Finley organized in October 1812, the year Finley moved his family to St. Clairsville. In 1811, Asbury had written to Thomas Coke, "Our camp meetings, I think, amount to between four and five hundred annually." He was referring to the entire country. Thanks to camp meetings, Methodist membership in the Miami district doubled in 1812. According to Charles Johnson, fifty-nine camp meetings were held in Ohio between 1804 and 1816. Those converted at an 1816 camp meeting near Marietta were mostly young people. Richard Wentz has aptly observed that camp meetings were places at which to find meaning and order in the midst of the frontier's chaos. In the summer of 1820 Finley held five of them, at one of which "the gathering of the people was immense." He recalled that scores of people who had previously paid no attention to the subject of religion flocked to church meetings.[57]

The camp meeting was a remarkable religious and social phenomenon that left its mark on frontier society. Successful camp meetings required extensive preparation. Large quantities of food were prepared and brought by the participants. Tents, wagons, and huts sheltered the worshipers. The preachers honed their most elequent sermons. The congregations sat on log benches, and, when a thousand voices were raised in song, the notes of the hymns echoed through the trees. At such a time Francis Asbury's grandson recalled that the din was "tremendous; at a hundred yards it was beautiful, and at a distance of half a mile it was magnificent."[58]

At services, those who were seeking conversion or who were worried about their lives or souls sat up front beneath the stern gaze of the assorted preachers. They sat on what was called the "mourners' bench," or, as the Irish traveler Simon O'Ferrall called it, "the penitents' pen." As they called the faithful to renewed fervor and the sinners to repentance and a spiritual awakening, the preachers' voices carried above the noise of the people's chatter, wagons being unloaded, camp utensils banging, and horses neighing.[59]

Singing was an important part of every service. Those ministers who could carry a tune and teach the lines of hymns to the congregation were considered especially blessed. Finley praised the singing of Rev. Robert

Manley at an Ohio camp meeting. "Before he had finished singing the fourth verse, the power of God came down, and pervaded the vast assembly, and it became agitated—swelling and singing like the sea in a storm." At least seventeen Methodist camp meeting hymn books were published between 1805 and 1843.[60]

One of Finley's favorite hymns began,

> Come poor sinners Christ invites you
> To partake His offered grace.
> Let His goodness now invite you
> Leave your sins and seek His face.

The services at night were illuminated by many fires. The dancing shadows made the group's confrontation with the preachers' words of warning all the more ominous and dramatic. Emotions became stronger. People reacted in a variety of ways, shouting, clapping their hands, screaming, and sometimes falling and swooning as they were caught up in the passions of the moment.

Church leaders were sensitive to the fact that emotionalism was associated with camp meetings. While they were seen as the work of God, the excesses in some of the services worried thoughtful ministers who sought to contain and channel the enormous outbursts of enthusiasm in some of the converted. Bishop Asbury wanted a "well-disciplined army." He disliked excessive emotions and called for "order, order, order."[61]

As the camp meetings became institutionalized, they grew less boisterous. The emotionalism and physical excitement were less excessive. But even in the 1830s, emotions could still run high at services. Maxwell Gaddis recalled hearing Finley preach at a camp meeting northwest of Russelville, in Brown County, in 1832. Finley's thunderous eloquence made him an ideal preacher for camp meeting services. At times, his enthusiasm produced lengthy sermons. His older colleague, John Collins, interrupted him during a service near Batavia in 1833 to say, "Now, brother, stop; keep the rest for another time, and throw out the Gospel net; it is now wet, and we shall have a good haul."[62]

Violence frequently occurred at the early camp meetings. Ruffians and roughnecks tried to break up the meetings, and sometimes the preachers retaliated by thrashing them. Jacob Young encountered violence at a camp meeting in 1809. "The rowdies annoyed us exceedingly. They pitched their tents on the hill-sides round about, and sold whisky, brandy, and cider. I visited and conversed with them til I found I could accomplish nothing that way. I then took a strong man with me and a hammer, went to their tents, knocked in the heads of their casks, and spilled their liquor on the ground."[63]

Samuel Hamilton's account of Methodism in Washington County, Ohio, described a Methodist class at worship "being assaulted by a lawless mob, [who] broke the windows, fired squibs, and covered the chimney, in order to annoy the worshipers with smoke, and drive them from the house of God." Finley described "the rabble" upsetting the Lebanon district meetings and cutting "the harness, saddles, bridles, and tents of the worshipers" to pieces.[64]

The Church tried to do something constructive to reduce the violence. At the 1819 Ohio Annual Conference a motion was passed, "Resolved that no Camp-meeting be appointed on the circuits, only by the direction of the Quarterly meeting Conferences & that they shall draft rules for the regulation of the same, and that the Presiding [Elder] of each Dist. have it inserted in the journal thereof." At the 1826 Ohio Annual Conference a committee was appointed "to write a memorial to the next General Assembly of the State on the subject of Amending the Laws respecting the prevention of unpopular conduct at meetings."[65]

Camp meeting accounts are filled with criticism of the excessive emotionalism that occurred. Daniel Drake was particularly critical of the camp meetings he attended. To him they presented "scenes of fanatical raving among the worshipers, and of levity and vice among the young men who hung about the camp, which was a disgrace to humanity." Although Isaac Holmes admitted that camp meeting promoters had the best of intentions, he thought the length of the meetings was "the height of folly." The caustic English traveler, Frances Trollope, devoted a dozen pages in her book to a probably distorted, critical description of a midnight camp meeting attended by two thousand near Cincinnati. Bayard Rush Hall considered a camp meeting in the West "the most mammoth picnic possible." According to James Flint, camp meetings were "like a menagerie of wild beasts." Peter Nielson, a British visitor for six years, called them "holy fairs."[66]

Finley's defense of them was simply, "Much may be said about camp meetings, but, take them all in all, for practical exhibition of religion, for unbounded hospitality to strangers, for unfeigned and fervent spirituality, give me a country camp meeting against the world."[67]

The meetings continued to be popular with the faithful. By 1811, there were more than four hundred in the country and by 1820 nearly one thousand. William Warren Sweet, who probably studied the subject more than anyone else, concluded that there has been too much attention placed on the emotional excesses and not enough on the routine work of the churches and preachers on the frontier. The social significance of the camp meetings in the 1800s has not been sufficiently appreciated.[68]

Not all camp meetings led to revivals; not all revivals were associated

Camp meeting by A. Rider. Copy of original painting, courtesy of the New York Historical Society.

with camp meetings. A revival was a period of religious awakening when large numbers of people were strongly moved to experience a profound conversion that resulted in a marked change in their living habits and value systems. Although the process of conversion was individualistic, revivals were group events in which large numbers of penitents made similar decisions in a public gathering at which singing, praying, and preaching occurred. The process of almost immediate conversion had a strong spontaneous quality to it.[69]

Revivals were emotional events. They were joyous occasions in that they marked an individual's turning away from habits considered sinful and moving in the direction of soul saving. In the early 1800s many revivals seemed spontaneous. Their success was attributed more to the working of God's spirit than to the preacher's efforts. Later, as they became institutionalized, revivals used methods that seemed to increase the likelihood of mass conversions. They were primarily a series of religious services in which energetic ministers used plain, persuasive language to convert people.

Historians have counted four major religious awakenings in American history. Why did one commence in 1800? According to William McLoughlin, who called them a mysterious folk art, they begin when there has been a serious crisis of values and beliefs. Were Americans in 1800 still adjusting to the upheavals of society brought about by the Revolution and the establishment of the new nation under the Constitution? Were the pressures of life so onerous that people needed a "restructuring" of these institutions and "redefinitions" of their social goals, as McLoughlin suggests? Or were revivals a "response to disestablishment, the religious liberty established by the Constitution, and the accompanying denominational pluralism," as John Hammond maintains? In any event, the famous Cane Ridge revival in 1801 was, as Baird pointed out, remarkably adapted to the circumstances of the time.[70]

These reasons may explain part of the phenomenon. Except for a small segment of the population rich enough to enjoy good living, life in 1800 was filled with uncertainty, crises, and almost unbearable pressures. Life expectancy was low. Few Americans lived beyond their sixties. Only about five-sixths of white infants survived beyond age one. The short life expectancy and the prevalence of sickness were also reasons for the success of revivals and of emotional religion. Many suffered from consumption. Bilious conditions and fevers were often epidemic. Many of the letters written to Finley over his career contained accounts of illness. Several times during his life he thought that he was close to death.[71]

Living conditions of the frontier encouraged the eventual popularity of revivals. Bernard Weisberger expressed this theme aptly when he wrote that inasmuch as the settlers worked and died hard, it was understandable that they would convert in a similar fashion. A revival was something radically different for those living in sparsely settled areas. It transformed their lonely lives, brought them into contact with others, provided a social connection as well as a religious one, and gave their routine a new level of meaning. A religious experience in a revival gave people license to face up to their fears and insecurities, to give vent to their emotions in a socially acceptable way. As Donald Mathews has observed, the Second Great Awakening was instrumental in giving meaning and direction to those who were suffering or struggling. We must remember that not all the converts were women. Buley has maintained that strong, passionate men were also susceptible to being influenced by revival methods. And Hardman has pointed out that the process by which conviction, despair, repentance, and conversion were compressed in a revival was bound to result in explosive emotionalism.[72]

We must remember too that periods of revival have led to enthusiastic reform movements. In the 1850s, James Porter saw religious revivals as "necessary to the triumph of moral reforms." He believed that people's sinful habits were so great that "nothing short of a profound sense of religious obligation and a thorough baptism by the grace of God can recover them."[73]

Revivals have been called anti-intellectual in that the basic approach was to the heart rather than to the head. A direct response was urged.

Little time was offered for contemplation. The pleas to renounce a sinful life were based on feelings more than on factual information. The preachers themselves preferred the emotional approach. In a revealing statement in *The Methodist Magazine* in 1819 Thomas Hinde declared, "Give me a sabel African, who has a knowledge of his sins forgiven, as my spiritual leader, in preference to all the sleek Doctors of Divinity, however learned they may be, if they are destitute of this knowledge."[74]

Conversion meant so much that it is understandable why revival meetings contained so much frenetic activity. The anguish experienced by those who were confronted with an awareness of the seriousness of their condition was almost unbearable. The potential converts were confronted with a difference in the demands of their secular roles and their religious ideals. Conversion meant turning one's back on the past and making a commitment to a different future. The break with what were called sinful ways had to be complete; the belief in the new way and in the word of God had to be unqualified. Furthermore, revivals were directed not only toward the unconverted; they also aimed at increasing the piety of those already converted.[75]

Whether revivalism permeated the secular as well as the religious life in the West, as Miyakawa has asserted, may be debated, but it certainly was "an expression of western religion and sociability." Furthermore, the movement contributed to a strengthening of democracy and to facilitating what Mathews has called the "acculturation in the West." This democratization resulted partly from the willingness to accept the religious impulses of the converted rather than relying solely on doctrines to preach the Word. The active involvement of the convert, regardless of how strong the Holy Spirit did or did not operate, often led to a participation in a variety of social and moral reform movements and to a renewed level of citizenship. Conversion in a revival encouraged what Dimond has called a "passionate confidence in personal and religious values, and in the possibility of social and moral redemption." Why not try to convert the world by changing individuals rather than institutions?[76]

Revivals were also an expression of the Romantic movement in the United States in the early nineteenth century. The reliance on emotion, the identification with nature as it was encountered in the Ohio forests, the affection for the individual, the subjective, the tendency to excess, those qualities so easily discernible in art and literature, had their religious counterparts. It was A.P. Mead who wrote, "The heart that has offered incense at the cross, is best prepared to kneel at nature's shrine." Revivalism has even been credited with helping to strengthen nationalism and a spirit of benign capitalism. There was also a connection between the success of revivalism and the rise of anti-Catholicism after 1820. Ray Billington has pointed out that Protestantism grew to be "venerated and protected" while Catholicism was resented and opposed as a threat to the Christianizing of the West.[77]

Although one cannot say that religion and religious fervor permeated Ohio society in the early 1800s, it must be realized that religious activity at that time was closely bound up with other aspects of people's lives. Religious services, camp meetings, even small class meetings met a social need as well. There were few secular institutions to bind people together. The cities of the East were far away in point of time. The ministers provided a cohesive element that went beyond their energetic efforts to save souls.

Revivalism sought to create a form of order in a disorderly world, to encourage a sense of community out of the loneliness of the frontier or isolated village and town. It sought to show how morality could give direction in an era of loose ends. Revivalism may even have served as a safety valve in society by syphoning off pent-up emotions and disaffections in praying, singing, and elevating personal standards, emotions that otherwise might have been directed in more violent and destructive ways.

Revivals in Ohio began shortly after the great Cane Ridge, Kentucky, event at which James Finley and thousands of others were converted. The first one occurred on the Miami circuit in 1801, according to the memoirs of Philip Gatch. He preached on a Sunday afternoon that year and, after he had dismissed the congregation, he went to another part of the cabin where he encountered a black boy whom he had raised leaning against the wall and crying. He asked why he was crying. The boy fell to the floor and begged for mercy in such a loud voice that members of the congregation returned to see what was the matter. The adults were so moved by the boy's concern for his soul that they called to each other to help him and the service was resumed. It lasted into the night and ended with several conversions. Frequent prayer meetings were held in the following weeks, and, according to Gatch, "This revival spread generally over the country." The next year Elisha Bowman was sent to the Miami circuit and continued the revival. Methodist church membership there increased in four years from 99 to 414.[78]

A Methodist revival occurred in Marietta in 1804 in which the majority of converts were women. They continued in other parts of the state throughout the decade. Finley helped produce a powerful revival the year he began to preach on the Scioto circuit in May 1809. He described it thirty years later in an article in the *Western Christian Advocate*. Four camp meetings had been held. The most dramatic was at Big Bottom below Chillicothe May 12, 1809.

Many fell to the ground and cried for mercy. . . . Upwards of sixty professed to find pardon at this meeting. This meeting made a strong impression on the neighborhood. . . . The next camp meeting was held on Eagle Creek . . . with many local preachers in attendance; and it did appear as if two great armies had met for a pitched battle . . . all went to work singing and praying, and the night was made glorious by the conversion of many souls to God . . . 500 fell to the ground. The work went on all night at the stand and in the tents . . . people were hungry for the word . . . [They] came out in their moccasins and hunting shirts and the sisters in their linsey and cotton dresses.[79]

In 1818-19, revivals were experienced in practically all circuits in Ohio. One of the biggest occurred in Chillicothe and began in October 1818 and continued through the following February. The Methodist church in that town gained 220 members, at least 80 percent of whom were young men and women. According to one account, by December the revival "reached the magnitude of a mighty torrent."[80]

A revival in Portsmouth in August 1818 attracted much attention. There the "mourners," as the potential converts were called, were advised after the service to go into the woods. John Collins, the presiding elder of the Scioto district, reported, "The lonely valley soon became vocal with bitter lamentations." One hundred were converted. At the end of the revival, "The tents struck; the wagons and carriages in readiness; weeping circles of young converts folded in each other's arms, ministers surrounded with weeping hundreds."[81]

Finley reported on a revival that began in Deerfield in July 1818 and continued for three months with a sizable increase in conversions. The following June, he was busy supervising revivals thoughout the Ohio district. "The work spread like fire in stubble."[82]

In 1820, Tallmadge was the scene of an unexpected revival in which Elizur Wright, Jr., participated and which continued for several months. Nearly one hundred were added to the church.

By the 1830s, revivals seemed less boisterous. Thomas Morris wrote Finley from Columbus January 26, 1833 to report, "The first principal subject is the Revival. Since you left us 125 have applied to join on trial; and we think it a safe calculation to say that as many have been "born again" during the same period. In this it differs from most revivals. . . . Many have been converted in class meetings, many in the secret chambers & some while praying in their families. Thus the full tide of salvation rolls on growing deeper and wider."[83]

The average number of Methodist revivals in Ohio between 1825 and 1828 was seventeen. Between 1829 and 1830 it was fifty-three, and between 1833 and 1835 it was twenty-five.[84]

They continued into the 1840s. A notice appeared in the *Ladies Repository* for January 1843 that announced, "Probably there has never been a period since time began, when revivals of religion were so general and so powerful as now. They spread nearly over the Christian world, and they sway the minds of men in an unusual manner." After 1840, however, the indoor protracted meeting replaced the great outdoor revival sessions which lost popularity as communities increased in size, transportation improved, church buildings increased in number, and social activities became more varied.[85]

The most immediate result of revivals was the great increase in those converted to religion. But the great significance to society was the more lasting result, the rise of reform movements designed to improve society. Many believed that once souls were saved, fundamental changes in society were bound to follow. It was a small step from an individual's conversion to group efforts to convert the world and purge it of its evils. If one individual could be saved, his or her life perfected, then many devout persons working together could improve conditions and institutions. Thus, voluntary associations were formed to undertake changes that could not be achieved by persons working alone. The great nineteenth-century reform movements in education, prison reform, temperance, women's rights, and antislavery were the logical results of all the revivalistic fervor.[86]

The career of Louis Dwight is an example of what the reform impetus could accomplish. Dwight intended to be a minister, but a chemistry experiment at Yale in 1813 ruined his voice and instead he became the first agent for the American Bible Society. In 1824, he traveled on horseback to give Bibles to persons. He was so moved by prison conditions that he organized the Boston Prison Discipline Society. (Even Daniel Webster contributed.) Thousands of Bibles were distributed to prisons so that eventually libraries could be formed.[87]

There was both cooperation and competition among the religious sects in Ohio. Methodists and Presbyterians worked together at the early camp meetings, but there was rivalry too. When Finley was presiding elder of the Ohio district in 1816, he campaigned actively against Calvinism and Universalism. He complained in his *Autobiography* that he found a Calvinist minister in almost every settlement in northeast Ohio and the Presbyterian influence "was so great that Methodism could scarcely live." Finley did not like "union" meetings. In one article, he criticized Eastern ministers from other sects who came out to Ohio to participate in services. "When they are among us," he wrote, "it is 'brother' and 'union'; but as soon as they are gone, we are all dead, wretched."[88]

Finley's strongest attack against other denominations appeared in an article he wrote titled, "A short record of the great revival at Oxford and in Miami University in May & June 1839." He attended services held by Lyman Beecher and in sarcastic words criticized Beecher's efforts to reconcile predestination with the call to the unconverted to take the first step toward saving their souls. Finley's jibes were unrestrained: "Now the Doctor, having traveled to these parts to stir up the luke-warm, and make converts, found that, notwithstanding all his heart stirring appeals, his benevolent warnings, . . . his pathetic persuasions, his rhetorical pauses, his solemn head shakings, his now and then elevated and eloquent vociferation . . . he could make no breech in the strong holds of Satan."[89]

Not all of the rapid increase in membership was the sole result of preaching, singing, and praying. It was devoutly believed that the conversions that occurred in revivals were the work of God. According to Finley, the great earthquake in December 1811 "was a time of great horror to Sinners." A comet was visible in 1811 and then beginning December 16 and 17 there were repeated earthquake shocks. The quake was centered in the Missouri area, but the series of shocks were felt as far east as Ohio, and they reminded people of their mortality and the fragility of their existence. Superstitious people considered them ominous portents. People in the Dayton area felt shocks again on January 23 and 27, and February 13, 1812. Finley was awakened in the early hours of February 13 by the shaking of a house in which he was sleeping. Another shock occurred February 16 when he was near Zanesville.[90]

One of the stories told of Finley was his experience staying in a cabin with a group of "sin-hardened" men when a heavy tremor shook the place. Finley jumped on a table and shouted, "For the great day of His wrath is come, and who shall be able to stand?" As he recalled the earthquake years later, "One day while I was preaching a funeral, the house began to rock and the cupboard doors flew open. The people became alarmed. . . . It contributed greatly to increase the interest on the subject of religion. Multitudes who previously paid no attention . . . now flocked out to meeting. . . . The number of converts was great, and the work extended almost everywhere."[91]

The next year, however, with the outbreak of the War of 1812, the spiritual development in Ohio slowed considerably. Religious zeal evaporated, replaced by a spirit of belligerency. Finley declared, "Wars and rumors of war are peculiarly fatal to a mild and peaceful spirit of the Gospel." Many converts who sought religion following the earthquake returned to their evil habits, according to Finley. In Ohio there was an almost 4 percent decline in Methodist church membership from 1812 to 1813. Finley's friend, David Young, wrote him on March 10, 1815, to say, "I congratulate you on the return of peace to our country. I hope now that the Spirit and Life of Religion will also return. However, we may expect that the effects of the unhappy and wicked war . . . will be long felt on morality and religion." Young's comment was prophetic. Methodist membership in Ohio remained under twenty-five thousand until 1817 when it resumed its upward march.[92]

Despite the problems of wars and economic panics, religion was a powerful cultural and social force in pioneer life and continued to be in the first half of the nineteenth century. Nevertheless, it probably was not as significant a force as the circuit riders believed. Perhaps crusaders always magnify the importance of their cause. Buley is probably correct in maintaining that religious conviction ruled many lives in 1800, a view repeated by Perry Miller, who called religious revivalism a dominant theme before 1860. Miller may have read more into the motivation of religious leaders when he asserted that the Second Great Awakening confirmed for Americans the belief that the 1776 Revolution had not been revolutionary "but simply a protest of native piety against foreign impiety." He is correct, however, in describing the early nineteenth-century interest in saving the West and the souls of its inhabitants as being more impassioned than the drive for independence from England. Ralph Gabriel's assertion that Americans before the Civil War held a strong belief in a fundamental moral order can be interpreted as recognition of the ultimate success of religious revivals.[93]

By 1850, it was claimed that one in seven persons was a church member. Methodists that year numbered 1.25 million. William Cooper Howells was on the scene in the 1820s and seems a reliable reporter of the era given his critical view of religion: "The religious feeling pervaded the whole community intellectually, and all accepted the general orthodox standard of faith. . . . The public mind was more largely employed with religious subjects than in later years, and it was the subject and object of nearly all public meetings to consider religion in some of its relations. . . . The leading question at issue was at all times the freedom of the will and the Calvinistic doctrine of predestination."[94]

Robert T. Handy has observed that one of the successes of Methodism in the West was its ability to confront creatively the "tension between order and freedom." The settlers struggling for economic security and some form of moral and ethical stability needed both. The Methodist system provided order; the Methodist message spoke of a certain freedom for one's soul within that order.[95]

3

Encounter with the Wyandots

> Missionary labor requires an energy and will that surmount all obstacles and brave all climates and all risks. . . . There is a species of moral heroism required for the true missionary.
>
> —Henry R. Schoolcraft

The Ohio Annual Conference that met in Cincinnati in August 1819 took a significant action in approving the sending of a missionary to the Wyandot Indians at Upper Sandusky. Finley was appointed presiding elder of the Lebanon district, which that year comprised eight circuits including the mission. Seventy dollars was collected for the mission support from the fifty-one preachers attending the conference.[1]

The Wyandot Indians were once a proud and powerful nation. Originally they called themselves Wendats or Ouendats. The name probably means "islanders" or "dwellers on a peninsula." Their earliest known location in the sixteenth century was on the north side of the St. Lawrence River in the area now known as Ontario, from Lake Ontario to Georgian Bay. When Jacques Cartier came up the St. Lawrence River in 1534 he found them near what is now Montreal. When Champlain arrived in the area in 1603 they were living south of Georgian Bay. It was Champlain who was reputed to have given them the name Huron from the French word, "huré," meaning "rough" or "wild boar." They belonged to the Iroquois linguistic family and considered themselves at the head of all tribes.[2]

The French had peaceful relations with them, and after 1615 missionaries sought to convert them to Christianity. Their population in 1600 is estimated to have been around ten thousand. French estimates in the seventeenth century ranged from twenty thousand to thirty thousand. Early in the seventeenth century, the Hurons provided about two-thirds of all the beaver traded in the St. Lawrence River area.[3]

The Huron tribes were matrilineal in that each family was ruled by the senior child-bearing woman. General governance was by a council of chiefs. The title of chief was hereditary within a family, but the particular person picked was selected by the child-bearing women of the family.

The Hurons had a well developed set of religious beliefs and myths, worshiped many spirits and had four types of annual religious festivals: singing feasts, farewell feasts, thanksgiving feasts, and prayer feasts for freeing one from sickness. Some feasts could last up to fifteen days. Their religious beliefs permeated their culture and probably influenced their way of life more than other people realized. Every decade or so they held a Feast of the Dead, which was their most important festival. At that time, the bodies of those who had died were taken from the village burial grounds and reburied in a common grave. Singing and dancing had important political and religious purposes. According to Henry Schoolcraft, "No grave act is performed without singing and dancing." They had several gods including the god of nature, the war god, the god of dreams, and the thunder god.[4]

Their economy was based on agriculture and trade, although they also hunted. In their trading trips they covered a wide area. The men would be gone on trade expeditions from June through September. They were adept at constructing birch bark canoes. The men made clubs, bows, and arrows while the women made pottery and wicker baskets. It has been said that they lived closer to the earth than Europeans.

The Hurons were attacked by the Iroquois in 1648-49, although some hostilities had occurred in 1641. There is some evidence that hostility between them dated from prehistoric times. The five tribes of the Iroquois were Cayuga, Mohawk, Oneida, Onondaga, and Seneca. The Iroquois sought to destroy the Wyandots, and they were forced to flee from their attackers for almost a century until 1701.[5]

There were several legends in the nineteenth century about the origin of this war and the subsequent Wyandot migration. One story told of an attack on the Senecas by some Wyandot braves. Another blamed the war on the scheming of a Wyandot woman. A more likely cause of the extensive hostilities was economic. The beaver supply was exhausted in the Iroquois territory by the 1640s. The Hurons were attacked because they had furs. Because the Iroquois possessed about four hundred Dutch firearms, they overwhelmed their foe, who had been weakened by a plague in the 1630s.[6]

After wandering over the northern forests, going as far west as the Wisconsin area, eventually most of the Wyandots settled in what became northern Ohio near Upper Sandusky. Some, however, moved as far south as Hocking County to an area one mile below Logan where the abundance of deer, bears, elks, buffalo, and fish made it an attractive place to live. Some settled along the shores of the Scioto River, opposite what was to become the city of Columbus, where they cultivated corn.[7]

The Wyandots were remarkably unlucky in the wars they fought. In the eighteenth century, while they were allies of the Algonquins, they were on the side of the French in their disastrous wars against the English. Their attacks on settlers along the Ohio River and in Kentucky were considered particularly ruthless. Three hundred Wyandots fought in the force against Wayne at the Battle of Fallen Timbers. In the War of 1812, the Wyandots in Canada supported the English. However, the chief, Tarhee, who had fought against Wayne, joined General Harrison's forces. Some Wyandots were with the American troops who invaded Canada. Others in Upper Sandusky stayed neutral.[8]

The Wyandots, who in 1800 numbered some twenty-two hundred, acquired a high status in the Ohio area. They had the right to light the great council fire at multi-tribal councils. They were recognized by the United States government as politically at the head of an Indian federation of tribes and were included in a number of treaties made with Native Americans in the old Northwest Territory. On September 29, 1817, Lewis Cass and Duncan McArthur, United States commissioners, concluded a treaty with the Wyandots near the Maumee Rapids. The treaty granted the Wyandot nation a reservation twelve miles square, the center of which was Fort Ferree at Upper Sandusky, and also a tract one mile square on the Cranberry Swamp on Broken Sword Creek in return for giving up claims to other lands.[9]

According to John Wesley Powell, in the 1840s, the Wyandots had eleven tribes or gentes known as Highland Turtle (striped), Highland Turtle (black), Mud Turtle, Smooth Large Land Turtle, Porcupine, Bear, Deer, Sea Snake, Hawk, Beaver, Wolf. Once a year, at the green corn festival, the council women selected names for the children born during the previous year. The names they received held a special significance.[10]

Before 1776, many of the Wyandots were converted to Catholicism. Between 1803 and 1810, the Presbyterians had a mission at Lower Sandusky under the leadership of the Reverend Joseph Badger. The War of 1812, however, ended that activity. Apparently, the Catholic Wyandots killed off the Presbyterian ones.[11]

John Stewart's preaching in 1816 was the beginning of what became the Methodist mission at Upper Sandusky. Stewart (or Steward, as some have spelled it) was a free-born mulatto who claimed to be part Indian. In 1815, while the Methodist Marcus Lindsey was preaching in Marietta, Stewart, who at that time was decrepit, dissipated, and on the verge of suicide, passed by and stopped at the meeting house door to listen. He was so moved that he became converted and felt that it was his duty to go and preach to the Indians even though he had no authorization from any church to do so.[12]

Stewart encountered resistance from many of the Wyandots, who initially were not receptive to missionary efforts. John Hicks, who was later converted, spoke out to defend his ancestors' religion and called it "a system of religion the Great Spirit has given his red children, as their guide and the rule of their faith, and we are not going to abandon it so soon as you might wish; we are contented with it, because it rules our conditions and is adapted to our capacities . . . we are willing to receive good advice from you, but we are not willing to have the customs and institutions which have been kept sacred by our Fathers, thus assailed and abused."

Another Wyandot who was later converted, Mononcue, raised objections that were not easy to refute. He declared that the Great Spirit never intended that Indians should be instructed out of a book. "Ours is a religion that suits us red people, and we intend to keep and preserve it sacred among us."

The head chief, Duon-Quot, was violently opposed to the preaching of Christianity to his people because he concluded that the Gospel, as taught by Stewart, would "result in the entire overthrow of the customs and religion of their ancestors." However, he subsequently became very sick and died. Opposition gradually decreased.[13]

Part of the opposition to Stewart, and later to Finley, came from white traders, some of whom sold whiskey to the Indians. Steward was called "no minister, a fraud, a villain" and denigrated because he was black.

Despite initial discouragement, Stewart was successful and continued preaching from November 1816 to early spring 1817. When he left, the Indians contributed ten dollars to help him. He returned in July but discovered that few of his conversions had been permanent. He remained there until spring 1818 and was finally licensed to preach in March 1819 after having been admitted on trial in 1817. The Ohio conference in 1819 assigned James Montgomery to help him and placed the Wyandot mission under the direction of Finley, who was named presiding elder of the Lebanon district. Montgomery was later replaced by Moses Henkle. Stewart and Henkle continued their work in 1820.[14]

At its meeting at Chillicothe in August 1820, the Ohio annual conference sent an address to the Wyandot Indians on the subject of religion. The conference also ordered each of its members to raise money for the support of the mission and voted two hundred dollars plus traveling expenses to Henkle.[15]

The missionary impulse among Methodists and other Protestant sects was a logical development given the widespread acceptance of the preaching in the Second Great Awakening. The Missionary Society of the Methodist Episcopal Church was organized in New York in 1819, and in the following year there was discussion at the general conference on forming auxiliaries. A total of nineteen dollars was collected at the Ohio conference for missions the first year that collections were authorized. Seeking to convert the unconverted became an imperative for the early nineteenth-century religious enthusiast.[16]

Although John Wesley recorded in his journal in Georgia January 24, 1738, "I went to America to convert the Indians," and although Thomas Coke in 1789 thought that some of the profits from the Methodist Book Concern might be used to "establish Missions and Schools among the Indians," the missionary zeal of most of the early Methodist pioneers did not include an effort to reach Native Americans. It was not until Finley's success that an increased number of Methodists saw the great need for missionary activities on this front. As Joshua Soule expressed it, the Indians had "a claim on American Christians paramount to all others."[17]

The task before the missionaries was enormous. They had to confront people different from them who had unfamiliar cultures, spoke unfamiliar languages, and they had to overturn existing religious customs in order to establish their own churches. Bishop McKendree wrote enthusiastically to Finley, "Our brethren here seem to regard the poor Indians as objects worthy of their most serious attention. We have appointed a missionary to travel through the bounds of the So. Carolina Conference to form societies etc. for the purpose of aiding in establishing schools among them." In the 1800s Americans considered Native Americans uncivilized. In addition, they expected them to become settled and accept their ways. Hunting required many more square miles than farming; therefore, whites considered farming more economical and intelligent. According to Roy Pearce, whites moving into the areas occupied by Indians expected them to move to insure a better life. Americans thought that their society could be sustained only if the savage past was obliterated.[18]

One of the debates that agitated Americans during the early years of the nineteenth century was the question of which should come first, civilizing the uncivilized or Christianizing the unconverted. Cotton Mather, in writing about John Eliot, the Puritan missionary to the Indians, had asserted that "they must be civilized before they could be Christianized." The federal government's policy in the 1800s assumed that civilization should occur first. The Protestant denominations were not united on this question. For the most part, Congregationalists, Presbyterians, and Quakers favored civilization first. The Moravians thought that Christianity should precede civilization. The Baptists and Methodists took varying positions. But most religious Americans before the Civil War favored both the conversion and the civilization of the Native Americans.[19]

One of the earliest statements on this issue was by Obadiah Jennings who, in a sermon in Pittsburgh in 1818, declared, "The Gospel is the only effectual means whereby they can be truly civilized. All other means . . . without this principle . . . must necessarily prove ineffectual." Finley's

Encounter with the Wyandots   45

position was clear-cut. "A man must be Christianized, or he can never be civilized. He will always be a savage till the grace of God makes his heart better, and then he will soon become civil and a good citizen." [20]

Little attention, however, seemed to have been devoted to defining what it meant to be civilized. Apparently, most people assumed it meant owning property, engaging in farming, commerce, or a profession, being able to read and write, wearing clothes, and, perhaps, repressing animal instincts. There seemed to be little awareness that Native Americans and whites perceived the world in different ways.

The Wyandot chiefs who were converted seemed to agree with Finley's insistence on conversion. At the Ohio Annual Conference in 1824, one of their number addressed the audience in these words: "Once we were wild, but the word of God has tamed us. Once we were afraid of you, and you were afraid of us, but now we meet as friends." [21]

Finley lost little time in getting heavily involved in the missionary effort. A six-page December 3, 1819, letter to *The Methodist Magazine* was published the following month and recorded in detail the first Methodist quarterly meeting held in the vicinity of the reservation. Finley wrote, "God through the instrumentality of Methodist preaching, has begun a most glorious work among the Wyandots." The meeting was held November 13 and 14, 1819, and included much preaching, singing, and praying. "Here are red, and white, and black men, of different nations and languages, sitting together under the Tree of life partaking of the most precious fruits and sweetly bathing their souls in the ocean of redeeming grace." The large audiences included about three hundred whites from nearby settlements. The Indians kept the service going all night. By its end, sixty Wyandots were converted.[22]

Finley experienced some opposition when he first arrived. Some weeks he would stay in the council house from Sunday morning to Monday evening responding to the Indians' objections against Christianity. In one of his sessions, he exposed the duplicity of one of the Wyandots' self-proclaimed prophets. Some Wyandot leaders told him that the Bible could not have been intended for them, because it had not been written in their language. Furthermore, as Finley recorded their reaction, the Bible "had a great many things that did not suit a people that hunted, but those who worked the earth. . . . When it speaks of plowing and sowing, and reaping, the whites understand these things, and the language suits them. But what does an Indian know of this." To the whites, the Wyandots were considered superstitious. They were described at the time as believers in magic and witchcraft who engaged in much religious dancing and feasting.[23]

Finley took it upon himself to acquaint American Christians with the missionary efforts among the Wyandots. The November 1820 issue of *The Methodist Magazine* contained a long article in which he described Stewart's work and various customs of the Wyandots. He depicted them as believing in a different god than the whites, "distinguished by color and dress" and asserted that another of their traditional customs was making feasts for the sick "and offering sacrifice to appease the wrath of the Deity, that the sick might be restored to health." He deplored their practice of "putting away their wives for very trifling considerations."[24]

In explaining the difficulty of his assignment, he wrote that the Indian god differed from that of the whites because he "is red, paints his upper parts, and dresses with the richest trinkets, such as bells, beads, rings, bands, brooches, and buckles, and that he requries them to imitate him in that respect."[25]

One of the first gifts to the mission was one hundred dollars collected mainly from blacks who had heard Bishop McKendree speak about John Stewart's missionary labors.[26]

The Methodist missionaries were not the only white men the Indians had to deal with. There were government agents, traders, settlers, and speculators. The clash of cultures was occurring on many fronts in the 1820s. The Wyandots reacted in understandable ways. In 1819, for instance, the Wyandots and Shawnees, concerned that their popular agent, John Johnston, might be replaced, wrote to the president asking him to keep Johnston, who had served them well for the eighteen years he was assigned to their area. In transmitting the Indian message, Johnston wrote, "Many of the Wyandots are Christians, they are the most promising of any Indians under my charge. I beg to ask for a portion of the annual appointment of $10,000 to enable me to establish a school at Upper Sandusky for their use." In the same letter, although later he became Finley's close friend, Johnston recommended that the Quakers be selected as missionaries at Upper Sandusky. Even at this early date Johnston recorded his preference for removing them out of Ohio "because I am convinced their interests as well as ours calls for the measure. I will remove them but I must have my own time and take my own method."[27]

A continuing problem for the Wyandots was the harmful effect of drinking and drunkenness on their tribe. The leaders regretted the negative influence whiskey sellers were exerting and in 1819 asked that their annuities for the federal government be given them in goods rather than in money so that they wouldn't have the cash to use in buying whiskey.[28]

Although the chiefs signed a statement asking that the mission be continued, Stewart's health was failing and Finley was not satisfied that enough progress was being made. He concluded that sporadic help from part-time ministers was not enough and that a more comprehensive plan was needed. He also realized that with their lands greatly reduced, the Wyandots had to farm in addition to hunting or else they would starve. He believed that they needed a full-time competent person in residence. In July 1821, on his way to Detroit, he stopped to persuade the chiefs to request a missionary and a school. The Ohio conference that year endorsed their request. Finley was the obvious choice for their expanded venture.[29]

Although as presiding elder of the Lebanon district (which included western Ohio and the territory of Michigan) from August 1819 until September 1821 Finley had general direction over the Wyandot mission, he was officially assigned as missionary to the Wyandots at the Ohio Annual Conference in Lebanon in September 1821. The following year he was reassigned as presiding elder of the Lebanon district and superintendent of the mission. Because both he and his wife were ill with a fever for a long period, Charles Elliott, who had initially been appointed to the Zanesville circuit in 1819, was appointed missionary. At the annual conference in September 1823, Finley's assignment was to the mission exclusively. The following year, however, he had to divide his time between the Sandusky district and the mission. At the annual conference in Columbus in October 1825 all of his duties were at the mission. But in October 1826 he picked up supervision of the Hillsborough district as well. Illness prevented him from continuing his connection with the mission after the fall of 1827.[30]

His eight-day move from Highland County to the Wyandot village in October 1821 was made in the face of many hardships. As he related it, "There was no plan of operation furnished me, no provision made for the mission family, no house to shelter them, nor supplies for the winter." Only two hundred dollars had been appropriated for the mission. Finley bought a yoke of oxen for the journey and had a wagon built to carry all his possessions. His party included, in addition to his wife and daughter (and perhaps also a grandson), two young hired men, one young woman and a volunteer teacher named Harriet Stubbs, John McLean's sister-in-law. One of his first tasks was to build a cabin, twenty by twenty-three feet, "without door, window, or loft." He rose at four in the morning and went to bed at nine in the evening. It started to snow the day he moved in his family.[31]

Two weeks after arriving on the scene, Finley was already seeking more funds and sharing his educational plans with some of his colleagues. On November 4, 1821, he wrote Joshua Soule,

Four of the chiefs have given me liberty to enclose as much ground for a farm as I please, and I can have the use of their Saw-mill to cut plank. . . . To put this establishment into complete operation, it will require for the first year between two and three thousand dollars. . . . If I had only the money which even the Methodists in your city, not to say in America, consume in smoking segars, chewing tobacco, and in other unnecessary expenditures, how many of these poor little naked savages could I feed and clothe and learn to read the word of God.[32]

Even this early in his tour of duty he was thinking of expanding his missionary endeavors. He wrote of visiting the Delawares, Senecas, Tarways, and Chippewas and declared that he felt a heavenly flame run through his soul.[33]

Finley put a high priority on educating the Wyandot children. He wrote to Soule: "I want to grasp all the children, and learn the girls to knit, sew, spin, weave and the art of housewifery; and the boys agriculture; and all of them to read the Holy Scriptures, and serve the true God. This I know is a hard task; but by the grace of God and the help of His friends I shall succeed. I know I have the confidence of these Indians."[34] Finley's primary task, of course, was to preach to the Wyandots and advance the cause of religion. He early decided to form the converted ones into classes, Methodist style, and, as he put it, "bring them under proper discipline." Initially, however, the Indians objected to having their names recorded on paper. It was not a practice to which they were accustomed. It took three months of Finley's persuasive skill and frequent readings of the General Rules for his will to prevail. Even that early in his work, he made as one condition for the Wyandots to join the church that they abstain from drinking alcohol. Even so, twenty joined at that time.[35]

He recalled later, "The temperance rule made a great stir among the whiskey-traders, and they tried to convince the Indians that in thus putting their names on paper, they had signed away their Indian liberty, and had become slaves of the white man. The lines, however, were drawn, and the national religion which allowed a man to be drunk one day and very religious the next, was entirely broken up."[36]

Finley was there to make the Wyandots good Methodists, and, in his opinion, there was only one prescribed way to do it. On February 19, 1822, he wrote to Martin Ruter revealing his discouragement that more had not been accomplished.

I am now trying to discipline our members which to some of the half-hearted is a grate scare now. . . . I have four chiefs and their wives with 35 others who have come under the yoke. I cannot live without discipline. I would rather have 10 who would be Methodist than 1000 that only bore the name. I have almost indescribable difficulties to surmount but by the grace of the Lord and Master I am determined to conquer. I have been launching all my artillery at whiskey, dancing, whoring, painting, feasting and now I have attacked witchcraft—this is a grate evil and does much harm.[37]

Finley also wrote three pages of rules for the regulation of the mission family.

Early in his tenure he received encouragement from Thomas McKenney, at that time superintendent for Indian Trade. "I wish you and all others who are at work in this great field of briars and thorns success."[38]

One of Finley's strongest assets was his willingness to live among the Indians and get to know them thoroughly. He believed that "it was impossible for any man, no matter what his conviction to have access to, or exert any good influence amongst the Indians, unless he can come down and associate with them in a very friendly way; for if he keeps at a distance, or shows any coldness or reserve of friendship, he can have no access to them."[39]

In June 1822, Finley conducted a camp meeting fourteen miles north of Delaware to which he brought sixty Wyandots. An observer wrote a long article describing the event and concluded that Finley "appears to possess the missionary spirit, and to be much engaged in the work; he now has fifty-three in the society belonging to the mission."[40]

The Wyandot chiefs were so impressed with Finley's first full year at the mission that they went to the Ohio Annual Conference meeting to ask that he be returned. The Wyandot chief, Between-the-Logs, who was converted by Stewart, declared, "When you placed my Finley amongst us in our own country, we rejoiced; and we have been much pleased with his living amongst us ever since. He is a plain man; he does not flatter our people; he preaches plain truth." Another chief, Mononcue, added, "He has a particular manner of teaching and preaching to us, different from other teachers who have been amongst us. . . . He was very industrious all the time he has been with us, and learns our people to work." Bishop McKendree, who presided over the conference, was deeply moved and responded, "If you will stand by us, we will stand by you."[41]

At that same conference in 1822 in Marietta, however, a sudden misunderstanding jeopardized the mission. Jacob Young gave a detailed account in his autobiography. The Indians became uneasy while meeting with all the ministers on the third or fourth day of the conference. They all sat in profound silence for half an hour. Between-the-Logs, whose name in the Wyandot language was Taruntne, finally spoke: "Brethren, we ourselves have full confidence in you, but some of our people have become uneasy; for certain white men tell them you keep a large book, and in it you charge us for all you are now doing; by and by, you will come and take away our land."

Bishop McKendree wrote an agreement between the Ohio Conference and the Wyandots in which he listed all the things the conference would do for them for which there would be no pay. The bishop and the chiefs signed the agreement and the crisis passed.[42]

By the summer of 1822, Finley was able to report that "God is with us in this wilderness, and His work is reviving gloriously among the natives." He described to his friends in the East his pleasure in administering the sacrament "to white, red, and black people who all sympathized together as members of the same spiritual family."[43]

Affairs at Upper Sandusky received attention at subsequent annual conferences. The chiefs attended the 1823 annual conference in Urbana and had another meeting with Bishop McKendree at which they ate bread and drank tea. One witness remarked, "The sagacity of the red brethren was quite observable; they . . . joined in singing several hymns in their own tongue." Mononcue held out his hands and the bishop embraced him.[44]

That year Finley was authorized to visit Governor Lewis Cass in the Michigan Territory to discuss establishing a mission among the Chippewas. The Conference also wanted a missionary employed to travel and preach, to establish missionary societies, and to collect money and food for the Wyandots. Reflecting Finley's interest in history, the conference action also urged all those engaged in missionary activity to keep journals to record what might be useful for the public to learn.

Conversions increased, and by 1823 over two hundred Wyandots had become church members; by 1826 their membership numbered 250. Finley must have taught them well. When Bishop Soule visited the mission in 1824 he was surprised at how well the Wyandots understood the doctrine of "trinity in unity."[45]

High on Finley's agenda was the establishment of a school for the Indian children. Writing to Martin Ruter January 2, 1822, he declared, "In this state of exile I am doing the best I can to promote the desire of the conference in establishing this school and mission, and though I have not progressed as fast as I could have wished, yet I have made some progress and am still laboring day and night . . . to bring it to full operation . . . am fully convinced that without suitable building we can do nothing with satisfaction or much success."

He asked for some books and to borrow two hundred dollars and promised to give Ruter a check for it in New York. The school started out in Finley's house but eventually was located a half mile northeast of the church.[46]

It took a while to get the school established on an official basis. In the Fall Finley was sick again but wrote Ruter on October 10 to say that he was about to leave for Upper Sandusky. He added, "I expect to be in your city about the first of Nov. Then I shall want more money." Earlier he had written Ruter to say, "The clothing you speak of I wish sent by the first opportunity."[47]

Finley arrived at the mission by October 20, 1822, to confer with the chiefs about the organization of the school. They agreed that a committee of five chiefs would inspect the school, that no children would be received for only a short time, that no child would have permission to go home without leave, that no student's complaint would be considered until it had been reviewed by the committee of chiefs. The conference also agreed upon a schedule for religious services. The diplomatic question of the choice of an interpreter to be employed by Finley was wisely left to the chiefs to determine. Both Finley and Charles Elliott, the missionary, proposed to the chiefs that the Scriptures be translated into the Wyandot language.[48]

Some of the Wyandots favored the school while others were opposed to it. The chiefs who had been converted hoped that eventually some of the educated children would become ministers. Charles Elliott recorded the missionaries' ultimate objective: "They shall, by early imbibing Gospel truths, be preserved from the superstitions of heathenism, and the practice resulting from them. The Indian god shall be neglected, the war dance shall be no more celebrated, and the idolatrous feasts shall be entirely done away and neglected."[49]

The school was founded on the manual labor system. Boys were taught farming. Girls were taught housework, sewing, knitting, spinning, and cooking. English and the Bible were also taught. Each class worked one day a week on the farm. From fourteen enrollment increased quickly and soon reached sixty. Finley divided the oldest boys into six classes so that some of them were in the field each weekday. A log meeting house was erected for the school and two additional teachers were employed. Five of the most important Wyandots were appointed a committee to supervise the school and the children's conduct. Finley was sensitive to involving the most influential Wyandots in his efforts. This committee was a particularly imaginative use of an advisory body.[50]

Finley used the manual labor system for both educational and political reasons. He saw the need to encourage the Wyandots to learn skills other than hunting. He also was aware that funds from the federal government and from individuals were more likely to come for vocationally oriented education than for a traditional classical one.

A second type of educational approach was tried in 1825 when some of the Wyandot children were placed with white families away from the reservation and attended local white day schools. Whether this approach originated with Finley is not clear, but, as early as January 7, 1825, one of the Wyandot boys was boarding with a Methodist family and attending a nearby school. The Ohio Annual Conference in 1825 passed a resolution recommending that the twelve largest boys be taken on the circuits or stations to improve their use of English. Finley took them to Urbana in December.[51]

John Johnston, the government agent in Piqua, who worked for a salary of twelve hundred dollars, had apparently been urging this arrangement on Finley for some time. On September 10, 1825, he wrote, "I am convinced more and more unless your scholars are scattered a part of the year in white families your labour and expense will be lost. As I once suggested to you they ought one half of the year to be placed, only one in a home, in the most correct exemplary families of white people . . . *take good heed to this suggestion* for I am fully persuaded if it is not adopted your mission and school will be added to the catalogue of failures, in attempting the civilization of the Indians." The following month Johnston wrote again, "I am glad to find that you intend bringing up the subject of dispersing your scholars before the Conference. I am more and more convinced that such a measure is indispensibly necessary to the success of any plan of civilizing and evangelizing the Indians."[52]

In December he wrote again to prod Finley on the matter. Writing from Worthington where he had observed a Wyandot boy whom he was supporting in school there he asserted that the lad "understands very little of what he reads, and this must continue to be the case so long as the scholars are kept so much of their time out of the society of the whites . . . there are many things to be learned to complete the character of man beside the knowledge of letters." Two days later Johnston sent a final note on the subject: "I am glad to find that the Conference has adopted the suggestions relative to the Indian scholars."[53]

One device popular at that time was to give the Wyandot children white names once they were enrolled in the school. According to Charles Elliott, their native names "sounded so strange and so harsh, and were withal so long, that we found it necessary to give them names in our own language." In a sense, it was partly a fund-raising practice inasmuch as donors could supply a name when they sent cash. Beyond that, however, it was an additional way to wean the child away from his heritage and help accustom him to American culture. John Johnston gave his own name to the child he was supporting. Others proposed the names of famous Methodists such as Francis Asbury and Mary Fletcher. The practice was started as early as 1822. On February 2, 1827, Edward Foreman sent fifty dollars from the Juvenile Wesleyan Missionary Society in Baltimore to name two Indian boys Job Guest and Joshua Wells.[54]

There was even the possibility of getting higher education for some of the more able Wyandot youth. The promise of a scholarship at Miami University finally came in a letter from Moses Crume November 17, 1825.[55]

Finley received many suggestions on conducting the mission and

Between-the-Logs was one of Finley's earliest converts and became a Methodist exhorter. He accompanied Finley on some of his fund-raising tours and was buried in the graveyard behind the Wyandot mission church.

school, some of which were helpful. Others were not. The corresponding secretary of the Methodist Missionary Society recommended that he employ the Lancasterian plan of teaching. "One teacher can as easily instruct 300 to 500 on that plan as 30 to 50 in the ordinary way, which would be a very great saving of labour and expense, not only in teaching but in the articles of Books & Stationery. This is not a visionary thing, it is reduced to demonstration in this city."[56]

Thomas Mason apparently ignored the differences between illiterate Wyandot children and New York students. He also probably did not realize that there was a weakness in using children to teach other children and that while the system worked for memorization, it failed when the subject taught required analysis or original thought.

One indication of Finley's widespread following in the early 1820s was the speed with which he was able to solicit support for the mission after arriving on the scene in October 1821. As early as 1822, he heard from Stephen Roszel that some young women in Baltimore had established a juvenile society to raise funds for "the education of the Indian children under your care." This organization reached a membership of 770 and had an initiation fee of six and one-quarter cents. Dues were two cents a month.[57]

Finley lost no time in acknowledging their work and provided the editor of the *Methodist Magazine* with a copy of their letter to encourage support from others. On February 15, 1822, he wrote to the Juvenile Finleyan Missionary Mite Society of Baltimore to thank them for their interest. The four-page letter was an example of effective direct mail fund-raising in which he described his situation in emotional detail: "The difficulty of communicating by interpreter, the avaricious disposition of wicked traders, who vend spiritous liquors among them; their violent opposition to having the minds of these sons of ignorance instructed, with the prejudices of the Indians against education, and their deep depravity of heart, are some of the most formidable barriers to the progress of religion against them. . . . Oh Lord! raise me up many friends to help in this work."[58] In that same issue of the *Methodist Magazine*, Finley supplied a detailed account of his daily routine.

Our family at present consists of thirteen. We rise at 5 o'clock, have family devotion before daylight, breakfast, and then to business. At 12 we dine; at 7 offer our thanksgiving for the mercies of the day, and retire to bed about 9. Our common fare is sassafras tea for breakfast, with some meat. At dinner, meat and hommoney, and at supper some take tea, and some water, sugar and bread. . . . We hope to soon have some milk. . . . I work hard every day, and sleep sound every night; but I want more grace. . . . I expect in one month to have twelve hundred pannels of fence up, which will enclose sixty acres. I have on hand a house, 48 feet by 38, of squared logs . . . and until I get this ready for occupation, I can do nothing to purpose in a school. I want almost everything; clothing, bedding, and money to pay my hired labourers. If you can do anything for us, I shall be thankful.[59]

Finding financial support for the mission had to be given a high priority. Finley was seeking funds even before he was appointed missionary. A letter from Steven Roszel on March 30, 1821, brought word of $436 from the missionary society. "May thousands of the tauney tribe be happily through your mission brought to a knowledge of the truth as it is in Christ Jesus. Your labours, sufferings and privations will not be forgotten. . . . In the midst of our pecuniary embarrassments I have been doing a little for you to aid you in your mission among the Indians."[60]

The Ohio Annual Conference in 1821 asked preachers to collect clothing and provisions for the mission. Supplies were sent from Cincinnati, Dayton, and Xenia. These included Bibles and other books but also blankets, wheels, cords, soap, kettles, bacon, dried beef, and sugar. Even before that action, people were sending money to Finley for the mission.

On January 20, 1820, William Swayze, who succeeded Finley in Deerfield, wrote promising to send funds: "I have not collected anything for the Indian mission yet but am in hopes to do something before the close of this year. It is hard times for money in the country at present."[61]

Finley's brother, John, who was a professor at Augusta College, raised fifteen dollars. Thomas Mason wrote frequently, once in 1823 to explain that the one-hundred-dollar gift for the support of the Wyandot boy, John Summerfield, was support for four years not just one. On August 21, 1824, he wrote with the news that the Juvenile Finleyan Missionary Mite Society of Baltimore had appropriated one hundred dollars for support for four years for a female Indian child to be named Hester Ann Rogers. Bishop R.R. Roberts sent seventy-five dollars.[62]

Bishop McKendree wrote April 14, 1823, with good news. "I insisted on drawing $400 in favor of the mission. . . . I send about $60 [for John Stewart.]" Greenbury R. Jones wrote April 28 to send $115. Finley's friend, Martin Ruter, wrote from Cincinnati April 5, 1823, to report that he had formed an independent missionary society to aid the Sandusky mission and that thirty dollars had been raised thus far. He went on to report that he had asked Jacob Young to collect one hundred dollars from a man in his district who owed it to the Methodist Book Concern and that sixty dollars had been subscribed in West Union in goods and articles of clothing. He ended, "I have requested Br. Jones to get you 100 or 200 yards of factory cotton cloth which he says he can do." In another letter May 10, 1823, he summarized the funds credited to Finley's account, which at that time totaled $529.46. Finley thanked him in a letter on June 27, 1823, for some money and for a twenty-five-dollar gift from a missionary society in Cincinnati. In 1825, Ruter collected a barrel of clothing and $125 from Tennessee contributors. In 1826, he sent fifty dollars.[63]

The most successful fund-raiser of all was Finley himself, especially when he mounted the rostrum at a religious gathering to describe in eloquent terms his missionary and educational efforts in Upper Sandusky. He was especially effective when he took along one of the converted Wyandot chiefs who spoke through an interpreter to supplement Finley's appeal. He sought support from many sources for money, food, clothing. What he could not beg he had to buy. Aaron Wood wrote him February 24, 1823, to say, "I have inquired for bacon and found it scarce . . . perhaps there may be some next summer." Nathaniel McLean, John's brother, who was in Columbus in 1823, bought a tub, buckets, and shoes for Finley at the Ohio Penitentiary and spent over $36. He wrote October 1, "I have filled your order in the best manner we could . . . this country at present presents but a scene of distress and affliction."[64]

Charles Elliott, who was named missionary in 1822, was another eloquent minister who sought support for the mission. In his letter for the fourth Annual Report of the Missionary Society, after reporting sixty Wyandot church members and 37 school students, Elliott wrote, "We are so ill off for beds and blankets, that I dread, as the approach of a deadly enemy, the coming winter. . . . Every sort of clothing is needed. . . . We need money; I have now only a few dollars and I owe, on the mission's account, twice that sum. . . . We will struggle on till we hear what the public will do."[65]

One of the most drastic efforts to get support for the mission was undertaken by Jacob Young, presiding elder of the Lancaster District, who was so disturbed at the poverty he found at the mission that he went about gathering food to send to it. On his return to his district he stopped en route to solicit provisions. Young then lobbied the state legislature on behalf of the mission. He called on Governor Allen Trimble, who formerly had been a Methodist minister, and described the mission's impecunious condition. He asked the governor to hold a meeting of the legislature. He then went to the Speaker of the House, a man named Richardson, and secured his consent. He prevailed upon Nathan Emery to preach a missionary sermon to the legislators after which he described what was being undertaken at the mission. He asked the speakers of the two houses to be collectors and, according to his autobiography, "raised a large collection, nearly all in silver."[66]

With that money he bought one hundred bushels of wheat, had it ground, sold the bran and shorts, and with that money bought flour barrels. As he recorded it, "While the preparations were going on, I went down to Zanesville, and begged from door to door, till I obtained about ten barrels of flour, some meat, and other good things." He paid a friend to take twenty barrels of the flour to the mission. The following spring he sent another twenty barrels to Upper Sandusky.[67]

Nathan Emery not only preached to the politicians; he also sent fifty bushels of potatoes. He explained to Finley, "I have had to use considerable exertions as most of our society are not wealthy and many of them who are not of our Church did not know there was a school or a mission established among the Wyandots and some are prejudiced. I think when you have leasure it would do well to write a short statement of the progress of the arts and religion among the Indians under your care and have it published." He offered to help Finley get something in the Columbus paper.[68]

Sometimes the goods sent were costly to collect. Toward the end of 1822, Thomas Mason sent a box of clothing and blankets from the Methodist Female Missionary Society of New York, but he sent it in care of a friend in Buffalo, New York. It was up to Finley to recover it.[69]

At times the donors had demands that added to Finley's duties. In the same letter, Mason complained that the Juvenile Finleyan Society of Baltimore had not yet been informed whether the two children they were supporting had been selected and named, "according to their wishes." He warned Finley that the society might change its mind about support and emphasized "the importance of giving immediately the necessary information . . . and of keeping up a correspondence with them on the subject, stating from time to time the conduct and improvement of the two children." He added that he wanted to receive monthly or quarterly reports for a publication being planned by the national body. "It will be in vain to expect to excite a general interest in behalf of our missions unless we can inform the people that something has been done and that more is doing."[70]

Elliott added a postscript to this letter, which he forwarded to Finley in Ridgeville informing him that he had written the Baltimore donors. He added, "I bought 200 bushels of corn for the high price of 35 cents per bushel. I paid 53 dollars for pork and beef, and we have no more than a supply for 2 weeks. . . . I must borrow money from somebody till I see you. . . . We *must* have a school mistress."

Others made similar demands on Finley. Thomas Jackson, a Philadelphia supporter, wrote him in 1824 and again in 1825 asking for detailed information on the mission's progress. "If you please, my dear brother, be *particular* when you write. It is, perhaps, necessary for us to be cheered with good news, to prevent our hearts from flagging." In 1825 he sent an "earnest" request: "give us a detailed account of the Mission under your charge . . . please to be particular." Franklin Strub wrote him February 2, 1825, to request information for the Baltimore Conference Missionary Society, "The Wyandot Mission is considered here to be of great importance." Indicative of his popularity was the fact that the first issue of the *Christian Advocate* on September 9, 1826, contained a two-column article on the first page on "Finley, the Methodist Missionary and the Converted Indian Chiefs."[71]

Not everyone was supportive. David Young wrote Finley October 7, 1823, to warn him of some opposition to the mission. "You perhaps are not aware of the narrow view of various dispositions indulged by a great many of the preachers and people of the O Conference; if not clearly against the mission, yet most assuredly against the agent whose immediate duty it is made to manage these affairs." He urged him to keep accurate regular accounts of mission income and expenses. At times Finley was troubled by criticism of his activities. John Johnston sent word April 14, 1824, "I wrote a reply to the publication which appears against you in the Urbana paper."[72]

Finances were a continuing concern for Finley and his assistants. During the year 1822-23 the mission's total expenses, including missionaries' pay, farm improvements, and the cost of feeding and clothing fifty to sixty children, were $2,254. The amount received that year from the Missionary Society was $1,899. A $93 deficit was a heavy burden to bear. An indication of the abject poverty of the enterprise was the report from Charles Elliott that "many of the children are half-naked or more. . . . We have only ten knives and forks for a family amounting to more than forty persons." To make matters worse, Finley was sick part of 1822.[73]

In 1823 Finley applied to the Department of War for a portion of the ten thousand dollars Congress had appropriated for civilizing the Indians. The year before he had been encouraged to expect support from the federal government, but Thomas McKenney wrote him March 23, 1822, to say, "No doubt a part of the public appropriation for civilizing and improving the Indians will be made to your establishment. But it will be necessary for the corresponding secretary of the Methodist operations for the missions to address a letter to the Hon. the Sec. of War, *in conformity* with the printed regulations which I have hitherto sent you."[74] Apparently no Methodist official followed up on Finley's request for he learned from his friend, John McLean, that "no regular application has been made . . . for any part of the annual appropriation for the benefit of schools among the Indians. I send the enclosed printed papers, that you may make the proper application, and hope that you will permit no delay to take place, as the annual distribution will shortly be made. You were better entitled to a portion of the ten thousand dollars last year, than many who received it."[75]

Finley was successful in getting approval in May 1823 for five hundred dollars for the Indian school, but no money was received from the government that year. (According to a Treasury Department audit on January 22, 1824, however, Finley should have received $250 that year.) Fortunately other contributions arrived, $400 that Bishop McKendree had raised and $115 from the Scioto district.[76]

The Wyandot children were not the only ones on the reservation who needed education. Finley cast about for ways to find books for the mission. He was finally successful when the Female Missionary Society of New York sent him a box of 256 volumes and some hundred tracts and pamphlets for the Wyandots. The gift did not come unencumbered, however. The Society sent instructions on how to run a library: "As some pains have been taken to collect the books, we are aware that some pains and method will be necessary to preserve the collection. We have sent you copies of some of our circulating library regulations here, which you may adopt or amend . . . have a large book-case made for the reception of these books . . . have each book with a uniform ticket inside the first cover: We have, therefore, for your convenience, printed one thousand, which are forwarded with the books. . . . P.S. We have also accompanied the whole with a catalogue in a bound book, and began by numbering them."[77]

The farm that Finley began and fenced in was an integral part of the mission effort. The food grown there was needed to feed the missionary family and the Wyandot children. He also wanted the farm to become a model for the older Wyandots to copy as he encouraged them to learn American agricultural techniques. The government agent, John Johnston, was so impressed on one of his visits that he wrote Bishop McKendree on August 23, 1823, to report, "The buildings and improvements of the establishment are substantial and extensive, and do this gentleman great credit. The farm is under excellent fence, and in fine order; comprising about one hundred and forty acres, in pasture, corn, and vegetables . . . the prospect of success here is greater than I have ever witnessed."[78]

In 1823, Finley received assistance from Jacob Hooper, who was appointed a missionary that year. Hooper taught the Indians the best agricultural methods and the mission loaned out oxen, plows, and wagons to help with the farm. His wife taught in the school. That year witnessed great improvements on the Indian farms as well. Many Wyandots built log houses with brick or stone chimneys. Fields were fenced in. Some purchased cattle and sheep. The process of civilizing was gaining momentum. Finley even toyed with the idea of raising sheep to provide wool for clothing. David Young encouraged him to explore the idea, although Young thought that raising hogs might be more profitable once the Erie Canal was completed.[79]

Another of Finley's dreams was to encourage the Wyandots to establish a store for themselves so that they would not be as dependent upon white traders. In his opinion, "white men have done more to prevent the conversion of the Indian nations than all their habits of ignorance, or prejudice have done. The influence of traders and agents has been, in many instances, exerted against their becoming Christians, or ever adapting the habits of civilization, for fear of losing the source of gain."[80]

It took a while, but the chiefs finally agreed to establish a store for the benefit of the nation. White traders were angry and blamed Finley for cutting their profits. The corresponding secretary of the Methodist Missionary Society applauded the effort. In a letter to Finley he wrote, "My only *solicitude* is about its being faithfully and prudently conducted." He did not need to worry. Finley wrote "Regulations for the Proper Government of the National Wyandot Store" with Cass's approval November 12, 1826.[81]

The Wyandots were especially grateful to Finley for proposing that they operate their own store. A chief told Bishop McKendree in 1827 that, because of this operation, the goods they bought cost them less and they received a fair price for their fur and skins. They were not exposed to the pressures from traders. "We have found this to be one of the best things for us. . . . From a nation of drunkards, we have become a sober people."[82] Thomas Mason sent additional advice: "I think it important to promote the comforts of civilized life among the nation, that the mechanic arts should be introduced as early as possible—Blacksmiths, carpenters, shoemakers, weavers, tailors, hatters, etc. and therefore men should be hired to come into the nation and teach the young men, or some of the young men should be placed with proper persons to learn these trades with the whites and then return to the nation to teach others. The former perhaps would be the better plan. And you will not forget the Lancasterian System of Instruction."[83]

Not all of Finley's correspondence contained criticism or suggestions of ways to improve. Much of it was supportive. John Johnston wrote on August 17, 1824, "I perceive you have had much trouble in regaining the ground lost in your absence & that your prospects are once more brightening. You have many difficulties to contend with but this is to be expected in all such undertakings. To civilize and evangelize the Heathen is no ordinary task."[84]

Much of his time had to be spent writing letters and reports. When the chiefs wanted to send communications, it was he who had to write them. He kept Bishop McKendree well informed of developments.

Finley had additional ideas for the mission. He wrote his brother, John, at Augusta College in 1825 to propose that he print a journal at Upper Sandusky. His brother was enthusiastic and wrote, "If there could be matter sufficient for a weekly paper it would be made interesting, especially in the East and South among the friends of the mission. . . . A good journeyman would have to be employed for awhile until some of your little Indians would learn the art. One great advantage . . . would be its tendency to excite the Indians to civilization and literature." He described what he would need to house his family and for his office. John died before Finley could pursue the matter further.[85]

Finley undertook a number of other civilizing efforts. In 1823, he proposed to the Wyandot Council that they keep a record of their acts and decisions. They agreed and he kept a journal account of every council meeting he attended. His rationale was simple. By this device, he wrote, "The means of introducing something like rule and law among them and of teaching them the notion of government" was undertaken. That same year he persuaded the Wyandots to brand their horses and other animals in order to prove their ownership in future disputes.[86]

At the chiefs' council meeting on May 2, 1825, Finley succeeded in getting four resolutions passed that reveal the scope of his influence by that time. The chiefs authorized him to employ someone to make and burn seventy thousand bricks and to contract with someone to attend the Indian mill for two years. The chiefs agreed not to divide their annuities "to anyone that is less than quarter blood Wyandot." The fourth resolution probably gave Finley his greatest pleasure. "If anyone is intoxicated and jeopardizes the life of someone, draws an unlawful weapon, threatens or disturbs any family or individual, they shall forfeit his share of annuities."[87]

Finley was frustrated in his efforts to expand his missionary activities to other Native American tribes. On February 8, 1823, he sent the editor of the *Methodist Magazine* an account of his preaching to the Senecas. "I am fully persuaded that the time is come for these tribes of men to come into the Christian fold. . . . My design is . . . to extend ourselves next spring and summer, among the neighboring nations." At the annual conference in September 1823 he was instructed to extend his labors to the Ottawas and Chippewas at Saginaw Bay. He wrote to Governor Cass, chief agent of the Indian department for the West, on October 23, 1823, on the question of establishing a mission there. He described them as "in the lowest state of moral degradation" and asked for two thousand dollars for the support of a blacksmith and the purchase of horses, cattle, and farming utensils. He also wrote to Elliott Goddard in Cincinnati September 19, 1823, about his expanded efforts. "I am looking to the wilderness of the North & the more I think and pray about it the better I feel. Bless God I am ready to march to the Rocky Mountains if Jesus says go for with Him at the helm I must succeed." He ended his letter with requests for a good coat and stout boots for his journey and gave his foot size.[88]

Initially, John Johnston was encouraging. He wrote on November 1, 1823, "You will not be so much confined now as formerly and will be able to extend your labours to other Tribes of the Natives." But he cautioned Finley that the Chippewas "will not easily be made farmers." A month later, however, he was less enthusiastic. "I think it will be altogether useless for you to visit that country before April or May as Governor Cass has intimated to you those Indians are a very degraded people, and will present to the missionary many discouraging appearances."[89]

Finley made a trip to Detroit anyway that winter, accompanied by two of the Wyandot chiefs and an interpreter. Finding the Chippewas widely dispersed, he gave up trying to visit them and went to see some of the Wyandots in Canada instead.[90]

One of Finley's most effective public relations moves was to take some of the converted Wyandot chiefs with him when he traveled. Chiefs Between-the-Logs (who had become a Methodist exhorter) and Mononcue accompanied him when he attended the dedication of the Second Methodist Church in Hillsboro in 1822. As early as that year he made inquiries about bringing some chiefs with him to the 1824 General Conference. Bishop McKendree, according to a letter his assistant wrote, was "unwilling to give advice" and suggested that Finley had to "judge of the propriety or impropriety of their attending." At the same time, he agreed that the Wyandots' appearance in the East could produce some salutary effects. By June of 1823, Finley had received from his good friend, John McLean, who was about to be named postmaster general, an invitation to stop in Washington on the way to the Baltimore Conference. The Baltimore Missionary Society held its anniversary meeting May 11, 1824. The chiefs were prevented from attending, but Finley spoke about the mission.[91]

By February of 1824 he had succeeded in getting an invitation from Nathan Bangs to bring the chiefs to the Missionary Society's anniversary meeting August 23 of that year. Bangs explained that the board could not cover the full expenses for the trip but had authorized fifty dollars. He suggested that Finley stop for fund-raising meetings en route.[92]

Finley brought five Wyandot chiefs to the 1824 Annual Conference to speak to the audience. Those in attendance contributed $24.75 for the mission. At the 1825 conference when action was taken to encourage the placing of Wyandot children in suitable white families, the preachers and presiding elders were also asked to collect clothing and other aricles for the benefit of the mission.[93]

Another invitation to go East came in 1826. Bangs promised that the missionary society would pay reasonable expenses but requested Finley to stop at the cities along the Erie Canal to raise money for the society. He left June 5 with Between-the-Logs, Mononcue, and Samuel Brown, an interpreter. They went on horseback to Portland and thence by steamboat to Buffalo. They took a canal boat east, Finley making certain that their boat carried no whiskey or rum. A stop in Ithaca was highly successful. A friend later wrote, "I was ever of the opinion that a visit from our Indian Wyandot friends would be of great benefit to our missionary cause. The results of your visit to New York has more than realized my expectations. Our people are now all alive to the great cause in which you are engaged." A meeting in Newburgh was equally successful. Thomas Mason informed Finley later that he had "seized upon the favorable moment and organized a missionary society. We had between 40 to 50 subscribers the first evening we met, and I think we shall raise to a hundred or more before the year closes."[94]

The party failed to arrive in New York City in time for the meeting of the national missionary body, but they were able to attend the anniversary of the Female Missionary Society of New York on July 24. The presentation by Between-the-Logs excited considerable interest. After describing Finley's arrival and the Wyandots' conversion he declared, "From that time a great change has taken place among us. Now all is peace and goodwill. . . . Before we knew not what relationship was; our women were negative, and our children grew up without government. Now, we know

Mononcue initially resisted conversion but later became a licensed Methodist preacher and accompanied Finley on some of his tours.

our relations, and cherish and love them. Before, we shaved and painted our heads, and put jewels in our ears and noses, and all the silver we could get was put in clasps on our arms. Now we have thrown them all away."[95] The collection that night totaled $160.

From New York the party journeyed to Philadelphia where large congregations heard Finley and the chiefs speak. They then went to Baltimore where they participated, at Bishop Soule's invitation, in a camp meeting. Here again, Between-the-Logs impressed the congregation. According to Finley, they were "in a flood of tears and expressed their feeling by shouts of joy." The chief took the Bible that was before him and handed it to Bishop Soule behind him telling him to give it to his preachers "to carry it to all nations."[96] They went on to Washington after Finley had bought a horse and wagon. He later reported that the contributions received on the trip were more than sufficient to pay all their expenses.[97]

Finley received very favorable evaluations when the Methodist bishops visited the reservation. Bishop McKendree visited for five days in June 1823 by which time more than two hundred Wyandots had been converted. He was impressed by the changes in the adults and was pleased to learn after a conference with the chiefs that they thought the school was in "good state."[98]

Both Bishops McKendree and Soule visited the mission in 1824. Finley met them in Columbus and guided them to Upper Sandusky that hot August day. They spent a week meeting the Indian families and inspecting the school. McKendree's diary recorded their conference with the chiefs, who described the changes that had taken place in their "creed, manners, morals, and condition." Bishop Soule, who was visiting the mission for the first time, heard praise for Finley from Mononcue, who told him "there were problems when he was away but they are better now that he has returned . . . let our brother Finley continue with us." Soule was especially impressed that the Wyandot Methodists had "so clear and consistent idea of the fundamental doctrines of the gospel."[99]

John Johnston, the agent for Indian affairs, was a frequent visitor to Upper Sandusky, sometimes walking the distance from Piqua. After several days' stay in August 1823 he sent a very favorable report to Bishop McKendree. He wrote, "A spirit of order, industry and improvement appears to prevail, with that part of the nation which has embraced Christianity: and this constitutes a full half of the population."[100]

Perhaps Finley's greatest achievement while serving the Wyandots was his feat in securing a grant from Secretary of War Calhoun to help build his mission church. He had already written Calhoun March 18, 1823, to report on the mission school's progress and to give him an estimate of building costs. Calhoun acknowledged his letter and agreed to allow five hundred dollars that year for the mission. In the fall of 1823 Finley went East accompanied by David Young to find more financial support. While in Washington he had an interview with President Monroe in which he described the state of the mission. He then met with John Calhoun. Using as his references Governor Trimble, members of Congress, and Postmaster General John McLean, Finley appealed to Calhoun for special support for the cost of the buildings needed at the reservation. Because of his own rigid orthodox Presbyterian background, Calhoun was undoubtedly impressed with Finley, who was slightly older. Finley probably stressed his own Southern Presbyterian roots in appealing to Calhoun's generosity. Calhoun agreed to grant him $1,333, two-thirds of his cost estimate.[101]

Finley's account of the interview is revealing. "I then asked him if it would be improper to take that money, and build a good church for the benefit of the nation. His reply was, that I might use it for building a church and he wished it made of strong and durable materials, so that it might remain a house of worship when both of us are no more."[102]

During his meeting he told Calhoun that "it was of little use to spend money on Indian schools, when they were not established on the manual system, and attended with religious instruction." He received official notification from Calhoun October 31, 1823, but the secretary of war changed the amount to $1,300 in his letter. In taking this action Calhoun ignored the guidelines, for funds were not supposed to be sent until the construction had begun. Finley raised five hundred dollars from another source to pay all the construction costs. It was one of the major achievements of his career. As he expressed it in one of his letters, "surely, the great God is opening our march into the wilderness." [103]

Thus it was that in 1823, federal funds—indeed, money for defense—was spent to construct a Methodist church for the Wyandot nation. No church-state objections seem to have been expressed. Perhaps Calhoun forgot that earlier President Madison had vetoed a bill granting land in the Mississippi Territory to the Baptists on first-amendment grounds. [104]

Finley rushed to send a thank-you letter to Calhoun along with a report on the previous year. He stated that fifty-three boarding pupils had been admitted along with eight day students. More than $2,100 had been spent the previous year. Gifts in-kind totaled $4,000. The total value of the mission property was placed at $7,500 including thirty head of cattle, fifty hogs, four yoke of oxen, four horses, and two wagons. [105]

Finley wrote Calhoun again January 5, 1824, to say he hoped to see him when he came to Washington in April. He described his plan to establish a new mission and school at Saginaw in the Michigan Territory and asked permission to use the vacant military buildings there. The agent, John Johnston, wrote Calhoun to affirm, "No Indian school can have stronger claims on the Government." [106] Calhoun must have been captivated by the Finley touch, for in April 1824, he increased the mission's allocation to eight hundred dollars. Later John McLean informed Finley that he had made a favorable impression. [107]

Naturally, Finley was the architect for the building, which was completed early fall 1824. The mission house was built approximately a mile from Upper Sandusky. It measured thirty by forty feet and was made of blue limestone. The masonry and plastering were done by John Owens and an assistant, who were paid eight hundred dollars. Some of the Wyandots also worked on the building, and from time to time Finley must have joined them in laying the stones. The church stood in a small enclosure surrounded by woods, had a graveyard nearby where John Stewart, Between-the-Logs, and others were later buried. [108]

Part of Finley's difficulties at the mission were caused by the subagent, John Shaw. Although initially when he arrived at the mission he was friendly to Finley, he began to make sweeping accusations against him. He even wrote Calhoun in an effort to get Finley removed. His Indian friends warned Finley that Shaw was his enemy. John Johnston had to come to Finley's aid in correcting misleading statements Shaw sent to Washington. On March 27, 1824, at the end of Shaw's trial, Johnston supplied Finley with a certificate clearing him of having anything to do with encouraging the Indians to complain to Washington about Shaw. Johnston, who had supervised Shaw twenty years before, thought that he could help the two to work together. John McLean, however, considered Shaw "unworthy of public confidence." [109]

Finley decided to involve Calhoun in his dispute with Shaw. He wrote May 24, 1824, from Baltimore where he was attending the general conference to explain that illness had accounted for the absence of the Wyandots from their recent meeting. He expressed the opinion that J. Montgomery would be able to help the Indians more than Shaw. He said that if there was any way he could lower Indian expenses or improve the actions he had taken he would appreciate Calhoun's suggestion. Calhoun was responsive to Finley's concerns, for on June 1, 1824, Thomas L. McKenney, superintendent of Indian affairs, wrote Johnston to tell him to arrange for him to have the agent he wanted. [110]

Shaw entered into an agreement with Johnston for the use of the mill and sawmill, which contained highly questionable provisions in Finley's opinion. He complained to Calhoun in a long letter. He reported that the moral and mental condition of the Wyandots had declined greatly since Shaw had been their sub-agent. He criticized him for encouraging dishonesty among the Indians and exercising a bad influence. He thought that Shaw's salary could be better spent by employing a mechanic to live and work among the Indians. He added that he would have to leave Upper Sandusky if Calhoun was unable to do more to help the mission. [111]

That threat was probably sufficient. Shaw was fired August 17, 1824. On the day that Shaw was fired, McKenney wrote to Finley to say that the secretary of war was highly pleased with his zeal and had entire confidence in his judgment. He reported that Finley's proposal for dividing the land among the Indians had been approved. On September 2, Cass wrote Calhoun to recommend that Finley carry out the duties normally performed by the sub-agent. Calhoun wrote Cass September 21 to agree. Cass informed Finley October 14 that he was confirmed as sub-agent (but without pay). The idea of a federal appointee working for no salary struck a favorable chord among some people. Joseph Ficklin wrote John McLean from Lexington, Kentucky, July 19, 1825, to observe, "I am very glad to find that so far from Mr. Shaw's removal being made for Mr. Finley that it was to reduce public expenditure here where an office was no longer necessary." [112]

Finley's extra duties added to his burdens. He quickly learned from

Encounter with the Wyandots

Postcard of a painting by F.M. Halbedel portrays Wyandots in front of the mission church in the 1830s. The card was published by the H.E. Kinley department store in Upper Sandusky. From a private collection.

Johnston in a letter October 26 that Shaw had overspent his allocation the previous year and that he had only eighty dollars to spend as sub-agent. He also had to draw up an inventory of all the government equipment on the reservation, most of which was in poor repair. His "Account of Publick Property left in my care by John Shaw and remaining yet" lists almost fifty items, including wagons and many tools.[113]

Becoming a sub-agent probably complicated his life more than he realized. John Johnston wrote on November 30, 1824, to caution him about separating his official duties from his conversion efforts. "You must be sensible however that in managing their affairs as publick men, we are to know no party or distinctions. The Christian and the pagan party are equally to claim our attention and regard. We are to be careful that the least partiality may not be perceptible in our publick acts. This I know will be sometimes difficult yet nevertheless it will be our bounded duty to adhere to this rule."[114]

Even in the 1820s federal employees had an affection for developing forms and gathering information. A circular sent May 22, 1824, from Thomas L. McKenney contained detailed instructions:

The enclosed printed forms have been adopted for the annual returns of the respective superintendents or persons in charge of the schools. These should be filled with great care, and forwarded to the department annually, on the 1st of October, accompanied by a report, setting forth, in detail, the prospects of the school; the dispositions of the Indians, whether more or less favorable to it; the names of the teachers and other persons; and the kinds of property belonging to the institution. Also noting anything remarkable in the progress of any Indian child, accompanied by his or her age, and the tribe to which he or she belongs; the general health of the children; their advances in the work of civilization, with such remarks as may be deemed useful, as to the climate, soil and productions of the surrounding country.[115]

McKenney wrote Finley on August 9, 1824, to request an alphabet, grammar, or a chapter on some subject "in the language of the tribe." His letter began with an expression of McKenney's views at that time: "with the view of preserving in the archives of the government whatever of the aboriginee man can be rescued from the ultimate destruction which awaits his race." Another communication from McKenney January 12, 1825, asked Finley to send to Samuel S. Conant of New York "such specimens of Indian oratory as you may be able to collect, and may deem worthy a place in the work which he proposes to publish." A printed memo dated August 22 of that year asked that information on the origins and language of Native Americans be sent to a professor at Transylvania University. Finley probably sent what was available. When Charles Elliott was at the mission he worked on the outline of an Indian grammar and collected a vocabulary of eight hundred words.[116]

A more friendly letter had come from McKenney February 22, 1825, with assurance of funding at the same level that year. He wrote, "There can be no doubt as to the result of your labors. The intelligence and industry which you keep in such perpetual operation cannot but produce a rich reward for your toils. It has ceased to be a matter of doubt among intelligent people that Indians can be Civilized and Christianized."[117]

One of Finley's last achievements at the mission was persuading the Wyandots to divide the land among individual families. It had been the custom for the Indians to hold the territory in common. Finley reasoned that individual land ownership would serve to speed up Americanization and encourage pride of ownership, increased responsibility, and industry. By the summer of 1824 the chiefs were leaning toward land ownership, but they wanted to go to Washington to meet with officials there. Finley wrote to Calhoun July 27, 1824, to report that the Wyandot chiefs would be requesting a meeting. McKenney replied for Calhoun to say the department had no funds for such a trip. He suggested that the chiefs write instead. He added that he thought placing the families on fixed premises would improve prosperity and harmony.[118]

Time passed, but Finley kept pressing the matter. In 1826 he added to his proposal. He suggested to Cass that the government lease land to the aging members of the tribe. Cass liked the idea but wrote him March 22, 1826, to say that he would suggest his good idea to the war department. "But I do not feel authorized to give my consent without the approbation of the government."[119]

The plan for giving each Indian family a farm of 160 acres was finally approved in 1827. The improvements which were made to the farms, however, made them more valuable and hence more attractive to those Americans who were seeking land in Ohio.[120]

In a sense, 1826 witnessed the culmination of Finley's work at the mission. On February 20, 1826, Captain C.L. Cass assumed the duties of sub-agent, relieving Finley of those duties. Lewis Cass wrote him February 6, 1826, to inform him that his brother had been appointed sub-agent; he recognized that the extra duties had been a heavy burden for Finley. On the same date Thomas McKenney wrote, "The Secretary of War has learned with regret that you are not in good health; and supposing your duties, which have been gratuitously and very satisfactorily rendered as Sub agent, may be oppressive, he has appointed Charles L. Cass to succeed, and relieve you from the duties of that office." But on May 1, 1826, Cass wrote to ask Finley to be prepared to take over again if necessary.[121]

In April, a successful quarterly meeting, the first held at the mission house, was so fervent that it lasted all night. By this time, 292 had been received on trial and 250 remained on the Methodist class roles. Sixty-five children were in the school. That figure was impressive in view of the fact that the total enrollment in the thirty-eight schools supported by the federal government in 1825 was only 1,159.[122]

That year the Missionary Society of the Methodist Episcopal Church supported twenty-one missionaries, two of whom were at Upper Sandusky and eight of whom were stationed among other Indian tribes. The Missionary Society sent $1,775 to the Wyandot mission in 1826.[123]

Fourteen of the older boys were living under the care of preachers on the various circuits and attending white schools in 1826. About two hundred acres of land were enclosed for the mission farm and provided corn, wheat, oats, potatoes, and other vegetables. According to James Gilruth, who became missionary in 1826, "many, both of the men and women, have laid by the Indian dress, and assumed that of the whites."[124]

Finances continued to be a problem. The fiscal year that ended September 30, 1826, left the mission with a deficit of $145. Thomas McKenney wrote on February 9, 1827, to report that because the Civilization Fund had overspent its allotment, the Wyandot allocation would be reduced to four hundred dollars.[125]

Finley finally had to give up the superintendency of the mission in

1827 because of ill health, a result no doubt of his heavy workload. He had been plagued with sickness through the 1820s. He claimed that the first time he was ill was July 14, 1822. His affliction then confined him a long time. He was so ill during the winter of 1825 that Nathaniel McLean sent a letter to say that he had heard he was "not long to be an inhabitant of the vail of tears." John McLean wrote February 7, 1826, to say that he was sorry Finley was "experiencing severe afflictions" He wrote again that summer to express concerns for his health. David Young wrote that he was glad to hear that he was too sick to continue for it saved Finley the trouble of resigning in order to "get rid of such burdens." The 1827 Annual Conference terminated his connection with the mission, and he was appointed presiding elder of the Lebanon district. Wyandot church membership reached three hundred in 1827, and there were seventy pupils in the school.[126]

Even after offically leaving the mission, however, Finley continued his ties with the Wyandots. Correspondence was frequent between him and his many friends. In August 1828, he conducted a camp meeting for the Wyandots at which, according to his description, "our Indian brethren evinced great zeal." A detailed account is contained in Finley's *Sketches of Western Methodism*. One hundred fifty Wyandots came to the camp meeting, and many were converted. Their "praise and prayer made the forest arches sing . . . and presently the tents of the whites were forsaken, and many might have been seen mingling with their red brethren and sisters in the exercises of the hour." By Saturday night, "the whole encampment was in a flame of religious excitement and the hours passed away in singing and prayer." Ten years later Finley was still being invited back to participate in camp meetings.[127]

Finley encountered more than the usual 1820s red tape after leaving the mission. On September 13, 1826, a W. Lee from the treasury department wrote him, "You stand charged on the Books of this Office with Three Thousand four hundred and eighty three dollars, advanced for account of the civilization of Indians from the 12th February 1824 to the 30th July 1826. I have to request that you forward with the least possible delay a statement of your disbursements accompanied with the necessary evidence of its proper application preparatory to the next meeting of Congress."[128]

Finley replied on October 23, but it took Mr. Lee until April 27, 1827, to respond. In that letter he wrote, "no records of your disbursements . . . has yet been received, and that consequently you stand charged with the whole amount transmitted to you." Lee's next letter was sent September 18, 1827. He wrote, "From the tenor of your letter of the 23rd October 1826 I have expected to receive long since a statement showing the disburse-

First part of the Lord's Prayer translated into the Wyandot language by Charles Elliott when he was a missionary. At Finley's suggestion Elliott began translation of the Bible. Courtesy of the Ohio Historical Society.

ments of the Funds received in your hands for the civilization of the Indians; but as yet nothing has been received at this office. I . . . urge your compliance, otherwise you will appear a Defaulter in the general statement of Indian affairs preparing for the ensuing season of Congress."[129]

Finley responded on October 1 to ask if a statement from Bishop McKendree would suffice. Lee replied on October 11 to say it would be sufficient. The bishop must have acted swiftly, for Lee wrote Finley on October 19, 1827, to report that his account was closed.[130] However, that was not the end of the matter. On June 20, 1829, W.B. Lewis, another employee of the treasury department, instructed Finley to transmit "with the least possible delay . . . a statement, accompanied by the proper evidence, of the application of the Funds transmitted to your account for the civilization of Indians."[131]

The exasperated Finley replied on June 27, 1829, to say that he would comply as soon as possible. He added, "I will send certificates for all that was drawn in my name but cannot until I can obtain them from the persons that were in charge as my health was such that I could not attend in person. Since last Sept I have had nothing to do with the School Establishment at the Sandusky mission nor have I drawn any money since."[132]

Collecting the proper documentation years after bills were paid was not a high priority for a busy preacher. Instead he secured the following certificate: "I hereby certify that the Rev. James B. Finley, Superintendent of the Mission among the Wyandot Indians has accounted to the Ohio Annual Conference for the three thousand and eighty-three dollars received from the Treasury of the United States in the years 1824, 25 and 26, which sum has been appropriated to the benefit of the school and the improvement of the buildings."[133] It was signed by William Walker and undated. It was not until July 26, 1831, two years later, that Lewis informed him "Your account. . . . Has been closed on the Books of this office in pursuance of the Certificates of R.R. Roberts and W. McKendree, Bishop of the Methodist Episcopal Church."[134]

Although illness had forced him to leave Upper Sandusky for Ridgeville, Finley continued close ties with the mission and with his Wyandot friends. James Gilruth, who replaced him, wrote frequently to keep him informed and to seek his advice.

4

Fight against the Federal Government

> The rage for investment in lands was now manifest in every visitor that came from the East to the West. Everybody, more or less, yielded to it.
> —Henry R. Schoolcraft

Throughout his career, James B. Finley was one of the most outspoken critics of the federal government's Indian policy. This policy sometimes reflected and at other times was in opposition to prevailing white attitudes on the rapidly moving western frontier. Decades of white-Indian hostility, a tradition of almost constant warfare as settlements moved westward, and a deep-seated fear of attack expressed by many in the Ohio River area ultimately influenced the shaping of government policy. Residents in the West could recall that it was the Wyandots who, during the American Revolution, defeated General Edward Hand's troops, unsuccessfully attacked Fort Henry, besieged Fort Laurens for nine months, and defeated Colonel Crawford's force and burned him at the stake. Even the most educated residents of Ohio were distrustful of the Native Americans in their midst.[1]

United States policy toward Native Americans in the first half of the nineteenth century was a combination of paternalism and exploitation. Initially, the government treated the tribes as independent nations. Treaties were made with them that were called permanent but which were broken shortly after they were made. In those treaties there was a consistent effort made to reduce the lands Indians claimed and occupied. Between 1795 and 1822 the government supported a program to sell goods to the Indians. They were encouraged to accept white civilization partly through an annual ten thousand dollar fund to support schools. After 1825, there was a concerted effort to get them all to move west of the Mississippi River.[2]

As the government's policy evolved after 1800, it was based on several principles. One was the desire to protect Native Americans' rights to their lands by agreeing to set definite boundaries for tribal lands and restricting white access to those areas. Another was to deny to individuals or local governments the opportunity to acquire land directly from the Native Americans, and still another principle was to regulate trade between the two groups. The government also sought to provide for the punishment of interracial crimes in order to prevent members of either race from engaging in hostilities. Promotion of civilization through education also gradually emerged as a government policy. This idea seemed to reflect the whites' expectation that the Native Americans would eventually become part of American civilized society.

The federal government's Indian policy was carried out initially by formal treaties made with the individual nations and later by a series of federal laws to regulate trade and to preserve the peace. However, as historians have pointed out, government policy was frequently thwarted by whites on the frontier whose hostility and greed made implementation of laws and treaties difficult and sometimes impossible. As Francis Prucha has stated, the conflict over land was the major issue in Indian-white relations.[3]

Government officials sometimes played down the subject of land hunger. In a speech to a number of tribes assembled at Vincennes October 5, 1792, Rufus Putnam promised, "The United States don't mean to wrong you out of your lands. They don't want to take away your lands by force. They want to do you justice."[4]

One of the fundamental questions in almost every discussion of Indian policy was whether or how to remove Native Americans from populated areas westward beyond the frontier. When Thomas Jefferson was president his concern was to move the Indians west in order to protect the nation's borders. Jefferson mentioned removal in his rough draft of a contemplated proposed constitutional amendment to legitimatize the Louisiana Purchase in 1803. Jefferson's draft read: "The province of Louisiana is incorporated with the U.S. and made part thereof. The right of occupancy in the soil, and of self-government, are conferred to the Indian inhabitants, as they now exist. . . . The legislature of the Union shall have authority to exchange the right of occupancy in portions where the U.S. have full rights for lands possessed by Indians within the U.S. on the east side of the Mississippi: to exchange lands on the East side of the river for those of the white inhabitants of the West side thereof and above the latitude of 31 degrees."[5]

Although Jefferson dropped his idea of a constitutional amendment, government officials after 1803 did try to persuade some tribes to exchange their lands for areas west of the Mississippi River. James Madison supported a similar policy in his attempts to pacify some of the tribes after the War of 1812. President Monroe adopted a removal policy in 1825 after being influenced by John C. Calhoun. When Andrew Jackson became president he followed a removal policy with a vengeance.[6]

When most of the treaties were made they were described as permanent and binding; yet, within a few years the government was forced to renegotiate new terms in the face of the inexorable march of settlement. The government made sixteen treaties with the Wyandots over the years. At a treaty January 21, 1785, at Fort McIntosh, the Chippewas, Delawares, Ottawas, and Wyandots were allotted reservations of land and agreed to cede other lands that they had claimed. Another treaty at Fort Harmar on January 9, 1789, spelled out certain provisions of good will and guarantees to the Wyandots and other tribes.[7]

On August 3, 1795, the Treaty of Greenville was signed with twelve Ohio Indian tribes in which they ceded large areas of their lands in the southeastern part of the Northwest Territory and agreed to a specific boundary line separating the remaining Indian land from that of the white settlers. The Treaty of Fort Industry concluded July 4, 1805, provided the Wyandots and other tribes with a permanent annuity but also provided for the sale of almost three million acres of land.

Under the provisions of a treaty signed by the Ottawa, Chippewa, Wyandot, and Pottawatamie tribes in Detroit November 17, 1807, more land was ceded to the government in northwest Ohio for the sum of ten thousand dollars. The Wyandot share was $1,666.60. The Wyandot chiefs were unhappy at their treatment by the government which had not honored previous treaties, and their loss of land and sent a long petition to the president and Congress February 4, 1812.[8]

On July 22, 1814, another treaty at Greenville was signed with the Delaware, Miami, Seneca, and Wyandot nations, who made peace with the United States and declared war on Great Britian. The government indicated that it wanted no grant of land, only peace. Three years later, however, Governor Lewis Cass of the Michican Territory and General Duncan McArthur of Ohio persuaded the Wyandots and several other tribes to give up several million acres of land north of the Greenville Treaty line in Ohio and west of a line drawn south through Put-in-Bay. The Wyandots were left with a twelve mile square tract at Upper Sandusky and a one mile square area on Broken Sword Creek about ten miles northeast of their main reservation. Ronald Satz has maintained that government officials used force, bribery, and deception to get the treaty signed.[9]

Cass and McArthur raised the question of removal during their negotiations. They wrote to Calhoun September 18, 1818, to report that "the proposition to remove to the west of the Mississippi was made . . . and enforced as far as we believed it politik to enforce it. It was received by them with such strong symptoms of disapprobation, that we did not think it proper to urge them too far upon the subject. The time has not yet arrived for them voluntarily to abandon the land of their fathers and seek a new residence in a Country with which they are unacquainted and among powerful and hostile Indians." They concluded their letter with the thought that the Indians would be better prepared to consider a move when they were surrounded by white settlements.[10]

The Wyandots signed the 1817 treaty under protest. Between-the-Logs went to Washington to plead his nation's cause and, as a result, on September 17, 1818, at the Treaty of St. Mary's, the Wyandot reservation was enlarged by 87 square miles and their annual annuity was increased by five hundred dollars.[11]

The Indian trading factories, which were established March 3, 1795, became one of the earliest efforts by the federal government to conduct a business in competition with the private sector. The act that year appropriated fifty thousand dollars "to the purchase of goods for supplying the Indians . . . and that the sale of such goods be made under the direction of the President . . . [who] had the power to establish trading houses anywhere within the limits of the United States and appoint the necessary agents for the houses."[12]

These trading outposts were included in George Washington's Indian policy and were designed to help the Indians and to benefit the United States. Establishing the factory system was an action designed to prevent unscrupulous traders from profiting from their contacts with the Indians, who resented being exploited. Washington intended the system to supply Indians with goods at reasonable prices and, at the same time, to gain their friendship.

As Francis Prucha has pointed out, the factory system had diplomatic, economic, military, and humanitarian objectives. It was expected that through the government trading posts, foreign influence over the Indian tribes would be thwarted, British traders would be eliminated from the competition, the Indians would be more readily controlled militarily, and American products would be made available at fair prices by honest traders.[13]

The factories purchased many furs from the Indians including deer, muskrat, beaver, bear, buffalo, mink, and otter skins. The government agents also bought deer tallow, bear oil, beeswax, snakeroot, lead, maple sugar, cattle, cotton, corn, and buffalo and deer horns.[14]

The War of 1812 dealt a severe blow to the factory system. Several of the posts, including the one at Sandusky, were completely destroyed by November of 1812. Beyond that, the factory system failed to create a profit. In 1815, seven of them reported a loss and only three a profit for the year. The loss at Sandusky was over eight thousand dollars. The system was subjected increasingly to criticism from private traders and companies. There were frequent congressional investigations. Even some of the Indians complained about the factories. Some of the manufactured goods that were supplied were not adapted to their needs, and, beyond that, the Indians were accustomed to receiving gifts and whiskey from private traders, who used this device to ingratiate themselves with their customers. The government agents supplied neither. In defense of government policy, John Johnston, the agent at Piqua, wrote on September 6, 1815, that the Indians had no right "by treaty, compact, or agreement of any kind" to receive gifts from the federal government.[15]

Complaints and criticism of the system increased each year. The trading industry found a friend in Senator Thomas Hart Benton, who led the fight to kill the system. Benton later admitted that it had been a "strenuous exertion" for him to kill the Indian trading houses. Thomas McKenney, superintendent of Indian trade, was opposed to closing them, but his arguments failed to convince a majority of congressmen. McKenney sought help from some of his missionary contacts. On March 13, 1821, he wrote John Emory, Methodist minister, to ask him to get people to send petitions to save the factory system.[16]

What has generally not been known is that the Methodist circuit riders in Ohio were supportive of the factory system, probably because they saw at first hand the greed of the white traders and what their profiteering had done to the Indian economy. In the same resolution that established the mission and school for the Wyandots at the 1821 Ohio Annual Conference, the following was included: "That an address be drawn up and sanctioned by the Conference and put into the hands of every preacher who has the charge of a Circuit or Station to obtain signatures petitioning Congress not to repeal the existing laws which regulate our commerce with the Indians. These petitions when signed are to be returned to the P[residing] Elder of each district and forwarded by him to Congress as soon as it can be done."[17]

One petition sent from Ohio contained 166 names. Many others were sent to no avail. In May 1822, Congress abolished the factory houses in an action some considered hasty. The system had too many powerful enemies including the Missouri Fur Company, Astor, and the American Fur Company. In pushing for its demise, Senator Benton called it "worse than useless."[18]

While politicians and lobbyists claimed the credit, there were other reasons for the system's failure. The government representatives did not go to the reservations; the Indians had to come to the trading posts. Credit was not extended to them nor were they sold liquor. The merchandise was frequently inferior in quality. The total loss to the government on the operation was estimated at over $146,000 according to an 1824 report.[19]

The charitable side of government policy was reflected in the efforts to "civilize" the so-called savages. As early as 1789 Secretary Henry Knox recommended that "the government send missionaries to reside among the aboriginees." The objective was to promote their "civilizing" by giving them domestic animals in order to encourage them to cultivate "a love for exclusive property." Congress followed up on that notion on March 30, 1802, when it authorized the president to spend up to fifteen thousand dollars annually to promote civilization among friendly Indian tribes.[20]

The treaties prior to 1817 made no mention of education. However, Rufus Putnam was sent the following instructions on May 22, 1792, when he went to negotiate with tribes near Lake Erie: "That the United States are highly desirous of imparting to all the Indian tribes . . . the blessings of civilization, as the only means of perpetuating them on the earth. That we are willing to be at the expense of teaching them to read and write, to plow and to sow, in order to raise their own bread and meat, with certainty, as the white people do."[21]

It seems reasonable to credit partially the great religious awakening after 1801 and the formation of missionary and tract societies with encouraging an increased interest in Indian civilization and education. The House of Representatives Committee on Indian Affairs submitted a report January 22, 1818, recommending that there be schools to educate Indians. "In the present state of our country, one or two things seems to be necessary. Either that these sons of the forest should be moralized or exterminated." The result was a major law March 3, 1819, that authorized ten thousand dollars annually to be spent for Indian education.[22]

This act created what was then called "The Civilization Fund." McKenney had wanted one hundred thousand dollars but Congress appropriated only ten thousand dollars for the president to use to advance the civilization of tribes who lived close to frontier settlements and introduce to them the "habits and arts of civilization." The president was authorized to "employ capable persons of good moral character, to instruct them in the mode of agriculture suited to their situation; and for teaching their children in reading, writing and arithmetic."[23]

President Monroe and Secretary Calhoun decided not to hire persons directly but to spread the money among benevolent societies that had or might in the future establish schools for the education of Native American children. Calhoun issued a circular in September 1819 that must have been one of the first requests for proposals issued out of Washington. It invited individuals or groups to apply for a portion of the fund and requested information on the sponsor's resources, number of students to be reached, and kind of education to be taught. Calhoun made it the policy to support only those schools which emphasized agriculture and "mechanic arts" for the boys and the domestic skills of sewing, spinning, and weaving for the girls. A second circular issued by Calhoun on February 29, 1820, stipulated that the federal government would pay only two-thirds of construction costs for buildings and that no money would be advanced until after construction was commenced. One-fourth would be reserved until construction was completed.[24]

Although the act creating the Civilization Fund had benevolent objectives, the government officials implementing it saw it as a means of further making the Native Americans dependent on the United States. Calhoun ruled in 1820 that those organizations receiving funds must "impress on the minds of the Indians, the friendly and benevolent views of the government towards them, and the advantage to them in yielding to the policy of the government, and cooperating with it, in such measures as it may deem necessary for their civilization and happiness." In this fashion, the federal government used annuities and subsidization to influence their settlements.[25]

The Wyandot school was granted five hundred dollars from the Civilization Fund in 1823. That year the entire expense for the school was reported as $1,950, so the federal support was slightly over 25 percent. That year the school contained sixty scholars, the fourth largest enrollment among the twenty schools receiving federal support.[26]

The fact that the schools were run by churches and missionary societies apparently posed no problem for government officials. These agencies seemed to be the only ones interested in the enterprise. The major considerations motivating political leaders were to do something to civilize the Indians and to avoid having the federal government actively involved. Church/state constitutional issues were left for another time.[27]

Five years later, however, as the pressure built to move all Native Americans west of the Mississippi, there were indications in Congress that some members wanted to abolish the Civilization Fund. William McLean wrote Finley on March 16, 1824, to give him the disquieting news:

The subject was introduced in the House of Representatives by a Mr. Cobb of Georgia and it has been referred to a committee of seven one of whom happens to be myself. Three of the committee are in favor of repealing it while four including myself are opposed to it. I am preparing a report to present to the House against the proposition which I shall offer in a day or two. I wish you were here to give me aid & information, an effort will be made to reverse my report in the House and should they succeed I shall lament it most sincerely. . . . It would disgrace the government to repeal the law and withhold from so important an object this pitiful sum.[28]

The threat to the fund that year was answered by Calhoun, who fought to preserve it. He assured Congress that the fund was helping the Indians and that stopping it would be harmful.[29] In 1825, however, government policy became less benevolent and more coercive. In his message to Congress in 1824 and again in January 1825 President Monroe advocated a plan of Indian removal. The days of peaceful persuasion were ending. Monroe declared that removal should occur in a way that promoted both the Native Americans' happiness and interests and United States' honor. Each tribe should get an adequate allotment of land to which they would agree to move. The government would preserve order, prevent outsiders from entering their property, and help civilize them. A report from Calhoun accompanied Monroe's message. In it he listed the number of Native Americans, the amount of land held, and the estimated expense of removal. For Ohio he listed 2,350 Indians and 409,401 acres of land. Calhoun thought that the Ohio Indians should be moved to an area west of Lake Michigan rather than to the region west of the Mississippi.[30]

Calhoun's attitude toward Native Americans was perhaps best revealed in a statement made in 1820 when he declared, "They must be brought gradually under our authority and laws, or they will insensibly waste away in vice and misery. It is impossible, with their customs, that they should exist as independent communities, in the midst of civilized society. They are not, in fact, an independent people." Two years later in one of his reports he commented on the prospects Native Americans faced when they were completely surrounded by white settlements. He expected them to succumb to a state of complete subjugation. He wrote, "The consequence is inevitable. They lose the lofty spirit and heroic courage of the savage state, without acquiring the virtues which belong to the civilized. Depressed in spirits and debauched in morals, they dwindle away through a wretched existence, a nuisance to the surrounding country." He thought that efforts to civilize them would ultimately fail.[31]

The Wyandots were considerably upset by the talk of removal. The chiefs sent a message to the war department in which they cited the provisions of the Treaty of Fort Meigs in which the Wyandots had been promised, in return for the lands they then ceded, that they would never be approached again on this subject. They said that the president had promised to maintain them in peaceful possession of their lands. They stated that they were progressing in religion; their children were in school; they were cultivating their lands, were becoming good citizens, and were happy and satisfied to remain where they were. Inasmuch as it was Finley's task to write down the chiefs' messages for them, he may have helped them strengthen their appeal.[32]

Government officials were not always forthright in communicating federal policy to the Native Americans. Thomas McKenney's March 24, 1825, letter in reply contained these instructions:

> You must teach them [your children] to love peace, to love one another, to be sober; you must instruct them how to make instruments of husbandry, and for all the mechanic arts; your young women you must teach to spin, and weave, and make your clothes, and to manage your household; your young men to labour in the shops and in the fields. . . . Brothers—your great father is glad that you have so good a man as the Rev. Mr. Finley among you. Listen to his words. Follow his advice. He will instruct you in all things. Brothers—Your great father will never use force to drive you from your lands. . . . But your great father will not compel you to remain where you are, if you think it better, at any time, to settle elsewhere . . . fear nothing from your great father. He is your friend, and will never permit you to be driven away from your lands.[33]

Lewis Cass kept Finley informed of developments. On March 25, 1825, he wrote to say that the removal law had not passed and that should it pass "there is nothing compulsory on the Indians. . . . I do not think this proposition should produce any effect upon your exertion in your establishment. . . . A very few years longer of improvement would place the Wyandots in a situation, from which no one would wish to see them removed."[34]

Finley was not persuaded by the words coming out of Washington. He was aware that the white neighbors of the Wyandots were becoming more troublesome. Some of them hoped to make life so miserable for the Native Americans that they would want to migrate. They sought to extend their laws over the reservation and to find ways to take their property. Finley wrote to Cass for advice. The October 26, 1825, reply was not encouraging. "I imagine there can be little doubt, but that the laws of the state of Ohio do not operate in any of the Indian reservations, and that, consequently, whoever attempts to execute process there . . . must be a trespasser . . . you are at liberty to employ some able lawyer, at the public expense, to conduct any proceeding which may be necessary."[35]

The correspondence from Washington was even more discouraging. Thomas McKenney wrote to Finley September 10, 1825, to say that "no steps will be taken to *compel* the Indians to emigrate. Believing, however, as I do, that their future happiness and prosperity depend very much upon their having a country of their own, in which they will be free, and for ever, from the encroachments and injuries to which experience demonstrates that they are now constantly liable. I think it advisable to prepare them to receive the proposition in the spirit in which it will be made." McKenney went on to suggest that Finley suspend any extensive improvements that might involve heavy disbursements until Congress had settled the issue. He advised the missionary to use the Intercourse Law of 1802 as his guide in assuring that justice was done to the Native Americans. McKenney's letter ended with the words, "*Do your duty.*"[36]

Finley reacted negatively to what he called the government's "honeyed phrases of diplomacy." He considered the reasons for wanting to remove them "moonshine pretensions." He believed that the government's position "was calculated to discourage and throw all our plans and prospects to the ground." He thought that the task of moving Indian tribes where they would be free from the encroachment of whites was "a flimsy vailing of the real object. Who can stop the march of the white populations? Neither mountains, deserts, seas, rivers nor poles. To talk, therefore, of giving the Indian a country where he will be delivered from the advances and impositions of the lowest and worse class of our citizens, is chimerical. . . . If the good of the red man was their object, is there not a much better opportunity to counteract the evils to which he is exposed, where the laws of the government can be enforced; and where morals and religion will come to the aid of the civil laws; where they can have the practical example of farmers and mechanics, and the blessings of religious society?"[37] The second attempt of the government to oust the Wyandots from Ohio in 1825 failed partly because of Finley's strong influence on the Christian chiefs.

The intensity of Finley's criticism of government policy is revealed in his correspondence in the 1820s. During that time he developed a close friendship with the nearby agent for Indian affairs, John Johnston. Johnston kept trying to persuade Finley to change his mind on the removal issue. On June 26, 1823, he wrote, "All good persons are pleased with the account of your progress in the cause of Indian reform. I fear, however, your subjects will ere long have to go the way of all their race, that is, that they will be compelled to move westward, where the Delawares and many others are gone since our Treaty in 1817. I find a great proportion of my Indians are looking to a remove. There is no such thing as preserving the Indians for any length of time on what is called "Reservation" . . . under the present arrangement of the Government, the Indians cannot be saved from destruction."

Two years later on February 12, 1825, Johnston pressed again. He wrote, "The Government is anxious to devise some plan for the welfare and happiness of this people. It will not be proper to say any thing to the Indians on the subject until we are instructed from the proper authority. If the Law passes, we shall have an unpleasant task to perform, more especially with the Wyandots. Whatever arrangement is made will be liberal. Congress and the President appear to view the Indians and their interests, in the most favourable light. We may confidently expect the same humane and liberal policy to be continued under Mr. Adams." Johnston's January 10, 1826, letter was the most forceful.

The Indians must all leave this country sooner or later. This is a position which every reflecting man must assent to. The Wyandots can form no exception to the rule. They may remain longer than the others, but they must go too and in as much as they must all go, the sooner the better, for those that will go first, will be best accommodated with a choice of country, and with liberal arrangements being made for them. Would it not be better for the Methodist Church to advise the measure, get the Wyandots out of the reach of bad white men and send them ministers and teachers with them where they would have a country which would be theirs forever. It is known that the Government in case of removal, would make the most liberal and permanent arrangements for the Indians and that the country is to be secured to them by the most solemn compact. If I was called upon with my dying breath to say which was the best for the Indians, go or stay, I should say go by all means.

In a postscript he warned, "it's wise for your society to acquiesce."[38]

One of Finley's more eloquent responses was contained in his April 26, 1826, letter to Johnston. "In your last you requested me to give my opinion with respect to moving the Indians. The reason I did not answer your request was I thought that you long since knew it and that you did it to try to involve me in some difficulty as I have the honor to differ very widely in this as well as in other respects from you." Finley criticized Johnston for saying one thing publicly to the Native Americans and favoring another approach when among whites. He continued, "Now would you sir like for Congress to pass a law to transport every Irishman to Botney Bay or out of the United States and with as much justice and with as much humanity. May you scare & persuade these poor helpless Indians to go to their own destruction to fortify a few covetous land holders. Such a nefarious thing God will not let prevail." He concluded by asserting that no power would compel him to advise the Wyandots to move.[39]

Others put pressure on Finley to modify his position. D.H. Beardsley wrote from Columbus on January 18, 1825, to say that he knew the missionary favored having the Christian Indians purchase their land but hoped that he would encourage the "Heathen Indians" to sell their land to the government. He explained that the Crawford County area did not contain sufficient territory to form a legal county and lacked a proper place for a county seat. "If the government could purchase one third of the Reservation it would then contain enough to form a county."[40]

The Monroe/Calhoun plan gained some support, but action was stalled in Congress for several years. Indicative of the view of many whites in Ohio were the words of John Johnston, who for several years had been engaged in removing some of the tribes. In 1826 he wrote a letter to the

Piqua Gazette, "The frequent removal of the Natives of the soil to make way for our population, and the consequent distress and misery entailed upon their race, calls loudly upon Congress to provide for them a country, from which they will not again have to be removed."[41]

Finley carried his pleas on behalf of preserving the reservation to Cass. On December 15, 1825, he wrote, "am happy to state to you that the work of civilization is progressing as fast as we could reasonably expect it." He asked Cass to use his influence to get more aid. Turning to the removal policy, he wrote,

In my judgment this people have some claims on us that none others of the Northwestern Indians have. . . . Much labor and money have been expended already by the Government & the Church on this People and if removed to the wilderness it might [be] considered lost in a grate degree and it would in the judgment of many driving out our own citizens to heathenism for they are certainly bones of ours & flesh of our flesh. I do hope that the Government will let us make a full trial on these People and also that the Government will continue our School Salary at what it was last year. Please to use your influence for this purpose.[42]

Finley complained to Martin Ruter that the "moving plan" had retarded his work and had caused much anxiety to the Christian Wyandots. He wrote that the area where the mission was situated "is much coveted by speculating white men and some have threatened to sacrifice us all for the publick good, as they call it." He admitted that he remained only because of a sense of duty. According to Wade Barclay, the whites clamored to free the fertile Sandusky region of Native Americans, which increased pressure on the Department of War to get Wyandot acceptance of cessions. Finley defended Indian rights so persistently that some of the government agents threatened his life.[43]

One of the government's methods for persuading Native Americans to move west was to finance the sending of "exploring parties" to examine the land available in the hope that they would be sufficiently impressed to sell the idea to their fellow tribesmembers. Finley was at Baltimore when William Walker wrote him from Upper Sandusky on July 15, 1826, to tell him of the arrangement. Walker shared his skepticism and wrote, "Oh ye fugitive sons of the forest where can ye find an abiding place to rest your wearied limbs and sing the songs of your fathers in peace! Unhappy people! never will the white man rest till the Pacific ocean drink of your blood."[44]

Finley added some remarks to the report form that he submitted to the Department of War for the year ending September 30, 1826:

Our Indians are improving the soil and begin to live above want and in a few years will be beyond the reach of savage life. They have been somewhat disturbed by the

Fight against the Federal Government

pressing of some of the agents to move them to the west but we have met and have entered into a national resolution not to go but to suffer death before they leave the present place of abode. It is the opinion of your Supt. that it would be very impolitick to remove them or to torment them on this subject. I heard one of the principal chiefs say that he would as soon take the cup of poison. I hope they will be left to make a full experiment. It has been doubted whether it would be practicable to Christianize & civilize those aboriginees but we have a good prospect at least of success for one if we are still protected & patronized by the government.[45]

His views received some confirmation from a report written by Judge John L. Leib, who was sent to Upper Sandusky by the secretary of war to evaluate the Wyandot mission school. Leib praised Finley and wrote, "The fruits of his labours are everywhere visible: they are to be found in every Indian and Indian habitation. . . . The Wyandots are a fine race and I consider their civilization accomplished. . . . They are the only Indians within the circle of my visits, whom I should consider it a cruelty to attempt to remove." Leib thought that the reservation was a model that could be copied by others. He commended the school and the store, which he found under good management.[46]

Public opinion, however, was increasingly in favor of removal. J.W. Campbell, one of John McLean's correspondents, wrote him July 10, 1828, to say, "I read your Indian speech with pleasure. Your view of the policy proper to be pursued in reference to the unfortunate aboriginees, seems just, every thing considered. They cannot long stay in the South. Their white neighbors will make it their interest to migrate and the sooner they go the better." There were only a few persons who shared the views of the Methodist minister, Thomas Hinde, that there should be an Indian Territorial Government.[47]

Even after Finley left the mission, he continued to plead the Wyandots' cause and to criticize government policy. On April 9, 1827, C.L. Cass, who had replaced him as sub-agent, wrote, "I have received your letter & am very sorry to hear of your slump but no doubt you are afflicted for some wise purpose. . . . The mission appears to be doing well. The Indians have behaved remarkably well this winter. I have not seen one intoxicated this winter."[48]

Finley had some support in Congress for his views. John Woods, Congressman from southwestern Ohio, wrote him on February 26, 1827, to report

We have before Congress a scheme for removing them beyond the Mississippi. This I believe to be a visionary project. It is a plan not for the benefit of the Indians but for the benefit of those who wish to obtain their lands. . . . I hope . . . to see you on the subject. . . . I am firmly of the opinion that the best mode for their civilization is to continue a proper system of education among them and as soon as possible bring them under our laws and give them their lands and property to be held in fee by each individual in his own right.[49]

The following autumn Woods continued his correspondence with Finley.

I have felt considerable interest in the measures about to be proposed in relation to the Indian tribes. The treaties which are formed every year are but a mockery of the compacts formed by independent nations. *The Indians are not independent.* They know this fact and so do we. . . . Our Indian negotiations have been and are a reproach and disgrace to the nation. The system partially adopted by the government of aiding the missionary establishments is in my opinion the only plan of civilizing the Indians by teaching them to plow & sow & reap & weave & spin at the same time that we enlighten their mind.[50]

The agitation for removal increased in fervor. By 1828, the Committee of Indian Affairs in the House of Representatives was ready for a report on moving the Native Americans westward. The author, Congressman Nathaniel McLean, sent Finley a copy a day after it was approved. In a January 18, 1828, letter accompanying the report, he wrote, "I am sorry it is not better done. You can't find fault with its sentiments or premises however much you may differ from my conclusions. You see I do not propose to touch your Wyandot folks nor any others except those who are anxious & determined to go."[51]

The report declared that while the Indians were "capable of employing the blessings of the civilized state, they remain, to this house, a miserable and degraded race." The report reviewed previous governmental actions to help them but concluded that they had not solved the problem. The committee recorded its preference for "the more agreeable task of removing them (that portion of them that are disposed to go) from the scene of controversy to a more peaceable and better regulated home." The report added that the committee opposed the government's use of "coercive measures" and favored letting the Indians "choose for themselves their future destiny." It concluded by noting that the committee was reporting a bill "confining its provisions to the appropriation of fifteen thousand dollars, for the expense of exploring the country—deeming it time enough to submit a bill embracing the object contemplated in this report, when it is known that the Indians shall be satisfied with the country, and the particular section of it they may select."[52]

A year later, however, the committee's action became stronger after reviewing the proposals of President John Quincy Adams and Secretary of War Porter. The committee agreed that removal of the Native Americans was necessary as a result of the growing crisis in some of the Southern states. The committee's report concluded, "The policy of urging them to leave their country for another would be deplored . . . if it were not believed to be the only effectual measure to secure the prosperity and happiness of themselves and their posterity." The committee recommended a bill to appropriate fifty thousand dollars to support Native American migration, but it was not approved by the House of Representatives.[53]

With the election of Andrew Jackson in 1828, forced removal became inevitable. Earlier in his career, Jackson had concluded that treaties with Native American tribes were failures and that it made no sense to treat them as independent nations. He wrote to James Monroe March 4, 1817, to indicate that he favored curtailing their territory and moving them west of the Mississippi River where the government would "circumscribe their bounds, put into their hands the utensils of husbandry, yield them protection, and enforce obedience to those just laws provided for their benefit, and in a short time they will be civilized."[54]

According to Satz and others, Jackson's position on Native American removal probably guaranteed his winning the Southern states in the 1828 election. In his March 1829 inaugural address Jackson said, "it will be my sincere and constant desire to observe toward the Indian tribes within our limits a just and liberal policy, and to give that humane and considerate attention to their rights and their wants which is consistent with the habits of our government and the feelings of our people."[55] However, the habits of government and the feelings of many people dictated only one solution. The Indian Removal Act of 1830 authorized the president to exchange public lands in the West for Native American lands in the East. Perpetual title to the new lands given to the Native Americans was promised, and the government also promised to pay for improvements made on the reservations and to assist in the migration westward. The sum of five hundred thousand dollars was appropriated to implement the law. Church groups sent memorials to Congress protesting the bill for ignoring Native Americans' rights. The bill passed the House of Representatives by a vote of 102 to 97 and the Senate on May 26, 1830, by a 28 to 20 margin. President Jackson signed it two days later, and it was quickly implemented. The Sioux, Sauk, and Fox tribes ceded their lands on July 15. The Choctaw Indians traded their land for an area in what later became Oklahoma on September 15.[56]

The act was extremely popular with those white Americans who were investing in land or moving westward to settle in new areas. It reflected the increased influence of economic considerations in public policy. Jack Larkin has maintained that this act made legitimate a campaign of economic and political pressure and that President Jackson carried out Indian removal "with unrelenting determination." Jackson, however, believed that he was treating Indians justly and thought that removal was the only way to protect them.[57]

Even the opposition of missionary and religious groups declined after 1830, partly, perhaps, because government officials gave assurances that help would be given in reestablishing missions and schools in the new Indian lands. Several key political leaders also changed their minds. McKenney reversed himself after an 1827 tour of the West. Lewis Cass came out in support of removal in an important article in the *North American Review* in January 1830. He believed that moving Native Americans was the only way to prevent their destruction. He was appointed Secretary of War in 1831. Schoolcraft, one of the most able Indian agents, also changed his views at about this time. Later he recorded in his journal a capitulation to the popular view: "It is now evident to all, that the salvation of these interesting relics of Oriental races lies in colonization west. Their teachers, the last to see the truth, have fully assented to it. Public sentiment has settled on that ground, sound policy dictates it; and the most enlarged philanthropy for the Indian race perceives its best hopes in the measure."[58]

Finley, however, remained unalterably opposed to the removal policy. He wrote a letter to the editor of one of the religious papers to say, "These unfortunate fellow creatures have been either neighbors or my companions for the best part of half a century . . . never will the situation be better than now to cultivate the mind, and improve the habits of these people . . . many of the tribes have made considerable improvements in religious habits and agriculture but I am much opposed to the plan of moving them at present indiscriminately to the other side of the Mississippi."[59]

Finley's close colleagues on the circuits agreed with his view of the government. David Young wrote from Zanesville March 9, 1825, to say that he could not understand the administration's actions against the Native Americans. "But they are men & perhaps are not scandalized enough by speculating on the poor creatures' lands!" On April 5, 1828, he wrote again to express relief that the Wyandots were not being snared by Congress's bait. He wrote, "How long would they improve jammed in the midst of forty other tribes—is the object to give the Indians a good chance to kill one another that we may occupy their lands without the scandal of killing them ourselves? I hope not. But will Arkansas and Missouri do them long! Where next? Oregon—Then they will be in the way & some may still think they ought to be coaxed & bribed & flattered & if necessary receive a little *salutary National shove into the western Pacific*."[60]

Finley's interest in the mission continued to be strong throughout the 1830s. Isaac Dane wrote him on April 13, 1831:

I received yours of March 30th on the 8th inst. and according to your request hasten to answer it. . . . The nation generally is well and tho some of those who were formerly members of the church and on the road to Zion have backslidden,

Fight against the Federal Government 89

still there are a number who are still . . . faithful to the good cause. I have to regret that there has been no revival for some time. I think there has been rather a decrease than increase in the numbers of the church for the last three years. During the last year some faithful members of the church have died. . . . There is more danger of the Wyandots selling out than there ever was. It seems to be a general conclusion among them that they will sell out and for that reason they are not making improvements as they would do.[61]

On April 22 of that year, Finley's old friend, William Walker, who was one-quarter Native American and an influential member of the tribe, sent him a four-page letter with news of individuals on the reservation. He reported that the youth who had been given James Finley's name had married. "With regard to religion at present, there is no particular excitement—the old members stand firm." He concluded by criticizing the administration's pressure on the tribe to move west.[62]

By this time the Wyandots were completely surrounded. President Jackson appointed James B. Gardiner to negotiate treaties with the remaining tribes in Ohio. Although he was successful in getting the Shawnees and Ottawas to cede their lands and move, he was unsuccessful with the Wyandots, who first asked for an inspection of the western lands and then refused to move.

In October 1831, William Walker led a party to inspect the area beyond what was then the western boundary of Missouri for a month. When the group returned to Upper Sandusky it submitted an unfavorable report which stated that there were not enough sugar trees nor game to sustain the tribe. The report claimed that Missouri politicians were opposed to their settling and called the whites living there "the most abandoned, dissolute and wicked class of people we ever saw." It concluded "that the interests of the nation will not be promoted, nor the condition ameliorated, by a removal to the country examined." The group's recommendation was "to cease all contention, bickerings, and party strifes; settle down & maintain their position in the state of Ohio."[63]

Gardiner who had expected a final treaty had to accept a partial purchase of land. In a letter to Lewis Cass January 4, 1832, he called the Wyandots "sagacious, intelligent and crafty." In a treaty on January 18, 1832, the federal government gained some sixteen thousand acres of Wyandot-owned land in Crawford County for $1.25 an acre, the land at the Big Spring, or Blanchard's Fork, which had been granted them in 1818. Their allowance from the Civilization Fund, which had been reduced from eight hundred to four hundred dollars in 1827, remained at that level. The Wyandot chiefs continued to resist agreeing to move because of Finley's strong influence.[64]

The government took one action in 1832 that even Finley could approve. In the law establishing a commissioner of Indian affairs, Congress stipulated that "no ardent spirits shall be hereafter introduced, under any pretense, into the Indian country."[65]

Finley was pleased that many Wyandots participated in a camp meeting after the annual conference at Dayton on September 19, 1832. According to one observer, "Their prayers, and songs, and exhortations, and shouts made an impression never to be lost by many."[66]

In 1834, major changes were made in government policy, none of which were contrary to the primary one of moving Native Americans west of the Mississippi. The Indian section in the Department of War was reorganized. A new trade and intercourse act was passed, but a bill to establish for all time boundaries for the Indian territory west of Arkansas and Missouri failed to pass. Without a permanent organization of the western area for the Native Americans, they remained as vulnerable as ever.

Pressures continued to mount against the Wyandots. One Irish traveler who visited Upper Sandusky was impressed by their determination to resist removal. He wrote, "Several attempts have been made to induce the Indians to sell their lands, and go beyond the Mississippi, but hitherto without effect. The Indian replies to the fine speeches and wily language of the whites, 'We hold this small bit of land, in the vast country of our fathers, by your written talk, and it is noted of our wampums. The bones of our fathers lie here, and we cannot forsake them.'"[67]

The Ohio legislature passed a resolution January 18, 1834, requesting Congress to arrange for the Wyandots' removal. Governor Robert Lucas was asked to negotiate a treaty with them and Congress appropriated one thousand dollars for his negotiations. His instructions authorized him to offer them an equal amount of land in the west, or if necessary, up to 50 percent more than their holdings. He was to offer supplies during the move west plus subsistence for a year and fifty cents an acre for their one hundred thousand or so acres. Some Wyandot chiefs went west again to evaluate the land proposed to them. Their report was unfavorable. Governor Lucas, assisted by his secretary, John A. Bryan, and the agent, John McElvain, tried to persuade them but failed. Lucas went to Upper Sandusky on August 6 and again on September 16. On September 18, the chiefs asked for payment of their annuities before discussing the question of a move. On September 26, Lucas tried to convince them to accept a treaty. The next day they informed him that they had concluded to postpone a final decision. The governor learned that their reluctance to move was based partly on advice from persons opposed to their leaving. Lucas wrote to Cass that the chiefs "maintained a degree of obstinate silence [and] could not be drawn into an argument on the subject of emigrating." Because all his federal funds were spent, Lucas gave up the effort.[68]

Fight against the Federal Government

In a treaty April 23, 1836, however, the Wyandots reluctantly agreed to sell a strip of land five miles wide west of their reservation that was annexed to Crawford County. Their condition appeared to be deteriorating rapidly. On March 15, 1837, William Walker, who had been reading proof sheets of Finley's manuscript, wrote him a five-page letter describing what he called deplorable conditions in the school and mission. On June 3, 1837, J.M. Armstrong wrote to say, "We have been peculiarly unfortunate in the appointments of the Government to the Indian work. The Superintendent of Indian Affairs at St. Louis is a wicked, reckless, profane, and has been a licentious man and ready and willing to uphold men of like character among the Indians as agents. . . . The agents manage to control the chiefs through disguising demagogues . . . they are frequently made to sanction the most flagrant injustice . . . vice, wickedness and drunkenness are on the increase. . . . The Wyandots are generally healthy. In a religious way there is a faithful few." [69]

Finley returned to Upper Sandusky in June 1837, for he received mail there inviting him to speak at a meeting nearby. That summer he and his wife were the only whites to participate in a camp meeting with 150 Indians near Delaware. He recorded his impressions in an article in the *Western Christian Advocate*. "The shouts of salvation made this wild, uncultivated valley ring, while the halo of heavenly inspiration sat on every tongue and was kindled to a flame in every heart." The service continued through the night. He wrote, "the spreading branches of the shady grove reflecting the light of our waxen candles; the gentle zephyrs moving the leaves, the rolling murmurs of the Scioto river, just on whose banks we were worshipping, and the echoes of the hallelueahs bursting from the lips of the converted red man, and hosanna from their children, was an era sufficient to overwhelm the contemplative mind." [70]

Another treaty was proposed that year to secure Wyandot approval for leaving Ohio. On August 8, 1837, William Walker wrote Finley to describe how support for the move was being acquired:

We the Council have recently addressed a strong appeal to the Secy of War opposing the conduct of the Commissioners from the commencement of their operations up to the date of our communication, and earnestly petition for their recall. . . . The Commissioners have ceased to hold open and public councils; the treaty they have made was in the first place signed by twelve persons, making the number including women and children about thirty-four. At another meeting a few more signed when drunk. After which the treaty has been at Mr. McCutchin's Bar, and as a straggling Wyandot happened along he was called into the house and if he was fond of drink, signing the treaty was then made the price of a glass of grog!. . . . They appear to be bloody bent on breaking up the nation.[71]

A different account is contained in T. Hartley Crawford's report to Congress in 1840. He wrote that an investigation of the charges exonerated the commissioners.

The result of the negotiations was the sale of more land but no acceptance of removal. Another attempt was made in 1839 but the government representative died during the negotiations.

On March 3, 1841, Congress appropriated three thousand dollars for new treaty negotiations with the Wyandots. John Johnston, who, of course, was well acquanted with them, was a close friend of the newly elected president, William Henry Harrison, and was probably his personal representative in Washington prior to his inauguration. Johnston had been removed from his office as Indian agent when Andrew Jackson was elected. On March 26, 1841, two days before President Harrison caught a cold that killed him, he appointd Johnston to negotiate treaties with some Indian tribes, including the Wyandots. Negotiations commenced in April and were lengthy and complicated. Johnston did not follow all his instructions from Washington because he felt that some of them would jeopardize the success of his assignment. He was determined to complete a fair and acceptable treaty. He found it especially difficult to substantiate Wyandot debts to whites because of, as he put it, "perjury, fraud and every species of corruption" from some white Americans.[72]

Although Johnston was pressured by representatives of the Mad River and Lake Erie Railroad, which planned a right of way though the reservation, he refused to be rushed. Apparently, he had received assurances from Harrison that he would request Congress to establish a territory that would be governed by Native Americans with white supervision and that ultimately would become a state. Neither President Tyler nor the Congress had any interest in that idea.[73]

The terms of the treaty, which he signed on March 17, 1842, a year after he had begun, stipulated that the Wyandots would surrender their 109,000 acres of land in Ohio and 6,000 acres in Michigan. In return, the United States granted the tribe 148,000 acres west of the Mississippi River. They were to receive a perpetual annuity of $17,500 and a permanent grant of five hundred dollars for the school. Their debts, amounting to $23,860, were to be paid by the government. They were also to be paid for improvements that they had made on their Upper Sandusky reservation. The Senate ratified the treaty August 17 and the Wyandots formally accepted it on September 16.[74] Some of the terms of the treaty were never fulfilled. The Wyandots never received all the money they had been promised.

Charles Dickens was one of the last foreign travelers to visit Upper Sandusky before the Wyandots left. He recorded that in April 1842 he met there some Native Americans who looked like gypsies, riding on shaggy ponies. He also had a long conversation with a man who must have been John Johnston.[75]

As the time approached for the Wyandots to leave Ohio, Finley received a letter from Gray Eyes written May 20, 1843, inviting him to visit Upper Sandusky one last time. "The cause of religion has prospered more abundantly than years heretofore, between 50 and 60 have been added to the church during the winter and spring. . . . We are now making preparations to remove to the West. It reminds us of the preparations we are all making for heaven. The 15th of next month is the time set to start for our new homes, and were it possible it would give me great pleasure to have you visit us before you leave. I think that you could be the means of doing good here, in the present state of feeling."[76]

Finley did return, for he preached at a second funeral for John Stewart, who was buried in the cemetery beside the mission house. Gray Eyes gave a farewell speech to a gathering of white neighbors as the Wyandots were about to depart. His fondest words were for the mission church where he had often worshipped and listened to Finley. Years later the mission church fell into disrepair but was restored in 1889. Services now are held Sundays at 8 A.M. during the summer.[77]

Some 664 Wyandots left Upper Sandusky Tuesday, July 11, 1843, 609 from Ohio, 25 from Michigan and 30 from Canada. Fifty, in families with sick members, remained to leave later. James Wheeler, the Methodist missionary, wrote two articles for the *Western Christian Advocate* describing the first several days of the journey. He wrote that many were leaving, "with a solemnity of countenance apparently as great as if they were attending the funeral of some departed friend." Wheeler reported that "whiskey pedlars" followed the band and made many drunk. Some whites stole provisions out of Wyandot wagons. Meanwhile, the principal chief, Henry Jacques, with a small party went to Columbus where farewell speeches were exchanged with Governor Shannon.[78]

The Wyandots marched through Bellefontaine, Urbana, Springfield, and Xenia before arriving at Cincinnati where they boarded two boats for Missouri, the "Nodaway" and the "Republic." The boats left on July 20. In what must have seemed a sad commentary on the missionary effort, on the day of departure from Cincinnati, the young man who had been known in his boyhood as James Finley became intoxicated in the afternoon and fell overboard at night and drowned.[79]

In his memoirs McKenney recounted a scene that occurred as the boats approached Harrison's grave at North Bend on the shore of the Ohio River. The principal chief asked the captain to load the gun and stop the boat. The Wyandots lined up silently on the hurricane roof. As they drifted past the tomb, they uncovered and waved their hats as the gun was fired. Then the chief stepped forward and called out, "Farewell, Ohio, and her brave!"[80]

The land offered the Wyandots was on the Neosho River. They thought it was unsuitable. They went to the forks of the Missouri and Kansas rivers, near the site of the future Kansas City, Kansas, where they purchased 39 sections of land from the Delaware Indians for $46,080, a tactical error since it jeopardized their allotment from the federal government. Their experience in their new home was disastrous. Nearly one hundred died within the year. The Kansas River flooded and many lost their houses, furniture, crops, and cattle. Many suffered from sickness. Bishop Morris, who visited the area in 1844, reported that the Wyandots were "among the greatest sufferers." They received less than one-sixth of the value of the improvements made on their land in Ohio. In addition, because they had bought lands from the Delawares, they were informed by government officials that there was no further obligation to furnish them the lands mentioned in the treaty.[81]

In his reports for 1843 and 1844 the commissioner of Indian affairs sought to get the government to pay the Wyandots the full amount owed them, but to no avail. The valuation placed on their improvements at Upper Sandusky was over $125,000 but they received only $20,000. The 1843 report contains words that reflected majority opinion at that time: "The state of Ohio, in a rising section of it, has thus been freed from a population that prevented the settlement of a large body of fine lands, and interposed a serious obstacle, the last of its kind in the state, to the advance of a thrifty district—while the Wyandots are also relieved from white influences that were destructive of any hope of Indian improvement."[82] Finley was prophetic in commenting on the fate of Native Americans in his *Autobiography*: "It is a melancholy reflection, that all those powerful tribes which once inhabited these plains, roaming at freedom where we now reside, and who sped with their light canoes over the surface of our rivers, the monarchs of all they surveyed, have now no claim whatever even to the graves of their fathers."[83]

Whites quickly filled the vacuum at Upper Sandusky, which became the county seat. Streets were laid out in 1843. By 1846, the town contained five hundred inhabitants, six stores, one newspaper printing office, and one Methodist church. It was not until July 1848 that Congress ratified the 1843 Wyandot agreement with the Delawares.[84]

Finley's correspondence with his old friends continued. Gray Eyes wrote him on November 30, 1847, to urge him to visit again. Finley responded to ask how many Wyandots were still church members. Gray Eyes replied that there were 180 who were still church members plus 43

Shawnee, 45 Delaware, and 30 Kickapoo Indians. He gave the names of the church leaders and wrote that he was glad that Finley intended to visit the following fall.[85]

Catherine and John Hicks wrote him on July 29, 1848, to say that they were looking forward to his visit. "Many years have passed since we first met in the wilderness of Sandusky and learned to sing praises to the Redeemer. Many changes have been brought about since we last met. . . . To take you by the hand once more before we push off from the shores of earth would fill our cups with joy."[86]

Two days later Gray Eyes wrote to acknowledge Finley's June 10 letter. He reported on the latest revival among the Indians and on the desire of the Wyandot church to leave the Methodist Church South and rejoin the Ohio Conference.[87]

In 1850, the Wyandot tribe lost the 148,000 acres of land given them in the treaty worked out by John Johnston in 1842. A covenant was negotiated with them in April of that year, giving them $185,000, or $1.25 per acre. Of this amount, one hundred thousand dollars was invested in government bonds yielding 5 percent interest with the interest paid to them annually. The remaining eighty-five thousand dollars was released to allow them to pay their debts, including compensation to the Delaware Indians for the land bought from them.[88]

The Wyandot tribal government was dissolved in 1855. That year they were given United States citizenship, and their land was divided among the tribe members. (In 1825, Finley proposed that the new generation of Wyandots be given citizenship.) The report of the commissioner of Indian affairs for 1850 praised the treaty that gave the Wyandots citizenship and terminated their annuities. "Their tribal organization has ceased . . . and they will soon no longer be known as an Indian tribe." In 1859, they were given thirty-three thousand acres by the Seneca-Cayuga on their reservation in northeast Oklahoma to which they later moved. Their 1970 population was one thousand.[89]

It is easy from the perspective of the 1990s to criticize the federal government for its harsh removal policy of the 1830s and 1840s. The government, however, was following a course supported by most white Americans at that time. No other policy was probably practical in the face of the pressures created by the spirit of manifest destiny and land hunger. Thus most nineteenth-century whites must share in the guilt of cheating the Native Americans and forcing them westward.

As early as 1821, the Indian agent, John Johnston, was well aware that Native Americans had much reason to hate members of the white race. Writing to Governor Ethan Allen Brown about the trials of the Delaware in being steadily pushed westward, he declared, "there is no man who is called upon to act on business with the Indians for any length of time but must feel for their distress. The increase of our population has brought to the Indians a long catalogue of evils." He concluded, "The wisdom of the National Government is loudly called upon to devise some other and better plan for progressing from total destruction this ill fated race of people."[90]

Reporting to Congress in 1826, James Barbour, the war department official then responsible for Indian affairs, wrote, "From the first discovery of America to the present time, one master passion, common to all mankind, that of acquiring land, has driven, in ceaseless succession, the white man on the Indian. . . . The department is continually pressed with applications, from New York to Arkansas, to adopt measures to extinguish the Indian tribes to their lands, and remove the Indians." Paul Stuart seems justified in observing that no matter how well intentioned the government's removal policy may have been, it was implemented in a coercive manner harmful to the Native Americans in many ways. Robert Shalhope included philanthropists in his criticism, for he believes that "the white man's love was as deadly as his hatred." Wilcomb Washburns's evaluation is more charitable in concluding that, given the system and the people involved, the destructive policy may have been inevitable and contained both malevolent and benevolent elements. John Quincy Adams, whose views on the removal policy changed over the years, finally wrote in his diary June 30, 1841, "It is among the heinous sins of this nation, for which I believe God will one day bring them to judgment." Henry Schoolcraft sadly concluded in his *Memoirs* that "the whole Indian race is not, in the political scales, worth one white man's vote."[91]

To pass judgment now on the actions of people over 150 years ago may be a futile exercise. Some of the federal officials responsible for the removal policy had genuine concern for the Native Americans' welfare. Thomas L. McKenney, for example, who was superintendent of the Office of Indian Trade from 1816 to 1822 and head of the Bureau of Indian Affairs in the Department of War from 1824 to 1830, believed that he had the highest motives. Although he was instrumental in getting Congress to pass the Indian Civilization Act, he also favored the Removal Act, for he wanted to separate Native Americans from the vices of whites.

Federal officials, philanthropists—even the missionaries—were caught in a seemingly impossible bind because of their attitudes, preconceptions, and prejudices. White Americans had been too ambivalent for too long. What they expected of Native Americans when they spoke of "civilizing" was naïve when part of American society was engaged in a rapid populating of the frontier and an unbridled materialism that threatened their very existence. Apparently white Americans at that time would accept no alternative to the brutally coercive removal plan. Finley and the other critics of the government were weak voices in the wilderness, a wilderness that was disappearing along with the Native Americans.

One ironic rationalization for wanting to move the Indians beyond the frontier was to get them away from the influence of the worst members of white society. As T. Hartley Crawford, commissioner of Indian affairs after 1839, wrote in his 1842 report to the Senate, "Removal from the lands that the whites wanted would bring to the Indians seclusion and protection from the contaminating influences of white civilization."[92]

Assessing Finley's accomplishments with the Wyandots is more difficult. On one hand, he was obviously very successful as a preacher and missionary. He was well loved by many members of the tribe, who named him "the old chief" in 1826. It was a major recognition for a white to be named an honorary chief. He not only brought many of them religious conversion but taught their children and helped to raise their standard of living through better farming. He helped many of them resist the greedy traders and land-hungry speculators. He urgued them to overcome alcoholism, and he secured federal funds for the building of their mission, a rare feat for 1823. He helped them resist government pressures to leave Ohio. On the other hand, he forced them, as their price of conversion, to give up many of their traditional customs and practices. He railed against dancing as well as drunkenness. He forced Indian children to take white names and white dress. As James Axtel and others have maintained, at its worst, conversion to Christianity meant cultural suicide.[93]

If we fault him for denigrating Native American heritage and for forcing his religious, social, and economic views on the Wyandots in the 1820s we must also recognize that he was representative of his age. He reflected the ideas, convictions, and prejudices of the frontier religious society that produced him. He spread the Gospel as he had been taught and inspired to do. He brought the benefits of civilization and Christianity to people white Americans thought were uncivilized. In his opinion, and in the opinion of many of his contemporaries, he was doing God's work.

What is remarkable is that he was able to accomplish so much in the face of so many handicaps. The Methodist itinerant system prevented him, or anyone else, from devoting exclusive, long-term attention to missionary activity. For three of the six years he was a missionary to the Wyandots he was also a presiding elder and a superintendent of the mission. And for sixteen months he was a sub-agent for the government as well! Furthermore, he was continuously the target of animosity from white traders and speculators.

Instead of criticizing Finley for what he did or did not do, it seems appropriate to observe that members of both races failed to comprehend

Postcard showing the ruins of the Wyandot mission church prior to its repair and restoration in 1889. The card was published by the H.E. Kinley department store in Upper Sandusky. From a private collection.

and accept each other's philosphy of life, structure of society, mores, and heritage. As Wade Barclay observed, "the attempt to evangelize the American Indians represented a conflict of radically different cultures." If Finley and other missionaries in the nineteenth century lacked sufficient appreciation of Native American culture and were not responsive to their ceremonies and customs, we must remember that, to them, the most crucial thing in the world was the salvation of souls. All else was less important.[94]

Even if Finley had been more successful, if 100 percent instead of 50 percent of the Wyandots had been converted, if they had somehow been exempted from the removal policy because of their special status, what then? Robert Berkhofer's conclusion cannot be ignored. He maintained that white Americans' racial attitudes are to blame for what happened. The Indians could not become integrated into white society because white civilized Christians would not accept them on equal terms. He concluded, "By discriminating against the aborigine upon a belief of white cultural superiority, Americans forced the Indians to remain savage and guaranteed the failure of the missionary program."[95]

Writing more recently, Ronald Satz agreed in his criticism of both

Fight against the Federal Government

Recent photograph of the Wyandot mission church in Upper Sandusky, which was restored in 1889. Behind the building is a small graveyard and tablets on the west wall list the missionaries and prominent converts. The property is maintained by the John Stewart United Methodist Church and the West Ohio Conference Commission on Archives and History.

government officials and missionaries. The former, he asserted, sought to eliminate Indian culture and force institutions and religious practices on the native tribes. He believed that the missionaries' success at conversion resulted in a weakening of Native American cultures. Other whites, he maintained, made things worse with their open disregard of Gospel teachings. Satz also has warned his readers not to confuse the rhetoric of politicians with the realities of implementing policies. Loring Priest's observation seems appropriate that prior to 1865 there was no meaningful effort made to help the Native Americans adjust to the white American style of life.[96]

James Finley deserves particular commendation for his forthright opposition to government policy and actions. It required unusual independence and zealous persistence to speak out against the removal policy for so long a period of time.

Finley contributed one more thing to the Wyandots. He wrote two books about them that acquainted many Americans in the mid-nineteenth century with their history and culture. His *History of the Wyandott Mission at Upper Sandusky, Ohio* was published in 1840. Even in his *Memo-*

rials of Prison Life he wrote caustically about the "injustice and dishonesty of the American government to these unfortunate and noble-hearted children of the forest." He described in detail the financial loss the Wyandots suffered in having to move west and ended the account with, "Let us repent in sackcloth and ashes."[97]

His book, *Life among the Indians*, was published in 1857 when he was almost 76. In his Preface he wrote, "No living man, probably, has seen and known more of the Indians in the north-west than myself. During almost seventy years I have been among them, as it were—have been acquainted with their principal men, studied their history, character, and manner of life. With me it has not been, as with most who have written about them, a mere matter of theory; for I have been among them, hunted and fished with them, ate and lodged in their wigwams, and been subjected to all the labors, excitements, perils, and privations of life among them."[98]

Finley's last words in his last book were an ominous prediction. After asserting that Indians were constantly annoyed with the thirst whites had for their lands, he wrote, "God will, in a coming day, settle the accounts of the Government and her agents and traders, for their conduct and treatment to the poor Indian; and eternal Justice will punish the worst and most inhuman of all our race."[99]

5

Power and Struggle

> If there is no fire of the Holy Spirit in the man, there will not be in the Word.
> —James B. Finley
>
> If there be any one characteristic by which this age is distinguished from another, it is that of excitement; and, generally speaking, an excitement on subjects that are intrinsically good.
> —Nathan Bangs

In 1827, as he turned forty-six years of age, Finley returned to being a full-time presiding elder. Although roads were better then than they had been and towns were increasing in size, the hardships of the traveling preachers continued to be severe. Finley observed the changes around him, regretted the loss of wilderness areas, and sought to adjust to the physical and economic developments he witnessed. After two years on the Lebanon district, he was assigned at the 1829 Annual Conference to the Cincinnati circuit along with Wesley Browning and William B. Christie, an assignment that he considered "anything but a desirable appointment." The transition from the woods of Upper Sandusky to a bustling city was formidable. He sought advice from Thomas Morris in Columbus on preaching to an urban population. He made the adjustment with little difficulty. After two years there he was appointed presiding elder of the Miami district. He purchased land in Warren on November 16, 1831. His schedule on the Miami district was rigorous. He attended the first quarterly meeting of the new Eaton circuit February 4, 1832. He must have been impressed with the area, for Eaton is where he eventually lived and died. He returned Sunday, September 25, 1842, to preach the dedicatory sermon in the new Methodist church in Eaton. He was instrumental in persuading 190 persons to pledge $1,074 to the church that day.[1]

In the spring of 1831 he briefly considered reviving his interest in medicine. He acquired a ticket of admission for the summer lectures and examinations at the Cincinnati Academy of Medicine. But his dedication to the ministry was too strong for him to make a mid-life career change. The old forests were disappearing; population was increasing; transportation was improving. In 1832, a canal from Cleveland to Portsmouth was completed. He found it a challenge to deal with change.

He and six other Ohio delegates had a serious accident returning from the 1832 General Conference. The party was crossing the Allegheny Mountains on a fast mail coach from Baltimore to Wheeling. It was a hot day on June 1, and, as the coach careened down the west side of Polish Mountain fourteen miles east of Cumberland, Maryland, it passed a train of heavy wagons. The frightened horses dashed off, and the coach was upset. Passengers and baggage tumbled down a steep embankment. One minister broke his arm, another a collarbone and several ribs. Finley had cuts on his face and almost fainted from loss of blood.[2]

In 1832 he was named presiding elder of the Cincinnati district. At that time the city was not divided into separate charges. The five ministers preached on successive Sundays in a circuit of the city's Methodist churches. They frequently met in Finley's office to discuss topics of concern, and they sought to visit all Methodist families. Finley's powerful preaching attracted large congregations.[3]

During the cholera epidemic there in October the Methodist churches were open day and night. Finley had to be in Ridgeville in Warren County, but Thomas A. Morris kept him informed. He wrote October 15 to indicate that although he had thought the epidemic was abating he was now experiencing one of the worst days yet. He wrote, "Seven of our members have already gone to eternity. . . . I have run from one scene of distress to another. . . . The confusion among our classes is fearful. . . . Many classes are locked out of their rooms the owners having escaped for life. The consternation is beyond what you would expect and families are flying by night & day." A revival began once the epidemic subsided. John Newland Maffit came from the East for four weeks of preaching after which Finley held a quarterly meeting. At the end of it one hundred persons were converted.[4]

By spring of 1833 Finley was sick again. Arthur W. Elliott wrote him on June 22, 1833, to bewail the fact that he was not expected to live. He expressed the wish that he and Finley could be buried "in one grave yard." Finley was convinced that he had cholera. He wrote a long plaintive letter to George Maley July 22, 1833, in which he apologized for missing a meeting and declared that he was close to death. "I want you to tell all my Christian friends at campmeeting that my soul is on stretch for home sweet home. . . . I have not had strength to preach since the 20th of April. . . . I cannot keep up with the itinerant gang but am seeking a shade & peaceful hour in which I may die."[5]

He continued to live, however, and became active once more. Later in 1833 he was placed in a Cincinnati church. For the period 1834-36 he was appointed presiding elder of the Chillicothe district. In 1834 he led the move to establish a Methodist paper in Cincinnati to report on western religious news. These efforts culminated in the weekly *Western Christian Advocate*. He was also influential in establishing the *Ladies Repository and Gatherings of the West*, the first Methodist periodical for women. The first issue was in January 1841. He proposed the creation of a German-language religious paper to serve the increased number of immigrants settling in Cincinnati. He wrote, in an article in the *Western Christian Advocate*, "Nothing in all our country is more needed. . . . Let me say, through you, to the Western World, that we have, in the providence of God, foreigners thrown amongst us, who are to be our future neighbors, and to marry with our children, in the helm of our government, and to bear a part in steering our political ship. Many of them want information necessary to all these purposes."[6]

He continued his interest in book details. At the first General Conference he attended in 1820, he submitted a motion instructing the Book Committee "to take into consideration the expediency of establishing a branch of the book business in the West." Although a similar petition had been refused in 1812 the General Conference yielded to the pressure from Western preachers and agreed to establish a branch of the Methodist Book Concern in Cincinnati. Martin Ruter was elected assistant agent but he was directed to serve under instructions from the New York agent. The move made sense financially. Because of the heavy discounting of Western currency the Book Concern had ten thousand dollars deposited in that area.[7]

At the 1827 Ohio Annual Conference Finley was appointed to a committee to consider the question of continuing the Cincinnati branch. Some Western ministers were opposed to it, but others believed that there was merit in allowing the Cincinnati branch to print books as well as process orders. Finley chaired the book committee, which took a strong role in recommending action.[8]

He submitted a lengthy report after his committee had reviewed the Book Concern's operation in Cincinnati. He concluded that the enterprise was in "a safe and prosperous condition." He referred to the deficiency in the supply of Sunday School books and deplored the fact that the West failed to receive sufficient and timely shipments. He claimed that Methodist preachers and agents could have sold fifty thousand dollars worth of books if they had had them available. He used the occasion of his report to repeat his recommendation that books be printed in Cincinnati. "Eastern men cannot calculate exactly for the west," he wrote, "as they are not intimately acquainted with its true condition, and therefore not with its wants." He regretted that agents had not been able to fill orders and asserted that schools should be furnished with books from Methodist writers. He thought that some of the Sunday School books from the American

Union were "somewhat tinged with Calvinism." His report ended with four recommendations, the last of which was to remove any obstruction "in the way of publishing any book of any description which, in the opinion of the Western Book Committee and Agents are necessary to be published."[9]

He was appointed to the book committee again in 1831. The 1832 General Conference passed a resolution to have a book agent and an assistant in Cincinnati to manage the Concern in the western country. The problem of delays in processing orders persisted. Finley and others believed that sales of the *Discipline* and other books were being lost because of these delays and slowness in the postal system. They also were unhappy with the subordinate relation of the Cincinnati branch to New York. John F. Wright, the book agent from 1832 to 1844, wrote Finley in February of 1836, "This is a favorable crisis in the history of the western agency. . . . The next general conference will furnish the very best opportunity to give it permanency and efficiency." The General Conference that year did remove some restrictions and gave the Cincinnati branch authority to publish some books. The Cincinnati agents were authorized to purchase ground and erect a building for printing and binding. They were allowed to receive gifts for this purpose. In less than three months a lot had been purchased for eleven thousand dollars and plans for a building were underway.[10]

Wright wrote Finley again on May 30, 1836, to tell him not to be discouraged at the slow progress. "It is true we are not at liberty to print any work stereotyped in N. York and on account of the failure of your resolution the agents at New York are not bound to send us any printed sheets unless they choose to do so." In another letter July 12, 1838, Wright reported further progress. "I think my visit to New York will exert a good influence in several respects. A majority of the bishops present were in favor of our construction of the paragraphs in relation to the western book concern." Further independence was achieved in 1839 when the Cincinnati branch was chartered as the Western Methodist Book Concern.[11]

Indicative of the fact that Finley was working toward the publication of his history of the Wyandot mission was the following paragraph in Wright's letter: "I ascertained that the price of a fine steel plate engraving of your portrait will be one hundred dollars. Copper plate $50. . . . Bro. Mason suggests that you ought to be on steel and that woodcut likenesses would answer for Mononcue and Between-the-Logs as well as some other Indian antiquity."[12]

Finley served on many committees at annual conferences and wrote many reports that helped shape the policies and practices of the church. One report he and G. W. Walker wrote in 1835 for the Ohio Conference to send to the other annual conferences clearly revealed his strong interest in enhancing the financial support for retired ministers and widows. The profits from the Book Concern were to be used for their future support. The General Conference in Cincinnati in 1834 had used some of these funds to pay the expense of its delegates. He and Walker wrote, "the multiplicity of duties imposed upon our Itinerant Ministers deprive them of the opportunity, and means, of securing a support for themselves and their families when they shall have worn out in the work. . . . We think therefore that it is of vital importance to the Connection, and to the institution that its proceeds should be inviolate for this purpose." [13]

Finley was transferred in 1836 to be presiding elder of the Lebanon district for three years, after which he held the same assignment in the Dayton district from 1839 to 1843. He presided at a quarterly meeting on April 20, 1839, when a committee was appointed to consider establishing a new church in Dayton. A lot was bought at Fifth and Jackson streets; money was raised, and the structure was dedicated August 10, 1842, with the name of Finley Chapel.[14]

His travel schedule for September 1839 quarterly meetings took him to Dayton September 9 and 10, Xenia September 16 and 17, Union September 23 and 24, and Troy September 30 and October 1st. The following spring he had eight quarterly meetings from April 25 to June 14. His father died at the age of ninety in his son's residence in Germantown December 8, 1840. In 1843 James was appointed presiding elder of the Zanesville district where he was to remain until his appointment as chaplain of the Ohio Penitentiary.

In the summer of 1844, however, he briefly explored the idea of settling down in Dayton. Thomas Brown wrote him from there August 17, 1844. "I am highly pleased with the idea of confining your ministerial labours to the Finley Chapel. . . . You say my old Homestead and the adjoining House would suit you." He could have bought both houses for twenty-five hundred dollars but decided against the move even though the prospect of preaching in a church named in his honor must have been appealing. He was probably still too restless to settle in one place.[15]

Finley's personality was acerbic to many people. He either liked a person thoroughly or disliked him extremely. There were rules to follow and he would hound a person who chose to ignore them. He was strongly emotional and would vent his anger when he was displeased. In 1826, he was irritated by the actions of one colleague, George W. Maley, and sent him a blistering letter. Maley, who was astonished at the rebuke he received, wrote to say, "I little expected to receive such an inflammatory letter from James B. Finley." Later they became good friends again.[16]

Finley's treament of Alfred Brunson reveals much about his personality and convictions. Brunson fought in the War of 1812. In December 1814, he was recommended by his Methodist class for a license to preach. Jacob Young, presiding elder in his district, opposed him. He persisted and was rejected again in 1816, this time because he had a family and was in debt. In 1817, Finley was his presiding elder. Finley opposed his being licensed because of his poverty and his being married. Finley was persuaded to relent at a quarterly meeting in Youngstown in November and gave Brunson some preaching assignments in Huron County, 150 miles from his home through what he called "an almost impassable wilderness."[17]

At a camp meeting in March 1818, Brunson felt that Finley was giving him "the cold shoulder" and pressed him for a reason. Finley lashed out at him petulantly and lectured him severely about his pride and self-conceit in front of older preachers. Later Finley told him that the conference had rejected him because he had three children. Brunson claimed that Finley asserted he had "more confidence in the pulpit than the bishop does, and I fear he will be hard to govern and control." Finley treated him harshly at a camp meeting in the summer of 1819, but Brunson retaliated by preaching such an eloquent sermon that people marveled at his abilities. At the annual conference in 1820 Finley reported that he was now satisfied that Brunson ought to be ordained.[18]

Finley's personality displayed extremes. He could be saintly, kind, and tolerant one instant and the opposite the next. Disputes and differences of opinion sometimes led to bitterness. William Burke was one of the early Ohio church leaders. Henry Boehm wrote that he "wielded a tremendous power in the pulpit." He had been secretary of the Western Conference and the first presiding elder of the Ohio district. He encountered trouble with his colleagues in 1813 when he was suspended for a year for treating a presiding elder "with contempt." The 1818 Ohio Annual Conference suspended him indefinitely. At the 1820 Annual Conference it was Finley who moved that Burke be expelled from the church "for contumacy," a motion that carried. Six years later Burke wrote him a pleading letter asking for clarification of his status looking toward a return to church membership. It was not until 1836 that the General Conference recommended that he be reinstated.[19]

Finley must have regretted some of his disputes. His friend and political contact, John McLean, often wrote to give him advice. "You have every thing that could be desired to encourage you in the good work," he once wrote. "By continued kindness to our radical friends or enemies, you have disappointed them, and encouraged the friends of the Redeemer."[20]

Finley's idealization of nature and his reflection of Romanticism permeated his social views and even his attitudes about the best type of preaching. In his *Sketches of Western Methodism* he wrote, "Nature is the fountain from whence the orator must draw his inspiration, and the field whereon he must develop his powers. As the eagle, who soars away from the homes and haunts of man, to bathe his undazzled eye in the sunbeam, and pillow his breast upon the storm, so the child of genius must become familiar with Nature in all her aspects."[21]

In writing about the career of the itinerant, Henry Bascom, Finley declared that he could only think freely "beneath the boundless skies and extended landscapes" and that he composed his greatest sermons at a Kentucky Indian mound. "Had his genius been cramped by the laws of the schools, which are often about as useful in making an orator as a notebook would be to a nightingale . . . we might have had . . . a Bascom polished with all the arts of elocution; but . . . there would have been a stiffness in his movements; and . . . we should have had nothing but the mimic artificial man."[22]

Typical of his generation, who lived, hunted, and survived in the forests of Ohio, Finley often contrasted the purity, boldness, and goodness of the west with the over-cultured, effete weakness and questionable values of the East. He was especially disparaging of the inhabitants of eastern cities. In writing about the ideal ministerial education for circuit riders he was critical of theological seminaries and questioned their relevance for the woods. He declared, "I am not opposed to literature but think that every citizen ought to be as learned in all the useful branches of Science. . . . But that a course of what is called Collegiate Education is necessary to qualify a man to be an able Minister of the Gospel I do not believe. The minister must be born again. . . . He must know that he is inwardly moved by the Holy Ghost. . . . He must be a Bible student, a Bible Christian in order to be a Bible Minister."[23]

At the least he was ambivalent on the subject of ministerial training. On a number of occasions he questioned the need for a well-educated ministry. He wrote, "If Princeton, Yale, Union, and Rochester, were emptied today, and scattered among the destitute of our frontier settlements, how long do you think, gentle reader, it would take them to acquire the efficiency of a backwoods itinerant in getting souls converted to God?" Some of his pronouncements on frontier life and preaching seem anti-intellectual in tone.[24]

He was appointed to a committee to study the expediency of establishing a theological seminary and shared in writing a report to the Annual Conference in 1834. The committee favored the status quo and considered seminaries unnecessary. He thought they would embarrass the itinerant operation.

Finley penned a long letter to the editor of the *Ladies Repository* in which he conveyed his suspicion of ministers who gained doctorates of divinity. He wanted to know where the degree had originated and by what authority it was conferred. He wanted a listing of the qualifications for the degree and asked why female institutions couldn't confer it on women. He went on to deplore the fact that no minister could receive the honor except from an institution of learning and supected that the distinction was conferred on a few favorites without reference to their preaching abilities. He concluded by expressing preference for the ranks of elder and bishop, which were earned properly within the church.[25]

Later in life, Finley was uneasy with the philosophizing that seemed to attract some of his younger colleagues. Perhaps he thought that for ministers to immerse themselves in philosophy would minimize the work of God in the process of conversion. One of his many letters to the *Western Christian Advocate* in July 11, 1855, addressed this topic. He reported on a preachers' meeting in Baltimore that discussed the will of man from metaphysical and theological perspectives.

I thought there was a danger of Methodist preachers refining too much on the plain old doctrines as taught by our Methodist fathers, and in so doing, darken counsel by a multiplicity of new words not easily understood. And I never knew a Methodist preacher who ran into the fog and mist of metaphysical reasoning but lost his usefulness, and frequently the balance of his own mind. . . . But there seems to be a special itching in some to preach some new thing . . . to write or copy some sermon, and read it. For myself, I have come to this conclusion: whenever a Methodist preacher commences reading a sermon, to get up and leave the house.[26]

He was always willing to give advice to his younger colleagues. In a March 24, 1837, article in the *Western Christian Advocate*, he declared that the first important thing was a preacher's own personal holiness. "Never act the boy. I advise especially not to be gallanting about with young females, or cracking jokes with them . . . be studious and attend to your books. . . . Study the Bible as the first book in the world; its doctrines, its history, its chronology, its geography. Next to your Bible is your Discipline. . . . Never miss your appointments. . . . Always beware of outside show."[27]

Finley's views were fairly representative of those of his colleagues who wrote him from time to time to agree with one of his pronouncements. James Gilruth wrote May 19, 1835, to say, "I feel we have much need to stand firm by our Discipline—there is so much innovation of one kind or another that unless we rally round the standard & bring every thing to the letter of the law there is no knowing where we shall land." He expressed pleasure with Finley's remarks on the subject of theological seminaries. Gilruth associated with them "pride, & pedantry—effeminancy, a cold lifeless ministry & a lukewarm church."[28]

While he objected to an overly educated ministry, Finley strongly favored education for the entire population. His attitude on this subject was strongly influenced by his own experience as a child. Having his own father as a teacher convinced him of the importance of early schooling. He declared in his *Autobiography*, "Every good man, every lover of his country, every bad man ought to use his influence to encourage and sustain, with his property and by the education of his children, every effort to banish the cursed monster ignorance from our happy country." He believed that everyone should look upon the improvement of the mind as "the most valuable acquisition within their grasp, both for here and hereafter."[29]

Finley frequently found occasion to emphasize the importance of education for the frontier area. He devoted several pages of his *Autobiography* to the subject.

The mind of man on his entrance into our disordered world, is destitute of knowledge of every kind, but is capable of vast acquirements and prodigious expansion; and on this his happiness and usefulness depend. But it must be acquired by education; and whatever opens the door to facilitate this object, will be productive of the greatest good, both to the individual and the community at large. The expansion of the mind makes the man. . . . On this depends the happiness of social intercourse, the enjoyments of all civil and religious privileges, the advancement in the arts and sciences, and the commerce of the world . . . if a poor man could be justified for theft on any principle, it would be to steal to educate his children.[30]

Finley was a strong proponent of education for women. In 1830 he joined G.R. Jones and Jacob Young in recommending support for a female academy in Cincinnati. He was instrumental in helping Jacob Young establish the school for girls in Worthington, Ohio, and was appointed visitor to the Worthington Female Academy in 1838. For the 1830s the notion that young women were worth educating was a radical one. According to Young, many people thought that a liberal education spoiled women. He claimed he had been told by some that "they never knew an educated woman that was a good house-keeper." Young believed that other female institutions in Ohio owed their origins to the Worthington Female Seminary. Finley was also president of the board of trustees of the Germantown Academy in 1840.[31]

Higher education was also of great concern to him. The idea of a Methodist college in the West was proposed to Finley in 1821 by George Houston of Dayton. Finley canvassed people in his Lebanon district and brought up the matter at the next annual conference. The Ohio Conference proposed to the Kentucky Conference a joint undertaking. Thanks to cooperation from the Bracken Academy and a grant of land, Augusta College was chartered by the Kentucky legislature December 22, 1822. Finley was given chief credit for pushing the idea. He was a trustee of Augusta College for several years and solicited on its behalf. In an 1834 article in the *Western Christian Advocate* he wrote, "The college has always been well supplied with students. . . . But it might be rendered more useful, if it were better endowed, and rendered more independent in its resources." The article described a plan in which the Ohio and Kentucky conferences might raise twenty thousand dollars in four years, the income from which could provide scholarships. "The signs of the times require, that we should be up and doing all we can for the rising generation. And so far as education is concerned, the best thing we can do is to patronize our own institutions."[32]

Finley found it difficult to attend trustee meetings, however, because of his busy schedule. Henry Bascom wrote him March 24, 1835, to urge him to attend but assured him that the board would not expect him to attend often "and would part with you very reluctantly." Joseph Trimble wrote him January 4, 1838, to ask him to attend the February meeting. "It will be a very important session."[33]

Finley also became one of the first trustees of Ohio Wesleyan University. He was one of three commissioners, along with Jacob Young and Charles Elliott, who were given power to negotiate a transfer of the Ohio Wesleyan Female College to the university. He continued as a trustee until 1852.[34]

In 1849 he received a letter from Solomon Howard of Springfield who wanted him to become a trustee of Miami University. Howard was concerned about conditions there and asked Finley to use his influence with the legislature to see that vacancies were filled with "suitable men," by whom he meant Methodists. "Why should one denomination have the sole management of one institution that belongs equally to all?" he asked. "It is admitted by all that the university is & has been for some time on the decline. Now we verily believe if a more liberal course should be pursued its halls would be filled with students and it will rise to an honor and glory to our state." Finley resisted the opportunity to get involved in affairs at Oxford, and he was not interested in Jacob Young's plan to take over Ohio University as a Methodist institution.[35]

Throughout his career many people turned to Finley for help. On July 26, 1819, Daniel Hitt wrote asking Finley to assist him in clearing up some financial difficulties involving Hitt and others with the Methodist Book Concern. James Hinthorn wrote him May 9, 1823, to request one of his medical prescriptions. James Montgomery sent him a letter February 16, 1824, when he was at Upper Sandusky, to seek his help in preventing the firing of John Johnston as Indian agent. Apparently, speculators were hatching a plot against him. Montgomery wrote, "With your friends at Washington I want you to throw all your weight and protest against the appointment of a new agent." On August 18, 1828, Thomas Morris wrote from Louisville, Kentucky, seeking Finley's aid in getting an appointment in Ohio. He thought a city life would be bad for his wife's health, but he was willing to accept any assignment west of the Scioto River. On January 8, 1829, Martin Ruter requested him to write a letter to a student's father to persuade him to let his son continue his studies in Cincinnati. James Gilruth wrote May 18, 1830, from Granville to ask Finley to inquire about his brother-in-law's death in Cincinnati and to find out the state of his religious feelings before he died. On March 7, 1837, William D. Barrett urged him to get Samuel Clark to pay his debts.[36]

His reputation for doing favors and for getting things done must have been statewide. The requests for help went beyond religious concerns. Some dealt with finances, others with lobbying the legislature. When he was a chaplain at the Ohio Penitentiary, many relatives and friends of prisoners wrote Finley asking for information or assistance. G.W. Johnston wrote him on January 13, 1849, to ask that he use his influence on behalf of the New Plymouth Church's fund-raising efforts to pay for a new building.[37]

There were, of course, many invitations to preach and speak at meetings. Thomas Morris wrote May 25, 1831, "This line is to inform you that our camp meeting is to begin Sept. 2nd three miles from Columbus on the Worthington road, & to request you to attend."[38]

Even his relatives sent requests for favors. Charles F. Brooke, his grandson, wrote to him while he was in Columbus to ask him to find a job. Finley succeeded in getting him a position in a dry goods store, but the youth wrote back that he was reluctant to give up his teaching job until he knew the terms of the new position. He finally notified his grandfather that he had married and wouldn't be coming to Columbus.[39]

Finley's political views during his lifetime were representative of most Ohio Methodist ministers in the first half of the nineteenth century. What conditioned him were his childhood in Kentucky, his family's identification with the National Republicans rather than the Federalists in Ohio, his closeness to Worthington and Trimble in Chillicothe, and his friendship with John McLean during his adult years. His dislike of Jackson was understandable. He supported the Whigs after 1834, opposed the Mexican War in 1846, and by 1856 was a Republican. He sent a letter to Bishop Hamline in support of Fremont for the presidency, which the Bishop used to convert others to the Republican cause.[40]

One of his colleagues, John Lewis Smith, called him "an enthusiastic

Whig" and witnessed an occasion when his political feelings produced an almost violent anger. Finley was presiding at a quarterly meeting in Xenia in 1848 when a congressman in the room stood up to declare that Finley had ridden into his town one Friday afternoon and had refused to stay at his house because he was a Democrat. Finley responded by declaring, "That's a lie!"

The congressman replied, "I say it's a fact."

Finley said, "I say it is false, and now, sir, if you have any religious experience to tell, let us have it, but as to your lugging politics in this love feast, it cannot be done."

The congressman asserted, "I will talk as I please, sir."

"Sit down, sir!" Finley roared.

"I'll sit down when I get ready," was the reply.

Finley picked up a large hickory cane, left the pulpit and started toward his heckler, who quickly sat down.[41]

Although politics was not a primary interest or concern, he communicated with many political figures and they with him. Many of his acquaintances assumed that he had considerable influence with legislators, especially when he lived in Columbus. Congressmen solicited his views on Native American affairs. He quickly sought government assistance for his mission once he knew of its availability.

Finley delivered an eloquent obituary in Fairfield at the time of President William Henry Harrison's death that clearly reflected his political leanings. He called the deceased Harrison "a man chosen by God to be the Washington of the Western Country." After chronicling Harrison's military and political career, Finley, his voice undoutedly charged with emotion, declared, "I have not only lost a president but a personal friend." Recounting Harrison's activity in protecting him and his mother against Indian attacks in the early 1790s, Finley cried, "I owe him a debt I can never repay. I weep for the death of a man who with his brave comrades stood between me and death."[42]

John McLean, who was appointed associate justice of the Supreme Court in 1829, wrote Finley frequently from Washington on political matters. Toward the end of 1846, W.L. Hand wrote him from Burlington to ask him to use his influence to keep a Baptist and a Presbyterian from being appointed to associate justice positions. The writer proposed instead two persons who were called true Methodists and true Whigs. "You must *log-roll* at a very early period," he wrote. He continued, "We think that duty to the cause we love urges us to bestir ourselves in behalf of Methodism, especially when we are convinced that we have better men."[43]

Another Whig, D. Fisher, wrote from Washington March 1, 1848, to say that he agreed with Finley's views on the war with Mexico. Two years later, another friend revealed in a postscript, "In politics you and I are of the same mind as much so as if one soul inhabited both our bodies."[44]

Finley also had particular views on who made the best legislators.

> God save us when our liberties and rights are intrusted to the hands of those who neither fear God nor regard man; for, though we could not make religion a test of qualification nor require a profession thereof as indispensable to a legislator, we would, nevertheless, require in the candidate for public favor, a decent respect for the opinions and rights of others. If it may be argued that men of infidel sentiments have been good statesmen and patriots, and have served their country with fidelity, we reply, their statesmanship and patriotism were not the result of their infidelity but they existed in spite of it.[45]

Secret societies, such as the Masons, were greatly disliked by Finley and many of his colleagues. The Ohio Annual Conference took action to criticize Masonry in 1816, Finley taking an active part. The conference approved a resolution "That it is inexpedient and imprudent for a traveling Preacher to dishonor himself by associating with the Free Masons in their Lodges." The 1817 conference action went further: "We are decidedly & sentimentally opposed to the practice & are determined . . . to set our Faces & lift our hands against it." The resolution concluded by calling Masons "deficient in Religion and good morals." On September 23, 1817, David Young sent Finley a copy of the conference committee's report on the subject of Masonry so that he would have extra information to use in his attack on it.[46]

Only two reasons were given in the committee's report for its opposition to the Masons:

> 1. Because it appears from observation that an union with this body of men is unfavorable to piety. Witness the multitudes who on being converted to God, have abandoned their Lodges & Festivals walking no more with them. Witness the decaying piety of those who have attracted themselves to them from amongst ourselves . . .
> 2. Whatever Masonry may be in itself, it is obvious to all the Masons are (in general) greatly deficient both in Religion and good morals.

David Young had his doubts about the action taken against the Masons. He thought that some in the conference were motivated by envy, but he realized that others had pure motives. "I hope good may result yet my fears are stronger than my hopes. . . . I hope however they will pity the weakness of our good intentions & just let us alone."[47]

Although the bulk of the anti-Masonic fervor occurred from 1826 to 1832, strong feelings continued through the next decade. On February 8, 1841, Finley wrote a three-page letter to David Whitcombe criticizing the

Masonic Order. He concluded, "perhaps it is necessary for me to make some apology for my sudden departure from Dayton but such was the wounded state of my feelings that I thought it best. I had not the least intimation of your having joined the Masons . . . and the news came on me like a clap of thunder. . . . I pray to God that you may yet see the great evils of this abominable flumary."[48]

In 1844, Finley was still trying to ferret out evidence of Masonic influence, especially among ministers. He sent a list of names to Uriah Heath, who was at Franklinton, asking him to check on those who admitted to membership in the Masonic Order. Heath replied January 1, 1845, to give him a detailed report. He added that the ones who were Masons agreed that it was better for Methodist preachers not to join because "they would lose more friends than they would gain."[49]

It is understandable that Finley should have held anti-Catholic views. Especially by the 1830s, practically every Protestant minister was convinced that the Catholic church was an institution undermining American democracy. Finley must have read Lyman Beecher's *Plea for the West*, published in 1835, which called for support and missionaries to save the area for Protestantism. Except for an occasional negative comment in his letters and articles, however, he did not mount an attack against Catholicism as extensive as his fight for temperance or his criticism of the sin of slavery. His most strident views were expressed in an 1855 article he wrote from New York after he had been shown where the Huguenots first landed and settled. He wrote,

These people, driven from their homes, and murdered by thousands, for no other crime than love to God and their fellow-men, proves the spirit and nature of Popery, whose appetite is never satisfied, except when glutted with the blood of their fellow-men, which the history of the past age fully proves; and even in this land of liberty and brotherly love she has come to lay, by her skillful executioners, the Jesuits, her dark and flattering gins, so that she may sweep from this glorious country her religious and civil liberties, bought with the blood and treasures of our fathers. . . . Let Americans take care; for, if Rome had the power, she would soon appoint a Bartholomew's day, and, like the poor Huguenots, we would be driven out before the Roman beast![50]

In his economic ideas Finley was fairly conservative and accepted the capitalist business ethic of antebellum America. Salvation was more important than financial security, and a man's wealth had nothing to do with the fate of his soul. He reflected the popular Whig notion that economic advancement would lead to individual moral and spiritual improvement. Nevertheless, having lived in poverty, Finley had a deep appreciation of the value of money. In 1826 he owned ten acres of land. He paid his father's debts when he died. He purchased land in Indiana, six miles from Newton, in 1842 while he was in Germantown, Ohio. In 1847, he leased ten acres of land he owned in Hancock County for four years but was late paying his land tax of $10.83 that year. During much of his career he had to devote time and energy to fund raising for a variety of causes, and he was not likely to engage in reforms that threatened his important sources of support.[51]

Despite his many life-threatening illnesses, Finley had a tremendous amount of energy and zeal and seemed constantly in motion. He was so outspoken and so convinced of the rightness of his thoughts and actions that, like a lightning rod, he frequently attracted criticism and attacks. Thomas A. Morris, when he was a bishop, wrote Finley on April 18, 1837, a long, perceptive letter that is probably the most useful in revealing what Finley's peers saw in him as his strengths and weaknesses. Morris began his letter by acknowledging receipt of one from Finley that elicited in Morris a blend of sympathy, admiration, and prayer. He wrote, "I am not at all surprised that the enemy has selected some grounds of attack referred to in your frank communication. There is a point in the history of every great man . . . when he is liable to peculiar trials." Criticism occurs, Morris believed, when a person's zeal continued and his strength began to ebb. "You are more liable on this ground than some others. You are formed for active life, yes more, for daring enterprise." Morris complimented him for pushing into the foremost ranks of those seeking to convert the world but reminded him that his uncommon labors and exposures had shattered his "once powerful constitution." He cautioned him to conserve his energies. He continued, "I sincerely hope God will spare your life and afford you strength to make a book, which may speak for you when you shall have gone to the land of your fathers." Finley must have heeded the bishop's advice for he managed to live for another twenty years, and at the time he read this letter some of his major accomplishments lay in the future.[52]

Of all the reform movements in the antebellum period, the one in which Finley was most involved was the temperance campaign. Early in his career he spoke out against drinking and drunkenness and continued his angry crusade against "ardent spirits" until his dying day.

6

Crusade for Temperance

> Little does the spirit of commerce care how many Indians die inebriates, if it can be assured of beaver skins.
> —Henry R. Schoolcraft

No subject received more vitriolic attack from James B. Finley than drinking and drunkenness. His crusade against alcohol consumption lasted his entire career. The fact that when he was a boy his father probably drank too much doubtlessly accounted for some of the intensity of his campaign. His father was deposed by a Kentucky presbytery because of drunkenness in 1795, although the official reason given was for contumacy, preaching after being suspended, and failing to attend his trial. His own church members had initiated the charge of drinking.[1]

James encountered plenty of heavy drinking as a fun-loving youth rollicking in the woods near Chillicothe and New Market before his conversion. He saw at first hand what ardent spirits did to Native Americans when greedy traders plied them with whiskey. He also met families in his ministerial travels who were made miserable because of someone's excessive drinking. He probably regarded alcohol as his greatest enemy because he was convinced that God's word was not likely to be heeded by those who drank too much.

Drinking habits in the early 1800s were heavy, especially in the frontier area. Alcohol there was often considered a necessity. Its use was important in social contacts, and its consumption even called an essential stimulant by some. One nineteenth-century Ohio historian described it as "a sort of panacea for all ills, a crowning sheaf to all blessings." Drinking in the morning was called an "eye-opener." Later in the day came the "eleven o'clocker" and the "four o'clocker." Before bedtime there was the "nightcap." Brandy was especially highly regarded as a remedy for many ills. In 1797, Massie's Settlement, later called Manchester, contained fewer than twenty cabins, but one was a tavern. "Liquors of every kind" were served at the Sign of the Ship in Chillicothe in 1808. A number of politicians in the state capital were known for getting "liquored up" there.[2]

Finley recalled in his *Autobiography* that "A house could not be raised, a field of wheat cut down, nor could there be a log-rolling, a husking, a quilting, a wedding, or a funeral without the aid of alcohol." In the west, whiskey sometimes served the same as money. Apparently, in Lexington, Kentucky, church contributions could be paid in whiskey. Travelers to this country in the early nineteenth century wrote at length about intoxicated Americans and tavern brawls. George Knepper has written that in some Ohio towns a distillery was one of the first buildings constructed.[3]

According to one account, by 1810 there were more than fourteen thousand distilleries in this country which were producing more than twenty-five million gallons of ardent spirits a year. The 1820 census revealed that distilling in Jefferson County, Ohio, was so extensive that it was not classified as a distinct industry. In 1820, 586 distilleries were operating in the state of Ohio, seventy-eight of them in Hamilton County and fifty-four in Jefferson County. Whiskey was also produced on many farms and sold in stores for fifteen to twenty-five cents a gallon. Some stores kept a barrel and tin cup available for customers to sample. "Dram taking" was a common practice in many occupations. John S. Wright visited Cincinnati in 1819 and wrote, "The inhabitants . . . are mostly of indolent slovenly habits, devoting the chief part of their time to hunting and drinking whiskey (the only liquor in use) and appear to be a meagre, sickly, spiritless and unenterprising race."[4]

By 1820, alcoholic consumption had risen to over seven gallons per person. The custom of drinking was so well established that critics of the use of alcohol were considered fanatics. Daniel Drake recalled that, "There were some families in the neighborhood, however, who did not drink or keep whiskey. They were Methodists, and it was a rule in the Methodist Church, at that time, that its members should not drink ardent spirits."[5]

There were scattered protests in the new republic. Anthony Benezet was effective among Pennsylvania Quakers, and Timothy Dwight carried on a crusade among Yale students. Benjamin Rush published his *An Inquiry into the Effects of Spiritous Liquors on the Human Body and Mind* in 1784. It was so widely read that the eighth edition was published in 1814. Wesley's orginial rule for Methodists, which had become the tradition in the American colonies, was to condemn "drunkenness, buying or selling spiritous liquors, or drinking them unless in cases of extreme necessity." After independence, Methodist conferences made revisions in the rule that weakened its effectiveness. In 1780, the Methodist General Conference went on record as disapproving the making and drinking of distilled liquors. In 1790, the rule was changed to condemn drunkenness or drinking unless in cases of necessity. A change in 1796 required preachers to take action against those who sold or gave spiritous liquors, but the rule created problems.⁶

In the 1820s, organizations began to encourage temperance activity. The Massachusetts Society for the Suppression of Intemperance was founded in 1813. The first organized national agency, the American Society for the Promotion of Temperance, was not founded until 1826. By 1834 it had some five thousand chapters. The first temperance society west of the Alleghenies was supposedly in Granville, Ohio, in 1828. The first Methodist temperance society was organized in Bangor, Maine, toward the end of 1831, and the New England Conference Temperance Society was formed in 1833. By the 1830s, articles on the evils of drunkenness began to appear more frequently.⁷

At the 1816 General Conference, James Axley of Tennessee offered a motion that read, "Resolved, that no stationed or local preacher shall retail spiritous or malt liquors without forfeiting his ministerial character among us." The motion was called up and tabled four times before it was defeated. Four years later, however, the same motion, minus reference to malt liquors, passed. At the 1820 General Conference a motion calling on church members who distilled ardent spirits to lose their standing was indefinitely postponed. A committee on temperance was appointed at the 1832 General Conference, and it submitted a report. It was not until the 1836 General Conference that ministers were prohibited from making or selling spiritous liquors, the penalty being loss of their standing.⁸

At the 1840 General Conference a proposal to strengthen the rule against drinking, buying, or selling liquor received 75 affirmative votes to 38 negative ones, one vote short of the two-thirds majority needed to pass. Henry B. Bascom voted for the motion after the secretary's count but Bishop Andrew, who was presiding, ruled that the motion lost, and the conference immediately adjourned. Apparently, the issue was not considered sufficiently vital, for no one challenged the ruling of the chair. It was not until the 1848 General Conference that the Northern Church returned to the original Wesley rule.⁹

Early in his career, Finley joined Axley, Cartwright, and Young in attacking drinking and drunkenness. He boasted, "Frequently I would pledge whole congregations, standing upon their feet, to the temperance cause." He claimed that on one of his circuits a thousand people had signed the pledge. But some of his congregations shouted back at him when he started to preach temperance.¹⁰

Finley asserted that he "suffered no opportunity to pass that I did not improve in portraying the physical, social, and moral evils resulting from intemperance." In 1810, the neophyte preacher preached a sermon in a tavern in Newark while his audience kept drinking. Later while preaching temperance in a Zanesville bar one of his listeners interrupted to tell him, "You go on with your business of preaching and we will mind ours." He returned several times to Dick's Tavern at the falls of the Licking River, where his thunderous voice competed with the noise of the customers.[11]

In 1811, while traveling on his circuit, Finley was guest in a house at Iron Mills, six miles from Zanesville. He discovered a keg of whiskey in his room, remonstrated his host and demanded that it be removed. His startled host refused, whereupon Finley left and spent a cold night sleeping in the woods. At the 1820 General Conference Finley was appointed to a committee on spiritous liquors. Action, however, was indefinitely postponed on a motion that would have expelled church members who distilled ardent spirits. When he traveled east with the Wyandot chiefs on their 1826 fund-raising tour Finley sought out a barge captain on the Erie Canal who was a teetotaler.[12]

John C. Brook wrote him May 12, 1823, from Ridgeville to tell him about some church members who were expelled for getting drunk at election time. Finley was probably disappointed to learn that his friend, Judge McLean, gave whiskey away on his campaign for office. Brook reported that several got drunk "and this has made considerable noise in the country."[13]

Finley's temperance fight consisted of preaching, lecturing, writing articles, and, after 1842, becoming active in an organization called the Sons of Temperance. He expressed his hatred of drinking and drunkenness frequently in the books he wrote. There are many references in his *History of the Wyandott Mission* to the efforts of whites to sell or give liquor to the Native Americans and the dire consequences of such activity. One of his most elequent statements on this theme was:

Yet the enemies of the cross of Christ, and of the Indians, were not asleep, but had their fatal poison in almost every house around the reservation; and wherever practicable, they set the Indians "on fire of hell" with it. They were not, nor are there any means, by which the devil, or his angels, the grog sellers, can so effectually destroy the happiness of man, in time and eternity, as with the fatal poison. How many thousand ruined families and individuals shall live to prove the terrible doings of this fell monster? . . . It is impossible to tell all the wickedness that has been committed on the Indians of North America, by the infernal practice of selling to them intoxicating liquors. . . . Tremble for the consequence, ye men who have caused nearly a million of human beings to be swallowed up in this vortex of destruction.[14]

The last anecdote recorded in this book was the story of a drunken Wyandot who killed another Indian. The moral of the story ends with another criticism of those who sold whiskey. "Committed, as they are, through the wicked practice of making and vending ardent spirits, I am almost brought to the conclusion that every man who makes and sells this destructive fire of hell, ought to be punished as a heinous offender, and be confined to the walls of a penitentiary, until he will reform, and cease to murder the souls and bodies of his fellow man."[15]

In his *Autobiography*, Finley found occasion to express his temperance views on several occasions. In relating his early experiences on the circuit, he described in detail his preaching in a tavern barroom in Newark. He climbed on a stool in the crowded room and spoke for thirty minutes, telling his audience they were "on their way to hell." When he left, some of the bar crowd searched for him and sent word they would roast him if he ever returned. On his next round, he preached in the Newark courthouse.[16]

Chapter 14 contains some of his favorite temperance anecdotes. He was preaching at an ironworks one day when he discovered many men drinking. He stood up on a large salt kettle and gave such a rousing temperance speech that a number of the workers signed the pledge. He wrote that he often met with opposition for advocating the temperance cause. He declared that his efforts aroused the indignation of those in the liquor business "and their curses were heaped on me in profusion. They would gladly have driven me from the country if they could."[17]

Finley recorded lectures he gave on temperance December 25, 1831, December 31, 1832, and July 30, 1847. In one of his lectures he declared, "Drunkenness is self murder. It destroys soul's body and property. It is a crime expressly forbidden in the word of God and will be punished with everlasting damnation . . . it is community murder . . . it is worse than horse stealing." In an article "On the Sin of Alcohol" he wrote, "Alcohol and all kinds of fluid that possess it is the worst bane of human nature and the great engine of hell for the destruction of our race both in time and eternity. It has destroyed more men, women and children than war, pestilence or famine every day and every year . . . it is written no drunkard can enter the kingdom of heaven." In one of his sermons he declared, "Alcohol is a poison. It destroys man in his physical, social and moral powers. It is a curse to society, and produces half of all the evils in the world. . . . Who oppose [temperance]? All its votaries who love money more than the good of our race."

In an address to a chapter of the Sons of Temperance he said, "The grand adversary of man has no weapon that he can employ with such success against our race as alcohol and it is the last that he will give up and he employs all that cold bloodless selfishness which belongs to the covetousness of our depraved status to poison his fellow man for the sake of gain and this same unhallowed spirit has been incorporated into the laws of our country."[18]

When he was presiding elder of the Dayton district in the summer of 1842, he heard about a movement to form a new organization to promote temperance. H.S. Thomas wrote him from New Albany August 20, 1842, to thank him for his encouragement. "Since I visited Germantown in company with Brother Sappington lecturing on the temperance cause, & since I seen you in the city I have traveled a great deal & laboured hard . . . but I don't know that at any time I have felt more gratified than when you signed the pledge, we are anxious to proceed and we feel the importance in the help of our religious."[19]

Thoughout the 1840s Finley was active in the Sons of Temperance organization, which was a fraternal order that sought out to enroll persons who had given up drinking or who were willing to sign the abstinence pledge. It was inspired by the popular Washington Temperance Society founded in Baltimore in 1840. Its leadership came from two groups. One consisted of former alcoholics who were zealous in believing that moral suasion efforts by those who had suffered from drunkenness were the most effective ways to win people to the temperance cause. The second group were those who had long preached temperance because of their convictions. The sixteen persons who founded the Sons of Temperance met most appropriately in a building called Teetotalers Hall at 71 Division Street in New York on September 29, 1842.[20]

The Sons of Temperance enjoyed a phenomenal growth. A charter was granted to the Ohio division August 1, 1844, and it became the largest in the number of chapters. The first national jubilee of the order was held in New York June 9, 1846, with a parade of ten thousand members. By that year there were fourteen grand divisions, 650 subordinates, and sixty thousand members. National membership reached 160,000 in 1848 and 245,000 in 1850. In 1852, Abraham Lincoln joined a chapter of the Sons of Temperance in Springfield, Illinois. After 1866, membership was open to women.[21]

The aims of the organization were "to shield us from the evils of intemperance; afford mutual assistance in case of sickness; and elevate our character as men." It was a tightly structured, centralized form of organization with an elaborate hierarchy, and its efforts were directed toward supervising its members' conduct.

No member was to make, buy, sell, or use alcoholic beverages. The organization sought "to reclaim inebriates, watch over them and aid them when they were sick." The National Division was the highest parliament of the order. It consisted of elected representatives who held high office, and it met annually. The grand divisions, statewide, were composed of elected representatives and met quarterly or semiannually. The subordinate divisions met weekly.[22]

There were initiation fees and weekly dues of six and one-quarter cents. If any member broke the pledge of abstinence he was considered expelled unless two-thirds of the membership voted to readmit him. If they did and the offender re-signed the pledge, he was fined one dollar. For a second offense the fine was two dollars. All the money collected constituted a fund from which sick members were eligible to draw a stipulated weekly sum of not less than one dollar. Members visited their sick brothers, and the widows of deceased members were also helped with a fifteen-dollar gift as a funeral benefit. If a member's wife died, he received ten dollars. In 1847 the income of all the subordinate divisions totaled over $176,000. The benefits expended that year totaled $48,452.

The constitution of the organization contained a suggested order of business for the weekly meetings. Three key questions were always asked: "Are there any brethren sick?" "Has any brother violated his pledge?" "Has any brother a friend to propose?" If any member knew that someone had broken his pledge he was honor bound to report him or pay a fine of one dollar for his neglect.

Once a person joined and contributed weekly to the organization there was a strong inducement for him to remain, for in withdrawing he would lose claim to any benefit for himself or his family in case of sickness or death. The welfare aspect of the organization undoubtedly appealed to Finley, who had a keen sense of the value of a dollar. According to one account of the order, "Our halls are also intended to be pleasant places of resort and of social intercourse, in which groups of young men especially may acquire habits of public speaking, and of transacting the business of a popular assembly."[23]

The order had colorful trappings. The Revised Rules for 1848 stipulated that "The regalia for members of the National Division shall be a blue velvet collar, with a rosette of red, blue and white; gold button in the center of rosette, two gold tassels suspended from rosette; and gold lace, half inch wide, around the inside and outside edges." The regalia for members of a grand division contained a red silk velvet collar and silver tassels and lace while that of the subordinate division had white linen collars and white tassels. The organization's colors were red, white, and blue—red for love, white for purity, and blue for fidelity.[24]

According to the constitution, all passwords were to be changed at the first meeting each October. "No concert, festival, or other public assemblage of any description shall be allowed without permission from the Grand Division, except funerals." Members were not allowed to wear their regalia publicly except by permission. In 1851 an article in the revised rule required that the music established by the National Division should be used for the opening, initiating, and closing ceremonies at all meetings.[25]

The Sons of Temperance received some criticism for being a secret society. As one publication explaining the organization put it, "They deem our ceremonies, processions, celebrations, titles and regalia, to be child's play, unworthy of the consideration and detracting from the dignity of an intelligent citizen." If Finley was uncomfortable about the secrecy involved, he never mentioned it. Most members made light of this element pointing out that the aims of the organization were public; it had only good objectives, and they claimed it was no more secret in its activities than a typical family. Finley was undoubtedly attracted to the organization's effectiveness in combating drunkenness and to the welfare aspect of the society. He may also have seen in it a way to reach future converts. Nevertheless, it seems inconsistent for him to object to the secrecy of the Masons and to defend that of the Sons of Temperance.[26]

One of the defenders of the Sons of Temperance claimed success in that "it descends even to the gutter, and lifts up the poor fallen brother from his degraded condition—strips off his rags—washes him from his filth—clothes him in clean and comfortable garments—administers to him the Pledge—restores him to sobriety, to his family and the world."[27]

The members had their own Alma Mater to sing:

All hail, ye Sons of Temperance, hail!
 Ye stand secure, a noble band;
Admitted but within your pale,
 The strong and weak united stand.[28]

Several temperance hymns could be sung at meetings and at other occasions. One of Finley's favorites must have been one he saved with his papers:

Great God, to thee a cheerful song
 Of thankfulness we raise:
We praise thee that we live to see
 These happy temperance days.
We meet, O Lord, to do thy will.
 Smile on the gracious plan,
To quench the flames of liquid fire,
 And rescue fallen man.[29]

The first anniversary of the Ohio Division was celebrated August 1, 1845, with a procession in full regalia through the streets of Cincinnati. Four bands played. A service was held in Wesley Chapel at which W.P. Strickland spoke. That was followed by a picnic in a grove at the head of Vine Street. Lyman Beecher was one of the speakers. Two thousand attended until a storm at 4 P.M. sent them home. A second anniversary celebration was held Saturday, August 1, 1846. The organization recognized Finley as one of its strongest advocates.[30]

The Ohio Division held a meeting in Columbus on January 13, 1847, and discussed petitioning the legislature on the issue of license laws. Finley was elected grand chaplain. At the beginning of 1847 he received the quarterly communication that contained the "Traveling Password and Explanation for the current year." The document listed four groups of numbers for him to memorize. Then on January 27, 1847, he received a document appointing him deputy grand worthy patriarch for the Ohio Grand Division of the Sons of Temperance. The document was "for purposes of opening, installing & inspecting Divisions for 3 months." A second document with similar authorization dated January 29, 1847, must have been sent to emphasize the importance of his assignment. On the side of this one were listed his subordinate divisions: "Good Samaritan, West Jefferson, Capital & London."[31]

Although Finley was chaplain of the Ohio Penitentiary at the time, he must have thrown himself eagerly into this extra activity on behalf of temperance. As spring approached, however, he became ill again and had to reduce his activities. Samuel F. Cary wrote him from Temperance Cottage, Cincinnati, to thank him for the work in which he was engaged. "I sincerely sympathize with you in the affliction you have suffered since we met. The divisions entrusted to your care have such unbounded confidence in you that they will regret your inability to perform your official duties."[32]

His health was better in the summer of 1847, and he was able to resume his duties. A quarterly session was held in Dayton July 28, followed by a procession in which Finley marched in full regalia behind the Springfield Brass Band. Finley concluded the exercises with a speech which an observer called "full of humor and good advice." He attended the Grand Division's third annual session in Cincinnati October 21-24 and submitted a resolution supporting the Cadets, a youth group of five hundred members who had pledged to avoid alcohol and tobacco. He also proposed a motion to make the initiation fee one dollar. He was reappointed deputy grand worthy patriarch in November. His commission described his duties. "It is requested of him—to visit officially each Subordinate Division aforesaid at least twice to exact a compliance with the established Constitutions, Laws, Rules, Ceremonies and Usages of the Order, and report any irregularity fairly, fully and promptly to the Grand Worthy Patriarch, under whose direction he shall act." At the annual session held in Columbus on Wednesday, October 18, 1848, Finley was elected grand worthy associate, the second highest position in the Grand Division.[33]

By the late 1840s, temperance leaders concluded that they had to increase their efforts if they were to accomplish real progress against drinking. They needed more ammunition than preaching, praying, meeting, and singing hymns. Finley and many others received a circular, dated February 7, 1848, from S.F. Cary and six others, who constituted an executive board of the Grand Division. The circular explained that "nothing is wanting to revolutionize our State, upon the great subject of Temperance, but to enlighten the public mind and energize the public heart. We also feel that the organization of the Sons of Temperance is preeminently fitted for this work."[34]

The circular stated that it was of major importance "to collect facts, arguments and statistics, on the manufacture, sale and use of intoxicating drinks." The authors indicated their intention to publish such information widely enough to reach every family in Ohio. The circular requested information on the number engaged in the manufacture and sale of alcoholic beverages as tavernkeepers, bartenders, or grocers; how many had become intemperate or had intemperate families; how many had acquired property through manufacturing or selling alcoholic beverages; the current number of liquor sellers; the number of town or county paupers and their expense for support; the proportion of crimes committed by intoxicated persons; the number of violent crimes and sudden deaths caused by intemperance in the last decade; and the probable consumption of grain in the manufacture of liquor. Unfortunately, there is no record of Finley's reply. Although he would have welcomed use of such statistics in his presentations, he felt that he found more compelling reasons for advocating abstinence in the word of God.

Finley was an active participant at the Sons of Temperance quarterly meeting in Zanesville April 25, 1849. He wrote a resolution that read, "Resolved, that for a Son of Temperance to sign a recommendation for any man to retail or deal out poison to his fellow man, in the shape of intoxicating drinks, violates his obligation."[35] This resolution was passed.

The next month the National Division met in Cincinnati and took several actions. The minimum weekly benefit for sick members was reduced from three dollars to one dollar. Subordinate divisions were authorized to abolish the benefit provision entirely by a two-thirds vote. The minimum weekly dues were reduced to five cents and subordinate divisions were authorized to expel a member if he voted, directly or indirectly, to support "the traffic in intoxicating liquors." A Sons of Temperance procession was scheduled for Columbus June 26, 1849, but because of sickness Finley left the city before that date.[36]

In October 1849, Finley received a long letter addressed to him as grand worthy patriarch from Edward Stevens, who reported on his division in Monroe, Butler County. The letter revealed much about the frustration of a colleague who was aware of how much more needed to be accomplished.

> I fear there is a prevailing apathy in the entire cause of temperance: I do not think there is a backsliding to older things but a sorry sort of indifference to the success of our principles. . . . We can easily work men into the order & reclaim them temporarily from the cup—but the devil has 10 agents . . . and the contest becomes too unequal hence our men . . . are disheartened & without wonder. I think then we must introduce some agency to labour for a Reformation of our laws. We must be allowed to have a voice in the sale of liquor before we can really effect much. . . . I think we might introduce many practices that would add interest to the Indoors work. Many are attracted within our Division Rooms by the polarity of mystery and do not find enough to gratify their curiosity & hence are easily dissatisfied with the work.[37]

Finley undoubtedly agreed that energies had to be directed toward changing laws. He also saw the value of coordinating efforts with other temperance organizations. The success of the efforts in Maine in getting a comprehensive prohibition law passed for the state in 1851 was an impetus for similar activity in Ohio. Finley drafted a proposed constitution for temperance alliance. Its object "shall be to promote in all possible ways the cause of Temperance; but its primary and definite object shall be to cause to be enacted and enforced a law which shall effectually prohibit the manufacture and sale of intoxicating liquors as a beverage. To secure this result, its members will use all lawful and honorable means to promote the election of such men to our Legislature, as are pledged to sustain and vote for a law similar in its fundamental principles to the Maine Liquor Law."[38]

Finley was pleased that the convention that revised Ohio's constitution also submitted for a separate vote a proposal that prohibited the licensing of "traffic in intoxicating liquors." The vote for the measure was 113,239 to 104,255 and was considered a victory for the temperance reformers, for a licensing system had long existed. Ohio, however, was not prepared to pass the Maine law.[39]

Ohioans were not as effective as the Maine reformers. It became evident that there had to be a concerted effort to run candidates pledged to pass prohibition legislation. In 1853, the Ohio State Temperance Convention distributed a circular calling for political action and for concentrating on electing candidates pledged to this objective. It was hoped that by uniting all the temperance organizations to this single issue the makeup of the legislture could be changed. The lobbying efforts failed.

Throughout the 1840s, Finley received many invitations to speak on the subject of temperance. A.N. Warwick wrote November 9, 1846, "I know of no one who has laboured longer & harder than you for temperance and I might add has borne more persecution than your self." On June 19, 1847, W.C. Roberts wrote inviting him to speak to the fifty members of the Jackson Division of the Sons of Temperance. John Sommerville wrote June 23 with a similar invitation from the Troy Division. "Come for we stand in great need of your assistance . . . many are anxious to hear you." Invitations came for July 1848 and April 1849.[40]

Finley accepted as many speaking invitations as he could. In 1853 he was chastised for missing a meeting of a county temperance organization. He wrote to C. Clark February 26, 1853, to explain that he was sick "with a palpitation of heart from over working." He added, "I want it to be perfectly understood that I do not yield to any man in Ohio as being a whole Soul temperance man up to the hilt." He informed his reader that he had begun his attack on what he called "the curse of our race" in 1811 and had pledged more than fifteen hundred persons in forty-two years.[41]

It was inevitable that in time a Daughters of Temperance would be organized. In 1847, Finley received a letter from H.S. Elliott, who wrote, "We are doing our best to get up a little publication in Dayton for the special benefit of the Cadets & Daughters of Temperance. We are trying to obtain subscribers enough to sustain the undertaking. . . . Now 'Old Pap'. You are the very man to give us a mighty impetus toward getting this little temperance gun into successful operation upon the battlements and fortifications of the grim Tyrant, Alcohol. . . . Will you add one more important Good Act to the thousands you have already done."[42]

Sometimes the temperance crusade turned from oratory to action. A colleague wrote Finley from Celina November 28, 1848, to report that the residents there "bought a tavern keeper's Bbl of whiskey and knocked the head in then set it on fire." The writer was pleased to report that the tavernkeeper had promised to keep no more whiskey. "It was a sink of drunkenness." At a temperance meeting there, seventeen signed the pledge. There were more positive activities. The Washington Union Daughters of Temperance established a House of Employment in Cincinnati "for Indigent Females" and sold them clothing.[43]

The aging preacher continued to press his crusade even while traveling. In 1855, he took a trip down the Ohio River to St. Louis. He wrote an article for the *Western Christian Advocate* recording his impressions. He praised the captain and first mate on the Mississippi River boat for not drinking or swearing but expressed dismay to find a bar on board and much gambling. He met a congressman on his trip and asked whether the temperance bill would pass. The man replied that it might, but he wouldn't vote for it. Finley continued his account. "One asked him if he would vote for a law to send a man to the penitentiary for stealing a horse if it was worth $10. 'Yes' was his reply. 'And you would not vote for a law to prevent a man from poisoning his neighbor, and robbing his family of father and husband, and stealing all their property and earthly happiness?' His Honor made no reply, but soon moved his seat."[44]

Later that year Finley took a ten-week tour to the East and spent four weeks in Brooklyn and New York. His report to friends in Ohio contained this comment:

There is now a mighty excitement among the rummies about the Maine law. Every morning paper is filled with their meetings, consulting and deliberating, and counseling lawyers; and it is enough to make a sober man laugh to look on and see the diversity of opinions of the sons of the bar. No doubt but it will make a good harvest for them; but the most ostensible gap is that it is unconsitutional . . . so these rummeyites when a law is made to stop their murderous traffic they cry out, "Unconstitutional!" and then they hope it will end. . . . But to ruin a family, rob them of their every earthly blessing, send the wife and children to the poor-house, and the man or woman to a drunkard's grave and a drunkard's hell, is too bad to be borne with, and a man must have the impudence of the devil that will claim that he has a right so to destroy his fellow man.[45]

Finley's reference to laws being called unconstitutional struck a chord for many of his readers. Some of the state prohibition laws, modeled after the Maine law, were declared unconstitutional. By the mid-1850s, the temperance movement was losing out for support to the antislavery cause.[46]

Finley attacked the "rummies" one final time after his brutal beating in 1856, when he was hit and knocked to the ground after attending a Republican party meeting. He claimed that his attackers must have been venting their ire over his campaign against drinking.

In respect to this reform movement, Finley was at least consistent throughout his career. His preaching and lecturing on behalf of temperance were effective in persuading many church members to take the pledge. His work in the Sons of Temperance organization was only a minor battle in the campaign, and his writings were not as influential as those of Benjamin Rush, Timothy Shay Arthur, Lyman Beecher, Albert Barnes, or Charles G. Finney.

Finley was also consistent in his views toward slavery, although his attitude toward abolitionists changed somewhat over the years. In the end, his activities in opposition to slavery turned out to be far more significant than his fight for temperance.

7

A Hero in Spite of Himself

> The action of the present General Conference will exert a powerful influence upon the destinies of this nation.
> —Uriah Heath

If James B. Finley was well known and respected as an effective church leader in Ohio, after the fateful day in June 1844 when his substitute motion in the general conference led to the division in the Methodist Episcopal Church between North and South over slavery, his fame spread throughout the nation. It must have seemed to him that year as though all his life experiences had prepared him for what he faced in confronting the issue of how to respond to a slaveholding bishop.

Finley grew up in Kentucky surrounded by his father's fourteen black slaves. The slaves had belonged to Robert Finley's father-in-law, who willed them to his daughter when he died. As a devout Presbyterian minister, Robert Finley was not inclined to want permanent possession of other humans. In his *Autobiography*, James described the log house his family occupied near Stockton in 1789:

> The house for our colored people was built the same way, and immediately adjoining the one in which the family lived. My father treated the slaves with great tenderness—more like children than servants. He never punished one of them, to my recollection. They were all taught to read, and we all joined together in praise and prayer to God. I have often thought that slavery existed in my father's family only in form, and that it was in the power of every master to enjoy all the benefits resulting from servitude, without the evils too often, alas! connected with it.[1]

When his father decided to move to Ohio in 1796, he offered his slaves their freedom. He also offered to those who wanted it free transportation to Ohio and a promise of support for a year afterward. Twelve of the fourteen accepted. Young James had the responsibility of leading them into Ohio.[2]

Finley's contacts with John Stewart when he was at the Wyandot mission served to give him a closer affinity with the black race and eliminated any prejudice he might still have had. His missionary experience with the Wyandots further extended his openness toward other races. Years later, in writing to Abel Stevens, he recalled the days when he lived with the Wyandots "and took their food eating and sleeping in their wigwams and in the woods often between a colored man and an Indian brother on dry bark or on a bear or buffalo skin."[3]

The official position of the Methodist Episcopal Church also served to influence Finley's attitude toward slavery. The General Conference in 1780 took action to instruct traveling preachers who owned slaves to free them. The action called slavery "contrary to the laws of God, man, and nature, and hurtful to society, contrary to the dictates of conscience and pure religion." The conference expressed its "disapprobation" on those who owned slaves and "advised their freedom."[4]

In 1784 the General Conference decided to expel local preachers who did not free their slaves in states where the laws permitted them to do so and at the 1785 conference a resolution was approved expressing "the deepest abhorrence the practice of slavery" and vowing to seek its destruction "by all wise and prudent means."[5]

The first Methodist *Discipline* in 1785 had a rule requiring slaveholding members to agree to free their slaves at some future time and requiring pastors to keep a record of these commitments. New members had to accept the requirement before being accepted into membership. An exception was allowed, however, for those in states prohibiting such action and, because of strong opposition, the rules were suspended at the conference in June 1785.[6]

The 1796 Conference passed several rules regarding slavery. The conference reaffirmed the Church's conviction that slavery was a great evil and urged caution in admitting slave holders to official stations in the Church and requiring them to promise emancipation "as the laws of the states, and the circumstances of the case will admit." The conference required that "no slave holder shall be received into [the] society till the preacher who has the oversight of the circuit has spoken to him freely and faithfully on the subject of slavery." Any member who sold a slave was to be expelled. Preachers and members were asked to consider slavery "with deep attention" in order to seek to eradicate "this enormous evil."[7]

Another step was taken in 1800; annual conferences were instructed to "draw up addresses for the gradual emancipation of the slaves" and traveling preachers who became slave holders were required to "forfeit" their ministerial connection unless they freed their slaves. William McKendree, however, was disappointed with the lack of antislavery progress. In a letter written October 10, 1802, he expressed pleasure at the rise of revivals but added, "Alas! as yet their united strength is utterly too weak to abolish slavery in Kentucky and Cumberland." In 1804 the Church retreated somewhat from its position.[8]

At the Western Annual Conference in 1808 the mood was more critical of slavery. Because the conference contained areas south of the Ohio River the issue was of practical concern. On the seventh day of the conference a motion was passed that "the subject of slavery be considered and some decisive rule be made." A committee was appointed to propose regulations. Subsequently the conference approved a rule requiring preachers to report on anyone found to have bought or sold a slave. A quarterly conference was given the responsibility of determining whether the slave transaction was "a case of mercy or humanity or from speculative motives." If the latter, the member could be expelled. Provision to appeal to the annual conference was spelled out.[9]

Four years later, the Ohio Annual Conference required the expulsion of any member who sold a slave. Church members were allowed to purchase slaves out of kindness, but a time limit was placed on such ownership. (This regulation, of course, did not apply to those living in the state of Ohio, where slavery and involuntary servitude had been prohibited by the Northwest Ordinance of 1787.) In any event, the provision was rescinded five years later. The 1828 General Conference passed a resolution approving "the objects proposed and the measures taken by the American Colonization Society." The Southern influence in the Methodist Episcopal Church seemed to increase in the early decades of the nineteenth century.[10]

Once he became a circuit rider, Finley familiarized himself with the Church's official position on this as well as on other issues. During the 1820s, he was probably too absorbed with the problems of the Wyandots to devote much attention to the subject of slavery. After returning to the circuits full-time, however, he became more aware of the increased "radicalism" in the churches and in society at large. Initially the radicals and reformers in the Methodist Church were agitating against the hierarchy. They believed that the bishops had too much power, that the church administration was too autocratic. This movement culminated in the creation of the Methodist Protestant Church in 1830. Finley was opposed to this action and did what he could to resist it. His friends in Pittsburgh kept him informed of developments. Mary Bayard wrote September 4, 1828, to express the hope that radicalism "will have a rest among us for awhile." William Fisher wrote in February 1829 to send him a list of twenty-two persons who withdrew from the Springfield church.[11]

On July 26, 1829, Samuel Brockmier wrote from St. Clairsville to report that three appointments had been lost to the radicals on that circuit. "I hope the Lord God of our fathers and of ancient Methodism will be with us and deliver us out of the hands of our enemies and restore peace and harmony to our Zion." There was better news from James Gilruth, who wrote from Granville February 7, 1830, to say, "The Radicals are doing us no harm of consequence, there has been but one . . . gone from us to them this year." John Bayard wrote him January 12 and December 11, 1829, to give details on the havoc wrought by the radicals in Pittsburgh. Charles Elliott wrote August 4, 1830, to confirm that the radicals were stronger in Pittsburgh than anywhere else in the United States.[12]

Elliott wrote again from that city March 1, 1832, to invite Finley to stop on his way to the general conference in Philadelphia. He criticized the ministers who were feeding their flocks "speculative theories and metaphysical disquisitions on church government; and then the wolves of reform pouncing upon them to scatter, tear, and slay." He ended by complimenting Finley, "If you have an old man's veins, a young man's blood runs through them."[13]

Although Finley could be innovative himself at times, he tended to resist novel ideas in others and was basically a conservative on issues of church government. This conservatism shaped his initial ideas on abolitionism and abolitionists. On January 9, 1828, he wrote his colleague, George W. Maley, a long letter in which he criticized radicalism for "going about like a roaring lion seeking who it may devour." He reiterated his opposition to slavery but added, "Popery & tyranny is the hue & cry from Georgia to Maine but it is no matter how many Negroes one drove to Orleans, how many husbands and wives, parents or children are parted, no matter how the bloody leash is wealded it is all perfectly consistent with Radical Liberty."[14]

Occasionally Finley heard from a Southern friend who gave him ample information on the negative impact of slavery. J.M. Early wrote from Mississippi May 13, 1830, to say "Slavery will & must ever be a barrier to the progress of religion. O! cursed bane when will it cease. My dear brother you have no conception of the state of society where perhaps two-thirds of the population are influenced by no other motive than the fear of the lash."[15]

In the 1830s, abolitionists increased their activities and, as radicals, were considered more dangerous by the bulk of conservative churchmen than those who opposed the authoritarian actions of bishops. The American Antislavery Society was founded in 1831 and the New England Anti-Slavery Society in 1832. The Lane debates occurred in Cincinnati in 1833, and in the same year the first Methodist abolition society was organized in New York. In 1835 the New England Conference created an antislavery society that advocated immediate abolition. The New Hampshire Conference also formed an antislavery organization.[16]

A Hero in Spite of Himself

In 1834, however, the *Christian Advocate*, in an editorial, condemned abolitionists for "irrational attempts to break up the existing relations of society." Its columns were closed to mention of slavery in 1837. In Ohio Methodist ministers held strong feelings against abolitionists. The Annual Conference on August 19, 1835, registered regret at the activities of the abolitionists in the East. The conference also commended the American Colonization Society. A week later the conference passed the following: "Resolved, that those brethren and citizens of the North who resist the Abolition Movement with firmness and moderation are true friends to the Church, to the slaves of the South, and to the Constitution of our common country, and that to encourage inflamatory lectures by foreign agents and sanguinary publications in favor of immediate abolition is injurious to Christian fellowship, dangerous to our civil institutions, unfavorable to the privileges and spiritual interests of the slaves, and unbecoming any Christian Patriot or Philanthropist, and especially, any Methodist.[17] In reporting on this action the *Western Christian Advocate* asserted that Methodist preachers in Ohio were agreed that slavery was an evil, that gradual, Constitutional methods were the best ones to use, and that the abolitionist approach was an evil worse than slavery.[18]

Against that background it is understandable that Finley was unhappy with the abolitionist agitation. Similar to so many of his conservative colleagues he feared that their extremist position would hurt the Church's main mission and increase the number of defections. Although there is no evidence that he ever joined the American Colonization Society, which was founded in 1817, the Finley Papers contain a copy of the "Constitution for a Home Colonization Society for the People of Colour, in the United States of America." This society's object was "to secure a home for all free people of colour, or who may be made free by the consent of their Masters." It was signed by Benjamin Boardman, and the document contained an announcement of a meeting in Plymouth, Richland County, "for the adoption of a Constitution, and the Organization of the Society."

More developments occurred at the 1836 General Conference in Cincinnati. That city, which contained many Southern sympathizers, was strongly opposed to antislavery agitation. In January a group of business leaders at a public meeting determined to suppress it. The Episcopal Address at the conference called on ministers "to refrain from the agitating subject" of slavery in order to preserve the peace of the Church and the "happiness of the slave." A two-day debate took place about the activities of two delegates, Orange Scott and George Storrs, who had lectured on abolitionism in the city. By a vote of 120 to 14, the General Conference recorded its disapproval of their conduct and in another resolution registered its opposition to "modern abolitionism." The resolution went on to "disclaim any right, wish, or intention to interfere in the civil and political relation between master and slave as it exists in the slave-holding states of the Union." That resolution passed unanimously. Finley did not participate in the debates on slavery. No changes were made in the *Discipline* respecting slavery.[19]

On July 7, 1836, Finley's niece in Virginia wrote to report, "Religion is in a very low state in the bounds of Brother's Circuit. The subject of Abolitionism appears to be the absorbing topic." She went on to say that church members wanted to separate from the Ohio Conference.[20]

The leadership in the Methodist Episcopal Church opposed the abolitionists in their midst more forcibly following the 1836 General Conference actions. Abolitionist ministers in the North, except for those in New England, were assigned to less desirable circuits or relieved from preaching duties. For example, Lucius C. Matlack, who was licensed as a local preacher in the Philadelphia Quarterly Conference in 1837, was refused renewal of his license in 1839 because he had assisted in the creation of a Wesleyan Antislavery Society and had become its secretary. Editors of religious periodicals who favored abolition were replaced. It was difficult to get antislavery articles printed. The Southern influence in the denomination continued to be strong.[21]

Throughout the country, however, abolitionism was increasing in acceptance. Some five hundred antislavery societies existed in the North. Antislavery conventions were held in Massachusetts and New York. More publications appeared criticizing the practice. La Roy Sunderland, Orange Scott, George Storrs, and others were being widely read. A meeting of the Ohio Anti-Slavery Society in Granville ended in a riot. On July 12, 1836, a proslavery crowd in Cincinnati destroyed the type that James Birney used in his antislavery newspaper, *The Philanthropist*.[22]

Finley, in concert with the majority of Ohio Methodist preachers, stayed on the sidelines. New England Methodists submitted a recommendation for change in the slavery rule at the 1840 General Conference to bar from any church office anyone who bought, sold, or held slaves. The Ohio Annual Conference rejected this recommendation by a vote of 130 to 10. The editor of the *Western Christian Advocate* commented, "We believe that there is not one slavery man in the Ohio Conference. And the great body of them highly disapprove of the measure of the recent abolitionists, they nevertheless are immovably fixed on their disapproval of slavery, and can never be induced to use their influence for it, though under the circumstances, they see no Gospel way, in which they can at present engage directly in removing this greatest of moral evils from our land."[23]

The issue of slavery was on all delegates' minds at the 1840 General

A Hero in Spite of Himself

Conference, but major action on the subject was postponed. Finley failed to get elected as a delegate because some people considered him too Southern in his views. Petitions on slavery were referred to a committee, which took no action. The conference upheld the powers of the bishops to decline to consider motions in annual and quarterly conferences that dealt with subjects other than those "prescribed for in the discipline."

Finley began to receive enquiries about his views. Some accused him of having Southern sympathies. To one correspondent who wrote asking for clarification after he had preached a sermon, he wrote that his views on slavery were clear:

I have from my boyhood stated as an evil and always looked upon it as a curse both civil and religious and contrary to the Natural & constituted law of God. . . . This question I look upon as settled by the discipline of the Church and the Constitution and Laws of the State of Ohio. The only difference is the question of expediency. What is the best & most successful way to get freed of it . . . and until God himself shall give the indications of the way . . . I fear there will be a difference of sentiment and thus to prevent action to any effect. But one thing I am sure of that God does not require us to do evil that good may come to pass.[24]

Finley's major address on the subject of slavery after 1837 was a rambling sixteen-page argument that condemned both slaveholders and abolitionists. He began by declaring that the current excitement on the subject was "fraught with great & important consequences to the republic and deserves a cool and impartial examination." He had waited for others to speak out but they had not done so, and he said it would be a crime for him to remain silent. He observed that the country was equally divided between thirteen slave states and thirteen free states. He reminded his audience that slavery had been introduced when the colonies were under British control and had no power over themselves. He summarized the reasons for the revolution. He asserted that in the compact creating the federal Constitution a commitment was made by the free states, namely that neither "the free states nor the federal government, was to interfere with that subject but the relation between master and slave was reserved by these states to their own control and their own legislative authority." He considered this pledge a sacred one on which the confederated republican government was created.[25]

He reminded his audience of the blessings of the Constitution, which had to be sustained and handed down to future generations. Then he declared, "Whatever question may now arise in the free states on the subject of slavery must be a question of expediency." He maintained that whatever the people in the free states did to ameliorate the condition of the slaves had to be with the consent of their masters and consistent with the free states' pledge. To interfere further, he warned, "would be a violation of the treaty, amongst the states, and rebellion against the federal government."

But modern abolitionism, he maintained, proposed to free all the slaves immediately and give them equal rights "in their present ignorant condition." Such rights would include suffrage, running for office "and of course a free amalgamation with the whites to marry our daughters to their sons and our sons to their daughters and become one people without distinction."

He asserted that people in the free states had no more power over the laws in the slave states "than we have in making the laws of England." He doubted that the abolitionists' abusive harangues and publications would soften the hearts of masters to free their slaves. What he thought more likely was a slave insurrection that would kill off all whites or a civil war.

Finley then focused on the question of what would happen if the abolitionists did accomplish their objective. He asked, "Will any sober minded citizen of this union be willing to give into the hands of these most ignorant and degraded of men his liberty, life and property?" He thought it unlikely that a majority would support such an action. What was more likely, he believed, was a division of the union.

He then returned to his main theme. "We cannot alter these laws" and have no right to do so. The slaveholding states existed before the compact and reserved to themselves control over their internal affairs. The slave states had no right to force those in the free states to become slaveholders, and those in the free states had no right to insist that those in the slave states all become free.

Finley questioned whether sending lecturers and publications to the slave states would to any good. He asserted that the books would not be read but burned. "You cannot enlighten them for they will not receive the light."

He then declared that the compact made at the time the constitution was written was "the foundation stone on which is based all our political and religious liberty." He criticized the abolitionists for not letting their neighbors alone "but under the pretext of brotherly kindness must manage their business for them." He questioned the value of abolitionist activity in the free states. He felt that people in the free states were already opposed to the principle of slavery and, therefore, had no need for enlightenment on this subject. He believed that people must feel insulted when they are accused of being slaveholders in principle because they refuse to be abolitionists.

He pointed out that some of the Easterners had been engaged in the slave trade "and much of the wealth of those states had their foundation in the blood and groans and tears of the enslaved Africans." He suggested that the Easterners give up their "ill begotten gain" before expecting the Southerners to relinquish their slaves. He also observed that some of the most vociferous abolitionists in the West were those who, before moving, sold their slaves and "purchased the rich lands of Ohio" with their profits. "Sell your rich homes," he declared, "and give back the principle and interest then tell your Southern Brother he is doing wrong."

Finley proceeded to criticize the ministers who were active abolitionists for failing to preach peace and ignoring the dictates of the Constitution. "Did Christ or any of his apostles go about the country preaching against the government," he asked, "forming societies and denouncing in the bitterest terms the civil authorities?" In his opinion, abolitionist ministers needed to be reminded that their main mission was to preach peace "to a fallen world" and that it was a mistake "while thousands are starving for the lack of their heavenly wisdom" they were agitating for violence.

He then indicated that colonization and abolitionism were both questions of expediency. He regretted that abolitionist activity had made the condition of the slave worse as slave masters became more severe and deprived slaves of many advantages they had once had. "It has riveted his chains faster, destroyed the confidence between master and slave and shut thousands out from hearing the gospel of their salvation." Abolitionism, he declared, "has in a great measure aimed its deadly dagger at all that is lovely amongst men and aroused the worst of passions that possess the depraved human heart."

He then praised the colonization movement for seeking to help blacks without attacking the principles of government. He thought that the idea of colonization would make Africa as attractive to blacks as America was to Europeans. Fanatic abolitionists, however, had hindered the success of the colonization idea. He regretted that they were trying to force their ideas on people who were opposed to their measures and suspected that their willingness to be persecuted was a device to gain sympathy.

He reviewed the reasons for opposing abolitionists' ideas. He suspected that they realized that they could not achieve their objectives without exciting mobs. He urged his audience to enlighten their neighbors and show them that it was not necessary to be an abolitionist to be opposed to slavery. His conclusion was a fervent plea. "I now lift up my warning voice against the principles, spirit and fanatical course of propagating modern abolitionism and ask all good citizens to use their influence peaceably to prevent your neighbors from being deluded."

Some of Finley's correspondents expressed their dislike of abolitionism. Samuel Pettit wrote from Piqua to criticize his minister and said he hoped he could be assigned to "an abolition circuit." He thought that if he returned another year "there would be a complete triumph of Abolitionism. . . . I do hope he may be Put on a Pair of Saddle Bags and try the Circuit somewhere if he can do any good." He expressed the desire that "we may get a man that is no abolitionist nor a Party man but a real Methodist Preacher not a proud vain Dandy."[26]

Another wrote to express regret at the organization of the Wesleyan Methodists. "A curse on slavery, I say, but I hope God will keep out of the M.E. Church the blighting . . . influence of discord, anarchy, and confusion." In May 1841 a small group in Michigan seceded to form a Wesleyan Methodist church. Finley was upset by the action taken by Orange Scott, La Roy Sunderland, and others to hold a convention May 31, 1843, which resulted in the formation of the Wesleyan Methodist Connection of America. Membership required a person not to hold slaves. Its six thousand membership grew in eighteen months to fifteen thousand. The movement initially increased Southern influence in the Methodist Episcopal Church and threatened to encourage additional secessionist movements in the North.[27]

Finley also heard from those with abolitionist sentiments. He was sent a statement signed by twenty-three persons who left the church over the issue of slavery. They declared,

The Methodist Episcopal Church has ceased to be an anti-slavery church and has become emphatically a slaveholding and slave-defending church . . . we are not permitted to discuss the sinfulness of slavery in our periodicals but are commanded "wholly to refrain." We are not permitted to meet in our own church which we have helped to build by liberal contribution of our money. . . . We cannot fully exercise our duty to pray for the slave of the slaveholder, in the regular meeting, of the church without feeling that we are sneered at by our brethren as abolitionist. . . . We are strongly, and decidedly opposed to the iron arm of the Episcopacy, as grown up in our church. We are opposed to a third order in the ministry, as our Bishops clearly have grown to be.[28]

As the fateful year 1844 approached, Methodists were divided into four groups: the Southerners who resisted the attacks on slavery from outside the region, the abolitionists in the North who were increasing in numbers and agitation, and the Northern moderates who refused to join the abolitionist cause because while they were opposed to the sin of slavery they saw no practical or legal way to abolish it. Moderate Methodists were also concerned about other reform issues that affected the society and were not yet ready to permit the slavery question to take all their energies and attention. Finley identified with the third group. There were also those in a fourth category who were uninformed on the slavery issue and had no strong views on the subject.

Throughout the early 1840s, however, the moderates were faced with an increased pressure to join the abolitionist cause. It was becoming more and more difficult to stay neutral. A total of sixty-five petitions, memorials, and statements on slavery were presented at the General Conference in 1844.

The conference became the most crucial in the history of the Church. It was also the most agonizing one for the delegates who, despite their efforts and oratory, failed to prevent the division between the North and South. The conference assembled at the Green Street Methodist Episcopal Church in New York on May 1. One hundred eighty delegates attended from thirty-three conferences. Some of the most eminent and talented preachers were in attendance. The *New York Tribune* editorialized that "few public bodies in our country . . . embrace a greater amount of effective talent than is comprised among the members of this Conference." Finley's preaching appointments for the conference were at the Willet Street Church May 26 with William Capers and H. Slicer, and on June 9 at the Eighteenth Street Church with A. Wiley and W.W. Redman.[29]

The subject of slavery and abolitionism was on everyone's minds. The sixty-five communications from annual conferences respecting slavery were referred to a committee on the third day. An appeal from a slaveholding preacher in the Baltimore Conference had to be heard. And early in the course of events it was learned that Bishop James O. Andrew was the owner of slaves. Peter Cartwright recalled, "This fact came upon us with the darkness and terror of a fearful storm, and covered the whole General Conference with sorrow and mourning."[30]

James Andrew was a highly respected minister. He joined the South Carolina Conference in 1812. Both he and James Finley attended their first General Conference in 1820 and were good friends. They were both in attendance at the sessions in 1824 and 1828. Andrew was elected a bishop in 1832. He was considered a very pious, humble person. His interest in the welfare of blacks was called "zealous and ceaseless." Joseph Mitchell checked the 1840 census and learned that the Andrew household consisted of three adults, seven children, and four slaves. Andrew's first wife had died in 1841 and he had married his second wife in Januray 1844. She owned fourteen or fifteen slaves who could not be freed because of Georgia law.[31]

Andrew's views on slavery were expressed in an 1831 article on "The Southern Slave Population."

The slave has a soul, and needs the faithful preaching of the Gospel as much as his master, or those who so busily seek to accomplish his earthly emancipation. . . . It is true that the blacks, in many places, heard preaching on the Sabbath, and in the towns the clergy could pay more attention to their instruction. But there were tens of thousands in the country who heard no Gospel. . . . We shall enter into no abstract speculations on the subject of slavery, perfectly satisfied that such discussions have been productive of much evil to the slaves of the South, without affording them any corresponding benefit. We look upon the blacks just as we find them, and our inquiry is, "What shall we do to accomplish for them the greatest possible benefit?"[32]

Andrew was convinced that emancipation was impractical for the slaves and that liberty would be no boon for most of them. Their souls were more important to him than their servitude and poverty. He was unhappy with his Northern abolitionist colleagues. He wrote Bishop Thomas Morris March 14, 1838, to say, "I should judge what I see weekly in the Advocate that the Church in the North and east is in a fair way to be revolutionized,—poor human nature how weak how erring how inconsistent. God be merciful to us in church and state." He concluded with a sarcastic list of predictions.

A Methodist anti-slavery convention to sit in judgment of the General Conference.—A Methodist anti-slavery missionary society—abolition prayer meetings and I suppose anti-slavery class meetings and love feasts and I suppose we shall shortly have *anti-slavery butter—abolition cheese* and *anti-slavery brooms* and *onions* and when they shall have turned all slave holders out of the church below I suppose there must be a committee appointed to go to the gate of paradise and demand as a prerequisite to their honoring heaven with their presence that Abraham and Philemon and diverse other worthies of the olden time be dismissed from the seats of glory.[33]

Later he wrote to Bishop Soule May 17, 1843, to tell him he was thinking of resigning because of health. He added, "The state of the Church, too, afflicts me. The Abolition excitement, I fear, has never presented an aspect so threatening to the union of the Church as it does at this moment. . . . I look forward to the next General Conference with no little apprehension."[34]

When Andrew heard in 1844 that his Northern colleagues were upset upon learning that he was a slaveholder, he offered to resign but the Southern delegates prevailed on him not to do so. Fifty of them met the day before the conference opened and unanimously approved a resolution asking him not to resign. The resolution declared, "it appears to us that his resignation would inflict an incurable wound on the whole South and inevitably lead to a division in the Church."[35]

Some Southern leaders were opposed to the practice of expecting bishops to have no connection with slavery. They wanted a slaveholding bishop elected in 1844. Other Southern leaders, including Capers, opposed this view. Bishop Soule had given assurance at the Baltimore Annual Conference in March 1844 that no slaveholder would be nominated. Bishop Andrew wrote his daughter May 14 to say, "I would most joyfully resign, if I did not dread the influence on the Southern Church. I shall therefore wait patiently a while longer. The clouds are dark, but God is in the whirlwind and guides the storm."[36]

It was the strong belief in the North that a slaveholder's effectiveness would be reduced in supervising traveling preachers and in chairing meetings. How could the circuit riders be consistent in their preaching, it was thought, when they were supervised by someone acting contrary to the traditional view of the Church? On the other hand, from the perspective of the South, to suspend or censure a bishop would be a new action never before taken by a general conference and might well be illegal in terms of ecclesiastical law.

The New England delegates anticipated action against slavery at the meeting. Otherwise it was expected that there would be mass secessions in that part of the country where abolitionism was strong. The middle ground was held by conservatives who sought to find a compromise that would keep the peace and hold the Church together. The main question, then, combined two issues, the moral one of the sin of slavery and the constitutional one of the role of the bishops in the Church.[37]

Early in the conference Dr. Stephen Olin of New York spoke at great length to try to prevent disruption. He had lived in both sections and empathized with both points of view. When Olin sat down it was evident that the audience had been moved.

The first issue to be settled was the appeal by a preacher named Harding who had been suspended by the Baltimore Conference for holding slaves. His appeal was denied.

Then from May 22 until June 1 the body deliberated the case of Bishop Andrew. What was especially remarkable about the debate was that it was the moderates and conservatives who took the lead. Those who were known to be abolitionists kept silent or were inconspicuous. What was also remarkable was that much of the debate focused on questions of church government, the power of the episcopacy, and the authority of the general conference, rather than on slavery. Through it all practically no criticism of Andrew's character or conduct was expressed. As the debate heated, many strangers crowded into the visitors' gallery to listen.[38]

The initial resolution calling on Bishop Andrew to resign troubled Finley and many others. It appeared to be too harsh, too judgmental, and likely to split the Church asunder. Finley decided to submit a substitute motion. His first draft, however, also seemed too harsh. His draft read: "We the undersigned Members of the General Conference do hereby present to said conference a charge against the Rev'd James O. Andrew . . . for improper conduct . . . 1st Specification of said charge is that he has become connected with slavery by marriage and otherwise.

2nd the Church has been thrown into great agitation. 3rd and by so doing he has greatly embarrassed his exercising the office of his itinerant general superintendency as Bishop if not in the greatest part of his field of labor totally prevents it."[39]

After some consultation and much prayer he submitted his final draft on May 23. It read: "Whereas, the Discipline of our church forbids the doing anything calculated to destroy our itinerant general superintendency, and whereas Bishop Andrew has become connected with slavery by marriage and otherwise, and this act having drawn after it circumstances which in the estimation of the General Conference will greatly embarrass the exercise of his office as an itinerant general Superintendent, if not in some places entirely prevent it; therefore, Resolved, That it is the sense of the General Conference that he desist from the exercise of this office so long as this impediment remains."[40]

In the ensuing debate Finley explained the reasons behind his proposal. He thought that the substitute motion "would meet the case better than any other. . . . The resolution does not impeach the character of Bishop Andrew in any way." He said that slave ownership would prevent the bishop's "circulation as an itinerant general superintendent." He added that he had a "warm attachment" to Bishop Andrew. "I hope the General Conference will give him a little time . . . to free himself from the incubus of slavery." Finley also hoped that his use of the word "desist" instead of the harsher one "resign" would keep the Southerners and the abolitionists within the Church.[41]

Finley spoke again in the debate on May 28. He said he thought his motion was based on the constitution of the Church in that the General Conference was "restricted against doing anything which will destroy our itinerant general superintendency." Because Bishop Andrew owned slaves, "it will embarrass his exercising the office." He claimed that the bishop couldn't travel at large and would, therefore, upset the rule requiring a general itinerant superintendency. He defended his motion as mild and moderate. He added, "this resolution was modified to meet the feeling of Southern brethren, and to cover the principle, and from this ground I will not be moved. No, sir, on this ground will I stand until I die." He declared that Methodist discipline had always stood "belligerent towards slavery." He did not see how it could be justified or sanctioned. "How any man can say it is right for him to hold his fellow being in bondage, and buy and sell him at pleasure, put him under an overseer, and drive, whip, and half starve him, and that this is connived by the Methodist Church, I cannot comprehend."[42] He concluded by saying, "By the Southern men I am taunted with being an abolitionist. So I am, sir, in the Methodist sense of that word, but none can say that I am a radico-abolitionist. I throw back the assertion with perfect contempt. By those rabid abolitionists I am called a proslavery man, and I treat them with the same disregard. I am a Methodist. . . . I never will agree that slavery shall be connected in any way with episcopacy."[43]

Andrew's defense of the situation didn't help matters. Instead of persisting in his determination to resign, he shifted to defending himself and maintaining that there was no obligation upon him to change his status as a slaveholder. He left New York for Philadelphia about 5 P.M. on May 25. The next day he wrote his wife, "If I would agree to free the slaves I would be a very clever man but how could I free them? Where would they go, and how support themselves? As a Christian and a man of humanity I could not let them go without some security for their support."[44]

Finley must have been disappointed with Bishop Soule's contribution to the debate. Soule declared that Methodist ministers could preach to blacks and seek to convert them but that they could not raise them to equal civil rights. "Let us not labour in vain, and spend our strength for naught," he said.[45]

On Saturday afternoon, June 1, Finley's motion was approved by a vote of 110 to 68. The Southern delegates voted against the motion except for one person from Texas who had recently moved from the North. Joseph Mitchell, who has studied the backgrounds of the Southern delegates, has revealed that all except one were married; most had large families and most were farmers. His assertion that they were "immersed in the Southern way of life" seems justified. Except for thirteen delegates, the North voted solidly for the motion. According to one account, "The votes were given amid the most profound stillness."[46]

Obviously, the division was not solely over the issue of slaveholding. There was also the constitutional issue of the authority of the General Conference over its bishops and the nature of the general superintendency. The delegates had much more to say on that subject than they had about slaveholding. Nevertheless, years after the event the abolitionist New Englander, James Porter, wrote an account of an agreement made before the conference between representatives of the abolitionists and the conservatives that resulted in having the former keep a low profile while the conservatives in the North and West led the attack on Bishop Andrew.[47]

Before the conference adjourned a Plan of Separation was approved, and Finley was appointed to a committee to work out details on the division of the assets of the Book Concern. In retrospect, the break appears inevitable. For sixty years the delegates in successive general conferences had wrestled with how to reconcile two ultimately irreconcilable forces, the moral imperative to deal with the evil of slavery and the force of self-defense among Southerners to whom the institution of slavery had become an inseparable part of their society. Finley himself reflected the upheaval resulting from the clash of these two forces. As a Southern born, deeply religious man, he hated the curse of slavery, but he resented the pressures of the abolitionists whose methods he considered uncharitable and possibly unconstitutional. He pictured his role on the stage at the 1844 gathering as a compromiser seeking to hold the two extremist divisions together, but he ended up as the catalytic agent whose motion precipitated the schism. Curiously, he omitted mention of the 1844 General Conference in his *Autobiography*, although he referred to it briefly in his *Memorials of Prison Life*.

Much of the debate may have focused on governance issues, but it seems clear that it was slavery that divided the delegates. For the Southerners, economic realities transcended adherence to the *Discipline*. Their financial security rested on the institution of slavery. They were Southern farmers more than dedicated religious zealots. The 1844 division of the Methodist Episcopal Church is significant evidence of the inevitability of the Civil War, for if these pious preachers defended the pernicious institution by their actions, the South was bound eventually to secede.

Three items that document this thesis are: Bishop Andrew owned a 550-acre farm, which in 1850 contained twenty-four slaves. Thirty-four of the forty-seven Southern delegates who were still in the South in 1850 owned 422 slaves, a valuation of over two hundred thousand dollars. In the 1844 debate Augustus Baldwin Longstreet, president of Emory College, declared, "If slaveholding disqualifies him [Andrew] for the office of bishop it disqualifies us all and our constitutional rights must stand or fall with him, and can we expect him to be silent and see him crushed knowing that we must be the victims of the next motion of the wheel."[48]

It should not have been a surprise that Southern ministers were slaveholders. The July 26, 1844, *Southern Christian Advocate* contained this statement: "The Methodist ministry in the Southern Conferences are for the most part slave-owners. By inheritance and marriage most of them have a legal ownership of the domestics at least who serve their families."[49]

A few of his Northern colleagues wrote Andrew after the General Conference not to agree with him but to bewail the prospect of division. John F. Wright wrote a prophetic letter from his Cincinnati post October 3, 1844. He stated, "I most firmly believe if the division takes place civil commotions will immediately follow, for there are certainly more reasons for the separation of the States than the division of the Church." He added in a postscript, "If the division takes place perpetual war will be declared and be carried on through all time."[50]

Although Donald Mathews may well have been correct in maintaining that the division in the Methodist Episcopal Church did not "portend" the

Civil War but merely was one of the many events leading to increased sectional antagonism, nevertheless that antagonism among ministers, presumably the most peace-loving members of society, became intense and destructive in the years after 1844.[51]

At the time, Finley himself may not have realized the consequences of the division to which he personally was opposed. The weary delegates departed without violence and in the spirit of charity toward one another, but this condition soon changed. One of the aftermaths of the division was a strengthening of Finley's attitudes against slavery. Another was a change in his relationship with some of his colleagues.

Once he returned home, a flood of letters arrived about the division. Much of his correspondence for the next several years was on the subject of slavery and the Southern secession. As early as June 4 Uriah Heath wrote from Newark, Ohio to observe, "The action of the present General Conference will exert a powerful influence upon the destinies of this nation." He responded to Finley's enquiry to report that many of the ministers and members of his district approved of the action in the Andrew case. He then added a prediction that was off the mark. "If this case issues as we most ardently hope it will, honorably to the Discipline of the Church, and to the cause of truth and righteousness, then I think that the work of abolitionism is about over."[52]

John McDonald, however, writing on July 22, said that he thought the states would try to divide over slavery. He praised Finley's eloquence but thought he had done the work of the abolitionists. A minister from Vicksburg, R.D. Smith, wrote on August 17 to say that he wanted an appointment in the Ohio Conference because he couldn't remain in the South because of his slavery views. "In the days of my boyhood I used to hear you make Methodist storms about Urbana; when I thought they afforded more fun for this life, than matter of serious consideration for life to come. Since that time I have had knowledge of your character as one of the old order of the itinerancy." He added that although he had said little about slavery he had probably said enough to turn people against him. "As you know, the subject is one of exceeding delicacy, and the slightest manifestation of disaffection creates suspicion, and excites more or less of unpleasant feeling . . . antislavery men and abolitionists are held here, to be the same genus, if not of the same species, and to call a man either, accounts to about the same thing as calling a dog mad."[53]

Finley's nephew, James, wrote from Wilmington August 25, 1844, to compliment him. "All eyes are on you now more than at any former period. . . . I never read or heard you with more delight than your effort on Bishop Andrew." Bishop Hamline also sent his felicitations on September 14 and reported that passage of Finley's motion had stopped the transfer of members to the Wesleyan Church and that Northern abolitionists were now "calm and loving to their Brethren." He indicated that if the Church "maintains its ground they have done with the subject forever."[54]

The Ohio Annual Conference was held three months after the meeting of the general conference. The division in the Church was uppermost on everyone's minds. Jacob Young submitted a resolution "approving the general conference action and the course pursued by the Ohio delegation in the Andrew case." A stirring debate occurred, and the motion finally passed. Despite the minority of Southern sympathizers, the Ohio conference was firmly in the Northern fold.[55]

During the fall of 1844 Finley was busy with his responsibilities as presiding elder of the Zanesville district. The November 8, 1844, issue of the *Western Christian Advocate* contained an article by Samuel Latta criticizing W.P. Strickland for his attack. The November 15 issue had a long article by Bishop Soule defending his position and one by Strickland responding to Latta. The November 22 issue contained statements from Andrew, Soule, and Finley. Finley wrote, "There are few, if any, who will consent to a division of the Church. . . . If it were left to the membership to decide . . . I firmly believe that two-thirds would go against it." He thought that the issue couldn't be settled by the ministers "with the present feelings and views. . . . I have but little hope of peace while hot flames burn men's hearts."[56]

At the beginning of 1845, however, he wrote again to the *Western Christian Advocate* to express his views on the schism in the Church. "The great excitements of Church and state have done us great injury in reference to religious progress and enjoyments; but the turbulent waters are again assuaging, and falling into their proper channels, and the work of God again thrives." He was wrong about the turbulent waters. Before the year was over he was caught up in the disputes which raged between North and South.[57]

A number of ministers in Kentucky and elsewhere just south of the Ohio River were upset at the prospect of a Southern secession from the Church. J.S. Tomlinson wrote on October 31, 1844, from Augusta, Kentucky to report

there is a strong and extensive feeling here against division. What is desired here is that if the South should determine on division, Kentucky, Western Virginia and Missouri may stand firm and we would all rejoice to learn your views of the question. . . . If we should be included in the division we feel as if we should be thrown into the arms of hightoned, proslavery Nullifiers, and that the cause of emancipation (which is silently but surely on the advance among us) would be thrown back to a far greater extent than it has been done by Abolitionism. . . . I do sincerely believe that you, and your colleagues of the Commission can do much for us in stemming the tide that threatens to overwhelm us. We feel as if the cause of American, of human liberty, were at stake.[58]

Finley's friend Leroy Swormstedt echoed his feelings when he wrote on February 1, 1845 to say, "Most of the preachers seem to think a division inevitable, and yet they deplore it. I must think with you, if it were left to the people we should not divide. Our brethren of the Arkansas and Mississippi Conf. are not as rabid as we would suppose. I believe the old men feel serious on the subject as the time draws nigh. For myself Bro F I deplore the prospect of division."[59] He added that he prayed the Church might still be saved from "the threatened calamity." Finley replied on February 10 to agree with him but objected to a circular he had sent. "Who knows but at their meeting in Louisville next May they (the Southerners) may take it into their heads to expel the North and general conference too. Then there will be no need of acting apart from them." He concluded with his objections about proceeding with the business of dividing the assets of the Book Concern. Swormstedt waited until August 8 to reply, "I need not tell you that we are in an awful fix as a Church."[60]

As the split widened between the two sections, forcing people to take sides, personal friendships were irrevocably broken. One of the most bitter breaks was Finley's with Bishop Joshua Soule. Soule, who was born in Maine, began preaching when he was seventeen years old. Early in his career he was a steward and agent for the Methodist Book Concern. He was a popular preacher and drafted the plan for a delegated general conference. He was first elected bishop in 1820 but declined that year when the general conference favored the election of presiding elders, an action he considered unwise and illegal. He was reelected bishop in 1824, the general conference having backed down from its previous action on presiding elders. At that time he decided to move to Lebanon, Ohio. He and Finley were such good friends that Finley offered to help him move his family west. Soule wrote him a long letter proposing the arrangements. He thanked Finley for furnishing two carriages and indicated that there would be ten in his party. "Nothing would be more gratifying than your company and aid on the journey. Yours in much affection." Soule was also very supportive of Finley's plans to write a history of the Wyandot mission.[61]

Soule's views on slavery were most cogently expressed in his episcopal address at the 1840 General Conference when he stated that there was little that the Church could do about that institution. He believed it was the Church's function to undertake its spiritual ministry and leave political affairs to the state. Soule thought that ministers should simply preach the Gospel and leave it to God's providence to bring about emancipation.[62]

Bishop Soule's action in supporting the South marred their friendship. Soule wrote several articles criticizing the action taken at the 1844 General Conference and had assigned work to Bishop Andrew. He invited Bishop Andrew to assist him in his duties in the Kentucky conference. Finley wrote a long letter that was published denouncing Soule for assigning work to Andrew "thus disregarding the sense of judgment of the General Conference, and the solemn decision of the college of bishops." He asserted, "To me there seems to be in this position something too boasting, and in these expressions something too taunting, and unbecoming a bishop." He accused Soule of putting himself above the authority of the general conference. He reiterated his antislavery position and declared, "where the law does not prohibit the freedom of the slaves, we will use all lawful means to extirpate this evil, and we cannot and will not ever give our consent to connecting this evil with the general itinerant supervision of our Church in North America." He concluded by stating that Soule would be held strictly accountable at the next General Conference.[63]

When Soule joined with the Southerners at the Louisville Convention and gave his approval to the organization of the Methodist Episcopal Church South, Finley rushed to print again. The June 27, 1845, issue of the *Western Christian Advocate* contained another criticism of Soule.

This man (and I speak with all due deference to his age and his former official relation to the Church) has done more to divide the Church of God, than any other man living. . . . I am pretty well assured, that J. Soule, in his present position, could no more preside in the Ohio annual conference, than any other Radical, or seceder in the land. . . . I do not believe that now is the time for the watchmen to keep silent. Our injured, insulted, and down-trodden Zion, . . . calls on every friend to stand firm in the defense of her purity, her Discipline, and her usages . . . we are called on, not only to make war against flesh and blood, but to war against "spiritual wickedness in high places."[64]

A further break occurred when Soule attended the Ohio Annual Conference in Cincinnati in 1845. He took the chair to preside at the meeting. Jacob Young and Finley immediately blocked him. As Young recalled the event, "About the time that the Bishop made his appearance, Finley walked up, and urged all the preachers to go to the conference room. They objected, and said Bishop Soule was going to preside. Finley told them he would not preside. . . . Finley was wide awake."[65]

When Soule was about to call the meeting to order, Young stood up and offered a resolution. When Soule indicated unwillingness to recognize it, Finley spoke up to protest the conference proceeding until action was taken on Young's resolution. Young's motion was to the effect that because Soule had declared willingness to become bishop of the Methodist Church South he had, in effect, severed his connection with them and that it was "inexpedient and highly improper" for him to preside. The motion passed 145 to 7.[66]

Finley was sufficiently upset by Soule's defection to the South that he drafted a long resolution to present at the next General Conference. It began, "Bishop Soule you are hereby notified that a charge will be preferred against you . . . for Improper Conduct." There followed five specifications including his calling on Andrew to exercise the office of bishop in contravention to the act of the General Conference, disregarding the decision of the other bishops in this case, betraying the trust committed to him by aiding the South in its secession, and by claiming an infallibility "which does not belong to man." Soule's final break with the North came in May 1846 when he publicly went with the Southern Church.[67]

Charges and counter charges filled the religious press. The Southerners accused Finley of inconsistency and referred to an 1839 letter he had written that was interpreted as proslavery. He had to deny the accusation. On May 15, 1845, Michael Marlay wrote to ask if the letter in question was a forgery. He reported that the Southern delegates going to the Louisville Convention had shown it to people in Cincinnati. "I know you are not an abolitionist, and I feel anxious that while you draw the line clearly between yourself and *Proslaveryism* that you would keep it *Equally Clear*, between you and *abolitionism* for this thing will have to be met by sane men, whether the South go off or not. Permit me to say again, keep your *two edged sword unsheathed* and while you oppose Slavery being connected with the Episcopacy, do not even *seem to strengthen Modern Abolitionism*."[68]

Another person with whom Finley broke was Samuel A. Latta, a minister with Southern sympathies. His friend Marlay wrote to say that while Latta disagreed with Finley he still held him in high regard. "You must not therefore erase him from your list of friends." Marlay also indicated that he agreed with Finley in saying that "Proslaveryism and Abolitionism were German cousins."[69]

Finley had harsh words for Latta after the division. He sent a letter that was published in the *Western Christian Advocate* defending himself against accusations made in the *Southwestern Christian Advocate* that referred to a letter Finley had written years ago that seemed to be sympathetic to the South. Latta wrote a long reply on August 1, 1845, immediately after reading Finley's charges against him. He complained that he couldn't respond in print because the columns of the *Western Christian Advocate* were closed to him. He declared that Finley's words were like an attack on a man in chains and unjustifed. "And although I have considered you greatly in error both with respect to spirit and sentiment yet there is no man for whom I feel a deeper interest than your self. . . . My wife sends her love to you. We are both very grieved with your course in this thing but we think you have been misled by an enemy & we are therefore still your friends."[70]

Other confrontations occurred at the time of the 1845 Ohio Annual Conference. The dispute between Latta and Finley became more bitter and friends of both men were drawn into the disagreement. Charles Elliott and Bishop Hamline supported Finley. A partial reconciliation was agreed upon, but later there were different interpretations of what had taken place. Samuel Latta submitted an account of the dispute to the *Richmond Christian Advocate* and George W. Walker sent a long article to the *Western Christian Advocate* to correct Latta's account. Charles Elliott, the editor, corroborated Walker's description of the controversy.[71]

Finley chose not to respond to Latta's charges but instead wrote an article that supported George Peck's review of Bascom's book, which was written as an answer to the reply to the protest of the minority in the 1844 General Conference. Finley called Peck's work "a complete triumph" over Bascom's "sophistry and misrepresentations." He thought it deserved to be in every Methodist family's library. Finley used his article to raise questions about the proposed division of the funds of the Book Concern and Chartered Fund. He observed that there had been three secessions, the Protestant Methodists, the Scottites, and the Methodist Episcopal Church South. He asked if the South had any more claim to the funds than the other seceders. "I will never give my consent, and I hope the Church never will, to divide her property with one party and not all." In concluding that there was no right in dividing the property he asserted, "The ministers and members of the Methodist Episcopal Church have given their money for a specified purpose . . . and it would be a gross perversion of the intentions of the donors."[72]

Finley's obdurate position received support in the North. T.W. Chandler thanked him for his views in an article published in the March 6, 1846, issue of the *Western Christian Advocate*. "I am much gratified, and many other brethren with me, that brother Finley had the independence to come up to this subject so boldly." Charles Elliott felt the same way and wrote that he was opposed to "any compromise with the system of slavery."[73]

Latta remained unsatisfied with Finley's actions and wrote him again March 18, 1846, a less charitable letter

I have waited long, for a fulfillment of the terms of the compromise, agreed upon between you, and myself, at the last Ohio Conference. (I told you you had been misled in charging me with the publication of your southern letter.) Subsequently, you admitted that you had been misled . . . and said you desired a correction of the statements contained in your letter. . . . You then threw your arms around me

& wept aloud, and I was also deeply affected and felt for you all the tenderness which a son feels for a father not once dreaming of disappointment in the non-fulfillment of promises thus solemnly made. . . . I cannot and will not believe you capable of the unmitigated hypocrisy.[74]

Finley finally replied July 28, 1846, and wrote, "I want you to send no more papers. I have lost all confidence in you as an honorable man. You have treated me badly as the best and finest friend you ever had. . . . I want nothing to do with you & all your hearsay about me. I know you will not injure me one iota. I want no controversy with you and hope you may yet have fortitude enough just to let me be."[75] Others rushed in to defend Finley. One wrote, "Well the Southern leaders seem to be very attentive to you, and pay lots of passing compliments!! . . . You can console yourself with the reflection that you have done what you could to sustain our long cherished institutions, and altho you may be cursed by "Bell book and candle" by the ultraists north & south, yet the great body of conservative Methodism will bless you for your firmness and love you for your unflinching devotion to the weal."[76] Finley's colleague, Michael Marlay, wrote again to advise, "You have nothing to fear" and assured him that the preachers were devoted to him and that publication of Dr. Capers' letter was an advantage to him.[77]

Letters continued to arrive that dealt with slavery and the division in the Church. Elizabeth Riddle wrote from Cincinnati November 4, 1845, to report that fifty members of her church were leaving to form a separate congregation with Southern ties "together with the illustrious few who immortalized themselves in so signal a manner at Conference." His close friend, Joseph Trimble, who had seconded his famous substitute motion, kept him informed of Latta's activities. On November 12, 1845, he warned him that Latta, who had transferred to the Kentucky conference, was preparing to publish a paper.[78]

Samuel Brown sent word from Charleston, Virginia, on January 6, 1846, that there was a strong current of Southern influence in the area and that one-fourth of the church members were proslavery. He wrote, "I think the great majority wish to stay in the M.E. Church but they want a conference of their own for there is strong prejudice here against Ohio. . . . I am as much as ever and more convinced of the great evil of slavery."[79]

On January 8, 1846, John Stewart of Salenes, Virginia, took two hours to write a six-page letter to Finley giving him details on conditions and attitudes at the various stations. He wrote, "every influence that can be brought to bear on us to injure us is now brought forward. . . . I have been thinking that we should have a western Virginia conference. The interest of the country and the interest of the church call for it." He thought that nine-tenths of the ministers and members would vote for it.[80]

J. Carpenter wrote June 20, 1846, to express his disappointment that Finley's assignment to the Ohio State Penitentiary precluded his being sent to London. "What think you of the South and their G. Con. by this time. I would like to spend an evening with you & know what thou thinkest about this sect—they have gone in for slave holding bishops . . . they have offered to the people some strange things under the sun to swallow."[81]

James Savage, who lived in Germantown, Kentucky, was representative of those ministers who suffered as a result of the schism because they didn't want to be part of the Southern Church. He wrote September 4, 1846, to express the hope that the next general conference would declare the plan of separation null and void. He believed that it "has done more harm than anything else to our beloved church."[82]

The division in the Church widened the chasm of animosity and mistrust between North and South. Finley was not the only one to engage in acrimonious disputes. Other examples of the bitter arguments over slavery and slaveholding filled the columns of the *Southwestern Christian Advocate*, *Zion's Herald and Wesleyan Journal*, *Richmond Christian Advocate*, and *Christian Advocate and Journal*. The war of words after 1844 was clearly a prelude to the Civil War itself to occur later. The moderates found themselves more and more in the same camp with the abolitionists as they were attacked by their erstwhile colleagues in the South. Finley was forced by events to review his feelings. He spent much of his time in those years trying to clarify his antislavery position. He was troubled by the fact that extremists in both North and South were criticizing him.[83]

He wrote long letters to Charles Elliott in which he modified some of his earlier ideas and intensified his criticism of slavery. One was a statement on the growth of the proslavery element. In this letter he began by declaring, "Surely we are on the approach of some mighty epoch in the order of a divine providence or standing on the verge of some volcanic eruption." He indicated that there were three great moral principles that mankind had to address: civil and religious liberty, temperance, and "the secret dark and damning spirit of Jesuitical Popery." These questions were agitating the world and everyone would soon have to choose "in which of these two armies he will stand." He repeated his conviction that slavery could not long exist.

the poor colored man is nobody; the slaveholder has got hold of him, taken him out of the hand of his God, and changed him into a brute; and now lives on his labor and sells him, his wife and children into bondage for life, as he would horses, jacks or mules, and calls this Christianity. . . . But slavery must die. The battle is now pitched and all men are now called on to take sides . . . we must be made slaves ourselves or we must take a firm and decided stand against it. . . . American liberty . . . has been trodden down into the heap of African slavery.[84]

Finley asserted that if the patriots who wrote the Constitution had been firm in their convictions they might have put an end to slavery then, but he believed that the slave states had made such a complaint that compromise was resorted to and the principles of liberty were weakened. He maintained that there was a contradiction between the principles fought for in the revolution and the legislation that doomed millions to eternal bondage. Just as the founding fathers compromised so did the Church, in his opinion. Methodism kept the sinning slaveholders within its pale and thus compromised with this great evil. In similar fashion, he declared, the Church compromised by letting whiskey makers and sellers into her communion. So it is with Jesuitical Catholicism, he asserted. "The world must compromise with her while she is aiming to destroy the foundation of all religious & civil liberty." He believed that compromising with evil was evil. He ended his statement with a plea that there should be no compromise by either the church or the state with these three evils.[85]

Finley wrote another letter to Elliott to defend himself against those Southerners who accused him of being an abolitionist. He gave the reasons he was opposed to slavery. He believed it was in opposition to the law of nature. Slavery, he wrote, "binds man's chains, deprives him of the right and prevents him in his pursuit, keeps him in ignorance to serve the purposes of others . . . is in opposition to God and man." He wrote that slavery took away the rights that God endowed. The slaveholder was a robber, brutalized the slave, separated families, deprived children of the benefits of parental love and instruction, deprived the slave of the benefit of his labor and sold people as though they were cattle. He added that he hated slavery because he was born and raised among it and knew that his facts were correct. He defied anyone to "palm this abomination on the world as a divine institution" and concluded, "if slavery is right then God is wrong."[86]

One of the provisions of the Plan of Separation was the appointment of Nathan Bangs, George Peck, and James Finley as commissioners to act along with three to be appointed by the Southern Church to estimate how much of the assets of the Book Concern should be allocated to the Southern Church and "to have full powers to carry into effect the whole arrangements proposed with regard to the division of property." Finley was a reluctant member of this commission. He was not only unhappy at the prospect of a split in the Church but also opposed to the way the Book Concern funds were to be divided. Earlier the general conference had stipulated that the profits of the Book Concern were not to be used except for the benefit of "superannuated and worn-out preachers, their wives, widows and children." The Plan of Separation action had abrogated this provision. It is understandable that Finley, at age sixty-three, would be sensitive to the implications of this action.[87]

He decided to resist calling a meeting of the commission and used as his main excuse the failure of three-quarters of the annual conferences to approve the Plan of Separation. The vote on the plan resulted in 2,135 votes in favor and 1,070 against, only a two-to-one majority. The vote in the Northern conferences was closer, only 1,164 to 1,067.[88]

Finley expressed his views on the Book Concern issue on several occasions. His most comprehensive rationale was published in the July 24, 1846, issue of the *Western Christian Advocate* under the title, "The Plan—Its Nullity." He began by pointing out that people had not understood the report of the Committee of Nine. He asserted that the report was not intended as a plan of division. The General Conference didn't divide the Church; it submitted the question of dividing the funds to the annual conferences.

Bishop Soule was the master spirit who mounted the whirlwind and directed the storm. I drew up charges against him in the case of Bishop Andrew, and other things . . . if he had not withdrawn, he would have been charged, and tried for his improper conduct. . . . I do not believe that any member of the Methodist Episcopal Church is in any way bound to pay attention to what they call the line of division; for the south have put it under their feet. . . . The great moral and civil course in our land is now glorified. . . . God bless all that will stand by the cause of truth and righteousness.[89]

He sent another long article in September that was a response to one in the *Nashville Advocate* that had published again his 1839 letter that criticized abolitionism. Finley lashed out scornfully at the Southern critics and attempted once more to set the record straight. He mocked his Southern opponents for being delighted that he had been appointed chaplain in a prison. "This must be pleasant to those hearts who are the bold advocates of oppression. They have the groans of the poor, abused and trodden down slave; and to sustain this system of robbery and oppression, they devote their time and talents in preaching, praying, and lifting up bloody hands with wrath and doubting." Finley declared that he felt honorably employed in preaching to unfortunate prisoners and was thankful that he was "not following the poor half-starved, half-naked negro or negress; with a bloody whip in my hand, through a cotton field."[90]

Despite his public objections to a meeting with Southern representatives on the Book Concern matter, however, he received a letter dated August 25, 1846, from Bascom, Green, and Latta requesting a meeting of the six commissioners. This letter prompted another article that he titled, "The Property Question," which ran in the November 13, 1846, issue of his favorite paper. He declared that he would have nothing to do with the request and gave several reasons. He asserted that the annual conferences had refused to authorize a division. "I would have as much authority to divide the property of any other firm without their consent, as I would the property of the Book Concern." He pointed out that the general conference had not given the commissioners the authority to collect the votes of different annual conferences so that any decision the commission might make would be illegal. Furthermore, the secretaries of the annual conferences were not required by any rule to disclose the vote. Another reason was, "The South have not complied with the conditions on which such a division was to be made . . . their leaving . . . was effected by the dictation of the proslavery preachers. Hence, the commissioners have no power or authority to act on the matter." The *Richmond Christian Advocate* reported on Finley's refusal in its December 31, 1846, issue.[91]

Finley received support for his views from Abel Stevens, who wrote, "It seems to me that we can never adjust the difficulty in any plan that will require a division of the property or recognition of the South as a Christian organization or relations of fraternity with them."[92]

Finley was fortunate that Charles Elliott, the editor of the *Western Christian Advocate*, shared his views, for he was able to command more space in the journal than any other minister. Elliott wrote him March 20, 1846, to say that he was opposed to "any compromise with the system of slavery." Other friends sent their support. Thomas Dickerson wrote August 22, 1846, "Thank God that you for one have been enabled to make a stand against slavery & that God whom you serve will support you."[93]

Elliott published another letter from Finley in the January 22, 1847, issue of his paper. Finley commented briefly on the slavery controversy and declared, "Methodism has always been . . . the friend of the slave, but the avowed and determined enemy of slavery." That year Finley wrote to Gray Eyes to learn about the progress of the Wyandots. Gray Eyes reported on the conversions among Shawnee, Delaware, and Kickapoo as well as his tribe. He complained about their connection with the Methodist Church South and indicated that he would prefer a missionary from the North.[94]

As the time approached for the 1848 General Conference, Finley asked his old friend, David Young in Zanesville, his opinion of the division in the Church. Young replied May 2, 1848, to record his disappointment with what had happened. "The plan for dividing the church is wholly contrary to all known laws either in heaven or earth." He concluded, "slavery can't last always." Elliott wrote him again on April 17, 1848, to express apprehension over the future of the Book Concern and to suggest a meeting before the start of the General Conference.[95]

Finley was an active participant at that conference. On its fourth day he opened it with religious exercises, was appointed to the Committee on

Law Questions, and submitted a motion asking Bishop Hedding to write and publish his views. He submitted a memorial from the members of the Wyandot church and helped persuade the conference to recommend that the Missionary Society refund the Wyandots five hundred dollars to pay the debt on their church and to refer their petition to transfer from the Methodist Church South to the Ohio Annual Conference.[96]

He went to the general conference prepared to submit his resolution against Bishop Soule if necessary. Soule had sent a long letter to the conference complaining about Finley and Elliott and had requested the conference to try him. When this letter was read, Finley was ready with another motion, "Resolved, That it is the sense of this General Conference that they have no jurisdiction over the Rev. Bishop Soule, and can exercise no ecclesiastical authority over him." Finley spoke at length to review his charges against Soule. He observed, "If we were now to exercise jurisdiction over him, and try him, and suspend him, he would not stay suspended; or if we would expel him, he would not stay expelled." The conference unanimously passed Finley's motion at the May 24th session.[97]

Finley also spoke in favor of abrogating the 1844 Plan of Separation. He said he had realized that he had upset many by his vote in 1844, but he felt the injury could be repaired if he now voted to renounce the plan. It was declared invalid by an overwhelming majority thus legitimatizing Finley's position on the Book Concern issue. The conference passed a modification of Finley's motion to submit the Book Concern issue to arbitration, Finley joining the majority. However, the Methodist Church South went to the United States Supreme Court and, in a unanimous opinion, won the case for division of the funds. Justice McLean had sought to facilitate the arbitration process, but John Wright and a few other Westerners refused on principle. The Southern Church received over $775,000.[98]

Finley must have been impressed by the work that McLean did to try to settle the Book Concern dispute out of court. McLean's judicial reasoning must have persuaded him to give up his earlier opposition to any division of funds. The two men continued to stay in contact in the 1850s. After a meeting on Friday, February 16, 1855, Finley wrote McLean, "After we departed last night I happened to go to the conference room and found there four of our Brethren . . . and it seems that some of them who I thought agreed with you & myself, were misunderstood by me." He advised McLean not to pursue a matter until they could be sure what the majority would do.[99]

After the 1848 General Conference Finley heard again from his Wyandot friends, who were unhappy at being part of the Southern Church. Eighteen of them sent a petition on July 29, 1848, that read, "The undersigned official members of the Methodist Episcopal Church in the Wyandot Nation wish to make known to you and through you to the Ohio Conference that we have this day officially determined to ask our old friends to take us under their pastoral care. We have heretofore determined not to go with the Southern secession and officially informed the Church South of our decision. . . . We consider it our natural right to belong to the church of our choice." [100]

Gray Eyes followed up with a letter on July 31 to respond to Finley's letter of June 10. Finley undoubtedly told him that he had submitted the memorial from the chiefs and church members at the meeting of the General Conference in Pittsburgh on May 12. Gray Eyes reported that the Kickapoos and Shawnees also wanted to remain in the Northern Church. He reiterated the desire of the Wyandots to return to the Ohio Conference. On September 9, Gray Eyes and John Armstrong wrote to say that "the enemy has been at work." They reported that their "slaveholding missionaries are willing to resort to any means whatever to maintain their grasp upon the Indians." They informed Finley that the Southern missionaries had arranged a meeting with "nonprofessors, slaveholders, infidels and backsliders" to get them to send a message to the Ohio Conference to counteract the legitimate one previously sent. They concluded, "Our present missionary has deeply gulled and betrayed us."

A week later John Armstrong wrote again with the news that the official members of the Church had formally declined to have anything more to do with the Southern branch. "You readily see our situation and the necessity of prompt action to relieve us from our embarrassment. If our brethren do not take us by the hand we are undone. We cannot and will not go with the new church but we cannot doubt that our old friend will come to our relief." [101]

Finley did all he could to help them. Although the Wyandot church wanted to be aligned with the Ohio Conference, the entire nation voted to remain with the Methodist Church South. And although the General Conference had authorized a Northern missionary, conflict continued between the Northern and Southern factions. James Gurley, the Northern missionary, was even forcibly removed. [102]

In the summer of 1848 Finley took up his pen to chastise Samuel Latta again. On August 18 he wrote, "I requested you once not to tar me with your sheet for reasons which I need not rehearse. I will have nothing to do with you if I can help it but if you do not let me alone you must take what will follow. . . . I ask you again to send no more of your stuff to me. I never read it but cast it from me as I would any other filthy thing." [103]

He received reassurances from his Kentucky friends for his actions at the 1848 General Conference. J.S. Tomlinson wrote from Augusta August

31 to say that there ought to be a Kentucky district in the Ohio Conference "and with such a man as you at the head of it." On September 23 W.C. Atmore wrote from New Richmond, "I admire . . . your Christian & manly procedure at the General Conference. . . . I have been one of those who have been injured by the actions of '44 & I appeal to your justice & charity to help me." Atmore had wanted to move north and preach in Ohio, but he was not accepted because he had taken appointments in Kentucky, another example of the hardening of feelings intensified by the division.[104]

The antagonisms continued on both sides. Finley held to his moderate position but increased the intensity of his attack on the evils of slavery. As the date approached for the 1850 convention for a new Ohio constitution, he wrote "An Address on Emancipation." In it he referred not to the abolitionists but to what he called a "Large and constantly increasing mass of our fellow citizens" who are demanding that a way should be left open for the "gradual extinction of this great moral, social, and political evil; for the gradual but thorough extirpation of the eating canker from our body politic." He commented on the recommendation that the 1833 law forbidding the importation of slaves into the state should not only be revived but also incorporated into the Constitution. He registered his support for such a move.[105]

Finley continued his attacks on slavery in the 1850s even though he devoted more of his time to writing books. On June 21, 1853, he penned a long letter to the editor of the Yellow Springs *True Presbyterian* giving his views on the subject. He declared that slavery destroyed the only work God made in His own image, made man a chattel, bought his soul, blotted out his will, and destroyed the "noble powers of his immortal mind." He asserted that slavery was in eternal opposition to God and nature. "It violates every principle of justice and mercy and humanity and aims its puny arm at the throne of God, the Bible, the religion of Christianity, the Constitution and government of these United States and all civilization," he wrote. He continued the letter by indicating that no one could have concocted a more villainous system and criticized those ministers who justified slaveholding and the fugitive slave laws. He ended with a warning: "I wish you to remember that this infernal traffic knows no bounds . . . and if the free people of this government do not wake up, for your indifference your children may yet be bought & sold in the market."[106]

Two years later he took a trip down the Mississippi River to New Orleans. This journey resulted in another article which the *Western Christian Advocate* obligingly published. Under the title, "The Barracoons—Stock Negroes" Finley wrote, "When I could stand on the boat and count from five to fifty cottages, where the poor slaves are pent up, brutalized, and driven by their overseer to and from their daily labor; bred and sold like mules to enrich the pockets of their inhuman and ungodly masters, a thick cloud seemed to hang over the country, and Nature herself seemed to put on mourning."[107]

He described his visit to a slave market and recorded his revulsion at the scene. He reported that he left with a feeling of indignation and contempt. He concluded that brutalizing humans through slavery was the worst of all villainies. He also described seeing prostitutes in alarming numbers and wrote that he considered them another feature of the institution of slavery.

Two weeks later another article appeared in which he shared his opinion of St. Louis. He wrote that he was disappointed with the city. Although it seemed to have the appearance of a healthy city it too suffered from the "incubus" of slavery hanging over it. He claimed that there was "a bitterness and antichristian and antiAmerican feeling against all persons from the free states." He was especially critical again of those who justified slavery on Scriptural grounds. He concluded that if more money could be made by freeing the slaves than by keeping them, they would soon be free.[108]

There was another long article the following week. He admitted that he had never persuaded a slave to leave his master but that if he saw one running away, he would not stop him nor feel compelled to do so despite the fugitive slave law. After calling slavery "the most unjust, unholy villiany in the world," he asserted that it had to be exposed "by agitating and keeping it before the minds of a wicked . . . world." He then addressed the question of what to do with the oppressed people once they were set free. His answer was to "take care of them, either in our own country or Africa, their native place." His solution for 1855 was not original, but it revealed how far Finley's views had evolved over the years.

How do we provide now for the ignorant foreign population pouring in upon us by the millions? Are we not under as much obligation to those born in our own country, as we are to foreigners? Surely we are. . . . I would that all of the slaves of the south should be paid for, and our Government is fully able to do it. . . . There are thousands of men and women too, both in the north and south, that would most willingly give of their property to aid the Government in providing freedom and a place for the poor downtrodden slave. And it must and will come, sooner or later, and when it does come, I hope it will be peacefully.[109]

The general conference met in Indianapolis in 1856. It was to be Finley's last one, and he took an active part in it. He was appointed to the Committee on Episcopacy, an indication of his continued interest and involvement. The slavery issue was still agitating Methodist ministers as well as many others in the North. Abolitionism was growing; the South was becoming more defiant. Twenty-nine of the thirty-eight annual conferences sent communications favoring antislavery action. The delegates, however, were deeply divided on what measures to take. The Committee on Slavery submitted a majority and a minority report. Several days were devoted to discussing the issue as it related to Methodist rules on slaveholding. Initially speakers were limited to fifteen minutes. That limit was changed to thirty minutes and later to one hour. Finley missed some of the debate because of family illness.[110]

Jacob Young submitted a substitute motion on May 27 that declared that "no man has a moral right to hold a fellow being as property." It reaffirmed the duty to preach to the slave, recommended prayers for peaceful emancipation and called for compensation to slaveholders for freeing their slaves. The motion was tabled, 104 votes to 70.

On May 28, Finley spoke at length on the subject. In defining what he meant by slavery he added a qualification that he had not mentioned before. He indicated that his wrath was not against the man who owned two or three worn-out blacks whom he treated kindly or against the one who treated a slave as a servant and freed him upon his death. To him, slavery "was the tyrannical usurpation of power of one man over another to crush his soul, and hold him body and soul for gain." He repeated a sentence that he had frequently used before about the brutalizing system that separated a husband from his wife and the mother from her child and treated them like horses, mules, or oxen. He firmly believed that any man who bought or sold another or who chased runaway slaves should not be admitted to the Church.

On May 29 the Committee on Slavery's first resolution received 122 votes in favor to 96 against, Finley voting with the majority. The motion lost since it failed to get a two-thirds majority. Although some of the younger members of the conference were eager for stronger action, the older leaders prevailed and the rule on slavery was not changed.

Finley participated in other conference issues. He moved to table a motion that proposed what documents were to be used in appeals cases, and it was tabled by a vote of 84 to 45. He voted with the majority to maintain the two-year term limit on assignments. He succeeded in a motion to invite Associate Justice John McLean to sit "within the bar of the Conference."

That summer Finley took an eight-week journey to Mt. Pleasant, Iowa. He encountered at first hand some of the proslavery agitators who were en route to fight in Kansas. The *Western Christian Advocate* published his article on his impressions in the September 17, 1856, issue. He declared that the "unhallowed and savage persecution" carried out against

A Hero in Spite of Himself

opponents of slavery in Kansas was the worst imaginable. "I have lived on the frontier of the west for sixty-eight years, and that too in the days of savage barbarity, but the savages of my day never treated the white man and his family worse than these savages have the emigrants to Kansas. A company of these barbarians passed through St. Louis while I was there, and their appearance showed that they were of the lowest caste of creation, armed to the teeth with rifles, and revolvers, and bowie-knives." He was convinced that they would never make Kansas a slave state, "not till the last drop of blood that runs in the veins of free men is spilled."[111]

His article prompted Bishop Hamline to write September 25 to compliment him on his words. Hamline was also glad to learn that Finley was supporting the Republican party. At about the same time that Hamline was writing, Finley was attending a Republican meeting in Lewisburg, Ohio, and was one of the speakers on the platform. He had come a long way toward abolitionism, even though that word was one he resisted embracing. And the most significant factor in the change was his major role in the 1844 General Conference.[112]

8

The Prison Years

> Your donations (of books) may seem small to yourself; but they are like the droppings of the sugar-camp. When all collected, they make a valuable treasure.
> —James B. Finley

On Thursday, April 2, 1846, James B. Finley, not quite sixty-five years old, walked along Spring Street in Columbus toward the Ohio Penitentiary. He was accompanied by his fellow minister, Granville Moody, and Dr. Gard. It was a cool spring morning and the sun must have glistened on the imposing walls that rose twenty-four feet high. He was about to start a new venture in ministerial service.

He had two official notices of his appointment, made partly because of his health and distance from his family and partly in response to the urgent pleas of the penitentiary's board. On March 10 Horatio Cox wrote him, "It is my duty to inform you that you have been appointed Moral Instructor to the Ohio Penitentiary, by the Board of Directors." On March 23 Bishop Leonidas Hamline wrote to release him from his duties as presiding elder of the Zanesville district to become "most moral instructor" at the prison. Hamline added that he believed Finley's labors "will prove a blessing to many forlorn souls for whom Christ died." It was appropriate that, having pioneered in preaching to Native Americans and in temperance agitation, Finley should become part of the nation's prison reform movement.[1]

In the early years of the republic, prisons were criticized by many for their miserable conditions and inhumane conduct. Concern for improving the treatment of criminals was part of the international humanitarian movement, but Americans seemed more successful than others in undertaking reforms. As early as 1787 a society for "Alleviating the Miseries of Public Prisons" was formed in Philadelphia. Benjamin Rush, William Bradford, and Benjamin Franklin were prominent leaders of prison reform in that city. Robert Vaux's report on prison conditions served to arouse public concern.[2]

In 1825, under the leadership of Louis Dwight, a Methodist minister whose handicap prevented him from preaching, the Prison Discipline Society was founded in Boston. Dwight devoted thirty years to prison reform. He was a firm believer in the proposition that a major cause for the increase in crime was "the inadequate supply of moral and religious instruction to prisoners."[3]

The strong religious fervor of prison reform is revealed in the motions taken at the annual meeting of the Prison Society in 1826. It approved resolutions declaring that one cause of the increase and frequency of crime was "the degraded character of the coloured population" and that "solitary confinement, at least by night, with moral and religious instruction, are an obvious remedy for the principal evils existing in prisons." Society members were appalled to learn that there was little or no provision for religious instruction in most state prisons. Massachusetts was the most generous in providing two hundred dollars a year for religious instruction, which was limited to "one short service on the Sabbath."[4]

A major advance in prison construction occurred after 1819 with the erection of a prison at Auburn, New York. The old Pennsylvania system had relied on solitary confinement with each prisoner provided with a small cell and exercise area. The Auburn system continued the solitary confinement concept but added larger dining areas, workshops, chapels, and yards. The Auburn system also was based on a hierarchy of control through surveillance. Isolation was still a foundation in that communication among prisoners was not permitted. The prisoners worked under a labor contract arrangement which was economical for the state to operate.

The debate between proponents of the two systems, traced by Thomas Dumm and others, seems archaic now, but the Auburn plan won probably because of its combination of enforced silence, surveillance, and an economical labor system. The Auburn plan sought little more than a change in prisoners' "habits." Orlando Lewis, an early twentieth century critic, however, concluded that the Auburn system reduced prisoners to being "automata."[5]

In 1831 the French government sent Gustave de Beaumont and Alexis de Tocqueville to the United States to study American prisons. They were favorably impressed with the Auburn system, especially with the prisoners' health and productivity, the economy of operation, and the encouragement to prisoners to reform their habits. Their publication, *On the Penitentiary System in the United States and Its Application in France*, was influential in solidifying support in this country for the Auburn plan.

The authors recognized that prison reform in the United States was primarily the result of religious concern for the reform of the prisoner and his soul's salvation. They observed that many of the heads of penal institutions and reformatories were former Protestant ministers. They stated in their report that "communication between prisoners renders their moral reformation impossible, and becomes even for them the inevitable cause of alarming corruption." The advantage of the Auburn approach, they believed, was that through labor the prisoner "will learn how to live honestly." Besides, the cost of detention was less burdensome when prisoners spent part of their time working.[6]

The authors were less complimentary in their comments about Ohio prisons that year. "Ohio, which possesses a penal code remarkable for the mildness and humanity of its provisions, has barbarous prisons. We have deeply sighed when at Cincinnati, visiting the prison, we found half of the imprisoned chained with irons, and the rest plunged into an infected dungeon."[7]

One of the keys to the success of Auburn, they believed, was the presence of a chaplain.

After the school and the services on Sunday, the prisoners return to their solitary cells, where the chaplain visits them; he visits them in a similar way on the other days of the week; and strives to touch their hearts by enlightening their conscience; the prisoners feel pleasure when they see him enter their cell. He is the only friend who is left to them; they confide in him all their sentiments; if they have any complaints against the officers of the prison, or if they have a favor to sue for, it is he who is interested in their wishes . . . the minister interferes in no respect with the discipline of the prison.[8]

It is understandable that prison reform should have been one of the benevolent activities spawned by the religious revivals. Conversion and spiritual regeneration, at least to Finley and his fellow ministers, were for all persons. Even the most corrupt or criminal individual was not to be denied the opportunity for conversion and access to salvation. Reformation of the criminal was as plausible as reformation of the drunkard or the unchurched.

By 1840 the United States could boast of twelve Auburn style prisons with capacities totaling nearly five thousand persons. They all had profitable industrial departments to encourage prison labor, but only four had permanent chaplains. The Auburn system had been widely accepted throughout the country.[9]

Construction of the Ohio Penitentiary, a quarter-mile northwest of the city, was completed in 1834 at a cost of $93,370.50. Over one million days of convict labor had gone into erecting the structure. Built mostly of limestone, the prison walls and three-story high buildings formed a hollow square. The wall on the Spring Street side ran for four hundred feet. It stood back from the street with terraced lawns that led to the entrance. The offices, residence for the warden, and the guard room were in the center. The building was modeled on the Auburn plan.[10]

Although the citizens of Ohio might have been pleased with their new prison, it shortly received criticism from an unexpected source. The annual report of the Prison Discipline Society of Boston criticized the practice of keeping prisoners in their solitary cells on Sundays. The report read, "Legislators of Ohio—ye fathers, ye brothers, ye sons—will you place men, sustaining these relations, week after week, month after month, and year after year, in solitary cells to spend their Sabbath? . . . May you never have your flesh and blood be the slow and consuming effects of unmitigated solitude and despair!"[11]

The following year this society condemned the state of Ohio for gaining twenty thousand dollars from the work of the convicts, "but giving them no Sunday suit!" Apparently, Ohio led the states in making money from the prisoners' work. The earnings in 1841 amounted to $21,897.

In the 1840s Dorothea Dix conducted a four-year investigation of American prisons. Her *Remarks on Prisons and Prison Discipline* was published in 1845. Part of her theory of prison reform was based on the belief that providing inmates with moral and religious instruction served both the prisoners and society. What she had to say about the new Ohio Penitentiary was highly critical. She called discipline at Columbus "exceedingly lax." She counted 460 convicts. Of the 140 committed to the penitentiary in 1842, twenty-one were sentenced to terms of ten years and over and five for terms of seventeen years. She reported that in 1844 the penitentiary received $1,038 from paying visitors which, at twenty-five cents apiece, she calculated, amounted to 4,150 persons. "It might be supposed," she wrote, "that the exposure of the convicts to such large numbers of spectators would not aid in the moral and reforming influences of the prison. This source of revenue would be better dispensed with." (Visitors could be admitted to the prison and observe the inmates without being seen.) She called the ventilation "exceedingly defective" and added, "There was no matron in the women's wing at the time I was there, the 19th and 20th of August, 1844, and they were not slow to exercise their good and evil gifts on each other."[12]

Continuing her evaluation of Ohio's institution, she wrote, "The supply of books at this, as at other prisons, is quite inadequate" and it "has no chaplain appointed by law." She concluded that the Ohio Penitentiary "is so totally deficient of the means of moral and mental culture directly imparted, that little remains to be said, after stating the fact."[13]

Things may not have been as bleak religiously as Dorothea Dix thought. The state legislature passed a law in 1821 that called for giving each convict a free Bible. It also provided that the director was authorized, if he thought it proper, to find a minister to preach in the prison. In 1828 a Presbyterian minister, the Rev. James Chute, was appointed chaplain at a salary of thirty dollars a month, a sum supplied by area Presbyterian ministers. That arrangement was changed when the legislature accepted the board's recommendation to provide a regular chaplain not only to preach but also to visit the convicts in their cells and counsel them. The Rev. Russell Bigelow was appointed chaplain in 1835.[14]

Two years later, however, that law was repealed and the penitentiary had to rely on volunteer help. The Young Men's Prison Society of Columbus supported a minister for a time. The Rev. Samuel Mills donated his services for a short period, but from 1840 to 1845 no provision was made for a chaplain.[15]

Inasmuch as Dorothea Dix's book was published in 1845 it is not surprising that the harassed directors in Ohio should have sought for the chaplain's position a person of Finley's caliber and prestige.

Finley entered the Ohio Penitentiary that day in 1846 and climbed to the warden's office on the second floor. He learned that the new warden had not yet arrived, but one of the guards gave him a tour of the five tiers and showed him the seven hundred cells, built of stone with iron barred doors, that an earlier visitor, Clark Guernsey, had measured as eight feet long, three feet wide, and six feet high, each containing a bed. Finley noted the heavy wide corridors, inspected the shops for making shoes and boots, for woodworking, for carriage trimmings. He walked through the mess halls and infirmary. At the time it was the largest penitentiary in the country.[16]

His first visit through the prison deeply affected him. The depressed, melancholic appearance of the prisoners led him to say to himself, "O, my God! . . . what a life, what a condition for an immortal creature."[17]

Having left his family in Eaton to live in the prison, he was not satisfied with his accommodations. They were too small and probably too damp. After he saw the large area allocated for the warden and his family, he wrote the new warden in Akron to ask if he might be assigned a room in that part of the building. Lamin Dewey replied on April 13 to say, "I am entirely unacquainted with that part of the prison, designed for the use of the Warden, but be assured, so far as I am concerned, it will give me great pleasure to comply with your wishes if at all consistent with the convenience of my own family, which, though small now, will necessarily be large when I remove. . . . You had better confer with the Directors. If they be of the opinion that there is room enough and if they desire you to reside in the prison, you had better make your arrangements accordingly."[18]

Dewey, who replaced General John Patterson as warden, had been a sheriff in Portage County and editor of the *Ohio Star* and the *Akron Beacon*, both Whig papers. Prison appointments at that time were political ones.[19]

The Prison Years

Illustration from Finley's *Memorials of Prison Life* shows convicts attending a service in the chapel at the Ohio Penitentiary in Columbus.

On Finley's second day at the prison he was briefed on his duties by the retiring warden, familiarized himself with his surroundings, and visited the female department. On his first Sunday in the prison many of his Columbus friends crowded into the building to hear his first sermon to the inmates. In his first days there he studied the rules for the "moral and religious instructor." They were much different from those of a circuit rider or presiding elder.

It shall be his duty to see that each convict that can read is furnished with a Bible or Testament.

To preach to the prisoners every Sabbath, or when necessarily absent, to engage some suitable person to fill his place.

To see that the Sabbath School is properly attended and supplied, as far as practicable, with suitable teachers and books.

It shall be his duty, as far as practicable, to have prayers with the prisoners every morning at the breakfast table, and to visit those that are sick in the infirmary, and administer to their spiritual wants.

To be present as far as he can, at all funerals of deceased prisoners, and to see that they are interred with proper religious services.

He shall have the liberty of visiting any prisoner who wishes to see him, and it shall be his duty to give them such advice as they seem to require.

He is to use his best exertions to promote the religious and moral welfare of the prisoner, as well as the harmony and general interests of the Institution.

All officers, contractors, agents and foremen, are required not to hold any conversation with the prisoners, except in relation to their respective duties, and while in the prison will be subject to all the rules and regulations established for its government.[20]

Word of Finley's new assignment quickly spread to his friends. Typical was Michael Marlay's response. "But among all the strange things that have taken place in this strange world, for some time past, is that my beloved Chief should be taken down from his elevated position, to be doomed to the State Prison there to pour out his manly eloquence upon those abandoned sinners that have been guilty of all the crimes that poor human nature is capable of." Finley's detractors also took note of his new assignment. One of his Southern former colleagues, still irritated at his 1844 antislavery action, wrote in the *Nashville Christian Advocate*, "Rev. J.B. Finley is now just where he deserves to be—in the Ohio penitentiary."[21]

During his early weeks in the prison he had considerable trepidation at what he was doing, for it was "entirely a new scene of action" for him. He decided that if he could not become well acquainted with the inmates and gain their confidence, he would be of little usefulness to them. He resolved to throw himself into the regular routine of the prison. He visited the prisoners often, ate with them, and conducted services as frequently as possible, with prayers at breakfast, a Sabbath school, and a Bible class.[22]

As he began his work he was aware of three theories about prisons. He described them in detail in his book, *Memorials of Prison Life*. One was that imprisonment was for the sake of punishment. Implementation of that theory, Finley believed, sometimes led to the conclusion that "the severer and more certain the punishment, the more sure it is to deter from crime." He indicated that the second theory was that punishment was for the improvement of the culprit and, therefore, should be "softened down by the spirit of unmixed love." He believed that a third view took a middle position between these two extremes in that society had to be defended against the repetition of crime and that punishment should somehow "benefit the criminal but unfortunate victim of the law." Finley clearly favored the middle ground. As he put it, "I have no cause to advocate but the cause of justice and humanity combined."[23]

Early in April Finley studied the prison's regulations, especially the "Duties of Assistant Keepers of the Ohio Penitentiary."

Assistant Keepers are required to be at the Prison at all times during Prison hours, unless prevented by sickness or having previously obtained leave of absence.

They are required, as they are bound by their oath of office, to enforce rigidly every rule and regulation of the Prison.

The preservation and the effect of the whole system of discipline depends upon non-intercourse between convicts. They will, therefore, make use of every exertion to prevent any communication between them.

They are required to say nothing in the presence of any of the convicts respecting the police of the Prison, unless it is for the purpose of directing them in their duty.

They are to hold no unnecessary conversation with convicts, nor allow them the speak unless it is absolutely necessary . . .

They are to require of convicts, labor in silence, and strict obedience.[24]

Finley must have realized that he was one of the few persons with whom the prisoners could converse freely during their incarceration. Access to the prisoners posed a privilege and a heavy responsibility. How could he convert these people, some of whom were illiterate, and all of whom were considered the dregs of the earth?

He spent his time visiting the prisoners and conducting services. He distributed tracts and sought to counsel those who wished help from him. Although his primary concern was the souls of his charges, he was also solicitious of their physical well-being. Not all of the inmates welcomed his inquiries, but he usually found a way to reach them. Frequently in afternoons he sat at the central well to talk with prisoners when they took a break from their shop work. Before the first month was over he became ill. "I was quite sick with a bilious attack. I was my own physician—bled myself—fainted—took boneset tea, and nursed myself."[25]

In his book on his years at the prison Finley took credit for a number of firsts in prison life. He abolished the custom of ringing a bell at the beginning of the chapel service. His view was, "if you wish to make a man really a man, you must treat him as a man." One day in May 1846, he visited the prison hospital. Instead of talking with the patients singly, he "constituted them into a sort of class meeting, asking them questions, receiving their answers, and giving them advice and consolation according to their circumstances. Perhaps it was the first meeting of its kind ever held within the walls of a state prison." He described the scene in vivid terms. The eloquence of his address produced many tears and much emotion. He compared his powers of speech with those of Demosthenes, Cicero, Burke, and Patrick Henry. The difference, to him, was that those orators were talking about tangible things; he was talking about "rewards and pleasures in the future." A minister's triumph, he observed, came in realizing the conversion of his hearers. "Something of this rapture I felt this day, when talking to these poor sinners in the hospital, while their silence, their attention, their tears, their cries of agony, their shouts of victory, gave assurance that the word of God was having its effect among them."[26]

Although Finley favored a humane treatment of prisoners, he did not view them as equals. He wrote, "Prisoners, in general, are far below the average of their race in mental character, as well as in moral condition. They must be treated accordingly."[27]

Finley supplied religious counseling to the few women prisoners as well as to the men. When he visited them on May 17 he concluded that they were much worse than the men. He wrote, "A woman when lost is lost entirely." He thought that they were more hardened in their "iniquity." On Sunday, May 31, he preached "in the Female Prison and they were much affected." He had the typical male attitude of his generation in expecting women to be more virtuous than men. He asserted, "As woman falls from a high point of perfection, so she sinks to a profounder depth of misery than man." He wrote in his journal, "I have hope for this part of my flock that God will break up the great despair of their hearts, and that they will yet find mercy." He must have been relieved when Mary Williams was appointed matron in 1846.[28]

Daily contact with the prisoners led Finley to realize that very little was done to improve their intellect. His own assignment focused on what was directly religious, which he believed was a mistake because, as he expressed it, "intellectual faculties play a momentous part in the moral reformation of a fallen human being."[29]

He concluded that because good books were a way to improve one's learning, the prison needed an adequate library. He visited his colleague, Uriah Heath, on May 13 and returned the next day with a supply of hymn books. After the new warden arrived on June 1, Finley intensified his efforts to collect books for the prison. His was not the first prison library, of course. The first one to contain more than Bibles was probably the one created in Sing Sing, New York in 1840. However, the first efforts to create a prison library apparently were in the Ohio River Valley. The Kentucky Penitentiary regulations in 1802 included the following: "The convicts shall be encouraged to employ any leisure time in reading; and donations of books will be thankfully received."[30]

Finley solicited his friends and used a variety of other fund-raising techniques. On June 11 he wrote an article under the title, "Books Wanted," published in the July 3, 1846, *Western Christian Advocate* and in which he made what he called a "feeble appeal." He informed his readers that he had been appointed to labor with "the most unfortunate of our race." He reminded them that the prison required silence of the inmates and described their conditions and state of mind. He asserted that prisoners were not devoid of moral or natural feelings and that they even had remorse for their past actions. "The mind, like the body, must have something to feed on, or it will become deranged." He eloquently described the sullen, gloomy melancholy into which the neglected prisoners sank when deprived of any intellectual encouragement.

His solution for preventing this mental disease was simple. He asked his readers' assistance in "furnishing a library of good books" and suggested that they supply books through their ministers. "Your donations may seem small to yourself; but they are like the droppings of the sugar-camp. When all collected, they make a valuable treasure."[31]

In a short time he had received over two hundred volumes. He was assigned a small room to serve as a library. He kept the project a secret within the prison until the books had been arranged on shelves. Then he told the prisoners to help themselves. As he recorded it, "never did I see such a rush of eager men."[32]

He spent Monday, July 20, calling on people in Columbus to collect more books, and his success was greater than he expected. He must have needed a wheel barrow to cart them all back to the penitentiary. He then went to Cincinnati to collect books there. Later, he recalled, "I got into my buggy, and rode from town to town, and from house to house. . . . Never was I turned away entirely empty. . . . Never in my life have I seen a charity so cheerfully and bountily supplied."[33]

He had lofty aims for his library. He believed that the prisoners needed "the best of books . . . the great master-pieces of human genius should be given them for perusal. Dull works will only weary and disgust them." In his *Memorials of Prison Life* he listed examples of what he sought: Herodotus, Homer, Livy, the Greek and Latin poets, Pope, Dryden, Petrarch, Washington Irving, Prescott, and works of a religious character.[34]

On October 21 his future editor, W.P. Strickland, wrote him from Dayton to report that the American Bible Society would soon send one hundred large testaments for the prison library. Finley's search for books continued throughout his stay at the prison. When he composed his annual report to the directors on December 7, 1846, he was able to claim two thousand volumes in the library with assurance of several hundred more. He reported that the inmates "have increased much in their desire to read and many have become interested in acquiring useful knowledge. The result is they are much more cheerful and contented."[35]

In June 1847 he wrote Uriah Heath asking him to solicit books in his area. On June 30, 1847, Heath wrote to report that he was sending two boxes containing 417 volumes, 362 pamphlets, and 4,409 pages of tracts. (They must have been large boxes!) He also sent seven pages of donors' names with the titles of the volumes they had contributed. He assured Finley that the books came from all sections of the Marietta community "without distinction of church or party . . . some of these books were given by poor persons." By the end of 1847 Finley had amassed for the library over four thousand volumes, twelve hundred pamphlets and a multitude of tracts. He continued his efforts the next year. On March 17, 1848, he and Heath rode to Groveport and collected thirty-one volumes.

By 1849 the prison library had increased to seven thousand volumes, fifteen hundred pamphlets and twenty thousand pages of tracts. Ohio's prisoners must have been the best read in the entire country. By this time, gas lights illuminated the building, and the prisoners could, according to the *Ohio State Journal*, "spend the long evenings in reading the books of the library, instead of as formerly, remaining in darkness and solitude."[36]

Finley shared his ideas on the treatment of prisoners with his new supervisor, Warden Dewey, after he arrived. Dewey was receptive to improving conditions. He must have started first by improving the quality of the food. On Friday, June 19, Finley recorded satisfaction in his journal at the improvement in the evening meal. "This great change from a piece of cold corn-bread for supper (after the poor fellows had worked from 10 o'clock to 7) to mush and molasses . . . I have not eaten a better supper since I have been here."[37]

More important than meals, however, was a relaxation of some of the harsh discipline observed in the penitentiary. At one point Finley was able to record, "I am glad that right notions are beginning to prevail on this subject; that it is no longer thought necessary to treat a convict as if he were a beast from the forest." To Finley's mind, the convicts were "only somewhat more fallen" than the rest of the unconverted in society.[38]

His book contains several references to prison discipline. He believed that he knew the reasons for serious crime in society. One reason was what he called "a system of lax family government. Industry and obedience are prime virtues in every well-regulated family. Where these are absent, there we find anarchy and misrule." A second reason was "the making and vending of spiritous liquors. Long as we have men in our midst to sell liquor, just so long may we expect to have iniquity and crime. The rum-seller, of all other wretches, is the greatest murderer."[39]

His major view of incarceration was summed up in his statement, "The great object of imprisonment is to protect community, and to reform the prisoner." But severe punishment did not accomplish this objective, in his opinion. He believed that the way prisoners were treated was characterized by "savage cruelty." He believed that there was "a great defect in our criminal code, which greatly retards the reformation of the prisoner—and this is the abuse of the pardoning power. Its frequent exercise seems to be almost absolutely necessary, however, in such cases as those where severe sentences have been pronounced on convicts for minor offenses; for example, ten years of hard labor for passing a few counterfeit dollars, or four years for stealing a young calf. Whenever the punishment is disproportioned to the crime there is a manifest injustice done; and it becomes a duty in the chief magistrate to exercise his pardoning power."[40]

He also favored separating youthful offenders from adult prisoners.

"There is a great defect in the prison arrangements concerning boys or young men; and this constitutes a large proportion of the prisoners." He thought they suffered when thrown in with older criminals and were given no help. "Boys and young men ought to be put to some kind of mechanical business which would afford them a respectable living."[41]

He conveyed his ideas on separating juvenile offenders in his 1846 report to the directors. He wrote, "These youths have been led off in an evil hour, by bad associations and by a milder treatment, might be reclaimed, without having a mark of disgrace fixed on them for all future life." He recommended that the legislature "provide a house of refuge, or correction" to which children under age eighteen would be sent and that it be a manual labor school.[42]

That idea was not a new one for prison reformers. New York had a house of refuge in 1825, Boston in 1826, and Philadelphia in 1828. Louis Dwight favored separating the youthful offenders from the older convicts, and Dorothea Dix commented favorably about the idea. But it must have been a new notion for Ohio. It was not until 1850 that Warden Dewey proposed that the legislature create a house of refuge. No action was taken in Ohio until much later.[43]

Finley was successful in gaining the prisoners' confidence. Many asked him to contact family members and sought his advice. A number requested special favors. He was especially pleased when he was able to convert one of them. One wrote home, "I have been in the prison hospital about two weeks having a serious attack from inflamation of the lungs. I have suffered much in bodily pain. . . . Father Finley is the Chaplain and preaches to the prisoners he comes to see me several times every day he has been very kind to me and labors faithfully with the prisoners to improve and elevate their moral condition and I have no doubt his exertions will in a great many instances be crowned with success."[44] Another wrote, "His ambition seems to be, as nearly as I can tell from his sermons, to turn the penitentiary into something like a church, for he is constantly telling us, that he shall never be at rest, till he sees every man a servant of the Lord."[45]

Toward the end of his book Finley supplied statistics on the number of inmates for the period from 1839 to 1848. The number admitted each year ranged from a high of 163 in 1846 to a low of 96 in 1847. The annual average for the decade was 144. Of 1,441 sentenced in that decade, 1,332 were whites, 108 were blacks, and one was a Native American.[46]

Finley's journal contains a table that is not printed in his book. It lists twenty-nine prison inmates who are identified in one place as "maniacs" and in another as "deranged." The table gives the prisoners' names, ages, dates when imprisoned, length of terms, offenses, and "supposed cause of insanity." The table is a useful window into the nature of serious crime in the 1840s and the notions of society at that time in respect to the causes of insanity. Finley was probably copying prison records, so it is doubtful that the causes listed originated with him. There is no indication whether he thought the reasons seemed logical or implausible.[47]

The youngest inmate in this category was eighteen years old, the oldest seventy. Sentences ranged from three years to life. Life terms were for murder. Horse stealing drew terms of three, ten, or twelve years depending probably on the judge or the horse. Terms for robbery ranged from seven to fourteen years. Counterfeiting received a ten-year term. Sentences for rape were three to five years. The supposed cause for insanity for these inmates were "epileptic, domestic affliction, hypochondriac, injury of brain, idiotic, and masturbation," the latter listed for five of the twenty-nine names. Apparently, the chaplains became prison statisticians.

Finley was strongly of the opinion that society had a responsibility to help former prisoners who had paid their debts for their crimes. In his book he told the story of a person about to be released who admitted that he was afraid to "enter again into the busy world" for he had nowhere to go. Finley's solution was to form organizations "whose object should be to take these poor outcasts by the hand, furnish them places of employment, give them a good word of encouragement, and send them along their way with a better prospect of an innocent, and prosperous, and happy life."[48]

Finley entertained visitors in his quarters from time to time. The author, Henry Howe, visited him in 1846 when he was collecting material for his book on Ohio. He recalled that "he took me under his wing. I had arrived with a severe cold and he cured me after the manner of the Wyandots. . . . He brought out a heavy buffalo robe, and spreading it before the fire in his room, I laid on my back and toasted my feet for about two days. . . . Those two days with the hunter were a rare social treat."[49]

Finley's prison duties did not prevent him from accepting preaching invitations and attending religious conferences and temperance meetings. He probably attended all the meetings he could of the Franklinton chapter of the Sons of Temperance. He spent part of each day adding to his journal. He wrote many letters, especially to his ministerial colleagues and Wyandot friends. Time was often spent on preparing sermons and on occasional visits to members of the legislature in Columbus. On October 30, 1846, he attended the ceremonies marking the founding of Chillicothe.[50]

It is curious that in his second year as chaplain he drafted a long message to use as his "adieu" to the Ohio Annual Conference. He wrote the lengthy message on March 13, 1847, when he must have been feeling extremely ill. He began, "Beloved Brethren, believing that my days are fast winding to a close and that I may never have the privilege of meeting with you again on earth I feel a duty I owe to you & myself to take this method of bidding you adieu." He reviewed his preaching career and asserted that he had never doubted his conversion or call to the ministry. He felt that he had been true to the *Discipline* and the mission of the Church but he regretted his shortcomings, "my often secret backslidings, and my heart wanderings from God." He continued by saying, "If I at any time have injured any of your feelings I have not done it with the intention of wounding you; and I hope that I may find with you forgiveness." He declared that he had always aimed at the good of the Church and added criticism of the Southern schism. He reiterated his opposition to dividing the Book Concern's funds, condemned slavery, and called for upholding the position of bishop. He ended, "Finally, Dear Brethren, I thank you for all your kindness to me, a poor unworthy laborer" and wrote that he looked forward to meeting them all in heaven. His gloomy mood soon passed, and he was very much alive once more at the next annual conference meeting. At that session a letter from the prison directors was read requesting Finley's reappointment. The conference obligingly asked the bishop to accept the directors' recommendation.[51]

At the end of 1847 he wrote his annual report to the prison directors. He reported that religious services had been held every week, that many prisoners had been attentive and were reading the Scriptures. He cited evidence that some who had served their terms had joined the Church and were now leading new lives but that he could not claim this result in every instance. He added his description of the conversion process. "The influence of the preaching of the Gospel is often invisible, often slow but it exerts a secret activity conveying its own properties progressively until like the measure of meal the whole mass is leavened and the change must become a matter of personal experience." He reported that the Sabbath School was progressing and gave the statistics for the increase in the library. He was convinced that the library "has proved a blessing to these men" and added that the majority were reading "with great interest and profit."[52]

His work continued at the penitentiary in 1848, but his record keeping declined. When he left Columbus to attend the general conference that year in Pittsburgh, Samuel Bradford, the deputy warden, wrote him on May 15 to say, "I miss you very much." He added that if he remained another year he hoped that Finley would decide to stay as well. "I know no man so well suited to the place. Excuse me, I do not mean to flatter you. I speak what is in my heart & you are an old man as much as myself. We can talk as Brothers."[53]

Warden Dewey also wrote Finley when he was in Pittsburgh. On May 21 he penned, "We have been glad to learn from your several letters that you reached the Conference in safety and that your health is again restored. . . . Remain quietly until the close of the Conference and then come home to us. . . . The health of the prison was never better."[54]

Throughout 1848 and 1849 Finley became ill more frequently. He finally left the penitentiary to recover his health among his family in Eaton. He left at a bad time. Cholera struck in June 1849, and he had to be replaced. Colonel Dewey wrote him July 21 to report that 110 inmates had died of cholera. He apologized for having to appoint another chaplain. "Come and see us as soon as you can. No one blames you for being absent, and the Directors intended no disrespect" by appointing another. "The emergency demanded speedy action and there was no time to consult or correspond with you in relation to the matter."[55]

The 1849 cholera epidemic was the worst in the penitentiary's history. More than one-quarter of the inmates died. The first cholera fatality in Columbus that year was on May 27. The first cases in the prison to die were on June 30. Almost all of the inmates were treated for some stage of the disease. Of the 413 prisoners, 116 died from cholera, five from other diseases. Two of the attending doctors also died. At the height of the epidemic, discipline was relaxed. The prisoners were not forced to remain in their cells. It was understandable that Finley had to be replaced by J.T. Donahoo, given the great need for ministerial service at such a time. Had Finley been there in June and July he probably would have died.[56]

Although he had received many commendations from the directors and warden during his tenure at the prison, some persons in Columbus criticized him for his sudden departure. One director even accused him of cowardice.[57]

If he had been unhappy about his sudden replacement at the penitentiary, he never openly complained. He continued cordial correspondence with both the warden and his deputy. On March 28, 1850, Dewey wrote to him in Eaton and complained about what he called disgusting conditions in the prison. He indicated that he favored the creation of a Prison Discipline Society and sought Finley's help with prison reform. He said that he was discouraged at the indifference in Ohio on the subject of prison discipline. He contrasted the good support received by temperance and antislavery efforts with the indifference in his area of concern. "Where are the friends of the poor heartbroken convict?" He asked Finley to help him and said that the legislature had requested that he study different systems of prison discipline.

Changing the subject, he continued, "What shall be done to secure us a proper person for moral instructor. It is a delicate subject for me to touch. The present incumbent has not the first qualification. I prefer to have no one. He does not do the least good in the world. Is it not a sin to keep such a man in such an important position?"[58]

On May 14, 1850, Samuel Bradford reported on personnel changes at the prison and predicted that there would be an effort underway to oust the Democratic staff members. He indicated that he was pleased that there seemed to be a more healthy feeling as to Whigery.[59]

Other causes demanded Finley's attention once he left Columbus and once his *Memorials of Prison Life* was published in 1850. His influence on inmates and on prison policy continued, however. It must have been partly the result of Finley's contribution that even as late as 1865 the Ohio Penitentiary was the only one in the country where, according to Blake McKelvey, "regular classes were conducted by the chaplain three evenings a week."[60]

In his final months at the Ohio Penitentiary, Finley, who was sixty-eight years old, cast about for another career. He was writing the book that was to become *Memorials of Prison Life*. Because his health was failing he knew that in a year or so he would have to retire, at least for awhile. There were more books he wanted to write and more sermons to preach. Perhaps something else could improve his finances.

He wrote Associate Justice John McLean to inquire about the possibility of an appointment to the postmaster position in Eaton. McLean's reply on February 20, 1849, was full of friendly advice. "I would suggest the propriety of procuring an expression of the citizens in your behalf. . . . I can entertain no doubt that the people of Eaton, if your wishes were known to them, would express themselves in your favor, and that would secure the appointment." He cautioned Finley not to let his congressman know of his interest because he was hostile to McLean and would oppose the appointment. He concluded, "You may rest assured that I will now and always exert myself to the utmost to promote your wishes." If Finley tested public opinion he probably learned that there was insufficient support in town for his candidacy for he never followed up on the idea.[61]

Nothing reveals the complexity of Finley's mind and behavior more than his role in an emotional issue which developed in the Methodist Church in the spring of 1849. He was invited by John S. Inskip, the pastor, to preach in the new Wesley Chapel in Dayton. The Dayton church departed from tradition by mixing men and women in the congregation. Finley's reaction was the opposite from what his earlier views and actions would suggest.

He had long been a firm proponent of having free pews in the churches. Unlike the situation in the East where a free church movement developed in the 1830s to democratize churches, among the Ohio Methodist churches the tendency had been not to rent or sell pews. The churches followed the instructions in the *Discipline*, "Let all our churches be built plain and decent, and with free seats." The churches also kept to the Wesley tradition that called for men and women to "sit apart."

In was consistent with Methodist doctrine for seats to be free at religious services. Otherwise, the rich would run the churches, and the institution could not well reach the poor and adhere to its claim that salvation was for all. In addition, it had been the tradition and rule ever since Wesley's time for the sexes to be seated separately. The most active circuit riders maintained a solid front in pushing to keep free pews and separate seating as part of the Ohio Methodist practice. The issue came up in the 1820 General Conference, which, after considerable debate, approved a resolution requiring that no future churches were to be built with "rented or sold pews." The resolution urged that efforts be made "to make those houses free which have already been built with pews." Finley had wanted a stronger statement.[62] Finley's friend, David Young, probably echoed majority opinion when he wrote, "I would sooner undertake to carry a "pew" to heaven on my back, as to carry a gang of negroes thither."[63]

By 1847 some of the younger ministers were becoming rebellious on the matter. That year the Ohio Conference appointed a committee to review the subject and make a recommendation. Finley was appointed chairman. The resolution he wrote called upon Methodists to hold to tradition. He declared that it was "our duty to adhere strictly to the letter of our Discipline . . . and under no pretense whatever to countenance an infraction of" the regulations. One of his resolutions passed by the conference read, "that if any such house should be built with pews to rent . . . that the Bishops of our church are hereby respectfully requested not to appoint any preacher to serve them."[64]

The report he submitted was criticized in the *Western Christian Advocate*. Finley defended his report. Several others rushed to print to express their views. Finley thought he was getting the last word when he wrote at length in the November 5, 1847, issue. "I do not believe the time has yet come, when the ministers of the Ohio annual conference, will renounce their allegiance to the Church, and to their country, so as to give up the Discipline or usages of the Church. . . . Methodism brings all her children, as Christians, to the same level. . . . The pewed system is antagonistic to the free institutions of our country. . . . Now make all the churches pewed, and will the masses of men hear the Gospel? No."[65]

John Inskip moved to Ohio in 1845. When he introduced "promiscious seating" in his new Dayton church, his presiding elder, George M.

Walker, wrote Finley with the news. "Free seats, but the men and women mixed up together." Walker expected Finley to take the lead in disciplining the upstart, but Inskip shrewdly invited Finley to preach in his new structure and he was impressed with what he saw. In an April 4, 1849, article, he admitted that he was startled at first to see men and women sitting together but came around to accepting the arrangement as a practice designed "by common consent, for the purpose of keeping the better order." He praised the congregation for its attentiveness. He concluded, "So long as the seats were free for all to come and hear . . . I for one, will not make serious objections." Thus Finley became one of the first in Ohio to divide the two issues: separate sex seating and free pews.[66]

Immediately after reading Finley's article, Joseph M. Trimble, who had seconded his friend's substitute motion in the 1844 General Conference, wrote to exclaim, "Oh my dear uncle Finley that letter of yours is giving pain to many hearts that love you, and that love Methodism better than men." He asked him to reconsider and called the Dayton move an "entering wedge" which, if not checked, would destroy "some of the most distinctive features of Methodism." He wrote that he regretted to see his old friend "taking sides with innovation of the rules."[67]

At the Annual Conference in 1849 Inskip was reprimanded for letting the sexes sit together. He promised to stop agitating the question and said that he would retire from his connection with the church if he failed to obey. A year later, however, he was charged with failing to keep his promise. Jacob Young and Granville Moody called for his censure. Finley was one of the few to defend him, but the conference ended up censuring him. Inskip appealed to the General Conference.[68]

Inskip was not the only one in trouble for favoring promiscuous seating. The Union Chapel in Cincinnati was without a pastor because of their pewed status. At the 1850 Annual Conference Finley himself submitted a petition "requesting action to allow the appointment of a preacher to Union Chapel a pewd church."[69]

Abuse was poured on Finley's head. He tried to separate the question of paying for pews and mixed seating. In an article in the April 23, 1851, *Western Christian Advocate* he wrote, "pewing churches is contrary to the genius of the Gospel, which is sent to every man, expressly. . . . God is no respecter of persons, the rich and the poor have equal rights." He felt that pewed churches were "contrary to the true spirit and genius of Methodism," but he was opposed to a penal law prohibiting them.[70]

Arguments continued at the 1851 Annual Conference held in Springfield, where Inskip had had the audacity to direct construction of the handsome High Street Church, where the sexes were permitted to sit together. Inskip's trial at the conference was lengthy. He was censured again. Granville Moody criticized Finley, who tried to clarify his position, but his remarks were not included in the minutes by action of the conference. W.P. Strickland, who was the conference recorder, sent Finley an affidavit to that effect. Finley wrote a paper on the "abuse" he received at the conference but could not get it published. Part of what he wrote was a listing of rules that had been discarded over time such as fasting, the wearing of old straight-breasted coats by men and plain Methodist bonnets by women. He did not believe that there was less religion in the church because these practices had disappeared. He believed that the ministers who favored family seating in churches were just as zealous and pious as those who insisted that the sexes should sit apart. He added that when he wrote his letter about preaching in Dayton, "I wrote the honest feelings of my heart." He concluded that what he would seriously object to was when the seats or pews were sold out and the poor man and his family were excluded.[71]

Finley found a friend in Abel Stevens, editor of *Zion's Herald*. He wrote him to thank him "for giving some of us poor ministers in the Ohio Conference, the privilege of defending ourselves against some of the most violent measures that in my opinion have disgraced a body of ministers . . . and no one has come in for more of their abuse than myself."[72]

The damage to his reputation, however, was done. In 1852 he complained to Jacob Young about Granville Moody's criticism of him as "a dying prophet, . . . the greatest traitor" and other epithets. Finley wrote that these criticisms were "heaped on me and not a man called [him] to order but it seemed to me that the old men of the Conference sicked him on."[73]

Inskip's appeal to the General Conference was debated at length May 12 to 15, 1852. Inskip himself spoke for six hours to a crowded room. Nathan Bangs, who had recently retired as editor of the *Methodist Quarterly Review* and the *Christian Advocate*, moved to reverse the action of the Ohio Conference, and his motion passed 87 to 64. At the same conference, the *Discipline* was revised to permit individual churches the right to decide their own seating. Although he was not there in person, Finley had the satisfaction of learning that the General Conference upheld his point of view.[74]

Finley's involvement in the promiscuous seating controversy was characteristic of the curious combination of traditionalism and pragmatism in his personality. His arguments may have seemed consistent to him, but others saw him as pugnaciously inconsistent. There is no doubt that his reputation and effectiveness were both diminished. It must have hurt Finley when the congregation of the Finley Chapel in Dayton changed its name to the Raper Chapel in honor of their pastor, who had just died.

The Prison Years

Inskip, who had left Ohio for Troy, New York, wrote two letters of consolation, the first on March 8, 1852. He indicated that he had been looking for a letter from Finley in *Zion's Herald* and hoped he still planned to go to Boston. "You must not on any account give up the idea. You can do more for the cause of 'toleration' than all the rest of us put together." His second, on March 20, was very supportive. "We cannot but feel indignant at the manner in which many have treated you in your old age. . . . The movement at Finley Chapel in Dayton, I have no kind of doubt was designed to be used as capital hereafter. It will no doubt be brought in to show that the people are so decidedly against us that even the "Old Chief" so far suffered in their judgment, that they were unwilling to continue his name in their congregation." [75]

One of the last letters that Finley wrote in 1857 was on the subject of free pews. "I have thought and still believe that pewing churches as a general thing is contrary to the genius of the Gospel which is for every man." [76]

9

The Occasional Historian

> The white man was as frequently the aggressor as the Indian, and many were the scenes of suffering, carnage, and massacre witnessed along the border line.
> —James B. Finley

James Finley had a great interest in history and recognized its importance. He started saving documents and letters early in his career and never stopped. The thirteen hundred letters he saved during his lifetime constitute a valuable resource of early nineteenth-century religious and social history. He encouraged his colleagues to preserve records and keep journals, and he devoted much of his time and energy to writing historical accounts.

He wrote many articles, some of them in the form of letters to the editor, for periodicals such as the *Western Christian Advocate*, *Methodist Magazine*, and *Ladies Repository and Gatherings of the West*. One of his earliest was in August 1819. His last was an article defending his concept of forgiveness, which was printed in 1857, a few months before his death. Some of his articles were translated into German.

One of his longer articles was a detailed account of an 1837 camp meeting near Delaware attended by 150 Indians that was printed in the October 6 and 13 issues of the *Western Christian Advocate*. The article was typical of Finley's effusive style and occasional hyperbole. It was one of the few times when he mentioned his wife in his writing. He described the gathering for the series of services, the pitching of tents, the lighting of candles, the prayers and singing, the many who came forward to be converted. He wrote, "The shouts of salvation made the wild, uncultivated valley to ring, while the halo of heavenly inspiration sat on every tongue and was kindled to a flame in every heart." He recorded that he tried to retire at a late hour but wasn't able to do so. "My wife was so filled with the Holy Spirit that she could not contain herself, but awhile praised God in our tent, and then broke forth to join her Indian sisters in the joyful circle." Finley rhapsodized about the scene which seemed to him like "the gate of heaven."[1]

He was so interested in preserving records of the past that on December 22, 1838, he wrote a proposal for the creation of a Methodist historical society. His ideas were published in the January 11, 1839, issue of the *Western Christian Advocate*. He wrote,

generations unborn should not be wanting in the knowledge of the days in which we have lived . . . now is the only time we can ever have to transmit to the succeeding generations an account of the work of God amongst us as a church, in the close of the eighteenth and the first of the nineteenth century. I now propose through you, to form a society in your city, to be called the "Historical Society of the Methodist Episcopal Church in the Valley of the West," or some such name; and that any person contributing to the stock of information required, shall be a member.[2]

He was probably not aware that Ezekiel Cooper had proposed a plan in Baltimore in 1811 to collect materials and documents to publish a history of the Methodist Episcopal Church. Finley's suggestion resulted in the formation of the Western Historical Society in Cincinnati. He couldn't attend the first meeting, but he sent a paper to be read. The organization collected letters, diaries, journals, manuscripts, and books about early Methodism and continues at present as the United Methodist Historical Society of Ohio.

It was in his five books that Finley made his major contribution to historical literature. Indeed, these books remain valuable accounts not only of early Methodism but also of the history of the Ohio River area. His first book, *History of the Wyandott Mission in Upper Sandusky, Ohio*, was published in 1840. Although he had left the mission in 1827, he had collected materials on the Wyandots and had kept in close contact with his friends there. Several of his published articles had been about the mission and his activities. He had long wanted to write a book about the Wyandots when he had the time. As early as 1822 he expressed this desire and in a letter Joshua Soule had encouraged him and offered assistance. He was most receptive, therefore, when Charles Elliott, the editor of the *Western Christian Advocate*, who had also been a missionary in Upper Sandusky, wrote him on January 4, 1837, to say, "You owe it to the public and the God, to collect, arrange and publish a history of the Wyandotts, or something amounting to this. I have looked for this for many years, but have been most grievously disappointed. . . . Please consider the matter, and examine what is your duty."[3]

Finley must have examined the prospect immediately. He contacted a number of church leaders to get their support. He quickly decided to undertake the project and was encouraged at the response from his friends at the Book Concern. He wrote to Messrs. Wright and Swormstedt, publishers, on March 2, 1837. He told them that he was "in some afflictions from my lungs & breast" and was not certain that he would be able to continue as an effective itinerant preacher. "I shall give myself wholly to the work that has been assigned me in reference to the Indians." He promised as soon as the roads permitted it, he and his wife would proceed to the Indian country. He also mentioned the possibility of traveling west of the Mississippi in the summer or fall.

He was worried, however, about finances. "As the Committee passed a resolution to pay me my support, I would like to have some understanding on the subject." He described his financial condition in detail and concluded, "I do not think I can get along on less than . . . 200 dollars besides my quarterage. . . . But I am not in debt. I have a constant pain & throbbing of heart which distresses me much." He added a postscript to ask that Elliott keep looking for Indian books for him.[4]

The publishers sent a discouraging reply on March 11 indicating that they could not estimate what his living expenses would be. "If the matter were presented as a *business transaction*, and we had been advised by the Book Concern to contract with you for a specific amount of materials to make a book, or for the manuscript copy made ready and prepared for publication we might have been authorized to enter in negotiation." They thought that the vague resolution "that your quarterly allowance and expenses be paid" was subject to various interpretations and could result in unpleasantness. They doubted that Finley should travel west or anywhere except perhaps Canada. They thought that information on tribes other than the Wyandot could be gleaned from books. In a postscript they asked whether the agents of the Western Book Concern had the authority to apply funds toward the purchase of a manuscript.[5]

Finley fired back a letter March 18 complaining about what he concluded was a misunderstanding on the financial terms and said that he was thrown into a predicament for he had had no idea that the publishers might not comply with the Book Committee's resolution for publication because of financial reasons. He wrote that since Wright had been at the meeting "and never uttered a syllable . . . if you had made the least hint that you would not have complied with the resolution of the Committee I would have been very far from accepting of their request so I place the whole blame on your silence in reference to your *Money Doubts*." He ended the letter with the kind of criticism authors should never level at publishers. "I think there is a meanness and contemptious of expression . . . in reference to myself and to the work." He asserted that he could not "lick the ladle" and had learned that there were some men who "when they get themselves into the publish corn crib do not love company."[6]

The publishers quickly replied on March 21 to assure Finley that they didn't mean any offense and had used respectful language in their correspondence, unlike his manner and style. They explained that Wright's first news of the idea was hearing Bishop Soule's letter read to the Book Committee. "All seemed to be greatly animated with the prospect of having a book." They reminded Finley that he had said that Bishop Soule and Judge McLean had promised to assist him and that Wright himself had actually drafted the preamble and resolution the Book Committee adopted. Their questions were designed to remove or confirm their doubts on the legality of the measure taken, and they regretted that a letter of abuse was returned to them.[7]

Finley replied immediately on March 25 to continue his complaints. He said he still felt that writing the history of the Wyandots was "a herculean task" and added, "this is a work that cannot be done in a week, month or perhaps a year." As to expenses, he informed them, "Bishop Soule has offered to bear all the expense of it himself and we have made an agreement that if you do not we will go in partnership and publish it ourselves." He added, "I want perfectly understood that I will take my own time and use what means I think necessary to make the work complete." He concluded by saying that a state of suspense was always disagreeable to him and that he would like to know as soon as conveniently "whether you will sustain the expense of the work or not."[8]

In the meantime Finley had written William Walker at Upper Sandusky to seek help in preparing the manuscript. Walker replied on March 15 to agree about the magnitude of the task. He saw some difficulties, one of which was "to obtain a complete connected history of the nation thro all their various wars, revolutions, migrations and reverses of fortune . . . prior to the arrival of the French in So. Canada." He added that the history had to include reference to the early Catholic and Presbyterian missions. He thought that the Methodist Church ought not to publish the history for it was not likely to be an impartial account. He promised to throw no obstacle in Finley's way.[9]

Finley spent much of 1837 writing his history of the Wyandots and in trying to resolve the impasse with his publishers. He must have been pleased to read an announcement about his work in the August 25, 1837, issue of the *Western Christian Advocate:* "History of the Wyandot Indians—We have the pleasure of announcing to our numerous readers, that brother Finley is vigorously prosecuting his labors in this interesting field of historical research. . . . The original sources of information will be resorted to, and the reader may expect to see in the forthcoming work, the picture of things as they are."[10]

He was eventually successful in that the Ohio Annual Conference meeting in Xenia on September 27 passed a resolution "that James B. Finley be requested to continue the composition of his Indian history

[and] that the Book Committee be requested to examine said work and if in their judgment it merits a publication the conference request the book agents to negotiate for the Copyright & publish said history."[11]

With that encouragement, Finley completed the manuscript by the end of the year and sent it to his friends on the Book Committee, Charles Elliott, W.B. Christie and L.L. Hamline. On February 2, 1838, the committee wrote to inform him that his manuscript had been examined and judged "valuable and worthy" of publication. "We therefore recommend the Book Agents J.F. Wright and L. Swormstedt to negotiate with Bro. Finley for the copy-right to publish said work." The agents must have sought Bishop Soule's advice, for on February 7, 1838, he wrote them a letter in which he said that on the one hand he felt "improperly prepared" to estimate a fair compensation but on the other hand admitted that he had told the author that he would receive three hundred dollars for the manuscript plus his salary for the year in which he had written it since he had received little or nothing from the Church. He ended his rambling letter by assuring them the book would have an extensive sale but that their financial affairs had to be given consideration.[12]

Bishop Thomas Morris wrote him on February 21, 1838, to indicate that he was glad his book would appear soon. He must have pleased Finley with his remark, "why shd Western people depend wholy on the East for their reading when they have ample materials, and abilities of their own?" He congratulated Finley for all that he was doing but cautioned him about his health. "As you seem to move under high steam pressure, I fear your boiler may collapse and leave you powerless [unless] you are aware of the danger."[13]

Troubles with his publishers were not over, however. An agreement was made on February 6, 1838, but the publishers had assumed that the manuscript was ready for publication. It was not. It needed editing, division into chapters, and transcribing. No printer could have comprehended Finley's penmanship! On March 8 Charles Elliott wrote him to report that he had finished "the first course of corrections on your manuscript." He wrote that he had worked on it two hours a day for about four weeks. "I expected to have received from you more matter before this time. . . . The time from 1827 to the present has to be filled in before the history goes to the press." Material expected from another source had not arrived. He thought that the subcommittee might decide that a more extensive revision was necessary.[14]

A second agreement had to be made with the publishers on March 26, which suspended the contract and allowed Finley to withdraw the manuscript for revision and preparation for the press. He returned to rewriting.

On April 20 he wrote Wright and Swormstedt to complain. "I have spent between two & three weeks at writing and revising the manuscript of the Wyandot Mission. I have added all the original matter that I have that is worth publishing and Mr. Brook is writing some account of the year he was there." He wrote that he had talked with Elliott and they had agreed that his part was to "furnish the matter and then you were to have it prepared for the press." He added, "I have done all I can for you know that I always disclaimed being able to make a book." Later in the letter he indicated, "If you think it will add to the sale of the book . . . I will pay for the imprinting of my likeness . . . out of what I am to receive." He concluded by saying he was willing to have Elliott's name on the title page and was prepared to give him his copyright.[15]

His publishers promptly replied on April 28. They reviewed the actions that had been taken on the manuscript and indicated that when it was returned to them with the Book Committee's approval and recommendation for publication, the February 6 contract would be binding. In the meantime, since the contract had been suspended they could do nothing. Finley must have worked more on the manuscript. By early June he was able to tell a relative that it was near completion. He also learned that month from John McDonald that he had enjoyed reading a few extracts of his book in the *Advocate*.[16]

The book was well received when it was finally published in 1840. It consisted of eighteen chapters and was 432 pages in length. In the preface, Finley explained that it was his intention to use the example of the mission at Upper Sandusky to show "the divine efficiency of Christianity to civilize the heathen nations." He may have hoped that his book could serve to help the Wyandots resist the pressure on them to move west or at least to encourage the missionary cause. He assured his readers that every word could be relied on as fact. He modestly claimed that he "has not aimed at a polished style, and seeks no literary fame." He had no ambition to shine as a writer. His main ambition was to advance God's glory and religious influence.[17]

The chapters follow a chronological order and deal first with the origins of the Indians, the Wyandots, and the introduction of religion into the tribe. There follow chapters on the establishment of the Methodist mission, Finley's arrival, and events related to his work as superintendent of the mission. Chapter 11 is devoted to a description of his meetings in Washington with Monroe and Calhoun. The last chapter consists of obituaries of fifty-four Indians. Some of the material in this volume also appears in his last book, *Life Among the Indians*.

Finley was comfortable writing in an anecdotal style that gave him opportunity to record incidents of unusual conversions, travels on behalf of the mission, and examples of the difficulties he faced. In one sense, it was his best book in terms of its organization and historical accuracy. He was generous in his use of superlatives, especially in describing the success in Christianizing the Wyandots. One theme that runs thoughout the book was his criticism of the exploitation of the Native Americans by the federal government and white traders.

Finley rarely had anything good to say about traders. At one point he wrote, "The heathen party made every exertion, however, to keep up their old Indian religion, and were much encouraged to do so by the counsel of the wicked traders and venders of spiritous liquors. Many things were circulated among them unfavorable to religion, the Bible, and to ministers." Later, in the context of describing the Wyandots' hunting activities, he wrote, "I well knew that the white settlers on the frontiers had great objection to the Indian hunting and killing the game in their vicinity, and would often do them mischief."[18]

One of his criticisms of his fellow whites was that they wanted to conduct business with the Wyandots on Sundays. To Finley and other pious Methodists, that practice was a serious fault. One of the incidents he recorded dealt with a reproach given by Between-the-Logs, while on a hunting trip, to white traders who sought to sell goods on a Sunday. He pulled out his Bible and asked one of the traders to read him the Ten Commandments. Finley recorded that "the man turned pale, and did not wish to touch it; but at the urgent request of the other, read the fourth commandment." Between-the-Logs reproved the whites for trying to get them to break God's word. He ended his reproof with the words, "My white brothers, go home, and never go to trade again on the Sabbath. You will find it better with you in this world, and in the world to come."[19]

Throughout his life, Finley was subjected to many threats. He referred to these attacks in his book. He wrote, "Many hard and evil reports were raised against me; and letters were written to Mr. Calhoun, Secretary of War, stating things that were false, and every effort was made to remove me out of the way." But the attacks came exclusively from the whites. He asserted, "I do not now recollect that I was ever insulted by an Indian, drunk or sober, during all the time I was with them; nor did any of them ever manifest any unkindness toward me."[20]

Toward the end of his history he wrote, "In the course of the last year some of my enemies, who never slept, tried to arouse the Indian nation against me." The charges against him were reviewed at the Annual Conference and he was exonerated. Later, on Bishop McKendree's visit, the Wyandots who had made the accusations against him relented and admitted that their charges were untrue.[21]

Because he had been, in his own words, "most bitterly persecuted," Finley felt it necessary to include in his account of the mission, a statement signed January 31, 1826, by eleven chiefs and leaders to the effect that he had done much for the nation and had done nothing wrong, that his conduct was that "of an honest and good man . . . and, we think, he cannot be guilty of a mean thing."[22]

Toward the end of his book, Finley described Bishop McKendree's third visit to the Wyandot reservation in June 1827. A council was held at which several of the chiefs reported on the state of the mission and on the progress of religion among them. One of them declared, "Religion has done much for us in another way. It has made us more industrious. In old times our women had to do all the work: raise our corn, cut our wood, and carry it; dress our skins, make and mend our moccasins and leggins; cook our victuals, and wash our clothes. The men did nothing but hunt and drink, feast and dance. But now men have seen it was their duty not to make packhorses of their wives and children, but to work themselves. . . . We are a happier people now than we ever were."[23]

Throughout his writing Finley extolled the virtues of the wilderness in contrast to urban life. In describing Bishop McKendree's trip in 1827 from Upper Sandusky to Urbana, the author told of a night spent in the woods. "How very different the condition and appearance of this itinerant, apostolic Bishop, from those mitered heads, who enjoy all the luxuries of life, and lord it over God's heritage! His pillow was the root of a tree, his bed the sheep skin on which he rode, his curtains the friendly boughs of the spreading beech, heaven his canopy, his coffee water, corn meal, and sugar, and his meat dried and pounded venison."[24]

The *History of the Wyandott Mission* sold well throughout the 1840s. Strickland wrote Finley November 25, 1848, to report that orders continued to arrive.[25]

Finley's opposition to the government's policy became better known as a result of the book, but he was not as well known in the East as was Jeremiah Evarts, the secretary of the American Board of Commissioners for Foreign Missions. Evarts supplied forceful legal arguments in his series of essays defending the right of the Cherokees to remain in Georgia. Finley's writing about Native Americans contrasts with that of Thomas L. McKenney and Henry R. Schoolcraft. McKenney's volumes are more autobiographical with justifications for his own actions and policies. Schoolcraft's book, *The American Indians, Their History, Condition and Prospects*, first published in 1848, is a more scholarly work. Finley's account of the Wyandot mission was written while the author's memory of events in the 1820s was still very good. His last work, however, *Life Among the Indians*, was published in 1857 when he was seventy-five years old. His writing then suffered from some lapses of memory.

Finley's second book was his *Memorials of Prison Life*, published in

1850. It was edited by the Reverend B.F. Tefft. Finley must have intended to write it from the beginning of his stay in the penitentiary for he kept a journal from almost his first day of work through 1847. A friend wrote him from Ohio Wesleyan as early as April 7, 1847, to offer help. "I am gratified to learn that you are still employing your pen for useful purposes. I can take your manuscript & prepare it for the press (if you desire) without putting you to any other expense than that of copying which I suppose would be but a trifle."[26]

Finley asked John McDonald to help him with the manuscript sometime in September 1847. He had completed a draft by early 1848 and sought publishing assistance from his close friends on the Book Committee. Charles Elliott wrote him on March 8 to say that the agents thought highly of it but that with the General Conference "so near at hand they do not feel at liberty to enter into a contract for a book which could not be issued in this term." He added that he and Tefft were in favor of publication.[27]

Later Finley complained to his publisher, Leroy Swormstedt, about the quality of paper he had been sent, but Swormstedt urged him to give it a trial. Tefft, who was editing the manuscript and who thought fifty thousand copies might be sold in Ohio, wrote Finley on March 15, 1849, to recommend the addition of several pictures to increase the book's sale. That spring Finley received several letters from Henry Howe in New Haven, Connecticut, who was interested in publishing the volume. Howe indicated in a letter April 11 that he wanted Finley to keep the copyright in order to help him to market the book by sending him names of persons throughout the country who were potential buyers.[28]

Negotiations with Howe fell though, however, and Finley settled with Swormstedt and Power in Cincinnati. On May 23, 1849, the publishers offered seven hundred dollars for the copyright and manuscript. "We have concluded for once to be generous to our old friend Finley." Of that amount, two hundred dollars went to Tefft for his editing. Finley was to receive three hundred dollars in cash and one hundred dollars in books at wholesale price or in cash if he preferred. His friend, John McDonald, wrote March 20, 1850, to report that his copy had arrived and complimented Finley on his accomplishment.[29]

The book was written in the same anecdotal style as his other volumes and contains frequent references to moral and religious themes. He used a journal form of narrative for most of the book and part of the work is a mini-autobiography. His descriptions of prison life were detailed and filled with human interest stories. Although his primary interest was obviously the prisoners' souls, the book reveals a continued concern for the physical well-being of the inmates. The book also served to publicize

Finley's humane ideas on prison reform. He assumed that his readers would be interested in stories about conversion, prison morale, and the ways in which he sought to make their lives bearable.

It was probably an easy book for him to write. As he indicated in the preface, "Having formed many years ago, the habit of journalizing the principal events of my life, I found myself at my old practice soon after entering my duties in the prison." He modestly denied having any literary skill. "In point of style, I have had no ambition to shine as a writer, my chief object being so to set forth my thoughts as to be clearly and easily understood."[30]

The volume contained Finley's characteristic use of hyperbole. In commenting on the work of Colonel Dewey and Captain Bradford, the warden and deputy warden, he wrote, "Never, perhaps, in any part of the world, was there a set of officers, having the management of a prison, who possessed and manifested more of a spirit of Christian philanthropy toward their degenerate but important charge, than the officers of this institution."[31]

The book contained twenty-two chapters and 354 pages. Several digressions break the flow of the narrative. This volume contains Finley's only reference in his books to his role in the 1844 General Conference. This digression led him to write one of his favorite antislavery statements to the effect that he would rather spend his life preaching to prisoners than to die with his hands bloodstained for holding slaves or defending slavery.[32]

Another digression was contained in his journal entry for Saturday, June 6, 1846, in which he recorded his attitude toward the Mexican War.

This morning I learned that one of our number, a lad lately released, had enlisted for Mexico, instead of going home to his parents as he had promised me. The city is filled with these recruits, who are drinking and swearing, and rioting in every lane and alley, as if they were just from Pandemonium. They are a fair sample of the majority of those engaged in this unholy crusade against a helpless nation, and their masters from the highest to the lowest, have shown themselves to be just fit for the wicked work of extending, by war and bloodshed, the area of human slavery.[33]

Slavery was often criticized in the work. At one point Finley wrote, "This is that venerable, patriarchal system, which southern Christians, and southern doctors of divinity, and the professed followers and admirers of John Calvin and of John Wesley, and the disciples of the meek and lowly Jesus in the South, defend at the hazard of every thing dear on earth.... Good God! Where are the consciences, where is the common sense of these misguided men!"[34] In another digression he indicated that he thought that criminal activity might be inherited rather than the result of environment. He called this theory the "law of descent."

I have myself seen, not merely the common physical and mental characteristics of parents pass down to their children, but even an inclination, a tendency, a besetment, to certain special habits, both good and bad, to children's children, to the third and fourth generation. I have seen the inclination to steal, to murder, to intoxication, to evil under several forms, with unerring certainty thus handed down. . . . The law of descent is just as fixed, as certain, as undeviating as any in the world around us; and it is one which has much to do with every position, public or private, which a man may occupy, from the cradle to the grave.[35]

Justice Department statistics in the early 1990s indicating that more than half of all juvenile delinquents in state institutions had family members who had been in prison seemed to lend some credence to Finley's theory.[36]

Finley's efforts at prison reform brought him up against the complexities of politics. He felt that if political leaders were more religious there would be greater concern for prison conditions. He concluded that most rulers were irreligious men who thought more of party than of morality or reform. He believed that until voters began to select a better class of representatives, "the first question with philanthropists will not be how we can best take care of and reform the wretched and abandoned, but how our lawgivers themselves can be converted to God, and rendered safe for the high trusts committed to them."[37]

He recorded a visit from the minister, who at that time was missionary to the Wyandots. That event gave him the opportunity to include in his book his strong criticism of the federal government's forced removal policy. He described at length "the injustice and dishonesty of the American government" in regard to "these unfortunate and noble-hearted children of the forest." He recorded his particular displeasure that the Wyandots received only a part of what had been appraised as a fair price for their land. "Let us repent in sackcloth and ashes," he concluded.[38]

His journal entry for Tuesday, January 19, 1847, was a notation that he had asked the staff to give him statistics on the number of convicts, their crimes, places of nativity, and the level of their education. He recorded that of 445 inmates, 297 could read and write, sixty could print only, thirty-seven had learned to read in prison, and twenty-three could neither read nor write. Of the men, 189 were married and 247 were single. Three hundred ninety-seven of the total were white. Of the ninety-one commitments in 1847, twenty-one were for horse stealing, sixteen for grand larceny, seven for burglary, and the rest for arson, forgery, bigamy, counterfeiting, and mail robbery. Columbus must have been free of murders that year or at least free of persons found guilty of the crime.[39]

Finley's many generalizations and aphorisms are scattered throughout the volume so that the reader learns much about the author's view of life as well as prison discipline. Some of his most pertinent statements were:

"The great object of imprisonment is to protect community and to reform the prisoner"; "The certainty of the punishment rather than the severity has undoubtedly the greatest influence in preventing crime"; "There is something degrading in the idea of a community endeavoring to enrich itself by the labor of the poor, unfortunate convicts"; "The means of acquiring useful knowledge ought to be large and full . . . every prison should be provided with a good library." He disliked the practice of contractors employing the prisoners, who were treated as though they were "so much capital." He disliked the use of the lash in punishment. He thought that a discharged prisoner should not feel that his hold on society was "lost." He also asserted, "The reform in prison discipline should discard all party-colored garments, the lock-step, and the shaven head."[40]

Finley concluded his 1846 report to the prison directors with one of his characteristically eloquent statements: "Having lost the confidence of society and all the sympathies of mankind; disgraced by imprisonment, and degraded by crime; and feeling its guilt, with the fearful amount of distress and disgrace brought on their decent relatives; with the dark forebodings of the future; was like the gall of wormwood drinking up their spirits. And nothing in the future to hope for."[41]

Finley's *Memorials of Prison Life* was reviewed in the *Methodist Quarterly Review* for July 1850. He must have been pleased with the kind words written about his book. The reviewer indicated that while the book professed to be simply a narrative of facts, it contained much of interest on the principles of prison discipline. He commended the book to his readers and called it one in which interest "never flags from the beginning to the end." The book remained in print with new editions through the 1850s and 1860s.[42]

Finley's major work was his *Autobiography*, subtitled *Pioneer Life in the West*, edited by W.P. Strickland and published in 1853. A comparison of the 1853 edition with those portions of the manuscript in the Finley Papers reveals that Strickland's editing was limited to adding punctuation, correcting some spellings, and rearranging some paragraphs. Beginning in June 1846, Finley wrote several articles on his early life which were incorporated into his book.

His autobiography was reprinted annually for many years. A second edition was brought out in 1857, and the last edition was printed in 1904. Henry Howe called it "a valuable contribution to the knowledge of western life in the beginning of this century, and gives an experience nowhere else so well told." The book contains twenty-eight chapters and 455 pages. Twelve of the chapters are about his life and career. The remaining chapters are what he called "contemporaneous history of the times in which I lived."[43]

The chapters are not in chronological order and most of the text is anecdotal in style. The preface begins with an uncharacteristic instruction: "Don't run; I shall not be long-winded. Just hold on a moment, as I have but few words to say." He promised the reader an "unvarnished narrative of the incidents of my life."[44]

The first chapter deals with his parentage and life in the late eighteenth century. He describes his family's hazardous trip down the Ohio River to Kentucky, a journey on which his grandmother died. He praises his father's treatment of the slaves he freed when he migrated to Ohio and ends with several pages in praise of education. It is clear that his early years were spent in almost constant danger for there are many references to hostile Indians in the vicinity of his home.

The second chapter, titled "Character of the Backwoodsman," shifts from family narrative to paint a glowing picture of frontier life around 1800. He describes some of the Indian attacks on settlers and the efforts of American armies to defeat them. He provides accounts of the exploits of some of the "spies" who roamed the woods to warn settlers of Indian incursions. This part of the story is continued in chapter 3, "Life in the Backwoods," in which he describes frontier dress, the building of log cabins, and the animals found roving the forests of Ohio. The chapter ends with an idealized portrait of the early nineteenth-century frontier dweller. "A more hardy race of men and women grew up in this wilderness than has ever been produced since; with more common sense and enterprise than is common to those that sleep on bed of down, and feast on jellies and preserves; and although they had not the same advantage of obtaining learning that the present generation have, yet they had this advantage—they were sooner thrown upon the world, became acquainted with men and things and entirely dependent of their own resources for a living."[45] Later he praised the hunter in these words:

A hunter's life is one of constant excitement. He is always on the lookout, and filled with constant expectation. . . . His wants are but few. . . . His employment does not lead him to covetousness and he is always characterized by a generous hospitality. His hut or cabin is always a sure asylum for the hungry and destitute. Whoever crossed its threshold, was turned away unfed and uncared for? The poor and the stranger will feel much better in the log-cabin, partaking of its hospitality by a cheerful fire, than when surrounded by the cold constraints of a nabob's table. With these sons and daughters of nature will be found the genuine hospitalities of nature's noblemen.[46]

Although these lines may approach exaggeration, the French traveler Michaux wrote similar words in 1805 when he observed, "The inhabitants . . . do not hesitate to receive travelers who claim their hospitality."[47]

Finley's own narrative is continued in chapter 4. He began with Wayne's victory in 1794, mentioned the flood of migration into Kentucky and told about his father's purchase of land near Chillicothe. This chapter is spiced with eloquent discriptions of the Ohio forests, the diseases affecting the early settlers, and a detailed account of a law passed by the first legislature designed to curb drunkenness among the Indians.

Although Finley recognized and approved of the progress that economic development and increased population brought to Ohio over the years, he still looked with nostalgia to the days of the first settlers. At one point he asserted, "there never lived a nobler race of men on the green earth than the pioneers of this great valley." He believed that the early Ohioans deserved admiration for all the hardships they faced and privations they endured as they transmitted to posterity "the inestimable blessings of civil and religious liberty." He was certain that the pious person could not help but see "a Divine hand overruling and conducting the whole."[48]

Chapter 5, "Backwoods Biography," interrupts the narrative to give sketches of some of the Kentucky and Ohio pioneers. Most of the accounts are highly laudatory. The focus is continued in the sixth chapter, which is devoted to Indian strife near Chillicothe. Finley justified his many anecdotal excursions with these words: "I have selected the above as one of the many tragical occurrences of those days . . . as a faithful chronicler of the times in which I lived, I think it due to posterity to know through what perils their fathers passed, and what were the circumstances by which they were surrounded."[49]

He returns to his own story in chapter 7, "Life In The Woods." He describes his carefree existence at the age of twenty and his hunting activities in the solitude of the woods in very positive terms. "A generous hospitality characterized every neighbor, and what we had we divided up to the last with each other. When anyone wanted help, all were ready to aid."[50]

Finley claimed that those who lived in the woods "enjoyed life with a greater zest and were more healthy and happy than the present race." He criticizes the current fashions in clothing and popular literature and was especially caustic in referring to the "sickly sentimentalism" of some of the "yellow-covered literature" he thought was infesting the land. His attitude at the time he was writing his autobiography can be summed up in his statement, "Alone in the deep solitude of the widerness man can commune with himself and Nature and his God, and realize emotions and thoughts that the crowded city can never produce." He believed that cities were "a desert of depraved humanity" where everyone was selfish, overly ambitious and reckless in their competition and grasp for prosperity."[51]

In chapter 8 he continues his narration and focuses on religious life. He describes his early critical views of predestination and his religious doubts. At times he even questions the existence of God. He wrote, "Thus I entered fully and freely into all parties of pleasure, except gambling. . . . Dancing constituted my chief joy." He recounts his experiences at the 1801 Cane Ridge revival and ends the chapter with the account of almost killing his brother.[52]

Chapter 9 continues the story of his religious conversion. He describes the visit he and his wife took to a Methodist prayer and class meeting and how, after his second conversion, he decided to commence preaching. He recounts how, after his success in converting family members and neighbors at prayer meetings in his home, a meeting house was constructed and his conversions increased. He describes how he was asked to exhort at a quarterly meeting in Hillsboro and was sufficiently encouraged to decide upon a preaching career.

Chapter 10, "Itinerant Life," continues the narrative at the point where he decides to travel the Scioto circuit in May 1809. He includes in this chapter information about his first Annual Conference, his appointment to the Wills Creek circuit, and about some of his early preaching experiences. One anecdote about the death of a drunkard gave the author the opportunity to express again his strong temperance views. He also describes a camp meeting on the banks of the Tuscarawas River and digresses to give an account of the massacre at Gnadenhutten in 1782. He ends this chapter with the observation that his first year on the circuit was possibly the most interesting in his career.

The next two chapters supply a digression. Once recounts a story about a woman who was miraculously saved after wandering in the forest for many days. The next records details about the death of an old Indian who had been accused of witchcraft. Although these pages interrupt the flow of the narrative, they serve to provide additional information on the insecurity and instability of life in the Ohio River area in 1800.

Chapters 13 and 14 continue the account of Finley's career as a circuit rider. These pages are filled with colorful anecdotes that reveal much about his piety, persistence in the face of adversity, and flamboyant personality. In these chapters the author provides an excellent picture of what it was like to be an itinerant in the thinly settled sections of southern Ohio in his first decade of preaching. Chapter 13 also contains a description of the earthquake of 1811-12 and its influence on the willingness of frightened people to turn to religion.

Chapter 15 contains information about his work from 1813 to 1816. In the following chapter he gives details of the 1816 Annual Conference at which he was made a presiding elder and assigned to the Ohio district. He describes his responsibilities in that district, which consisted of eight circuits, and recounts how he supervised ten traveling preachers and a membership of 4,050. This chapter is rich in colorful stories. He writes about one woman who interrupted his sermon to say she wanted to exhort. He reveals how he deplored the rivalry between Methodism and Calvinism in the area. He also describes one camp meeting at which some rowdies tried to disturb the service, forcing him to throw the leader on the ground, disarm him, and turn him over to an officer.

The next three chapters again interrupt the narrative of his career. One contains descriptions of backwoods preachers, another a curious account of a missionary and a stranger who is thought to be a thief but who turns out to be a friend, and a third which is an idealized portrait of a circuit rider in the story of the life of Richmond Nolley.

Finley resumes telling about his career in chapter 20 with a description of the Annual Conferences in 1818 and 1819. He goes into detail describing the debates at the 1820 General Conference. He indicates that he thought 1820 was one of the best years of his itinerant life. He writes that Governor Cass sent a petition asking the bishops to send Finley to Detroit but that Bishop McKendree thought the Wyandot mission was more important. Because of his other publications about his years at Upper Sandusky, Finley limited the account in his *Autobiography* to five pages. What he selected to write about is revealing. He asserts that "it required great wisdom to manage affairs so as not to prejudice the Indians." He affirms that the whiskey sellers were seeking to expand their influence and opposed him constantly. He describes his efforts to form a religious society and how he explained to the Wyandots that the papers he wrote included reference to total abstinence.[53]

With chapter 21, Finley breaks the chronology and returns to an account of the great revivals of 1800-1801. He characterizes them as the most astonishing and powerful ever known in the West. His details about the Cane Ridge revival are a highlight of this chapter. Some of these pages have been extensively quoted by historians in both the nineteenth and twentieth centuries.

Chapter 22 is the last one to continue the personal narrative. Finley lists his assignments following his appointment as presiding elder of the Lebanon district where he labored for two years. He carries the narrative forward for the remainder of the 1830s. In the summer of 1842, he recalls, he was exhausted with fatigue. He was suddenly attacked with "bilious fever" and he reached home with great difficulty. He sank rapidly, and after seven nights of sickness his family expected him to die. He records that he had a vision that "a heavenly visitant" arrived to escort him to heaven. He dreamed that angels were all around him. At the end of his dream he began to shout, clapped his hands, sprang from his bed and was well again.[54]

He resumes the listing of his appointments and carried the story to 1853 when he was at the Clinton Street Church in Cincinnati. The chapter ends with a reference to the removal of the Wyandots from Ohio, although he records the year inaccurately.

The rest of the book, over sixty pages, is devoted to sketches of prominent ministers and others. A respectful description of Francis Asbury is contained in chapter 23. Finley inserted one of his typically sweeping statements: "That Providence which has ever presided over the Church perhaps was never manifested more signally, so far as Methodism in America is concerned, than in the selection, at that time, of an agent whose peculiar fitness for the work of organizing, giving direction, and imparting efficiency to the system of means already set in operation for evangelizing the continent, was so marked."[55]

Subsequent chapters contain descriptions of Bishop McKendree, David Young, Finley's brother John, and William B. Christie. The last chapter is devoted to portrayals of eminent chiefs of the Wyandot nation. In this chapter Finley reviews the history of the federal government's attempt in 1817 to extinguish Indian title to lands in Ohio.

Finley ended his autobiography with a note: "I have many reminiscences concerning the Indians which have never yet been published, and which can not be inserted in this volume. At some future day, should Providence spare my life, I may be able to give them to the public. Till then I bid my readers an affectionate adieu."[56] It was characteristic of Finley that he should have ended his *Autobiography* with a chapter containing positive information about Native Americans. He believed that they deserved fairer treatment. He was convinced that those who had been converted to Christianity were on their way to becoming upright citizens, even productive landowners. Although his books are filled with gory tales of Indian attacks on the frontier, that era, in his judgment, was behind as he labored as a missionary in the 1820s. He witnessed the detrimental effects which speculators, traders, and others were having on Native American society. In respect to the time when Indians were feared, he once wrote, "Much has been said about the barbarity of those tribes in their mode or warfare; but let it be always recollected that they were nobly engaged in the defense of their country, their families, and their natural rights, and national liberties. Never did men acquit themselves with more valor, nor, according to their means, made a better defense."[57]

It is worth noting what Finley left out of his autobiography. He made no mention of his participation in the 1844 General Conference. He mentioned his wife and daughter infrequently. Perhaps the events and persons he omitted were too important to him to put to paper.

Many of his friends were eagerly looking forward to reading his book. John Inskip, who had left Ohio for New York, wrote on January 17, 1853, to say, "I hope you and Strickland will make a good book. You must bring some on with you. No doubt some could be sold here. Put plenty of "Indians" - "coons" - "Possums" - "Cabins" - "Camp Meetings" - "Revivals" etc. etc. in it. If you can make a good selection from your great fund of anecdotes etc. you will have one of the most popular books that has emanated from the press for many years."[58]

The *Methodist Quarterly Review* praised the book in its October 1853 issue as "full of the stirring incident that characterizes every truthful record of American frontier life. It is among the many wonderful phenomena of this country's history, that the man is yet living and labouring, who was himself one of the pioneers in the colonization of the West. . . . He tells his story in a simple and straight forward style, which carries one inevitably along with the narrative."[59]

John McLean wrote the *Western Christian Advocate* to record his pleasure at reading it. A more detailed review in the March 1, 1854, issue called the work "intensely interesting." The reviewer wrote, "my attention was so completely absorbed that I scarcely ate, drank, or slept, till I devoured its contents." The reviewer in the *Quarterly Review* urged Finley to write more on his reminiscences about the Wyandots.

According to a May 1854 communication, eleven thousand copies of the *Autobiography* were printed of which 9,990 had been sold. The balance due Finley from the Book Concern at that date was $894.10. Apparently, he had hoped to make enough in royalties to help pay off a debt carried by the Clinton Street Methodist Church in Cincinnati. He spent part of his time seeking money for this church and wrote a stirring appeal in the January 30, 1856, issue of the *Western Christian Advocate* asking for funds for this building.[61]

Except for a few errors in dates, most of the events chronicled in the book were fairly accurate. The book also contains information on some church leaders not found elsewhere. Finley's habit of keeping a journal and preserving so many of the letters he received paid off. The volume has two major flaws. His overpraising at times led to exaggeration. His nostalgia for the frontier days tended to make him gloss over the meanness and hazards of life in the early 1800s.

The most scathing criticism of the book and of Finley's philosophy was made in 1957, a century after his death, by Arthur K. Moore. Moore's book, *The Frontier Mind: a Cultural Analysis of the Kentucky Frontiersman*, pictured Finley's "chronological primitivism" as being "magnificently absurd." Moore equated Finley's glorification of the frontiersman with a return to the mindset of the Stoics and eighteenth-century naturalists, and he faulted him for his criticism of 1850 industrialized society. Finley's view of nature and of progress, however, seems closer to a Christianized transcendentalism, if one may use such a term.[62]

Finley's fourth book was his *Sketches of Western Methodism: Biographical, Historical, and Miscellaneous, Illustrative of Pioneer Life*, printed in 1854. It was a work he had long wanted to write and for which he had long been collecting materials. Back on November 29, 1844, in a postscript on a letter to Charles Elliott, he wrote, "I have commenced my book as you advised me and having put my hand to the plow I do not mean to look back and hope to gather some things which would have been lost. I want to get an account of many of the old preachers." He indicated that some of them had sent him material and asked Elliott to put a notice in his paper requesting preachers to send him a few sheets. He wrote that he wanted to hear from Burke, Lakin, Quinn, Collins and Jacob Young. (He also offered Elliott twelve and a half cents for the skeleton of his steam boat sermon.)[63]

Sketches of Western Methodism reflected Finley's concern with preserving the early religious history of the area in which he lived and worked. In forty-five chapters and 551 pages he recorded the lives and careers of over thirty Methodist pioneering itinerant preachers and recounted noteworthy incidents from the late eighteenth and early nineteenth centuries. The book was edited by W.P. Strickland. It was reprinted in 1857 and reissued in 1969.

In his preface Finley expresses regrets that much of the history of early Methodism had already been lost and writes, "the waves of oblivion were rapidly washing out the few traces that remained." He felt strongly that more records should be published of the early history of western Methodism. He adds that he had extracted promises from a number of colleagues to record what they remembered of the past.[64]

In his first chapter he describes the first years of Methodism in this country in terms of "heroic deeds." He emphasizes the fact that the first generation of ministers faced much hardship as they traveled through the western forests.

The second and third chapters record the autobiography of William Burke, described by Finley as "the oldest pioneering preacher now living in the west." Burke's autobiography recounts his own career as well as that of others and also confirms Finley's assertion that the itinerants faced heavy challenges. "The pioneers . . . suffered many privations, and underwent much toil and labor, preaching in forts and cabins, sleeping on straw, bear and buffalo skins, living on bear meat, venison, wild turkeys, traveling over mountains and through solitary villages, and, sometimes, lying on the cold ground, receiving but a scanty report, barely enough to keep soul and body together, with course home-made apparel."[65]

Burke was one of the ministers at the Cane Ridge revival. He asserted that when he preached on Sunday morning ten thousand people assembled to hear him. Later he estimated total attendance at twenty thousand.[66]

Burke also provided statistics on the number of circuits and church members for each year during the first decade of the nineteenth century. He listed 1798 as the first year in which itinerancy was introduced north of the Ohio River and declared that in fifty-six years Methodist membership increased from 99 to 150,000 in Ohio.[67]

Chapter 4 focuses on the career of Michael Ellis, one of the first inhabitants of Maryland to be converted to Methodism. He started preaching in 1784. Finley comments on the prejudice against married ministers at that time and argues that they deserve ample support and should not have to worry about their family's poverty. In commenting on the Methodist system of rotation in assignment every two years, Finley writes, "Every minister should study the character of his hearers." His approach to preparing for a sermon discounted the value of extensive reading and study. Instead, he favored, "prayer and close, laborious thought." Ministers should study a subject out "in all its connections and bearings," and then go into their pulpits "pouring out the garnered truths with their full hearts." In 1813 Finley and Ellis were both appointed to the Barnesville circuit, so the author's description of the other's personality is based partly on close personal knowledge.[68]

Finley closes this chapter with one of his praises for the frontier settler, with whom he identified during his lifetime. "The inhabitants, like all backwoods people in those days, lived by the chase, yet we have often seen in their rude log-cabins as powerful exhibitions of the power of Christianity as ever we witnessed in the more refined circles of society."[69]

Chapter 5 deals with the origins of Methodism in Cincinnati. His description of Collins's preaching is partly based on an interview with one of the members of his original congregation. Finley praised the structure and intent of the class system in the course of his description of the first regular church. "This mutual interest in the spiritual welfare of each member of the church was what constituted the true secret of the early character of Methodism; and the great success which marked its progress in every country where it has been established, is to be attributed more to the recognition of this wholesome, social regulation than to any other peculiarity of doctrine or church government."[70]

Finley's mention of the many Methodist Church buildings in Cincinnati includes one in the Methodist Church South. His comment ten years after the fateful division in which he played such a significant role seems mild and nonjudgmental: "God forbid that the time should ever come when we shall be so cramped by a headless and heartless bigotry, destitute alike of thought and feeling, that we can see no good beyond our narrow domicile, and have no emotions of brotherly kindness for those of another fold."[71]

Chapter 7 describes Barnabas McHenry, who was one of the first preachers in the West. In this chapter Finley comments on the prejudice people in the 1800s displayed toward Methodist preachers, who, he maintained, were "a special object of ridicule. Every conceivable method was resorted to for the purpose of caricaturing the preachers and their doctrines. Songs were written and sung, while specimens of Methodist sermons, perverted and distorted, were published broadcast, to bring odium upon the society."[72]

This chapter contains one of Finley's criticisms of what he considered "overly-educated ministers": "The preachers of those days did not suffer themselves to be carried away into the endless mazes of metaphysical speculation, or to be lost in the fogs of an occult philosophy; but bathing their vision in the eternal sunshine of God's truth, they came down, like Moses from the burning mountain, full of love and radiant glory."[73]

Chapter 10 addresses the career of Benjamin Lakin, who was born in Maryland but grew up in Kentucky. In listing the places where Lakin preached Finley omitted mention of his 1810 two-week journey to northwest Ohio to preach to blacks and Native Americans. Of a circuit rider's life, Finley writes, "Each step of such a mission was connected with danger and toil." He added that a change had occurred in the ministry and in society so that he believed that ministers in the 1850s did not feel the same degree of responsibility that the men did in 1800. He regretted the fact that men seemed to enter the ministry at the time he was writing "with no great anxiety or interest than they would enter upon any learned or business profession for the purpose of honor and emolument." He also regretted that so much emphasis was being placed on "mere literary training and scholastic attainments." He objected to exalting learning at the expense of zeal and wisdom.[74]

He describes Lakin's itinerant career, which began in 1794. After mentioning Lakin's marriage, Finley criticizes again the Church's view of married itinerants. He writes, "It was almost out of the question for any man to continue in the work if he had a wife." The fact that he himself did so he did not mention. He deplored the fact that no provision was really made for a wife and that she was generally considered "an incumbrance." He adds however, "only one or two had courage and endurance enough to travel when married."[75] Finley became acquainted with Lakin when the latter was on the Scioto and Miami circuit in 1802. He describes him as one of the ministers who "guided the Church through that most remarkable revival of religion, which swept like a tornado over the western world."[76]

Chapter 11 is devoted to John Sale, who played an important part in Finley's career. Sale was born in 1769 and was converted in his youth, a typical occurrence. When he became a Methodist minister he was subjected to much criticism. According to Finley, "To become a Methodist at that time . . . was to enter upon a profession which would ensure the contempt and scorn of the ungodly, and, of many professors of another faith." Finley digresses in this chapter to write about himself. He records that in 1809 Sale employed him to travel four months on the circuit before he was licensed.[77]

The subject of chapter 13 is Samuel Parker. Finley describes a huge religious service which he and Parker held in Cincinnati in 1813, a service with a congregation so large it was held on "Lower Market-Street, between Sycamore and Broadway." Many were converted. He also writes about what he called "one of the most powerful camp meetings" ever held on Deer Creek that same year. Thousands attended, including the author and his father.[78]

Chapter 14 is about Learner Blackman. The author points out that the first Methodist preachers paid particular attention to doctrinal preaching. "In all their sermons the distinctive doctrines of methodism occupied the chief place. Repentance, faith, justification, the possibility of falling from grace, with the doctrine of the atonement as contra-distinguished from the Calvinian view, and occasional brushes of Church polity and ordinances as held by other denominations, formed the staples of the sermons of those early preachers. But not only was Calvinism attacked; Arianism, Universalism, and other forms of error were made to feel the lash of those sturdy pioneers of the faith of Wesley." Then he adds that the next generation of preachers lost sight of polemic theology and became enamored with oratory and interlarded their sermons with poetry. "Nicely-rounded periods, beauty of expression, and the fine rhetorical flourishes, were regarded as of more importance than orthodoxy itself." That phase was followed by more attention to didactic preaching. As for the style in the 1850s, Finley asserted that the Methodist pulpit contained more learning but not necessarily as much zeal, devotion and wisdom as in the former days.[79]

Chapter 15 tells a story about a lost child and a sixteen-day search for her in the forest by a large body of men. Subsequent chapters deal with the careers of James Axley, Joseph Oglesby, William Beauchamp, Governor Edward Tiffin, and John A. Grenade.

Chapter 21 is on the Western Book Concern, which was created in 1820 as a branch of the body originally founded in 1789. Finley praises its head, Martin Ruter, who later became president of Allegheny College. In 1836 the concern was authorized to publish books. The second one published was Finley's *History of the Wyandott Mission*. He listed the titles of the other works.

John Collins is the subject of chapter 22. Finley began the chapter with a description of his first meeting with Collins, who in 1803 settled on the East Fork of the Little Miami River. His horse strayed away and arrived at Finley's cabin thirty miles away. When Collins came to claim his horse, he invited Finley to his service in Hillsboro and prayed with him before leaving. The author wrote, "Our heart was strangely and wonderfully drawn toward him, and we were won by his sweetness and gentleness." It was Collins who converted John McLean and his brother, Nathaniel, in Lebanon in 1811.[80]

Chapter 24 is titled "The Conversion of a Family" and is a seven-page account of the conversion in Bowling Green of a prominent man and his entire family following one of Finley's sermons. Finley recounts how the man apologized to the community for his earlier lack of religion and precipitated a revival. In this chapter Finley castigates the theater, opera, and dancing salon as centers of vice.

Chapter 25 is on John Crane. In connection with an account of this man's career, Finley asserts that circuit riders, or "swaddlers," in the West were "despised by black-gowned and white-cravated clergymen, with the lore of a theological seminary in their brains, and the powder and perfume of the toilet on their hair."[81]

William Young's career is described in chapter 26. Although Finley tended to praise everyone he mentioned, one of his few negative comments was about Young. "Though not a very pleasant speaker, or agreeable in his manner in the pulpit, he was, nevertheless, a burning and a shining light."[82]

Finley changed the pace in chapter 27, titled "The Conversion of an Infidel." He recounted an experience when he was on the Cross Creek circuit in 1814. There was a "Mr. P.," member of the state legislature who, according to Finley, belonged to the French school of infidelity and renounced all religion. This man had a charming daughter who one day went to a Methodist service. She returned to another against her mother's instructions and was converted. Her father learned of it, came home, "whipped her out of the gate" and banished her. She walked through the town and was taken in by a neighbor. The father relented after a tortuous night, sent for the daughter, welcomed her back, and then he and his wife were converted too.[83]

"The Conversion of a Cruel Master" is an eight-page account of a Virginia plantation on which a black became an eloquent exhorter after being converted. When the kindly master of the plantation died, Cuff was given to the son, who squandered his wealth and who eventually had to sell his slave. Cuff's new owner was an infidel who whipped him for praying. That night he felt remorse and regretted what he had done. The next day he called for Cuff and asked him to pray for him. The cruel master was converted and freed his slave. This story ends with the statement that the master himself even became a successful minister.[84]

Marcus Lindsey is the subject of chapter 30. Lindsey converted John Stewart in Marietta. Finley describes Stewart's conversion in detail and his subsequent travels to preach to the Delaware and Wyandot tribes.

The following chapter is about the conversion of a German settler. There follow accounts of the careers of John Strange and William P. Finley, Robert's third son, who was born in 1785. James was instrumental in his brother's conversion. It is in this chapter that the author tells of his father's loss of several tracts of land to unscrupulous speculators when he moved to Kentucky. After describing some of the circuits on which his brother, William, preached Finley gives an account of the accident in which William's skull was fractured. According to the author, eventually his brother's mind gave way and he died after an operation. Finley describes his brother's preaching as "nothing very brilliant or showy."[85]

Russell Bigelow is the subject of chapter 34. He is described as "gifted, devoted, and zealous." He started preaching at the age of twenty-three. One of his assignments was to the mission at Upper Sandusky, but Finley thought he was not suited for that work. In 1833 he was stationed in Columbus for two years but had to stop preaching because of poor health. He became chaplain of the Ohio Penitentiary. Finley wrote, "He entered upon his labors . . . with a zeal and devotion characteristic of his truly benevolent heart. He visited every cell, and conversed with every prisoner. . . . Many an obdurate and sin-steeled conscience was touched by the eloquence of his tears and entreaties to win them from the wages of sin. . . . Under these labors he broke down, and before the year had expired it was necessary for him to resign his post."[86]

Bigelow became very depressed. The fact that he had seven children to support probably contributed to his low spirits. He visited with Finley, whose son-in-law, J.C. Brooke, gave him all the cash he had. Bigelow returned shortly and threw his horse collar and harness into the yard. Apparently it was all he had "to leave as a memento." He went home to die after working incessantly for twenty years.[87]

Henry B. Bascom is the subject of chapter 36. Finley praises him highly. He writes that Bascom "rose above all sectional views, soared beyond all sectional lines, and embraced his entire country in the arms of his benevolence." Finley claims that Bascom had a remarkable youth. He began preaching in 1812 having been recommended by Finley's father. Later he was a professor of moral science at Augusta College. The author called him a "pulpit orator" and asserted that oratory was a gift of nature, "not the product of education." In an aside, Finley recorded, "We once kneeled down on the verge of an overhanging cliff, and turned our ear to take in the full thunder of Niagara, as it rolled, a hundred feet below us, its everlasting bass, and such a sense of the majesty and power of God possessed us, as we were never conscious of before. We rose from our knees and shouted, 'God' " [88] Finley was full of admiration for Bascom's preaching talents and writes at length about his eloquence in the pulpit. He asserts that "for sublimity and grandeur" Bascom was without a rival. Finley inserted another comment on "the knowledge and eloquence which is to be derived from the study of nature." He writes, "In this age when books and colleges are flooding the land, it would be well for us to call ourselves back a little to the study of nature." He repeats his criticism of theological education for ministers. "We have absolutely been sickened at the stereotype process by which preachers have been made in our colleges. They are the merest casts from some model teacher, and every thing about them is an imitation. . . . Nature is smothered to death, and buried beyond the hope of a resurrection. And yet we would not eschew books nor colleges. God forbid! We want them all, but we want natural men, whose flash and thunder in the pulpit come from the Bible and the great battery of nature." [89]

In his account of Samuel Hamilton in chapter 36, Finley pictures Hamilton's conversion at a camp meeting in 1812 when he was twenty-one. Finley was preaching and stayed with the young man while he went through an anguishing conversion experience in the woods. This chapter also contains statistics on the state of religion in Washington County.

The succeeding chapters have records of William H. Raper, John Ulin, and William Phillips. Chapter 40 is titled "The Intrepid Missionary" and is about the career of Daniel Poe. Finley begins this chapter with one of his characteristicly sweeping statements. "The Methodist Church has furnished missionaries, who for zeal and courage, in planting the standard of the cross on the battlements of heathendom, have not been excelled by any other denomination." [90]

Chapter 41 is about Thomas Drummond. In reviewing his career Finley generalizes about ministerial achievement. "Some preachers at first give but little promise, and develop slowly, yet in the end become learned, talented, and useful. . . . Others at once seem to flash over the horizon of life as the sun when he crosses the threshold of the ocean." Perhaps he was thinking of his own career.[91]

The following chapter contains an account of a camp meeting for the Indians that Finley held in 1828, a narrative he had published earlier as an article. The next one is about another Indian camp meeting at which a general was converted.

Chapter 44 is about pioneering women. In recording some of their achievements Finley declared that their "zeal, courage, and self-sacrificing devotion [were greater than] the heroism of the patriot mothers of olden time." He related an account of two women in Georgia who were instrumental in converting many backwoodsmen. Finley extrolls their accomplishment and ridicules the criticism of those who objected to women speaking in public. He writes, "God's ways are not our ways. . . . He has chosen the weak things of the world to confound the mighty . . . selected these two females as the chosen instruments of mercy and salvation to that dark and destitute region."[92]

The last chapter is on the Indian chief, Rhon-Yan-Ness. At his death he was the oldest Wyandot chief and he had been one of the first to be converted to Methodism. After telling about Rhon-Yan-Ness's life, Finley concludes the chapter with one of his criticisms of the federal government. "The Indians have been cruelly treated, and it is high time the Government should interpose more effectually its authority in their behalf. How much we owe them as a nation none can tell; but it is high time that some move was made to repay the debt."[93]

What has impressed many readers of the book was Finley's ability to portray the Indian warfare of the late 1790s and to convey so accurately a sense of frontier living. Although not all the praise he gave the preachers in his book may have been deserved, his accounts of their careers supplied valuable information about Methodism in the old West at a crucial time in its development. His editor, W.P. Strickland, added some of the biographical sketches written by other ministers. Some of the chapters containing digressive anecdotes might have been omitted to strengthen the volume. Even so, the work was a major achievement for Finley at that time of his life. No other nineteenth-century writer left as extensive and detailed an account of the religious life of the early Ohio pioneers as did Finley.

His book, *Life Among The Indians; or, Personal Reminiscences and Historical Incidents Illustrative of Indian Life and Character*, was his last and was published in 1857. It was edited by Davis W. Clark. The price was one dollar. In the preface Finley maintains that he had been acquainted with Indians for almost seventy years. He also claims that no one else had seen and known more about them in the old Northwest than he, perhaps another Finley exaggeration.

He declares that what he writes is not a matter of theory but of first-hand knowledge. "I have been among them, hunted and fished with them, ate and lodged in their wigwams." He calls the area of Kentucky, Ohio, Indiana, and Michigan "the greatest battlefields between barbarism and civilization in the west," and declares "there is scarcely a spot celebrated in Indian warfare that I have not visited again and again." He acknowledges a debt to Drake, Schoolcraft, and others in preparing his manuscript.[94]

The book consists of twenty chapters and 548 pages. Although most of the volume focuses on American Indian history, several key pages are devoted to autobiographical information. He begins the first chapter by recounting his migration into Ohio in 1796. He tells about his father preaching to two congregations in Kentucky, freeing his slaves, and incurring the ill-will of his neighbors for doing so. He denounces the "unprincipled" speculators who defrauded many of the early settlers. He mentions the negotiations his father had with Nathaniel Massie to purchase lands in Ohio for his two congregations.

The bulk of this chapter is devoted to accounts of Indian attacks on the Massie settlement and on his explorations into the wilderness. Finley includes his account of the incident in 1795 when a party of sixty whites, including his father, encountered and fought a group of unfriendly Shawnees and Senecas near Paint Creek. According to Finley, the Indians had refused to agree to the Treaty of Greenville. According to Wayne's account, however, the clash occurred before the treaty was signed. The second attempt at settlement was made the following year when forty moved into the area near Chillicothe. Finley described the region in great and glowing detail.

The second chapter contains accounts of Indian warfare in the period from 1760 to 1794, most of which occurred near Chillicothe. He includes vivid accounts of Daniel Boone's exploits including his captivity in that area in 1776.

The third chapter focuses on Indian cruelties. It seems strange that a person of Finley's forward-looking views on Native Americans should have filled so many pages with gory accounts of Indian depredations. His pages, however, are about conflicts in the eighteenth century and appear to be factual ones that he, as a historian, felt obliged to report. He begins this chapter with reference to the butchery of the Moravian Indians by whites in 1782, an account that serves to remind his readers that not all the plunder and violence were by the Indians. As he indicates "these acts of savage cruelty were not all on the side of the Indians. Indeed, had the acts of the pioneers toward the Indians always been characterized by kind treatment and fair dealing, it is doubtful whether the savage cruelties inflicted on them would have occurred." The account of the murder of the Moravian Indians is followed by a description of the attack in June 1782 on Colonel Crawford near Upper Sandusky. Crawford's torture and death are pictured in great detail. The next account is of an Indian raid on a family at Cooper's Run in April 1787. Several others follow.[95]

Chapter 4 contains a survey of the Native American tribes that lived in the Northwest Territory. He assured his readers that the Wyandots were "always a humane and hospitable nation." Their humane treatment of their prisoners was another evidence of their humanity, in his opinion. He included the history of the Five Nations. The chapter ends with a list of the amounts appropriated in 1857 to the various Indian tribes, a sum totaling $2,350,385.[96]

Chapter 5 deals with the siege of Detroit in 1763 and the death of Pontiac. The account is a modification of the record found in B.B. Thatcher's *Indian Biography*. Chapter 6 summarizes the capture of Mackinaw as recorded by a Mr. Henry, whose travels were published in 1809. Henry was captured and almost killed. Chapter 7 is about Tecumseh and his war. According to Finley, Tecumseh "was the soul and leader of the last great effort of barbarism, to check the swelling tide of civilization in the west." In following Tecumseh's exploits, Finley concluded, "It must be admitted that the Indians had too many just issues for complaint . . . they were often subjected to indignities and wrongs." Chapter 8 records the death of Tecumseh in 1813. In this account, Finley borrowed heavily from Drake's *Life of Tecumseh*.[97]

Chapter 9 is devoted to the activities of his old colleague, John Stewart. The author claims that by 1815 the Wyandots, as a result of their drunkenness, lewdness, and gambling, had become "the most degraded and worthless of their race." He summarizes Stewart's early life, conversion, and first efforts to preach to the Wyandots. The chapter ends with a long letter Stewart wrote to the Indians after he left them in which he encouraged them to continue to follow his religious teachings.[98]

The next chapter deals with Stewart's return to the mission and his service there before he was licensed to preach. At this point the narrative becomes autobiographical. Finley writes about his own appointment at the 1819 Annual Conference to the Lebanon district, which extended into Michigan and which included the Wyandot mission. He reviews his eight years of close contact with the mission. The author goes into great detail about the first quarterly meeting held at the mission and the first service at which he preached with the aid of an interpreter. Sixty Indians and three hundred whites from nearby settlements attended. The account includes quotations from some of the Wyandots who spoke at the meeting. Either Finley recorded them at the time or he had a prodigious memory. After giving additional details about his work with the Wyandots Finley emphasized the main point of his book:

This was the first Indian mission under the care of the Methodist Episcopal Church, and the beginning of a saving work of God on the hearts of the aboriginals of our country, in the Mississippi Valley. The doctrine always taught, and the principle acted upon, were, that they must first be civilized before they can be Christianized. Hence the Government and individual societies labored to civilize them, by teaching them the art of farming. But the labor was in vain. A man must be Christianized, or he can never be civilized. He will always be a savage till the grace of God makes his heart better, and then he will soon become civil and a good citizen.[99]

Finley goes into considerable detail about his work at the mission and repeats some of the events about which he had already written. Chapter 12 contains an account of his travels to neighboring tribes and records some of his sermons to convince them that Christianity was the true faith. He also wrote about his difficulties enforcing the *Discipline*. Chapter 13 includes a story of Bishop McKendree's visit to the mission, a description of the mission school, and one of John Johnston's letters commending the mission. The book's second theme is advanced at this point in that Finley asserts, "White men have done more to prevent the conversion of the Indian nations than all their habits, or ignorance, or prejudice have done."[100] Throughout this part of the book, Finley's portrait of the Indian was extremely laudatory. As he put it, "We found in the Indian character a great sense of independence, and a strong opposition to any thing that looked like slavery or subjection. They glory in their native liberty; and for a person to show any thing like a feeling of superiority, was the most effectual way to bar all access to them. . . . They seldom use corporeal punishment, believing it to be too great a degradation."[101]

In chapter 14 Finley describes his trip to the Ottawas and Chippewas, the discouragement he received from Governor Cass in regard to his plan for a mission, and the offer from him of two thousand dollars to aid the Indians in their agricultural activities. This chapter contains a eulogy to John Stewart, who died of consumption in 1823. It also contains an account of Finley's preaching in Detroit in late December 1823. He writes that the day following his sermon "all business was suspended." He went from house to house and even visited the army barracks to seek converts.[102]

Chapter 15 continues the record of activities at the Wyandot mission including a winter hunt. Finley recounts the actions of traders and the subagent who plotted against him and describes the three-day trial after which he was exonerated. He recalls that he had never been insulted by an Indian nor was any unkindness ever displayed against him. "I do not believe that there are a people on the earth, that are more capable of appreciating a friend, or a kind act toward them or theirs, than Indians. Better neighbors, and a more honest people, I have never lived among.

They are peculiarly so to the stranger, or to the sick or distressed. They will divide the last mouthful, and give almost the last comfort they have, to relieve the suffering." [103]

Finley fought against the revival of Indian dances when three or four were held each week. He would ask his Christian Indians where they would rather die, at a dance or a prayer meeting. Since "prayer meeting" was always the answer, he seldom failed to get his flock to conform. He declared, "There are no people that appreciate kindness more than the Indians; and the man that expects to do any thing with an Indian, must do it by kindness." In this chapter the author describes his trip to Washington to see Monroe and Calhoun and secure a grant to build the mission church. [104]

Chapter 16 is concerned with the visit of bishops McKendree and Soule to the mission in 1824. The story, however, takes a different tack in the next chapter, which deals with the federal government's proposal to move the Wyandots west of the Mississippi River. Finley explains that there were two things required to promote the Indian's civilization. One was the establishment of a permanent school; the other was the division of land so that individuals might have ownership and be motivated to improve their property. His opposition to removal was based on five reasons. First, "As a conquered, subdued enemy, who were once a strong and powerful nation . . . they have strong claim on our generosity." Second, ever since the Treaty of Greenville, the Wyandots had been friends of the government. Third, in battle "they were more merciful than their neighbors." Fourth, their prospects for becoming fully civilized were promising; the act of removal was cruel. Fifth, the government had made promises that should not be broken. [105]

Chapter 18 contains an account of Finley's trip east with two Wyandot chiefs for a series of fund-raising meetings. Their visit drew large crowds in Eastern cities and the tour was a great success. He also describes in this chapter the arrangements made to place twelve of the most promising Indian boys with white families for a short time to improve their education.

In chapter 19 Finley describes the division of the Wyandot lands into 160-acre plots to encourage productivity and frugality. The experiment in capitalism apparently worked well. Houses were built, livestock increased, and many improvements were made. He also mentions his efforts to get the Wyandots to operate a store for their own economic benefit.

The last chapter consists of eleven biographical sketches of famous Indians not published elsewhere. The brief paragraphs serve to emphasize the differences among Native Americans and, in that respect, to partially correct some of the stereotypes held by whites in the 1850s. On the whole, the portrayals are sympathetic. Finley ended his book with a final criticism of federal policy and the land hunger of Americans. This final condemnation could have been strengthened had Finley added the actual details of the Wyandot's move from Upper Sandusky and had he included the financial figures on their situation.

Life Among The Indians contained more accurate early history of Native Americans than Finley's first book. At times the volume is marred by his tendency to treat everyone in highly idealistic terms. The *Western Christian Advocate* gave the book favorable attention twice in its April 29 and May 20, 1857, issues and a review was in the May 6 issue. The reviewer noted that the portrait of Finley in the book was one from 1824 and that he looked different in 1857. A great sale for the book was predicted.

The review in the *Christian Advocate and Journal* called it "invaluable for its data respecting our early Indian missions" and said it would have a popular run. *Zion's Herald* called the book "of real intrinsic merit, valuable as history." The most detailed evaluation was printed in the *Methodist Quarterly Review* in July 1857. The reviewer was particularly impressed with the biographies of Indian leaders and the author's ability to provide a powerful contrast between "Pagan savagism and Christian civilization."[106]

Finley's book did not deal in detail with tribes in the far West as did George Catlin's two-volume work, *Letters and Notes on the Manners, Customs, and Conditions of the North American Indians*, also published in 1857. Catlin, who had visited forty-eight tribes, wrote a very sympathetic account of Indian life and conditions. Unlike Finley, he changed his mind about federal removal policy and condemned it by the 1850s.[107]

Finley had remarkable success getting his work published. A number of chapters from his books first appeared as articles in periodicals. He must have been disappointed, however, that the sermon he submitted to two of his colleagues in 1846 was not accepted for publication in their volume of notable Methodist sermons.

Finley was no Prescott or Parkman; he lacked the objectivity of a trained historian, but he based most of what he wrote on original sources and had a remarkable way with words. His writing reveals much about his generation's religious zeal and the difficulties faced by people who experienced extensive change as their wilderness disappeared and towns and cities expanded around them.

10

The Last Years

> I would rather die than be a fruitless preacher.
> —James B. Finley

Finley's last years were spent in Eaton, the site of Fort St. Clair, which is about as far west as one can go and still remain in Ohio. He still traveled and preached and, on occasion, raised money for special causes, but his circuit riding habits were far behind him. He took pleasure in seeing his eleven grandchildren and six great grandchildren. His wife was still living as was his daughter and her husband, John C. Brooke, a fellow Methodist minister. The evils of slavery and drinking continued to get his attention, but the fires were ebbing, the pace was slowing.

Following his replacement as chaplain of the Ohio Penitentiary in July 1849 his health continued to be poor and he was superannuated on September 19th that year at the Ohio Annual Conference. He had recovered sufficiently by the next fall that he was assigned to Yellow Springs. He participated in the dedication of the new Methodist church in Chillicothe on September 8, 1850.

He had to retire again because of health at the 1851 Ohio Annual Conference, against his wishes. He left the conference early and wrote Bishop Thomas Morris to ask about his appointment because he wanted to remain active. Bishop Morris wrote him on September 30 to give him the details. He explained that originally the council had tried to form a small district for him near his home, but it had not worked out. He wrote, "As the last resort I enquired whether we could not give you Dayton Dist. as it is; but there were difficulties." Morris listed Finley's health and the fact that Elliott, who had been there only one year, was expected to return. He assured Finley, "But you must not infer from the conclusion that the brethren were indifferent to your case. Br. Elliott offered to take a circuit for your accommodation if necessary. Bro Young also felt much for his old friend and former colleague, and all appeared well disposed to you, but judged your request could not be granted consistently with the good of the whole work." He continued to explain that if he had been able to solve the problem he would have done so, but no solution was practicable. He added, "I doubt not it is a sore trial to be compelled by family affliction, as you are, to restrict oneself to a corner of the Conf. and to give up the general work in which you have been so long engaged." He then wrote a postscript, "When your name was called, Br Grover asked for you a Superannuated relation, which the Conf. readily & cheerfully granted."[1]

Although this action allowed him to improve his health and devote time to writing, he was back in action the following September. From 1852 to 1855 he served the Clinton Street Methodist Church in Cincinnati, which was later named the Finley Chapel. After two years of building up the congregation he became superannuated again but served part time raising funds to pay off the church debt. His last appointment in 1856 was as conference missionary.

When he resigned from the board of trustees at Ohio Wesleyan University in 1852 he was still upset over the abuse he had received over his support of "promiscuous seating" in churches. A friend there assured him that he was still "beloved & valued as ever. . . . Your name will go down to posterity as that of one of Ohio's favorite sons & one of Methodism's strongest & most honored champions."[2]

He continued to supply his favorite newspaper with long articles. The *Western Christian Advocate* for August 10, 1853, carried a piece titled "Car Traveling," which contained descriptions of incidents he witnessed while riding from Cincinnati to Eaton. Part of it was personal. "I have been a half invalid for some months past. . . . I found all well at home, and had the pleasure to sit down in my own house, where there were four generations of us. I am mending up again. I have nothing to complain of. I have enjoyed my share of the blessings of a gracious Providence for seventy-two years, and I look forward constantly for the end of my journey with an unshaken confidence in the God I have tried to serve, and the Gospel I have preached to others."[3]

On Sunday, September 26, 1853, he returned to Hillsboro to attend the dedication of the new Methodist church. It was a joyful time of reunion, for Charles Elliott and W.P. Strickland were there as was Governor Trimble to hear his son, Joseph, preach the sermon.[4]

Finley still became involved in controversial disputes. He was the prosecutor in the charges of immoral conduct against L.D. Harlan, who had claimed that Bishop Hamline had seduced a woman. Finley wrote six specifications in his charges against Harlan, who was accused of circulating slanderous and false reports about the bishop who, he claimed, was insane as well as immoral. The trial before a committee of ministers took place in October 1854. Harlan wrote a ninety-page defense of his conduct.

In his defense he declared, "I am fully persuaded, sir, that in my arrest, Mr. Finley was actuated by an intemperate, misguided and maddened zeal." He called Finley's efforts to malign his character "folly, not to say madness" and claimed that he was determined to support the interests of Hamline. At one point in his trial he said, "I desire you to bear in mind that I have been arrested by an aged minister in our itinerant ranks, now sustaining a superannuated relation to the Cincinnati Conference of the Methodist Episcopal Church. Allusion has already been made to the fact Mr. Finley has served his generation, and must soon be gathered in the land of his fathers. He is now, from the infirmities of age, unable to render effective service in the work of the ministry."[5] Finley, in response, explained to the committee hearing the case that he had no personal dislike of the accused. The committee ruled that Harlan was not guilty of immoral conduct but was guilty of imprudence. He appealed the decision to the 1856 General Conference, and the conference on May 9 voted to affirm the decision of the Cincinnati Annual Conference.[6]

Finley engaged in another dispute in 1857 over his concept of forgiveness, which produced hard feelings. He wrote an article published in the March 4, 1857, issue of the *Western Christian Advocate* in which he maintained that God did not require one to forgive someone who had injured him until the person repented. "Not one word is said about forgiveness without repentance," he asserted. William H. Sutherland disagreed with him in a long article in the April 1 issue. Sutherland cited many Biblical references and declared, "It is a duty to forgive everyone that is indebted to us, under pain of the Divine condemnation . . . for an unforgiving spirit cannot possibly be a happy one."

Finley responded May 6 with an attack on Sutherland and must have thought he had the last word when he wrote that he could not conceive of forgiveness without repentance. Sutherland responded in the May 20 issue and expressed regret that Finley had assailed him. He showed how his opponent had mistaken the point at issue.[7]

Finley was still active raising money for different causes. In the summer of 1855 he preached twice in Philadelphia. He wrote, "It was an open time, and the brethren and sisters with one accord opened their purses and gave me the best collection I have made at any one church in my visit."[8]

Sometimes the pressures on him to raise money became too heavy. He complained in an article that "wayworn and weather-beaten" as he was, he was still being asked to do "what neither my age nor my present circumstances will allow." He referred to requests that he continue to beg for money to pay off the debt at the Clinton Street Church, which he proceeded to do in eloquent words.[9]

He never hesitated to express his views about practices in the Church with which he disagreed. That year he rushed to print a criticism of the use of an organ in services. He did not like it playing between the verses. "Singing is one part of divine worship that ought never to be dispensed with," he wrote, "and I have no doubt but choir singing has a tendency to formality in worship, and does away all the benefit of devotion in our congregations." He also criticized the practice of the congregation sitting during prayers, calling it "rude" and "disgraceful." "Kneeling is the Scriptural position of the body in prayer," he asserted.[10]

Another of Finley's letters was printed in the July 4, 1855, issue of the *Western Christian Advocate* and a longer one from Mt. Pleasant, Iowa, in the August 20, 1856, issue. He had dedicated a church in Lockport, Illinois, and went on to Iowa, which he praised. "This is a most beautiful country of rich, open prairie . . . [but] it lacks in majesty, compared with the grand old woods, covered with the lofty oak, walnut, ash, and sugar-tree." Nevertheless, he admitted that he had been trying to prepare to move west for fifty years. "By faith, I see a better land, a permanent home and rest. . . . There I hope to emigrate."[11]

Another tour west in the spring of 1857 inspired three articles for the same paper. In the April 1 issue he wrote, "I write you amid the shaking of the boat, the noise of screaming children, and not far from the card table. A boat journey to the west is now the world in miniature. Here we are crowded with subjects of all nations. The Emerald Isle is specially and well represented." He recorded a delay of eight hours getting through the canal at Louisville and utilized the time to walk the streets of the city. He deplored the contrast between the church spires and the slave market and criticized "the professional followers of the meek Jesus holding the purchase of the Savior's blood as chattels, and selling them as swine or cattle." He wrote, "To see these poor, ignorant, crushed human beings drudging out their lives to their so-called Christian masters, is most horrible in the sight of God and humanity. . . . The city looked gloomy as do all other places where this sum of all villainy exists."[12]

The April 8, 1857, issue contained an account of his experience preaching on board as his boat passed Evansville, Indiana. "At ten o'clock I commenced singing, and the crowd began to settle down, and in a short time I had the attention of most of the passengers—except the Catholics. . . . I had . . . an open time, and tears fell from many eyes."[13]

The April 15 issue contained another article praising Iowa. He concluded it, however, with seething criticism of the "Border ruffianism" and of the Dred Scott decision and asserted that "we have no more any Constitution nor laws."[14]

Finley's life was one of superlatives. He worked hard, preached eloquently, and won many religious victories. He had many close friends and some bitter enemies. When he disagreed with someone, he could be extremely vituperative. David Jordan wrote him from Piqua July 29, 1842, to exclaim, "Sir, the very unkind and extraordinary treatment I have received from you today, as well as for the last one or two years, has been exceedingly grievous to me indeed. . . . I can not help but feel aggrieved at the unkind, and uncourteous manner in which you appeared disposed to treat me in the Conference room this afternoon." He went on to assure Finley that he was not the cause of his salary reduction.[15]

Yet he could be generous with his assistance to a friend when he wanted to be. John McDonald wrote him to seek his help getting his books and articles published. In a letter on August 28, 1841, McDonald thanked him for his assistance. "Had not providence sent you to me, I certainly would not have been an author. You spurred me on to the attempt." Bishops from time to time sought his advice on colleagues' appointments.[16]

People might have faulted him for breaking up a Quaker meeting in 1841, but others praised him for his action. Samuel A. Latta wrote March 17, 1841, to compliment Finley for his letter. "In some parts of it you are extremely eloquent & learned. I cannot see why the plague you have not been dubbed DD." He was always very generous to his very close friends. He had wanted to push Charles Elliott's name for bishop until Elliott asked him to stop. He wrote him January 9, 1844, to declare, "I have not the necessary qualifications for so responsible and important an office in our church."[17]

Because of the rigorous life he led he was frequently sick and sometimes close to death. In 1853 some people thought he was about to die. John M. Bradstreet wrote him from New York to say he realized that Finley was "coasting Jordan & near your departure from this tented field." Bradstreet wrote that Finley was more favored than Moses because he would be permitted "to enter the happy land."[18]

He must have been feeling ill at that time, for in 1854 he wrote a farewell letter to the bishops and members of the Cincinnati Conference. He declared, "This morning I feel it my last privilege to take my leave of you. I thank you all for your kindness to me and pray that you may fully accomplish the glorious work to whitch you have been called." He asked them to forgive his imperfections and wrote that he regretted any difference of opinion he might have had with some of them. He asked them to help the congregation on Clinton Street to finish their church. He concluded, "Now I bid you all farewell. I shall see you no more until we meet in the spirit world."[19]

Finley attended his last General Conference meeting in Indianapolis in 1856 and was active as usual. It was his last opportunity to exercise leadership at a national level, his last effort to criticize slavery to a large assembly of his fellow ministers.

Later that year Finley was violently attacked in an incident that may have shortened his life. On Monday evening, September 15, 1856, he attended a meeting of the new Republican party in Lewisburg, Ohio. He sat on the platform and probably was one of the more eloquent speakers that night. After the meeting adjourned, he must have been one of the last to depart. As he left the church, he was surrounded by a group of about a dozen yelling and cursing persons who were demonstrating against the Republicans. One of them suddenly struck Finley on the back of his head with a rock or bludgeon that knocked him to the ground where he lay unconscious for some time. The rowdies quickly disappeared. When he regained consciousness he stood up unsteadily and tried to cross the street to his grandson's house. When he reached the gutter he fainted and fell a second time. He lay there until some friends found him and nursed his injuries. Finley explained for the *Western Christian Advocate* that "it must have been done by some who hated me for my firm and unyielding opposition to the whiskey and slavery cause. I know I am hated by many. . . . I know they would have murdered me, but, thank God! I still live, and hope to live still, and to preach liberty to the captives, and the opening of the prisons to those who are bound. I go for the greatest liberty of conscience in religion; for free grace, free speech, free press, and free territory," The last line may have been his adaptation of the 1848 Free Soil party slogan, "Free soil, free speech, free labor, and free men." [20]

When his last book was published he probably was pleased with the favorable reviews. He continued to accept preaching invitations when his health permitted. He preached at a quarterly meeting in Liberty, Indiana, in August 1857 and attended a camp meeting near Winchester, Indiana, where he preached his last sermon on Saturday afternoon, August 22. The following week he was preparing to attend a missionary meeting in Indiana but became seriously ill. After being paralyzed by a series of strokes, he died Sunday evening, September 6. His last words were, "I have enjoyed perfect peace; I have it now." The lion of the forest would roar no more. [21]

Finley was buried in the Mound Hill Union Cemetery in Eaton. His wife, Hannah, died in 1861. A twelve-foot monument marks the family graves.

The *Western Christian Advocate* obituary described Finley as a highly qualified person accustomed nearly all his life to the frontier, someone who in his prime "possessed physical strength and agility not equaled, perhaps, by one in a million." It concluded, "He was characterized by a plain outspokenness, which, to those who did not know him, sometimes

The Last Years

appeared blunt, but which those best acquainted with him knew to be the honest utterance of a heart that despised and shunned all disguises."[22]

James H. Anderson described him as a "celebrated preacher whose burning zeal and moving eloquence gave him power over the masses." Henry Howe called him "one of the greatest of the itinerant Methodist ministers" and declared that he had personally converted five thousand persons over a forty-year period. John Barker named him "one of the crown princes of the Methodist itinerancy."[23]

Throughout his career Finley placed a high priority on reaching out to the lowly and marginalized members of society—Native Americans, blacks, prisoners, the struggling settlers he first encountered in his preaching. He made a conscious personal sacrifice to be a circuit rider that resulted in his neglecting his health, his family, his own economic well-being.

By 1857 Finley's world had changed dramatically from what it had been fifty years earlier. In the first year of President Buchanan's administration he must have felt ill at ease in the face of increased urbanization and industrial growth. The struggles in Kansas between antislavery and proslavery forces must have depressed him. The Dred Scott decision must have convinced him more and more of the evil of slavery, although he was pleased with John McLean's dissent in that opinion. What he thought of the hoop skirts coming into woman's fashions we will never know.

The forest through which he roared as a youth disappeared by the time he was a man, but he continued to look back to those frontier days thoughout his life. One of his colleagues recalled him as "a man made of God on purpose for hard times." Another wrote that he "exerted a wide influence for good in this state than was exerted by any man of his day and generation." He preached his way across Ohio and touched many lives. He attended every annual conference from 1809 to 1856 and eight general conferences, the first in 1820 and the last in 1856. He did what he thought best for the Wyandots and was ahead of his time in defending Native Americans against unscrupulous, land-hungry whites and a callous government. In helping to initiate the division in the Methodist Church between North and South over slavery he contributed to intensifying the avalanche of righteous fervor that carried Americans into the Civil War seventeen years later, a war he feared was coming but did not live to see. For a man to be so warmly loved and so bitterly disliked must mean that he produced on everyone he met a lasting, deep response. Perhaps there have been too few Finleys in our history.[24]

Notes

Unless otherwise indicated, all letters, diaries, and documents cited are in the Finley Papers, United Methodist Archives Center, Ohio Wesleyan University Library, Delaware, Ohio.

1. The New Market Devil

Epigraph from James B. Finley, *Autobiography of the Rev. James B. Finley: Or Pioneer Life in the West*, ed. W.P. Strickland (Cincinnati: Cranston and Curts, 1853), p. 177.

1. Finley, *Autobiography*, p. 174.
2. Ibid., p. 177; John M. Barker, *History of Ohio Methodism*, (Cincinnati: Curts and Jennings, 1898), p. 157.
3. Nelson W. Evans and Emmons B. Stivers, *A History of Adams County, Ohio* (West Union, Ohio: E.B. Stivers, 1900), pp. 477, 624.
4. Finley, *Autobiography*, pp. 15-26.
5. Ibid., p. 38.
6. Robert W. Finley to Massie, Dec. 12, 1794; David M. Massie, *Nathaniel Massie: A Pioneer of Ohio* (Cincinnati: Robert Clarke, 1896), pp. 58-59; William H. Smith, *The St. Clair Papers: The Life and Public Services of Arthur St. Clair* (Cincinnati: Robert Clarke, 1882), 2:374-76; Finley, *Autobiography*, pp. 101-2.
7. Elsie Johnson Ayres, *The Hills of Highland* (Springfield, Ohio: Skinner, 1971), p. 163; James B. Finley, *Memorials of Prison Life*, ed. B.F. Tefft (Cincinnati: Swormstedt and Power, 1850), p. 72.
8. Finley, *Autobiography*, pp. 105-6.
9. Ibid., p. 111.
10. Ibid., p. 113; Lyle S. Evans, *A Standard History of Ross County* (Baltimore: Gateway, 1987, reprint of 1917 ed.), 1:228; John L. Smith, *Indiana Methodism* (Valparaiso: n.p., 1892), p. 184; Finley, *Autobiography*, p. 147.
11. Finley, *Autobiography*, p. 147.
12. Ayres, *Hills of Highland*, p. 112; Evans, *History of Ross County*, p. 149; D.W. Williams, *A History of Jackson County, Ohio* (Jackson: n.p., 1900), p. 90.
13. *Western Christian Advocate*, Nov. 22, 1832.
14. Evans, *History of Ross County*, pp. 155, 163; Eliza's birth date is on her grave.
15. Pauk K. Conkin, *Cane Ridge: America's Pentecost* (Madison: Univ. of Wisconsin Press, 1990), pp. 15-17.

16. Peter Cartwright, *Autobiography of Peter Cartwright: The Backwoods Preacher*, ed. W.P. Strickland (New York: Carlton and Porter, 1857), pp. 30-31.
17. Conkin, *Cane Ridge*, p. 80; Hadley Cantril, *The Psychology of Social Movements* (New York: John Wiley, 1941), p. 63.
18. *Methodist Magazine* 2 (July 1819): 272.
19. Finley, *Autobiography*, pp. 166-67.
20. Smith, *Indiana Methodism*, p. 184.
21. Ayres, *Hills of Highland*, p. 165; F.A. Michaux, *Travels to the West of the Alleghany Mountains in the States of Ohio, Kentucky, and Tennessee* (London: B. Crosby, 1805), p. 103.
22. Emilius O. Randall and Daniel J. Ryan, *History of Ohio: The Rise and Progress of an American State* (New York: Century History, 1912) 3:106; Julian M. Sturtevant, *An Autobiography* (New York: Fleming H. Revell, 1896), p. 44.
23. James M. Miller, *The Genesis of Western Culture: The Upper Ohio Valley, 1800-1825* (Columbus: Ohio Archaeological and Historical Society, 1938), p. 37; Daniel Drake, *Pioneer Life in Kentucky, 1785-1800* (Cincinnati: Robert Clarke, 1870), p. 176.
24. Henry Boehm, *Reminiscences, Historical and Biographical, of Sixty-Four Years in the Ministry* (New York: Carlton and Porter, 1865), p. 260.
25. Jesse Lee, *A Short History of the Methodists in the United States, Beginning in 1766, and Continued till 1809* (Baltimore: Magill and Cline, 1810), p. 354; Finley, *Autobiography*, pp. 190-94.
26. Elmer T. Clark, ed., *The Journal and Letters of Francis Asbury* (Nashville: Abingdon, 1958), 2:647.
27. James B. Finley, *Sketches of Western Methodism: Biographical, Historical, and Miscellaneous, Illustrative of Pioneer Life*, ed. W.P. Strickland (Cincinnati: Methodist Book Concern, 1854), p. 323.
28. William Warren Sweet, ed., *The Rise of Methodism in the West: Being the Journal of the Western Conference, 1800-1811* (New York: Methodist Book Concern, 1920), p. 205n; Robert A. Rutland, *The Presidency of James Madison* (Lawrence: Univ. Press of Kansas, 1990), p. 86.
29. Dempsey Sheppard, *The Story of Barnesville, Ohio, 1808-1940* (Barnesville: F.J. Heer, 1942), p. 144; Finley, *Sketches of Western Methodism*, pp. 322-23.
30. Albert H. Redford, *The History of Methodism in Kentucky* (Nashville: Southern Methodist, 1870), 2:172-73.
31. Rev. Stephen R. Beggs, *Pages from the Early History of the West and North West* (Cincinnati: Methodist Book Concern, 1868), p. 293; Lowrey, "Recollections of James B. Finley" in Williams, "Early Methodism," United Methodist Archives Center, Ohio Wesleyan University Library, Delaware, Ohio; Abel Stevens, *A Compendious History of Methodism* (New York: Phillips and Hunt, 1867), p. 471.
32. John Stewart, *Highways and Hedges: or Fifty Years of Western Methodism* (Cincinnati: Hitchcock and Walden, 1870), pp. 59-60.
33. Randall and Ryan, *History of Ohio*, 3:24; Stewart, *Highways and Hedges*, p. 35.
34. Young to Finley, Mar. 13, 1815.
35. Finley to Sale, Mar. 15, 1816.

36. William C. Howells, *Recollections of Life in Ohio, from 1813 to 1840* (Cincinnati: Robert Clarke, 1895), p. 39.

37. William B. Sprague, *Annals of the American Pulpit*, vol. 7, *The Methodists* (New York: Robert Carter, 1873), p. xvii; James B. Finley, "Memorandum Book for the District of Ohio."

38. Alfred Brunson, "History of Methodism in the Western Reserve," *Methodist Magazine* 14 (July 1832): 255-74; McKendree to Finley, Mar. 21, 1817.

39. James B. Finley, "Diary," Apr. 2, 1818; Young to Finley, Nov. 18, 1818.

40. William Warren Sweet, ed. *Circuit Rider Days Along the Ohio: Being the Journals of the Ohio Conference from Its Organization in 1812 to 1826*, (New York and Cincinnati: Methodist Book Concern, 1923).

41. Soule and Mason to Finley, Jan. 23, 1818.

42. Leland R. Johnson in Robert L. Reid, ed., *Always a River: The Ohio River and the American Experience* (Bloomington and Indianapolis: Indiana Univ. Press, 1991), pp. 185-86; *Western Herald and Steubenville Gazette*, Feb. 18, 1819; Andrew R.L. Cayton, *The Frontier Republic: Ideology and Politics in the Ohio Country, 1780-1825* (Kent: Kent State Univ. Press, 1986), pp. 131, 128.

43. John Finley to James Finley, July 12 and Oct. 17, 1818.

44. John Finley to James Finley, June 3, 1819 and Aug. 29, 1821.

45. Houston to Finley, Nov. 22, 1829.

2. The Expansion of Methodism in Ohio

Epigraph from Isaac Holmes, *An Account of the United States of America* (London: H. Fisher, 1823), p. 388.

1. Stephen C. Fox, *The Group Bases of Ohio Political Behavior, 1803-1848*, (New York: Garland, 1989), p. 157; Roscoe C. Buley, *The Old Northwest: Pioneer Period, 1815-1840* (Indianapolis: Indiana Historical Society, 1950), 2:468n.; Maxwell P. Gaddis, *Foot-prints of an Itinerant* (Cincinnati: Methodist Book Concern, 1855), p. 540; John M. Barker, *History of Ohio Methodism* (Cincinnati: Curts and Jennings, 1898), p. 123.

2. Robert Paine, *Life and Times of William M'Kendree* (Nashville: M.E. Church, South, 1868), 1:180; Wade C. Barclay, *Early American Methodism, 1769-1844* (New York and Nashville: Board of Missions and Church Extension of the Methodist Church, 1949), 1:152-53, 239; Bernard A. Weisberger, *They Gathered at the River: The Story of the Great Revivalists and Their Impact upon Religion in America* (Chicago: Quadrangle, 1958), p. 46; T. Scott Miyakawa, *Protestants and Pioneers: Individualism and Conformity on the American Frontier* (Chicago: Univ. of Chicago Press, 1964), p. 45.

3. Barker, *History of Ohio Methodism*, p. 123; Nathan O. Hatch, *The Democratization of American Christianity* (New Haven: Yale Univ. Press, 1989), p. 87; Abel Stevens, *Essays on the Preaching Required by the Times*, (New York: Carlton and Phillips, 1855), p. 181.

4. Paine, *Life and Times of William M'Kendree*, 1:181.

5. Sweet, *Circuit Rider Days*, pp. 24-25.

6. Joseph B. Doyle, *20th Century History of Steubenville and Jefferson County, Ohio* (Chicago: Arnold, 1910), p. 402; Sweet, *Rise of Methodism in the*

West, p. 17; Emory J. Bucke, ed., *The History of American Methodism* (New York and Nashville: Abingdon, 1964), 1:395; "Journal of the Rev. John Kobler," *Western Christian Advocate*, Aug. 9, 1839; Ayres, *History of Highland*, p. 153; Henry Smith, *Recollections and Reflections of an Old Itinerant* (New York: Lane and Tippett, 1848), p. 328; John Sale quoted in William Warren Sweet, *Religion on the American Frontier, 1783-1840*, vol. 4, *The Methodists*, (Chicago: Univ. of Chicago Press, 1923), p. 154.

7. See Frederick A. Norwood, ed., *Sourcebook of American Methodism* (Nashville: Abingdon, 1982), pp. 31-43.

8. Finley, *Autobiography*, p. 178.

9. Jacob Young, *Autobiography of a Pioneer* (Cincinnati: Swormstedt and Poe, 1857), p. 97; Barclay, *Early American Methodism*, 1:238; Stevens, *Essays on Preaching*, p. 207.

10. William C. Howells, *Recollections of Life in Ohio, from 1813 to 1840*, (Cincinnati: Robert Clarke, 1895), p. 152.

11. *The Methodist Preacher: or, Lights and Shadows in the Life of an Itinerant*, (Philadelphia: Bedford, 1844), p. 17.

12. Heath to Finley, Jan. 1, 1845.

13. Charles W. Ferguson, *Organizing to Beat the Devil, Methodists and the Making of America*, (Garden City: Doubleday, 1971), p. 82.

14. Stevens, *Essays on Preaching*, pp. 109-12.

15. Samuel W. Williams, *Pictures of Early Methodism in Ohio* (Cincinati: Jennings and Graham, 1909), pp. 97-98.

16. *Methodist Preacher*, p. 12.

17. Elizabeth Nottingham, *Methodism and the Frontier: Indiana Proving Ground* (New York: Columbia Univ. Press, 1844), p. 169.

18. Cartwright, *Autobiography*, p. 96; Finley, *Autobiography* p. 297.

19. William Burke in Finley, *Sketches of Western Methodism*, p. 112.

20. Buley, *Old Northwest*, 2:451.

21. *The Doctrines and Discipline of the Methodist Episcopal Church* (New York: Mason and Lane, 1832), pp. 60-61.

22. Robert Baird, *Religion in America* (New York: Harper, 1845), p. 250; Cartwright, *Autobiography*, p. 243.

23. Thomas Hinde, *Methodist Magazine* 4 (June 1821): 228.

24. Quoted in Charles A. Johnson, "The Frontier Camp Meeting: Contemporary and Historical Appraisals, 1804-1840," *Mississippi Valley Historical Review* 37, 1 (June 1950): 103.

25. Timothy Flint, "Religious Character of the Western People," *Western Monthly Review* 1 (1827-28): 269.

26. Finley, *Autobiography*, p. 171; Samuel G. Goodrich, *Recollections of a Life Time* (New York: Miller, Orton and Mulligan, 1857) 1:196-97.

27. Friis in John F. McDermatt, ed., *The Frontier Re-examined* (Urbana: Univ. of Illinois Press, 1967), p. 76; Finley, *Sketches of Western Methodism*, pp. 179-80.

28. John McLean, *Sketch of Rev. Philip Gatch* (Cincinnati: Swormstedt and Poe, 1854), p. 185.

29. Perry Miller, *The Life of the Mind in America from the Revolution to the Civil War* (New York: Harcourt, Brace and World, 1965), p. 49; Harrison quoted

in William H. Milburn, *Ten Years of Preacher-Life: Chapters from an Autobiography* (New York: Derby and Jackson, 1859), p. 76.

30. I.F. King, "Introduction of Methodism in Ohio," *Ohio Archaeological and Historical Quarterly* 10 (July 1901): 190; Sweet, *Circuit Rider Days*, p. 34; Finley, *Autobiography*, p. 194; Andrew Carroll, *Moral and Religious Sketches and Collections* (Cincinnati: Methodist Book Concern, 1857), p. 41.

31. M. Cucheval-Clavigny, "Peter Cartwright and Preaching in the West," *Methodist Quarterly Review* 55 (Jan. 1873): 84; Finley to Davis, July 18, 1846.

32. James P. Pilkington, *The Methodist Publishing House: A History* (Nashville and New York: Abingdon, 1968), 1:2; the *Discipline* quoted in H.C. Jennings, *The Methodist Book Concern: a Romance of History* (New York: Methodist Book Concern, 1924), p. 59.

33. *Journals of the General Conference of the Methodist Episcopal Church* (New York: Carlton and Phillips, 1855), 1:349.

34. Paul H. Boase, "The Fortunes of a Circuit Rider," *Ohio History* 72 (1963): 107.

35. Sweet, *Circuit Rider Days*, p. 114.

36. Hitt and Ware to Finley, Oct. 18, 1815.

37. Hitt and Ware to Finley, Nov. 18, 1815 and Jan. 4, 1816.

38. Soule and Mason to Finley, Aug. 19 and Dec. 10, 1816.

39. Sweet, *Religion on the American Frontier*, p. 70; Soule and Mason to Finley, May 17 and Dec. 8, 1817.

40. Finley, *Sketches of Western Methodism*, p. 216.

41. Barclay, *Early American Methodism*, 1:x; Sweet, *Rise of Methodism in the West*, p. 102.

42. T.M. Eddy, "Influence of Methodism upon the Civilization and Education of the West," *Methodist Quarterly Review* 39 (Aug. 1857): 286.

43. Ernest G. Bormann, *The Force of Fantasy: Restoring the American Dream* (Carbondale and Edwardsville: Southern Illinois Univ. Press, 1985), p. viii; *Methodist Quarterly Review* 34 (Jan. 1852): 74.

44. Bormann, *Force of Fantasy*, p. 130; Cartwright, *Autobiography*, p. 358.

45. Catharine C. Cleveland, *The Great Revival in the West, 1797-1805* (Chicago: Univ. of Chicago Press, 1916), p. 120; Charles A. Johnson, "Early Ohio Camp Meetings, 1801-1816," *Ohio State Archaeological and Historical Quarterly* 61 (1952): 44.

46. Nottingham, *Methodism and the Frontier*, p. 39.

47. Williams, *Pictures of Early Methodism in Ohio*, p. 52.

48. Howells, *Recollections of Life in Ohio*, p. 103.

49. Russell E. Richey, *Early American Methodism* (Bloomington and Indianapolis: Indiana Univ. Press, 1991), pp. xiii-xiv; Boehm, *Reminiscences*, pp. 206-7.

50. Kenneth O. Brown, "Finding America's Oldest Camp Meeting," *Methodist History* 28, 4 (July 1990): 253; William H. Venable, *Beginnings of Literary Culture in the Ohio Valley: Historical and Biographical Sketches* (Cincinnati: Robert Clarke, 1891), pp. 206-7.

51. Walter B. Posey, *The Development of Methodism in the Old Southwest, 1783-1824* (Tuscaloosa, Ala.: Weatherford, 1933), p. 20.

52. Lee, *Short History of the Methodists*, pp. 360-62.

53. B.W. Gorham, *Camp Meeting Manual: A Practical Book on the Camp Ground* (Boston: H.V. Degen, 1854), p. 155.
54. Charles A. Johnson, *The Frontier Camp Meeting: Religious Harvest Time* (Dallas: Southern Methodist Univ. Press, 1955), pp. 57, 102; Francis Asbury, *Journal of Rev. Francis Asbury* (New York: Eaton and Mains, 1852), 3:286.
55. Cartwright, *Autobiography*, p. 76; James B. Finley, "Annals of Methodism in the West," *Western Christian Advocate*, Nov. 22, 1839; William Warren Sweet, *Revivalism in America*, (New York: Methodist Book Concern, 1923), p. 131; Asbury, *Journal*, 3:321; Johnson, *Frontier Camp Meeting*, p. 38; Boehm, *Reminiscences*, pp. 317, 363, 405.
56. James B. Finley, "Diary."
57. Finley, *Autobiography*, pp. 239, 349-50; Johnson, *Frontier Camp Meeting*, p. 105; Richard E. Wentz, *Religion in the New World: The Shaping of Religious Traditions in the United States* (Minneapolis: Fortress, 1990), p. 158; *Western Christian Monitor* (Aug. 1816): 425.
58. Quoted in Jack Larkin, *The Reshaping of Everyday Life, 1790-1840* (New York: Harper and Row, 1988), p. 253.
59. Simon A. O'Ferrall, *A Ramble of Six Thousand Miles Through the United States of America* (London: E. Wilson, 1832), p. 524; Emilius O. Randall and Daniel J. Ryan, *History of Ohio: The Rise and Progress of an American State* (New York: Century History, 1912), 3:22.
60. Finley, *Autobiography*, p. 228; Johnson, "The Frontier Camp Meeting," p. 109.
61. Quoted in Martin E. Marty, *Pilgrims in Their Own Land: 500 Years of Religion in America* (New York, Penguin, 1985), p. 176.
62. Quoted in Joseph B. Wakeley, *The Heroes of Methodism, Containing Sketches of Eminent Methodist Ministers, and Characteristic Anecdotes of Their Personal History* (New York: Carlton and Lanahan, 1856), p. 390.
63. Quoted in Barclay, *Early American Methodism*, 1:86.
64. Quoted in Finley, *Sketches of Western Methodism*, p. 458; Barclay, *Early American Methodism*, 1:219.
65. Sweet, *Circuit Rider Days*, p. 280.
66. Daniel Drake, *Pioneer Life in Kentucky, 1785-1800* (Cincinnati: Robert Clarke, 1870), p. 194; Isaac Holmes, *An Account of the United States of America* (London: H. Fisher, 1823), p. 388; Frances Trollope, *Domestic Manners of the Americans* (London: Whittaker, Treacher, 1832), pp. 233-46; Hall quoted in Buley, *Old Northwest*, 2:459; Flint, "Religious Character of the American People," p. 231; Peter Neilson, *Recollections of the Six Years' Residence in the United States of America* (Glasgow: David Robertson, 1830), p. 195.
67. Finley, *Autobiography*, p. 315.
68. William Warren Sweet, *The American Churches, an Interpretation* (New York: Scribners, 1947), p. 54.
69. See Wentz, *Religion in the New World*, p. 166; William G. Doyle, *The Social Order of a Frontier Community: Jackson, Illinois, 1825-1870* (Urbana: Univ. of Illinois Press, 1978), p. 164.
70. William G. McLoughlin, *Revivals, Awakenings, and Reform* (Chicago: Univ. of Chicago Press, 1978), p. xiii; John L. Hammond, *The Politics of Benevo-*

lence: Revival Religion and American Voting Behavior (Norwood, N.J.: Ablex, 1979), p. 200; Baird, *Religion in America*, p. 201.

71. Larkin, *Reshaping of Everyday Life*, pp. 74-75; Williams, *Pictures of Early Methodism in Ohio*, p. 25.

72. Weisberger, *They Gathered at the River*, p. 29; Donald G. Mathews, "The Second Great Awakening as an Organizing Process, 1780-1830, An Hypothesis," *American Quarterly* 21, 1 (Spring 1969): 27; Buley, *Old Northwest*, 2: 455; Keith J. Hardman, *Charles Grandison Finney, 1792-1875: Revivalist and Reformer* (Syracuse: Syracuse Univ. Press, 1987), p. 9.

73. James Porter, *Revivals of Religion: Their Theory, Means, Obstructions, Uses and Importance, with the Duty of Christians in Regard to Them* (Cincinnati: Swormstedt and Poe, 1853), p. 261.

74. *Methodist Magazine* 2 (Sept. 1819): 350.

75. See Dickson D. Bruce, Jr., *And They All Sang Hallalujah: Plain-Folk Camp Meeting Religion, 1800-1845* (Knoxville: Univ. of Tennessee Press, 1974), pp. 135-36.

76. Miyakawa, *Protestants and Pioneers*, p. 159; Mathews, "Second Great Awakening," p. 29; Sydney G. Dimond, *The Psychology of the Methodist Revival* (London: Oxford Univ. Press, 1926), p. 257; Nathan O. Hatch, *The Democratization of American Christianity* (New Haven: Yale Univ. Press, 1989), pp. 9-10.

77. Mead, *Manna in the Wilderness*, p. 415, quoted in Frederick A. Norwood, *The Story of American Methodism* (Nashville and New York: Abingdon, 1974), p. 158; Ray A. Billington, *The Protestant Crusade, 1800-1860: A Study of the Origins of American Nativism* (New York: Macmillan, 1938), pp. 41-42.

78. Quoted in Barker, *History of Ohio Methodism*, p. 93.

79. *Western Christian Advocate*, Nov. 22, 1839.

80. Williams, *Pictures of Early Methodism in Ohio*, p. 143.

81. *Methodist Magazine* 2 (June 1819): 233, 235.

82. Ibid. (Aug. 1819): 308.

83. Morris to Finley, Jan. 26, 1833.

84. Hammond, *Politics of Benevolence*, p. 51.

85. *Ladies Repository and Gatherings of the West* 3 (Jan. 1843): 32; Johnson, "Frontier Camp Meeting," p. 99.

86. See Miyakawa, *Protestants and Pioneers*, and Alice Felt Tyler, *Freedom's Ferment: Phases of American Social History from the Colonial Period to the Outbreak of the Civil War* (St. Paul: Univ. of Minnesota Press, 1944).

87. Blake McKelvey, *American Prisons: A Study in American Social History Prior to 1915* (Chicago: Univ. of Chicago Press, 1936), pp. 9, 12.

88. Finley, *Autobiography*, p. 287; *Christian Advocate and Journal and The Zion's Herald*, Jan. 9, 1829.

89. Finley Manuscript.

90. Finley, *Autobiography*, pp. 238-39; Henry Howe, *Historical Collections of Ohio*, 2d ed. (Norwalk, Ohio: Laning, 1904), 2:277; Lyle S. Evans, ed., *A Standard History of Ross County*, reprint of 1917 ed. (Baltimore: Gateway, 1987), p. 262.

91. Finley, *Autobiography*, pp. 238-40.

92. Ibid., p. 258; Young to Finley, Mar. 10, 1815.

93. Buley, *Old Northwest*, 2:419; Miller, *Life of the Mind in America*, p. 7;

Miller in James W. Smith and A. Leland Jamison, eds., *The Shaping of American Religion*, (Princeton: Princeton Univ. Press, 1961), 1:350; Ralph H. Gabriel, *The Course of American Democratic Thought*, 2d ed. (New York: Ronald, 1956), pp. 17, 38-39.
    94. Fox, *Group Bases of Ohio Political Behavior*, p. 116; Howells, *Recollections of Life in Ohio*, p. 120.
    95. Robert T. Handy, "American Methodism and Its Historical Frontier," *Methodist History* 23, 1 (Oct. 1984): 44-53.

3. Encounter with the Wyandots

Epigraph from Henry R. Schoolcraft, *Personal Memoirs of a Residence of Thirty Years with the Indian Tribes on the American Frontier* (Philadelphia: Lippincott, Grambo, 1851), p. 512.
    1. Sweet, *Circuit Rider Days*, pp. 176, 177, 183; I.F. King, "Introduction of Methodism in Ohio," *Ohio Archaeological and Historical Quarterly* 10 (July 1901): 202.
    2. John R. Swanton, *The Indian Tribes of North America* (Washington, D.C.: Smithsonian Institution, 1952), p. 233; Bruce G. Trigger, *The Huron: Farmers of the North* (New York: Holt, Rinehart and Winston, 1969), p. 6; William E. Connelley, *Wyandot Folklore* (Topeka: Crane, 1899), p. 17.
    3. Wade C. Barclay, *Early American Methodism, 1769-1844* (New York and Nashville: Board of Missions and Church Extension of the Methodist Church, 1949), 1:203; Nathan Bangs, *A History of the Methodist Episcopal Church*, (New York: Lane and Tippetts, 1851), 3:166; Howe, *Historical Collections of Ohio*, 1:893; *Methodist Magazine* 13 (Jan. 1831): 94-101; James Axtell, *The Invasion Within: The Contest of Cultures in Colonial North America* (New York and Oxford: Oxford Univ. Press, 1985), p. 46.
    4. Henry R. Schoolcraft, *The American Indians, Their History, Condition and Prospects*, rev. ed. (Buffalo: George H. Derby, 1851), p. 195; Connelley, *Wyandot Folklore*, p. 17.
    5. Helen Hornbeck Tanner, ed., *Atlas of Great Lakes Indian History* (Norman: Univ. of Oklahoma Press, 1986), p. 29.
    6. Barbara Leitch, *A Concise History of Indian Tribes of North America* (Algonac, Mich.: Reference, 1979), pp. 186-87.
    7. Howe, *Historical Collections of Ohio*, 1:609, 927.
    8. William Galloway, *Old Chillicothe* (Xenia, Ohio: Buckeye, 1934), p. 296; Clark Wisler, *Indians of the United States* (Garden City: Doubleday, Doran, 1940), p. 130.
    9. Leonard U. Hill, *John Johnston and the Indians in the Land of the Three Miamis* (Piqua, Ohio: Stoneman, 1957), p. 156; Thomas L. McKenney and James Hall, *The Indian Tribes of North America* (Edinburgh: John Grant, 1934), 3:23; Elias D. Whitlock, Nathaniel B.C. Love, and Elwood O. Crist, *History of the Central Ohio Conference of the Methodist Episcopal Church* (Cincinnati: Methodist Book Concern, 1913), p. 85.
    10. John Wesley Powell, *Wyandotte Government: A Short Study of Tribal*

Society (Salem, Mass.: Salem, 1881), pp. 3, 9; see also *Methodist Magazine* 13 (Jan. 1831): 95.

11. Hill, *John Johnston*, pp. 186-87.

12. See Thelma R. Marsh, *Moccasin Trails to the Cross, A History of the Mission to the Wyandot Indians on the Sandusky Plains* (Upper Sandusky, Ohio: John Steward United Methodist Church, 1974); and James B. Finley, *History of the Wyandott Mission at Upper Sandusky, Ohio* (Cincinnati: Wright and Swormstedt, 1840), pp. 74-108, for accounts of Stewart's preaching.

13. Quoted in Joseph Mitchell, *The Missionary Pioneer: or a Brief Memoir of the Life, Labours and Death of John Stewart* (New York: J.C. Totten, 1827), pp. 31-32.

14. Finley, *History of the Wyandott Mission*, p. 94.

15. Sweet, *Circuit Rider Days*, p. 193.

16. Walter B. Posey, *The Development of Methodism in the Old Southwest, 1783-1824* (Tuscaloosa, Ala.: Weatherford, 1933), p. 81; John F. Marlay, *The Life of Rev. Thomas A. Morris* (Cincinnati: Hitchcock and Walden, 1875), p. 323.

17. Quoted in Pilkington, *Methodist Publishing House*, 1:6, 81; Soule in *Methodist Magazine* 5 (Jan. 1822): 31-33.

18. McKendree to Finley, Jan. 24, 1821; Roy H. Pearce, *The Savages of America: a Study of the Indian and the Idea of Civilization*, rev. ed. (Baltimore: Johns Hopkins Press, 1965), pp. 67, 168.

19. Robert F. Berkhofer, Jr., *Salvation and the Savage: An Analysis of Protestant Missions and American Indian Response, 1787-1862* (Lexington: Univ. of Kentucky Press, 1965), p. 5n; Mather quoted in Lucy Maddox, *Removals: Nineteenth-Century American Literature and the Politics of Indian Affairs* (New York and Oxford: Oxford Univ. Press, 1991), p. 181, n. 11.

20. Jennings quoted in John R. Bodo, *The Protestant Clergy and Public Issues, 1812-1848* (Philadelphia: Porcupine, 1980), p. 91; Finley, *History of the Wyandott Mission*, p. 109.

21. Quoted in *Methodist Magazine* 13 (Oct. 1831): 384n.

22. Ibid. 3 (Jan. 1820): 39-40.

23. *Christian Advocate*, Sept. 9, 1826; Finley, *History of the Wyandott Mission*, pp. 237-38; Whitlock, Love, and Crist, *History of the Central Ohio Conference*, p. 89.

24. Finley, *History of the Wyandot Mission*, p. 434.

25. Finley to editors, *Methodist Magazine* 3 (Nov. 1820): 431-36.

26. McKendree to Finley, Jan. 24, 1821.

27. Quoted in Hill, *John Johnston*, p. 104.

28. Ora B. Peake, *A History of the United States Indian Factory System, 1795-1822* (Denver: Sage, 1954), p. 115. (Peake cites Indian Department Letter Book, F 249.)

29. Barclay, *Early American Methodism*, 2:118-19.

30. Ayres, *Hills of Highland*, p. 167; Sweet, *Circuit Rider Days*, pp. 204-5.

31. Finley, *History of the Wyandott Mission*, pp. 115-17.

32. *Methodist Magazine* 5 (Jan. 1822): 30.

33. Sweet, *Circuit Rider Days*, p. 75.

34. *Methodist Magazine* 5 (Jan. 1822): 30.

35. Finley, *History of the Wyandott Mission*, p. 120; Sweet, *Circuit Rider Days*, p. 75.

36. Finley, *Autobiography*, p. 360.
37. Finley to Ruter, Feb. 19, 1822.
38. McKenney to Finley, Jan. 21, 1822, quoted in Peake, *History of Indian Factory System*, p. 179.
39. Finley, *History of the Wyandott Mission*, p. 206.
40. *Methodist Magazine* 5 (Sept. 1822): 360.
41. Ibid. 6 (Mar. 1823): 115-17.
42. Jacob Young, *Autobiography of a Pioneer* (Cincinnati: Swormstedt and Poe, 1857), p. 366.
43. *Methodist Magazine* 5 (Nov. 1822): 430.
44. G.R. Jones quoted in Bangs, *History of the Methodist Episcopal Church*, 3:236.
45. *Methodist Magazine* 8 (Jan. 1825): 32-38.
46. Finley to Ruter, Jan. 2, 1822, Finley Papers, Hayes Presidential Center Library, Fremont, Ohio.
47. Finley to Ruter, Oct. 10, 1822, Finley Papers, Hayes Library.
48. Charles Elliott, *Indian Missionary Reminiscences: Principally of the Wyandot Nation* (New York: T. Mason and J. Lane, 1837), pp. 68-84.
49. Ibid.
50. Finley, *History of the Wyandott Mission*, p. 184; Berkhofer, *Salvation and the Savage*, p. 39; Elliott, *Indian Missionary Reminiscences*, pp. 70-71.
51. Barclay, *Early American Methodism*, 2:277; Ruter to Finley, Jan. 7, 1825; Finley, *History of the Wyandott Mission*, p. 336.
52. Johnston's salary from *American State Papers*, Class 2, Indian Affairs (Washington, D.C.: Gales and Seaton, 1832), 2:365; Johnston to Finley, Sept. 10 and Oct. 6, 1825.
53. Johnston to Finley, Dec. 3 and 5, 1825.
54. Elliott, *Indian Missionary Reminiscences*, p. 94; Mason to Finley, Dec. 10, 1822; Foreman to Finley, Feb. 2, 1827.
55. Crume to Finley, Nov. 17, 1825.
56. Mason to Finley, Aug. 15, 1827.
57. Roszel to Finley, Jan. 21, 1822.
58. *Methodist Magazine* 5 (May 1822): 189-93.
59. Ibid.: 189-90.
60. Roszel to Finley, Mar. 30, 1821.
61. Sweet, *Circuit Rider Days*, p. 78; Swayze to Finley, Jan. 20, 1820.
62. John Finley to James Finley, June 28, 1823; Summerfield to Finley, Aug. 21, 1824.
63. McKendree to Finley, Apr. 14, 1823, Finley Papers, Hayes Library; Jones to Finley, Apr. 28, 1823; Ruter to Finley, Apr. 5 and May 10, 1823, Jan. 7, Feb. 2, Dec. 6, 1825, Jan. 19, 1826; Finley to Ruter, May 10, 1823, Finley Papers, Hayes Library; Roberts to Finley, Aug. 30, 1825.
64. Johnson, *Frontier Camp Meeting*, p. 130; *Western Christian Advocate*, Feb. 23, 1838; Wood to Finley, Feb. 24, 1823; McLean to Finley, Oct. 1, 1823.
65. Quoted in Barclay, *Early American Methodism*, 2:122.
66. Young, *Autobiography*, pp. 370-71.
67. Ibid.
68. Emery to Finley, Apr. 16, 1823.
69. Mason to Finley, Dec. 10, 1822.

70. Ibid.
71. Jackson to Finley, Dec. 20 and 30, 1825; Strub to Finley, Feb. 2, 1825, Finley Papers, Hayes Library.
72. Young to Finley, Oct. 7, 1823; Johnston to Finley, Apr. 14, 1824.
73. *Methodist Magazine* 6 (Jan. 1823): 37; Finley, *History of the Wyandott Mission*, p. 198.
74. McKenney to Finley, Mar. 23, 1822.
75. McLean to Finley, Feb. 12, 1823.
76. Thomas C. Cochran, ed., *New American State Papers* (Wilmington, Del.: Scholary Resources, 1972), 1: doc. no. 102, p. 664; McKendree to Finley, Apr. 14, 1823; Jones to Finley, Apr. 28, 1823; Finley to Ruter, Nov. 17, 1823.
77. Lamplin to Finley, quoted in *Methodist Magazine* 10 (Mar. 1826): 108-9.
78. Finley, *History of the Wyandott Mission*, pp. 193-94.
79. Young to Finley, Feb. 16, 1824.
80. Finley, *History of the Wyandott Mission*, p. 196.
81. Mason to Finley, Oct. 5, 1826; Finley's "Regulations" for the store, Finley Papers, Hayes Library.
82. Quoted in Finley, *History of the Wyandott Mission*, pp. 375-76.
83. Mason to Finley, Oct. 5, 1826.
84. Johnston to Finley, Aug. 17, 1824.
85. James Finley to John Finley, Feb. 22, 1825.
86. Finley, *History of the Wyandott Mission*, p. 200.
87. Ibid., pp. 202-3.
88. *Methodist Magazine* 6 (Apr. 1823): 153; Finley to Cass, Oct. 23, 1823; Finley, *History of the Wyandott Mission*, pp. 212-13; Finley to Goddard, Sept. 19, 1823, Finley Papers, Hayes Library.
89. Johnston to Finley, Nov. 1 and Dec. 9, 1823.
90. Finley to the editor, *Methodist Magazine* 7 (May 1824): 195.
91. Ayres, *Hills of Highland*, p. 22; Hitt to Finley, May 4, 1822; McLean to Finley, June 25, 1823; Finley, *History of the Wyandott Mission*, p. 262.
92. Bangs to Finley, Feb. 13, 1824.
93. Sweet, *Circuit Rider Days*, pp. 245, 249, 267.
94. Bangs to Finley, Feb. 16, 1826, Finley Papers, Hayes Library; Hall to Finley, Aug. 5, 1826; Mason to Finley, Oct. 5, 1826.
95. *Methodist Magazine* 9 (Sept. 1826): 352.
96. *Christian Advocate*, Sept. 4, 1826; Finley, *History of the Wyandott Mission*, p. 357.
97. Barclay, *Early American Methodism*, 1:281n.
98. McKendree to Mason, Aug. 12, 1823, quoted in *Methodist Magazine* 6 (Oct. 1823): 393-96.
99. Joshua Soule, "Wyandot Mission," *Methodist Magazine* 9 (Jan. 1825): 32-38.
100. Quoted in Ibid. 6 (Oct. 1823): 396.
101. Calhoun to Finley, May 1, 1823 in W. Edwin Hemphill, ed., *The Papers of John C. Calhoun* (Columbia: Univ. of South Carolina Press, 1976) 8:42-43; Finley, *History of the Wyandott Mission*, pp. 274, 324.
102. Finley, *History of the Wyandott Mission*, p. 257.

103. Calhoun to Finley, Oct. 31, 1823; Finley to Ruter, Nov. 17, 1823, Finley Papers, Hayes Library.
104. See Robert A. Rutland, *The Presidency of James Madison* (Lawrence: Univ. Press of Kansas, 1990), p. 77.
105. Finley to Calhoun, Oct. 31, 1823, in Hemphill, *Papers of John C. Calhoun*, 7:336-37.
106. Finley to Calhoun, Jan. 5, 1824, in Hemphill, *Papers of John C. Calhoun* 8:445; Johnston to Calhoun, Dec. 20, 1823, in ibid., 8:417.
107. McKenney to Johnston, Apr. 26, 1824, in Hemphill, *Papers of John C. Calhoun*, 9:54-55; McLean to Finley, June 27, 1824.
108. Marsh, *Moccasin Trails to the Cross*, p. 23; Barclay, *Early American Methodism*, 2, 116n; Howe, *Historical Collections of Ohio*, 2:898.
109. Finley, *History of the Wyandott Mission*, p. 241; Johnston certificate in Finley Papers, Hayes Library; McLean to Finley, Sept. 27, 1824.
110. Finley to Calhoun, May 24, 1824, in Hemphill, *Papers of John C. Calhoun*, 9:112-13; McKenney to Johnston, June 1, 1824, Johnston Papers, Ohio Historical Society Archives, Columbus, Ohio.
111. Finley to Calhoun, July 17, 1824, in Hemphill, *Papers of John C. Calhoun*, 9:231.
112. McKenney to Finley, Aug. 17, 1824; Cass to Calhoun in Ibid., 9:298-99, 322; Cass to Finley, Oct. 14, 1824; Ficklin to McLean, July 19, 1825, McLean Papers, Manuscript Division, Library of Congress.
113. Johnston to Finley, Oct. 26, 1824; Finley, "An Account of Publick Property left in my care by John Shaw."
114. Johnston to Finley, Nov. 30, 1824.
115. Finley, *History of the Wyandott Mission*, p. 259.
116. McKenney to Finley, Aug. 9, 1824; McKenney to Finley, Jan. 12, 1825, Finley Papers, Hayes Library.
117. McKenney to Finley, Feb. 22, 1825, in Hemphill, *Papers of John C. Calhoun*, 9:585.
118. Finley to Calhoun, Feb. 27, 1824, in Hemphill, *Papers of John C. Calhoun*, 9:247.
119. Cass to Finley, Mar. 22, 1826, Finley Papers, Hayes Library.
120. John H. Vogel, *Indians of Ohio and Wyandot County* (New York: Vantage, 1975), p. 59.
121. Cass to Finley, Feb. 6, 1826; McKenney to Finley, Feb. 6, 1826; Cass to Finley, May 1, 1826, Finley Papers, Hayes Library.
122. *Methodist Magazine* 9 (July 1826): 275.
123. Ibid., 269.
124. Ibid, (Aug. 1826): 308.
125. Finley, *History of the Wyandott Mission*, p. 142.
126. McLean to Finley, Jan. 26, 1826; McLean to Finley, Feb. 7, 1826; Young to Finley, Feb. 13, 1827.
127. Finley, *Sketches of Western Methodism*, pp. 517-18; Allen to Finley, May 21, 1838.
128. Lee to Finley, Sept. 13, 1826.
129. Lee to Finley, Apr. 27 and Sept. 18, 1827.
130. Lee to Finley, Oct. 11 and 19, 1827.

131. Lewis to Finley, June 20, 1829.
132. Finley to Lewis, June 27, 1829.
133. William Walker Certificate.
134. Lewis to Finley, July 26, 1831.

4. Fight against the Federal Government

Epigraph from Schoolcraft, *Personal Memoirs*, p. 520.

1. Earl P. Olmstead, *Blackcoats among the Delaware: David Zeisberger on the Ohio Frontier* (Kent and London: Kent State Univ. Press, 1991), pp. 26-29, 57-58; Robert W. Steele and Mary Davies Steele, *Early Dayton* (Dayton: U.B., 1896), p. 118.

2. The most useful books on federal government Indian policy are Richard Drinnon, *The Metaphysics of Indian-Hating and Empire Building* (Minneapolis: Univ. of Minnesota Press, 1980); Francis P. Prucha, *The Great Father: The United States Government and the American Indians*, 2 vols. (Lincoln: Univ. of Nebraska Press, 1985); and Ronald N. Satz, *American Indian Policy in the Jacksonian Era* (Lincoln: Univ. of Nebraska Press, 1975).

3. Francis P. Prucha, *American Indian Policy in the Formative Years* (Cambridge: Harvard Univ. Press, 1962), p. 139.

4. *American State Papers*, Class 2, Indian Affairs (Washington, D.C.: Gales and Seaton, 1832), 1:319.

5. Dumas Malone, *Jefferson the President: First Term, 1801-1805* (Boston: Little, Brown, 1970), p. 273; Annie Heloise Abel, "History of Events Resulting in Indian Consolidation West of the Mississippi," *Annual Report of the American Historical Association for the Year 1906* (Washington, D.C.: G.P.O., 1908), 1:241-42.

6. John R. Bodo, *The Protestant Clergy and Public Issues, 1812-1848* (Philadelphia: Porcupine, 1980), p. 92.

7. Prucha, *Great Father*, 1:34, 44; Charles J. Kappler, comp. and ed., *Indian Affairs: Laws and Treaties* (Washington, D.C.: G.P.O., 1904), 2:6, 18.

8. Cochran, *New American State Papers*, (Del.: Scholarly Resources, 1972), 1:124, 3:193; *American State Papers*, Indian Affairs, 1:795.

9. Buley, *Old Northwest*, 1:109-10; Satz, *American Indian Policy in the Jacksonian Era*, p. 1.

10. Cass and McArthur to Calhoun, Sept. 18, 1818, quoted in Abel, "History of Events," p. 289.

11. Kappler, *Indian Affairs*, 2, 164.

12. Quoted in Prucha, *American Indian Policy in the Formative Years*, p. 2.

13. Ibid., pp. 84, 87.

14. Peake, *History of Indian Factory System*, p. 132.

15. Ibid., p. 189; *American State Papers*, Indian Affairs, 2:68.

16. Herman Viola, *Thomas L. McKenney: Architect of Early American Indian Policy, 1816-1830*, (Chicago: Swallow, 1974), p. 64.

17. Sweet, *Circuit Rider Days*, p. 207.

18. Quoted in Hemphill, *Papers of John C. Calhoun*, 7:xxxix.

19. Peake, *History of Indian Factory System*, p. 205.
20. Quoted in George D. Harmon, *Sixty Years of Indian Affairs* (Chapel Hill: Univ. of North Carolina Press, 1941), pp. 57, 58, 59.
21. Quoted in Alice Cunningham Fletcher, *Indian Education and Civilization* (Washington, D.C.: G.P.O., 1888), p. 162.
22. Ibid.
23. *U.S. Statutes at Large*, 3:516-17; Viola, *Thomas L. McKenney*, p. 43.
24. *New American State Papers*, 2:576-77, 581.
25. Prucha, *American Indian Policy in the Formative Years*, p. 222.
26. Harmon, *Sixty Years of Indian Affairs*, p. 374, table 3.
27. Barclay, *Early American Methodism*, 2:115n.
28. McLean to Finley, Mar. 16, 1824.
29. Harmon, *Sixty Years of Indian Affairs*, p. 165.
30. Buley, *Old Northwest*, 1:113-14; Harmon, *Sixty Years of Indian Affairs*, p. 106; *American State Papers*, Indian Affairs, 2:541-47.
31. *American State Papers*, Indian Affairs, 2:200-201; *New American State Papers*, 2:588.
32. James B. Finley, *Life Among The Indians: Or, Personal Reminiscences and Historical Incidents Illustrative of Indian Life and Character*, ed. Rev. D.W. Clark (Cincinnati: Cranston and Stowe, 1857), pp. 442-43.
33. McKenney to Four Wyandot Chiefs, Mar. 24, 1825 in Hemphill, *Papers of John C. Calhoun*, 9:274-75. (Also in *Methodist Magazine* 9 (July 1825): 275-76.)
34. Cass to Finley, Mar. 25, 1825, Finley Papers, Hayes Library.
35. Cass to Finley, Oct. 26, 1825.
36. McKenney to Finley, Sept. 10, 1825, in James B. Finley, *History of the Wyandott Mission* (Cincinnati: Wright and Swormstedt, 1840), p. 305.
37. Quoted in Vogel, *Indians of Ohio and Wyandot County*, p. 58; Finley, *Life Among The Indians*, p. 451.
38. Johnston to Finley, June 26, 1823, Feb. 12, 1825, Jan. 10, 1826.
39. Finley to Johnston, Apr. 26, 1826.
40. Beardsley to Finley, Jan. 18, 1825.
41. Quoted in Buley, *Old Northwest*, 1:184n.
42. Finley to Cass, Dec. 15, 1825.
43. Finley to Ruter, Dec. 19, 1825, Finley Papers, Hayes Library; Barclay, *Early American Methodism*, 2:124.
44. Walker to Finley, July 15, 1826.
45. Finley Report to the Department of War for the year ending Sept. 30, 1826, Finley Papers, Hayes Library.
46. *Methodist Magazine* 11 (Sept. 1827): 414-15.
47. Campbell to McLean, July 10, 1828; Hinde to McLean, Sept. 5, 1827, John McLean Papers, Manuscript Division, Library of Congress.
48. Cass to Finley, Apr. 9, 1827.
49. Woods to Finley, Feb. 26, 1827.
50. Woods to Finley, Nov. 10, 1827.
51. McLean to Finley, Jan. 18, 1828.
52. 20th U.S. Congress, 1st sess., rep. no. 56, House of Representatives, "Indians Removing Westward," Jan. 7, 1828.

53. Quoted in Prucha, *American Indian Policy in the Formative Years*, p. 233.

54. John S. Bassett, ed., *Correspondence of Andrew Jackson* (Washington, D.C.: Carnegie Institution, 1927), 2:279-81.

55. Quoted in Satz, *American Indian Policy in the Jacksonian Era*, p. 12.

56. *U.S. Statutes at Large*, 4:411-12; Francis P. Prucha, "Andrew Jackson's Indian Policy: A Reassessment," *Journal of American History* 56, 3 (Dec. 1969): 538.

57. Larkin, *Reshaping of Everyday Life*, p. 5; Edward Pessen, *Jacksonian America: Society, Personality and Politics* (Homewood, Ill.: Dorsey, 1978), p. 296; Prucha, "Andrew Jackson's Indian Policy," p. 531.

58. Satz, *American Indian Policy in the Jacksonian Era*, p. 54; Prucha, *American Indian Policy in the Formative Years* pp. 89, 120; Elizabeth Gaspar Brown, "Lewis Cass and the American Indian," *Michigan History* 37 (Sept. 1953): 286-98; Schoolcraft, *Personal Memoirs*, p. 629.

59. Finley manuscript.

60. Young to Finley, Mar. 9, 1825, and Apr. 5, 1828.

61. Dane to Finley, Apr. 13, 1831.

62. Walker to Finley, Apr. 22, 1831.

63. J. Orin Oliphant, "The Report of the Wyandot Exploring Delegation," *Kansas Historical Quarterly* 15, 3 (Aug. 1947): 248-62.

64. Ibid., 248; Kappler, *Indian Affairs*, 2:339; Prucha, *Great Father*, 1:247-48; Harmon, *Sixty Years of Indian Affairs*, pp. 280, 379.

65. Quoted in Prucha, *American Indian Policy in the Formative Years*, p. 127.

66. Stewart, *Highways and Hedges*, p. 174.

67. O'Ferrall, *Ramble of Six Thousand Miles*, p. 308.

68. Dwight L. Smith, Ed., "An Unsuccessful Negotiation for Removal of the Wyandot Indians from Ohio, 1834," *Ohio State Archaeological and Historical Quarterly* 42 (July 1949): 305-31.

69. Vogel, *Indians of Ohio and Wyandot County*, p. 63; Carl G. Klopfenstein, "The Removal of the Wyandots from Ohio," *Ohio Historical Quarterly* 66 (Apr. 1957):122; Armstrong to Finley, June 3, 1937.

71. Walker to Finley, Aug. 8, 1837.

72. Klopfenstein, "The Removal of the Wyandots from Ohio," p. 125; Johnston quote in Hill, *John Johnston*, p. 120.

73. Kenneth W. Duckett in "Introduction to the John Johnston Papers," Ohio Historical Society Achives.

74. Kappler, *Indian Affairs*, 2:534-37; Hill, *John Johnston*, p. 120; Harmon, *Sixty Years of Indian Affairs*, p. 299.

75. Charles Dickens, *American Notes* (London: Chapman and Hall, 1842), 2:133.

76. Gray Eyes to Finley, May 20, 1843.

77. Charles S. Van Tassell, *Story of the Maumee Valley: Toledo and the Sandusky Region* (Chicago: S.J. Clarke, 1929), 1:43; Thelma R. Marsh, *Daughter of Gray Eyes* (Upper Sandusky, Ohio: n.p., 1984), p. 60.

78. *Western Christian Advocate*, Aug. 11, 1843.

79. Ibid., Aug. 18, 1843.

Notes to Pages 94-102   235

80. Thomas L. McKenney, *Memoirs, Official and Personal, with Sketches of Travels among the Northern and Southern Indians* (New York: Paine and Burgess, 1846), 2:89.

81. Oliphant, "Report of the Wyandot Exploring Delegation," *Kansas Historical Quarterly* 15, 3 (Aug. 1947): 252; Marsh, *Daughter of Gray Eyes* p. 37; T.A. Morris, *Miscellany: Consisting of Essays, Biographical Sketches and Notes of Travel* (Cincinnati: L. Swormstedt and A. Poe, 1852), p. 347; James Wheeler in *Western Christian Advocate*, Dec. 27, 1844.

82. *New American State Papers*, 2:51.

83. Finley, *Autobiography*, p. 379.

84. Klopfenstein, "Removal of the Wyandots from Ohio," p. 136.

85. Gray Eyes to Finley, Nov. 30, 1847.

86. Catherine and John Hicks to Finley, July 29, 1848.

87. Gray Eyes to Finley, July 31, 1848.

88. Kappler, *Indian Affairs*, 2, 587.

89. Prucha, *Great Father*, 2:349-50; Finley to Cass, Dec. 15, 1825; *New American State Papers*, 2:430.

90. Johnston to Brown, July 31, 1821, Ethan Allen Brown Papers, Ohio Historical Society Archives.

91. *New American State Papers*, 2:665, 668; Paul Stuart, *Nations Within A Nation: Historical Statistics of American Indians* (New York: Greenwood, 1987), p. 70; Robert E. Shalhope, *The Roots of Democracy: American Thought and Culture, 1760-1800* (Boston: Twayne, 1990), p. 131; Wilcomb E. Washburn, *The Indian In America* (New York: Harper and Row, 1975), pp. 168-69; Lynne Hudson Parsons, "'A Perpetual Harrow Upon My Feelings': John Quincy Adams and the American Indian," *New England Quarterly* 46 (Sept. 1973): 339-40; Schoolcraft, *Personal Memoirs*, pp. 318-19.

92. *Senate Document No. 1*, 26th Congress, 3d sess. sec. 413, 379.

93. Axtel, *Invasion Within*, p. 330.

94. Barclay, *Early American Methodism*, 2:268.

95. Berkhofer, *Salvation and the Savage*, p. 159.

96. Satz, *American Indian Policy in the Jacksonian Era*, pp. 275-76; Ronald N. Satz, "Indian Policy in the Jacksonian Era: The Old Northwest as a Test Case," *Michigan History* 60 (Spring 1976): 93; Priest in Cochran, *New American State Papers*, 1:17.

97. Finley, *Memorials of Prison Life*, pp. 83-84.

98. Finley, *Life Among The Indians*, p. 3.

99. Ibid., p. 548.

5. Power and Struggle

Epigraphs from James B. Finley, *Western Christian Advocate*, Oct. 6, 1837, and Nathan Bangs, *Methodist Magazine and Quarterly Review* 17 (1835): 356.

1. Finley, *Autobiography*, p. 374; R.E. Lowry, *History of Preble County* (Owensboro, Kentucky: Cook & McDowell, 1981), p. 105.

2. Marlay, *Life of Rev. Thomas A. Morris*, pp. 121-22.

3. J.M.D. Mathews, "Thirty-Five Years Ago," *Western Christian Advocate*, Sept. 30, 1868.

4. Morris to Finley, Oct. 15, 1832; Marlay, *Life of Morris*, p. 116.

5. Elliott to Finley, June 22, 1833; Finley to Maley, July 22, 1833, George Maley Papers, United Methodist Archives Center, Ohio Wesleyan University Library.

6. *Western Christian Advocate*, Mar. 30, 1838.

7. *Journals of the General Conference of the Methodist Episcopal Church* (New York: Carlton and Phillips, 1855), 1:184; Whitlock, Love, and Crist, *History of the Central Ohio Conference*, p. 39; Pilkington, *Methodist Publishing House*, 1:171.

8. Sweet, *Religion on the American Frontier*, p. 697.

9. *Western Christian Advocate*, Oct. 4, 1839.

10. *Journals of the General Conference*, 1, May 26, 1832, 415; Wright to Finley, Feb. 1836; Pilkington, *Methodist Publishing House*, 1:263.

11. Wright to Finley, May 30, 1836 and July 12, 1838.

12. Wright to Finley, July 12, 1838.

13. "To the members of the Several annual Conferences, belonging to the Methodist Episcopal Church in North America," Methodist Episcopal Church in Ohio, Miscellaneous Papers, Ohio Historical Society Archives.

14. Charlotte Reeve Conover, *Dayton and Montgomery County Resources and People* (New York: Lewis Historical, 1932), 2:394-95.

15. Brown to Finley, Aug. 17, 1844.

16. Maley to Finley, Feb. 8, 1826.

17. Alfred Brunson, *A Western Pioneer* (Cincinnati: Hitchcock and Walden, 1872), 1:167-69.

18. Ibid., pp. 200-12.

19. Boehm, *Reminiscences*, p. 260; Barclay, *Early American Methodism*, 2:356-57; Sweet *Circuit Rider Days*, pp. 168, 190; Burke to Finley, Jan. 28, 1836.

20. McLean to Finley, Dec. 16, 1830.

21. Finley, *Sketches of Western Methodism*, pp. 432-33.

22. Ibid., p. 433.

23. Finley Manuscript.

24. Finley, *Autobiography*, p. 340.

25. Finley to Simpson, n.d.

26. *Western Christian Advocate*, July 11, 1855.

27. Ibid., Mar. 24, 1837.

28. Gilruth to Finley, May 19, 1835.

29. Finley, *Autobiography*, p. 39-42.

30. Ibid., pp. 40-42.

31. Young, *Autobiography of a Pioneer*, pp. 442-43.

32. Redford, *History of Methodism in Kentucky*, 3:98-99; *Western Christian Advocate*, July 11, 1834.

33. Bascom to Finley, Mar. 24, 1825; Trimble to Finley, Jan. 4, 1838.

34. Gaddis, *Foot-prints of an Itinerant*, p. 510; Thomson to Finley, July 29, 1852.

35. Howard to Finley, Feb. 6, 1849; Young, *Autobiography*, pp. 432-33.

36. Hitt to Finley, July 26, 1819; Hinthorn to Finley, May 9, 1823; Mont-

Notes to Pages 111-118

gomery to Finley, Feb. 16, 1824; Morris to Finley, Aug. 18, 1828; Ruter to Finley, Jan. 8, 1829; Gilruth to Finley, May 18, 1830; Barrett to Finley, Mar. 7, 1837.
37. Johnston to Finley, Jan. 13, 1849.
38. Morris to Finley, May 25, 1831.
39. Brooke to Finley, May 29, June 6, Nov. 1, 1846.
40. Hamline to Finley, Sept. 25, 1856.
41. Smith, *Indiana Methodism*, p. 184.
42. Finley, "Discourse on the Death of President Harrison."
43. Hand to Finley, Dec. 3, 1846.
44. Fisher to Finley, Mar. 1, 1848; McDonald to Finley, Dec. 18, 1848.
45. Finley, *Sketches of Western Methodism*, p. 362.
46. Sweet, *Circuit Rider Days*, pp. 143, 158.
47. Young to Finley, Sept. 23, 1817.
48. Finley to Whitcombe, Feb. 8, 1841.
49. Heath to Finley, Jan. 1, 1845.
50. *Western Christian Advocate*, Jan. 20, 1855.
51. Wright to Finley, July 19, 1826; Corwin to Finley, Feb. 16, 1836; McCollach to Finley, July 12, 1842; Eaton to Finley, Mar. 12, 1847; George to Finley, June 24 and Dec. 16, 1847.
52. Morris to Finley, Apr. 18, 1837.

6. Crusade for Temperance

Epigraph from Schoolcraft, *Personal Memoirs*, p. 326.
1. Joseph A. Thacker, Jr., *James B. Finley: A Biography* Ph.D. diss. (Lexington: Univ. of Kentucky, 1967), p. 15; Conkin, *Cane Ridge*, p. 78; Sweet, *Religion on the American Frontier*, pp. 149-61.
2. Howe, *Historical Collections of Ohio*, 2: 827; Rhea Mansfield Knittle, *Early Ohio Taverns* (Ashland, Ohio: privately printed, 1937), pp. 13, 14.
3. Finley, *Autobiography*, p. 248; Tyler, *Freedom's Ferment*, p. 311; George W. Knepper, *Ohio and Its People*, (Kent: Kent State Univ. Press, 1989), p. 180.
4. Larkin, *Reshaping of Everyday Life*, p. 281; Adam Seybert, *Statistical Annals* (Philadelphia: Dobson and Son, 1818), p. 463; *Digest of Accounts of Manufacturing Establishments in the United States and of Their Manaufactures, Fourth Census* (Washington, D.C.: Gales and Seaton, 1823), pp. 101-16; Buley, *Old Northwest*, 1:370; John S. Wright, *Letters from the West: Or a Caution to Emigrants* (Ann Arbor: Univ. Microfilms, 1966), p. 21.
5. Posey, *Development of Methodism in the Old Southwest*, p. 105; Larkin, *Reshaping of Everyday Life*, p. 286; Drake, *Pioneer Life in Kentucky*, p. 84; Bucke, *History of American Methodism*, 1:257.
6. Henry Wheeler, *Methodism and the Temperance Reformation* (Cincinnati: Walden and Stowe, 1882), pp. 51, 57, 58.
7. John A. Krout, *The Origins of Prohibition* (New York: Knopf, 1925), p. 90; Knittle, *Early Ohio Taverns*, p. 14; Tyler, *Freedom's Ferment*, pp. 313-15; Richard M. Cameron, *Methodism and Society in Historical Perspective* (New York: Abingdon, 1961), p. 136.

8. Wheeler, *Methodism and the Temperance Reformation*, p. 62; *Journals of the General Conference*, 1:106, 107, 168, 239.
9. Wheeler, *Methodism and the Temperance Reformation*, pp. 104, 108.
10. Finley, *Autobiography*, p. 251.
11. Ibid., pp. 250-51, 247; Knittle, *Early Ohio Taverns*, p. 19.
12. Finley, *Autobiography*, p. 249; *Journals of the General Conference*, 1:182, 239.
13. Brook to Finley, May 12, 1823.
14. Finley, *History of the Wyandott Mission*, pp. 329-30.
15. Ibid.
16. Finley, *Autobiography*, p. 229.
17. Ibid.
18. Finley Manuscript.
19. Thomas to Finley, Aug. 30, 1842.
20. Samuel Ellis, *The History of the Order of the Sons of Temperance* (Boston: Stacy, Richardson, 1848), p. 15.
21. Abel Fletcher, *The History, Objects and Principles of the Order of the Sons of Temperance* (Philadelphia: Gihon and Porter, 1845), p. 5; Orlando Lund, *The Order of the Sons of Temperance* (New York: Barns, Smith and Cooper, 1847), p. 11; Philip S. White and Ezra Stiles Ely, *Vindication of the Order of the Sons of Temperance* (New York: Oliver, 1848), pp. 27-31.
22. White and Ely, *Vindication*, p. 32.
23. Ibid., p. 33.
24. Sons of Temperance, *The Revised Rules of the National Division of North America* (Philadelphia: Craig and Young, 1848), pp. 17-18.
25. *Constitution of the Order of the Sons of Temperance of North America* (Philadelphia: Craig and Young, 1849).
26. White and Ely, *Vindication*, p. iv.
27. Fletcher, *Sons of Temperance*, p. 15.
28. Lund, *Order of Sons of Temperance*, p. 40.
29. Finley manuscript.
30. P.R.L. Peirce, *A History of the Order of the Sons of Temperance in the State of Ohio* (Cincinnati: J.A. Collins, 1849), pp. 19, 57, 67; Ellis, *History of Sons of Temperance*, p. 149.
31. Sons of Temperance Document.
32. Cary to Finley, Apr. 15, 1847.
33. *Proceedings of the Annual Session of the Grand Division of the Sons of Temperance of Ohio Held in Cincinnati, October 27, 1847* (Cincinnati: Clark and Collins, 1847); Peirce, *History of the Order of the Sons of Temperance*, pp. 92-96, 115; Sons of Temperance Document; *Proceedings of the Annual Session of the Grand Division of the Order of the Sons of Temperance, 1848* (Cincinnati: Clark and Collins, 1848).
34. Sons of Temperance Circular.
35. *Proceedings of the Quarterly Session of the Grand Division of the Sons of Temperance, Held at Zanesville, April 25, 1849* (Cincinnati: Hastings, Yerkes, 1849).
36. *Ohio State Journal*, May 23, 1849.
37. Stevens to Finley, Oct. 6, 1849.

38. "Constitution of the—Temperance Alliance," Oct. 6, 1849.
39. *Ohio State Journal*, July 7, 1851; Eugene H. Roseboom, *The Civil War Era, 1850-1873* (Columbus: Ohio State Archaeological and Historical Society, 1944), pp. 220, 224.
40. Warwick to Finley, Nov. 9, 1846; Roberts to Finley, June 19, 1847; Summerville to Finley, June 23, 1847.
41. Finley to Clark, Feb. 26, 1853.
42. Elliott to Finley, Dec. 1, 1847.
43. Bradford to Finley, Nov. 28, 1848; *Proceedings of Sons of Temperance, 1847*.
44. *Western Christian Advocate*, Mar. 14. 1855.
45. Ibid., June 20, 1855.
46. Tyler, *Freedom's Ferment*, p. 348.

7. A Hero in Spite of Himself

Epigraph from Heath to Finley, June 4, 1844.
1. James B. Finley, *Autobiography of the Rev. James B. Finley, or Pioneer Life in the West*, ed. W.P. Strickland (Cincinnati: Cranston and Curts, 1853), p. 35.
2. Ibid., p. 111.
3. Finley to Stevens, 1851.
4. *Minutes of the Annual Conferences of the Methodist Episcopal Church, 1771-1828*, (New York: Mason and Lane, 1840), 1:12.
5. Ibid., pp. 20, 24.
6. Ibid., p. 24.
7. *Journals of the General Conference of the Methodist Episcopal Church* (New York: Carlton and Phillips, 1855), 1:22.
8. Ibid., pp. 41, 44, 62-63; McKendree quoted in Cleveland, *Great Revival in the West*, p. 205.
9. Sweet, *Rise of Methodism in the West*, pp. 147-48.
10. Barclay, *Early American Methodism*, 2:89; *Journals of the General Conference*, 1:357.
11. Bayard to Finley, Sept. 4, 1828; Fisher to Finley, Feb. 1829.
12. Brockmier to Finley, July 26, 1829; Gilruth to Finley, Feb. 7, 1830; Bayard to Finley, Jan. 12 and Dec. 11, 1829; Elliott to Finley, Aug. 4, 1830.
13. Elliott to Finley, Mar. 1, 1832.
14. Finley to Maley, Jan. 9, 1828.
15. Early to Finley, May 13, 1830.
16. Thomas B. Neely, *American Methodism, Its Divisions and Unification*, (New York: Fleming H. Revell, 1915), p. 52.
17. Barclay, *Early American Methodism*, 2:99; "Manuscript Journal of the Ohio Conference, August 19, 1835, "United Methodist Archives Center, Ohio Wesleyan University Library.
18. Paul H. Boase, "Slavery and the Ohio Circuit Rider," *Ohio Historical Quarterly* 64 (Apr. 1955): 197.
19. Randall and Ryan, *History of Ohio*, 4:126; *Journals of the General Con-*

ference, 1:446-47, 475; *Methodist Magazine* 20 (Jan. 1838): 32-55; Charles Elliott, *History of the Great Secession from the Methodist Episcopal Church in the year 1845* (Cincinnati: Swormstedt and Poe, 1855), p. 159.

20. Pellican to Finley, July 7, 1836.

21. John R. McKivigan, *The War Against Proslavery Religion: Abolitionism and the Northern Churches, 1830-1865* (Ithaca: Cornell Univ. Press, 1984), p. 46; James M. Buckley, *A History of Methodism in the United States* (New York: Harper, 1898), 2:6-7.

22. Lucious C. Matlack, *The Antislavery Struggle and Triumph in the Methodist Episcopal Church* (New York: Phillips and Hunt, 1881), p. 122.

23. Thacker, *James B. Finley*, pp. 240-41; *Western Christian Advocate*, Oct. 4, 1839.

24. Finley to Jordan, Nov. 25, 1841.

25. Finley Manuscript.

26. Pettit to Finley, Sept. 25, 1842.

27. Peat to Finley, Nov. 1, 1843; Thacker, *James B. Finley*, p. 243.

28. Twenty-three persons to Finley, Dec. 22, 1843.

29. *New York Tribune*, May 2, 1844.

30. Cartwright, *Autobiography*, p. 415.

31. George G. Smith, *The Life and Letters of James Osgood Andrew* (Nashville: Southern Methodist, 1883), pp. 312-13, 336-38; Joseph Mitchell, "Traveling Preacher and Settled Farmer," *Methodist History* 5, 4 (July 1967): 7; *Journals of the General Conference*, 2:63-64.

32. *The Methodist Magazine* 13 (July 1831): 314-315.

33. Andrew to Morris, Mar. 14, 1838, Morris Papers, United Methodist Archives Center, Ohio Wesleyan University Library.

34. Andrew to Soule, May 17, 1843, in Smith, *Life and Letters of Andrew*, p. 325.

35. Smith, *Life and Letters of Andrew*, pp. 341-42.

36. *Methodist Quarterly Review* (July 1851): 405; Andrew to daughter, quoted in Gross Alexander, "The General Conference of 1844," *Methodist Review Quarterly* 59, 1 (Jan. 1910): 80.

37. John N. Norwood, *The Schism in the Methodist Church, 1844: A Study of Slavery and Ecclesiastical Politics* (Alfred, N.Y.: Alfred University, 1923), pp. 59, 63.

38. Donald C. Mathews, *Slavery and Methodism: A Chapter in American Morality, 1780-1845* (Princeton: Princeton Univ. Press, 1965), p. 260.

39. Finley Manuscript.

40. *Journals of the General Conference*, 2:65-66.

41. *Western Christian Advocate*, June 7, 1844; Mathews, *Slavery and Methodism*, p. 260.

42. *Journals of the General Conference*, 2:151-52.

43. *Western Christian Advocate*, June 14, 1844.

44. Andrew to Mrs. Andrew, May 26, 1844, in Smith, *Life and Letters of Andrew*, p. 359.

45. *Journals of the General Conference*, 2:152.

46. Mitchell, "Traveling Preacher and Settled Farmer," p. 4; Bucke, *History of American Methodism*, 2:59.

47. Bucke, *History of American Methodism*, 2:56.

48. Mitchell, "Traveling Preacher and Settled Farmer," pp. 7, 12-13.
49. Lewis M. Purifoy, Jr., *The Methodist Episcopal Church, South and Slavery, 1844-1865*, Ph.D. diss. (University of North Carolina at Chapel Hill [Ann Arbor: University Microfilms, 1965]), p. 31n.
50. Wright to Andrew, Oct. 3, 1844, in Smith, *Life and Letters of Andrew*, p. 371.
51. Mathews, *Slavery and Methodism*, p. 282.
52. Heath to Finley, June 4, 1844.
53. McDonald to Finley, July 22, 1844; Smith to Finley, Aug. 17, 1844.
54. James's nephew to Finley, Aug. 25, 1844; Hamline to Finley, Sept. 14, 1844.
55. "Manuscript Journal of the Ohio Annual Conference, September 1844," United Methodist Archives Center, Ohio Wesleyan University Library.
56. *Western Christian Advocate*, Nov. 8, 15, and 22, 1844.
57. Ibid., Jan. 24, 1845.
58. Tomlinson to Finley, Oct. 31, 1844.
59. Swormstedt to Finley, Feb. 1, 1845.
60. Finley to Swormstedt, Feb. 10, 1845; Swormstedt to Finley, Aug. 8, 1845.
61. Horace M. Du Bose, *Life of Joshua Soule* (Nashville: Smith and Lamar, 1911), p. 171; Soule to Finley, n.d.
62. James Dixon, *Personal Narrative of a Tour through a Part of the United States and Canada with Notices of the History and Institutions of Methodism in America* (New York: Lane and Scott, 1849), p. 90.
63. *Western Christian Advocate*, May 23, 1845; Purifoy, *Methodist Episcopal Church*, p. 68n.
64. *Western Christian Advocate*, June 27, 1845.
65. Young, *Autobiography of a Pioneer*, pp. 477-78.
66. *Western Christian Advocate*, Sept. 12, 1845; Bucke, *History of American Methodism*, 2:153.
67. Finley Manuscript; Albea Godbold, *Forever Beginning, 1766-1966: Historical Papers Presented at American Methodism's Bicentennial Celebration, April 21-24, 1966* (Lake Junaluska, N.C.: Association of Methodist Historical Societies, 1967), p. 25.
68. Marlay to Finley, May 15, 1845.
69. Marlay to Finley, Apr. 3, 1845.
70. Latta to Finley, Aug. 1, 1845.
71. *Western Christian Advocate*, Jan. 16, 1846.
72. Ibid., Mar. 6, 1846.
73. Ibid.
74. Latta to Finley, Mar. 18, 1846.
75. Finley to Latta, July 28, 1846.
76. Eddy to Finley, Aug. 4, 1845.
77. Marlay to Finley, Aug. 21, 1845.
78. Riddle to Finley, Nov. 4, 1845; Trimble to Finley, Nov. 12, 1845.
79. Brown to Finley, Jan. 6, 1846.
80. Stewart to Finley, Jan. 8, 1846.
81. Carpenter to Finley, June 20, 1846.
82. Savage to Finley, Sept. 4, 1846.

83. Purifoy, *Methodist Episcopal Church*, pp. 76-80.
84. Finley Manuscript.
85. Ibid.
86. Finley to Elliott, n.d.
87. *Journals of the General Conference*, 2:175-77.
88. Norwood, *Schism in the Methodist Church*, p. 118.
89. *Western Christian Advocate*, July 24, 1846.
90. Ibid., Sept. 4, 1846.
91. Bascom, Green, and Latta to Finley, Aug. 25, 1846; *Western Christian Advocate*, Nov. 13, 1846.
92. Stevens to Finley, Dec. 30, 1847.
93. Elliott to Finley, Mar. 20, 1846; Dickerson to Finley, Aug. 22, 1846.
94. *Western Christian Advocate*, Jan. 22, 1847; Gray Eyes to Finley, Nov. 30, 1847.
95. Young to Finley, May 2, 1848; Elliott to Finley, Apr. 17, 1848.
96. *Journals of the General Conference*, 2:42, 68, 118.
97. Ibid., 2:173.
98. Francis P. Weisenberger, *The Life of John McLean: A Politician on the United States Supreme Court* (Columbus: Ohio State Univ. Press, 1937), pp. 176-80.
99. Finley to McLean, Feb. 17, 1855, McLean Papers, Manuscript Division, Library of Congress.
100. Wyandot Petition, July 29, 1848.
101. Gray Eyes to Finley, July 31, 1848; Gray Eyes and Armstrong to Finley, Sept. 9, 1848; Armstrong to Finley, Sept. 16, 1848.
102. *Western Christian Advocate*, Aug. 23, 1848; Frederick Norwood, "Strangers in a Strange Land: Removal of the Wyandot Indians," *Methodist History* 13, 3 (Aug. 1975): 57.
103. Finley to Latta, Aug. 18, 1848.
104. Tomlinson to Finley, Aug. 31, 1848; Atmore to Finley, Sept. 23, 1848.
105. Finley, "An Address on Emancipation."
106. Finley to editor, *Yellow Springs True Presbyterian*, June 21, 1853.
107. *Western Christian Advocate*, Mar. 7, 1855.
108. Ibid., Mar. 21, 1855.
109. Ibid., Mar. 28, 1855.
110. *Journals of the General Conference, 1856* (New York: Carlton and Porter, 1856), pp. 77, 78-79, 119.
111. *Western Christian Advocate*, Sept. 17, 1856.
112. Hamline to Finley, Sept. 25, 1856.

8. The Prison Years

Epigraph from *Western Christian Advocate*, July 3, 1846.
1. Cox to Finley, Mar. 10, 1846; Hamline to Finley, Mar. 23, 1846.
2. Tyler, *Freedom's Ferment*, pp. 265-85.
3. Louis Dwight, *First Report of the Board of Managers of the Prison Discipline Society: Boston, June 2, 1826* (Boston: T.R. Marvin, 1827), p. 51.

4. Ibid., p. 51.
5. Thomas L. Dumm, *Democracy and Punishment: Disciplinary Origins of the United States* (Madison: Univ. of Wisconsin Press, 1987), pp. 87-123; Orlando F. Lewis, *The Development of American Prisons and Prison Customs, 1776-1845* (Montclair, N.J.: Patterson Smith, 1967), p. 78.
6. Gustave de Beaumont and Alexis de Tocqueville, *On the Penitentiary System in the United States and Its Application in France*, Trans. Francis Lieber (Philadelphia: Carey, Lee and Blanchard, 1833), pp. 13, 21.
7. Ibid., p. 31.
8. Ibid., p. 59.
9. Tyler, *Freedom's Ferment*, p. 282.
10. Howe, *Historical Collections of Ohio*, 1:644; Osman C. Hooper, *History of the City of Columbus* (Columbus: Memorial, 1920), p. 148; Clara B. Hicks, *The History of Penal Institutions in Ohio to 1850* (Columbus: F.J. Heer, 1924), pp. 381-82.
11. Quoted in Lewis, *Development of American Prisons*, p. 263.
12. Dorothea L. Dix, *Remarks on Prisons and Prison Discipline*, 2d ed. (Philadelphia: Joseph Kite, 1845), pp. 2, 22, 26, 29, 43, 48.
13. Ibid., pp. 55, 57, 59.
14. Hicks, *History of Penal Institutions in Ohio*, pp. 390, 399.
15. Ibid., p. 401.
16. Merton L. Dillon, ed., "A Visit to the Ohio State Prison," *Ohio Historical Quarterly* 69, 1 (Jan. 1960): 70; Hicks, *History of Penal Institutions in Ohio*, p. 381; Hooper, *History of Columbus*, p. 148; Howe, *Historical Collections of Ohio*, 1:644.
17. Finley, Memorials of Prison Life, p. 28.
18. Dewey to Finley, Apr. 13, 1846.
19. *Ohio State Journal*, Apr. 4 and 28, 1846.
20. Hicks, *History of Penal Institutions in Ohio*, pp. 419-20; Finley, *Memorials of Prison Life*, p. 23.
21. Marlay to Finley, Apr. 9, 1846.
22. Finley, "Report to Directors, 1846."
23. Finley, *Memorials of Prison Life*, pp. 16, 20.
24. Finley Manuscript.
25. Finley, *Memorials of Prison Life*, pp. 39, 77, 84.
26. Ibid., pp. 68-69.
27. Ibid., p. 70.
28. Ibid., p. 99.
29. Ibid., p. 100.
30. Heath, "Journal," May 13-14, 1846, Ohio Historical Society Archives; Blake McKelvey, *American Prisons: A Study in American Social History Prior to 1915*, (Chicago: Univ. of Chicago Press, 1936), p. 42; Enoch C. Wines and Theodore W. Dwight, *Report on the Prisons and Reformatories of the United States and Canada*, (Albany, N.Y.: Van Benthuysen, 1867), p. 228.
31. *Western Christian Advocate*, July 3, 1846.
32. Finley, *Memorials of Prison Life*, p. 101.
33. Finley, "Journal," p. 6.
34. Finley, *Memorials of Prison Life*, p. 159.

35. Strickland to Finley, Oct. 21, 1846; Finley, "Report to Directors, 1846."
36. Heath, "Journal," June 14, 1847, and March 17, 1848, Ohio Historical Society Archives; Heath to Finley, June 30, 1847; *Ohio State Journal*, Mar. 29, 1849.
37. Finley, "Journal, June 10, 1846."
38. Finley, *Memorials of Prison Life*, p. 159.
39. Ibid., p. 291.
40. Ibid., pp. 291-92.
41. Ibid., p. 308.
42. Finley, "Report to Directors, 1846."
43. de Beaumont and de Tocqueville, *On the Penitentiary System in the United States*, pp. 108-9; Dwight, *Report of Prison Discipline Society*, p. 15; Dix, *Remarks on Prisons*, p. 90; Hicks, *History of Penal Institutions in Ohio*, p. 413.
44. Anonymous letter, n.d.
45. Quoted in Finley, *Memorials of Prison Life*, p. 220.
46. Ibid., pp. 344-45.
47. Table listing twenty-nine prison inmates.
48. Finley, *Memorials of Prison Life*, p. 209.
49. Howe, *Historical Collections of Ohio*, 2:456-58.
50. Evans, *Standard History of Ross County*, 2:301.
51. Finley to Ohio Annual Conference, Mar. 13, 1847; "Manuscript Journal of the Ohio Annual Conference, 1847," United Methodist Archives Center, Ohio Wesleyan University Library.
52. Finley, "Report to Directors, 1847."
53. Bradford to Finley, May 15, 1848.
54. Dewey to Finley, May 21, 1848.
55. Dewey to Finley, July 21, 1849.
56. *Ohio State Journal* May 28, 1849; Jacob H. Studer, *Columbus, Ohio: Its History, Resources and Progress* (Washington, D.C.: Office of Librarian of Congress, 1873), pp. 374-77; William T. Martin, *History of Franklin County* (Columbus: Follett, Foster, 1858), pp. 328-29, 363.
57. J.H. Matthews, *Historical Reminiscences of the Ohio Penitentiary, 1835-1884* (Columbus: Chas. M. Cott, 1884), p. 127.
58. Dewey to Finley, Mar. 28, 1850.
59. Bradford to Finley, May 14, 1850.
60. McKelvey, *American Prisons*, pp. 41-42.
61. McLean to Finley, Feb. 20, 1849.
62. Paul H. Boase, "Let the Men and Women Sit Apart," *Bulletin of the Historical and Philosophical Society of Ohio* 15 (1957): 33-48; *Journals of the General Conference of the Methodist Episcopal Church* (New York: Carlton and Phillips, 1855), 1:210.
63. Young to Finley, Mar. 25, 1826.
64. *Manuscript Journal of the Ohio Annual Conference*, Sept. 1, 1847, United Methodist Archives Center.
65. *Western Christian Advocate*, Nov. 5, 1847.
66. Walker to Finley, Feb. 14, 1849; *Western Christian Advocate*, Apr. 4, 1849.
67. Trimble to Finley, Apr. 6, 1849.

68. John Stewart, *Highways and Hedges: or Fifty Years of Western Methodism* (Cincinnati: Hitchcock and Walden, 1870), pp. 276, 280.
69. "Manuscript Journal of the Ohio Conference, September 1850," United Methodist Archives Center, Ohio Wesleyan University Library.
70. *Western Christian Advocate*, Apr. 23, 1851.
71. "Affadavit of W.P. Strickland, Reporter at the Ohio Conference at Springfield in 1851"; "Paper in reference to the abuse I received at conference."
72. Finley to Stevens, n.d.
73. Finley to Young, June 28, 1852.
74. *Journals of the General Conference*, 3:46, 47, 49, 53, 107.
75. Inskip to Finley, Mar. 8 and 20, 1852.
76. Finley to editor, *Western Christian Advocate*, Mar. 29, 1857.

9. The Occasional Historian

Epigraph from Finley, *Autobiography*, p. 124.
1. *Western Christian Advocate*, Oct. 6 and 13, 1837.
2. Ibid., Jan. 11, 1839.
3. Elliott to Finley, Jan. 4, 1837.
4. Finley to Wright and Swormstedt, Mar. 2, 1837.
5. Wright and Swormstedt to Finley, Mar. 11, 1837.
6. Finley to Wright and Swormstedt, Mar. 18, 1837.
7. Wright and Swormstedt to Finley, Mar. 21, 1837.
8. Finley to Wright and Swormstedt, Mar. 25, 1837.
9. Walker to Finley, Mar. 15, 1837.
10. *Western Christian Advocate*, Aug. 25, 1837.
11. "Manuscript Journal of the Ohio Annual Conference, 1837," United Methodist Archives Center, Ohio Wesleyan University Library.
12. Book Committee to Finley, Feb. 2, 1838; Soule to Wright and Swormstedt, Feb. 7, 1838, Methodist Episcopal Church in Ohio, Miscellaneous Papers, Ohio Historical Society Archives, Columbus, Ohio.
13. Morris to Finley, Feb. 21, 1838, Finley Papers, Hayes Library, Fremont, Ohio.
14. Elliott to Finley, Mar. 8, 1838.
15. Finley to Wright and Swormstedt, Apr. 20, 1838.
16. Wright and Swormstedt to Finley, Apr. 28, 1838; McDonald to Finley, June 5, 1838.
17. James B. Finley, *History of the Wyandott Mission at Upper Sandusky, Ohio* (Cincinnati: Wright and Swormstedt, 1840), p. 4.
18. Ibid., pp. 137, 248.
19. Ibid., pp. 249-50.
20. Ibid., pp. 241, 242.
21. Ibid., pp. 385-87.
22. Ibid., p. 388.
23. Ibid., pp. 373-74.
24. Ibid., p. 380.
25. Strickland to Finley, Nov. 25, 1848.

26. Thomson to Finley, Apr. 7, 1847.
27. Elliott to Finley, Mar. 8, 1848.
28. Tefft to Finley, Mar. 15, 1849; Howe to Finley, Apr. 11, 1849.
29. Swormstedt and Power to Finley, May 23, 1849; McDonald to Finley, Mar. 20, 1850.
30. Finley, *Memorials of Prison Life*, pp. 3, 4.
31. Ibid., p. 5.
32. Ibid., p. 44.
33. Ibid., p. 110.
34. Ibid., p. 179.
35. Ibid., p. 175.
36. *The New York Times*, Jan. 31, 1992.
37. Finley, *Memorials of Prison Life*, p. 202.
38. Ibid., p. 84.
39. Ibid., pp. 344-45.
40. Ibid., pp. 292, 304, 306, 310, 318, 319.
41. Finley, "Report to the Directors, 1846."
42. *Methodist Quarterly Review* 32 (July 1850): 491.
43. Howe, *Historical Collections of Ohio*, 2:458; Finley, *Autobiography*, p. 218.
44. Ibid., p. 3.
45. Ibid., pp. 69-70.
46. Ibid., p. 96.
47. Michaux, *Travels to the West*, p. 109.
48. Finley, *Autobiography*, p. 118.
49. Ibid., p. 142-43.
50. Ibid., p. 151.
51. Ibid., p. 158.
52. Ibid., p. 164.
53. Ibid., p. 359.
54. Ibid., pp. 376-77.
55. Ibid., p. 381.
56. Ibid., p. 455.
57. Finley, *Life Among the Indians*, p. 97
58. Inskip to Finley, Jan. 17, 1853.
59. *Methodist Quarterly Review* 35 (Oct. 1853): 595-96.
60. *Western Christian Advocate*, Oct. 19, 1853 and Mar. 1, 1854.
61. "Rev. James B. Finley in account with Methodist Book Concern;" Joseph A. Thacker, Jr., *James B. Finley, A Biography*, Ph.D. diss. (Lexington: Univ. of Kentucky, 1967), p. 314; *Western Christian Advocate*, Jan. 30, 1856.
62. Arthur K. Moore, *The Frontier Mind: A Cultural Analysis of the Kentucky Frontiersman* (Lexington: Univ. of Kentucky Press, 1957), p. 207.
63. Finley to Elliott, Nov. 29, 1844.
64. Finley, *Sketches of Western Methodism*, p. 4.
65. Ibid., pp. 20, 58.
66. Ibid., pp. 78, 79.
67. Ibid., p. 89.
68. Ibid., pp. 71, 97, 99.

69. Ibid., p. 100.
70. Ibid., p. 109.
71. Ibid., p. 116.
72. Ibid., p. 144.
73. Ibid., p. 150.
74. Ibid., p. 179.
75. Ibid., pp. 180, 181.
76. Ibid., p. 183.
77. Ibid., pp. 186, 188.
78. Ibid., pp. 208, 209.
79. Ibid., p. 216.
80. Ibid., p. 318; Weisenberger, *Life of John McLean*, p. 7.
81. Finley, *Sketches of Western Methodism*, p. 347.
82. Ibid., p. 357.
83. Ibid., p. 368.
84. Ibid., p. 385.
85. Ibid., p. 410.
86. Ibid., p. 412.
87. Ibid., p. 414.
88. Ibid., pp. 428, 431.
89. Ibid., pp. 440, 441.
90. Ibid., p. 495.
91. Ibid., p. 511.
92. Ibid., pp. 531, 536.
93. Ibid., p. 550.
94. Finley, *Life Among The Indians*, pp. 3, 4.
95. Ibid., p. 68.
96. Ibid., p. 95.
97. Ibid., pp. 182, 197.
98. Ibid., p. 233.
99. Ibid., p. 277.
100. Ibid., p. 369.
101. Ibid., p. 373.
102. Ibid., pp. 400-401.
103. Ibid., p. 409.
104. Ibid., p. 420.
105. Ibid., pp. 447-49.
106. *Methodist Quarterly Review* 39 (July 1857): 494-95.
107. George Catlin, *Letters and Notes on the Manners, Customs, and Conditions of the North American Indians*, 2 vols. (Philadelphia: Willis P. Hazard, 1857).

10. The Last Years

Epigraph from "Reminiscences of James B. Finley" in S.W. Williams, "Early Methodism," United Methodist Archives Center, Ohio Wesleyan University Library.

1. Morris to Finley, Sept. 30, 1851.

2. Thomson to Finley, July 24, 1852.
3. *Western Christian Advocate*, Aug. 10, 1853.
4. Ayres, *Hills of Highland*, p. 160.
5. L.D. Harlan, *Defense of L.D. Harlan before a Committee of Seven Ministers of the Cincinnati Annual Conference of the Methodist Episcopal Church* (Cincinnati: A. Watson, 1855), pp. 18, 89.
6. *Journal of the General Conference*, p. 54.
7. *Western Christian Advocate*, Mar. 4, Apr. 1, May 6 and 20, 1857.
8. Ibid., July 11, 1855.
9. Ibid., Jan. 30, 1856.
10. Ibid., June 27, 1855.
11. Ibid., Aug. 20, 1856.
12. Ibid., Apr. 1, 1857.
13. Ibid., Apr. 8, 1857.
14. Ibid., Apr. 15, 1857.
15. Jordan to Finley, July 29, 1842.
16. McDonald to Finley, Aug. 28, 1841.
17. Latta to Finley, Mar. 17, 1841; Elliott to Finley, Jan. 9, 1844.
18. Bradstreet to Finley, Jan. 20, 1853.
19. Finley to Bishops and Members of the Cincinnati Conference, 1854.
20. *Western Christian Advocate*, Sept. 16, 1856.
21. *Minutes of the Annual Conferences of the Methodist Episcopal Church* (New York: Carlton and Porter, 1860), 6:441.
22. *Western Christian Advocate*, Sept. 16, 1857.
23. Anderson quoted in Jacoby to Hirsch, May 12, 1924; Henry Howe, *Historical Collections of Ohio*, 2d ed. (Norwalk, Ohio: Laning, 1904), 2:456; John M. Barker, *History of Ohio Methodism* (Cincinnati: Curts and Jennings, 1898), p. 177.
24. Lowry, *History of Preble Country*, p. 326; S.W. Williams, "Early Methodism Newsclippings," p. 194, United Methodist Archives Center, Ohio Wesleyan University Library.

Bibliographical Essay

Primary Sources

The most important source for this study is the James B. Finley Papers in the United Methodist Archives Center, Beeghly Library, Ohio Wesleyan University, Delaware, Ohio. This collection of over twelve hundred letters, addresses, diaries, documents, sermons, and miscellaneous materials is a valuable treasure of religious and social history.

Another collection of James B. Finley Papers is in the Hayes Presidential Center Library, Fremont, Ohio. Most of these letters and documents deal with the Wyandot Mission at Upper Sandusky, Ohio. The 1810 diary attributed to Finley, however, although apparently written by him, is a copy of a portion of the journal of Benjamin Lakin.

Additional letters related to Indian affairs, especially those written by Finley, John C. Calhoun, Lewis Cass, and Thomas L. McKenney, are printed in Edwin Hemphill, ed., *The Papers of John C. Calhoun*, vols, 7, 8, 9 (Columbia: Univ. of South Carolina Press, 1973, 1975, 1976). Other collections consulted in the United Methodist Archives Center are the George W. Maley Papers and the Thomas Morris Papers.

The Ohio Historical Society Archives, Columbus, Ohio, contain several relevant collections. They include; the Ethan Allen Brown Collection, the Uriah Heath journal, the John Johnston Papers, and the Miscellaneous Papers of the Methodist Episcopal Church in Ohio.

The Papers of John McLean in the Manuscript Division, Library of Congress, were also reviewed.

Documents Related to Methodism

The minutes of Methodist Annual Conferences and journals of General Conferences are indispensable in tracing the expansion of Methodism and the changes in policy. In terms of the Ohio scene, one should consult William Warren Sweet, ed., *The Rise of Methodism in the West: Being the Journal of the Western Conference, 1800-1811* (New York: Methodist Book Concern, 1920) and *Circuit Rider Days Along the Ohio: Being the Journals of the Ohio Conference from Its Organization in 1812 to 1826* (New York and Cincinnati: Methodist Book Concern, 1923). Both volumes contain good introductory chapters. The Manuscript Journal of the Ohio Annual Conference, 1840-1867, is in the United Methodist Archives Center. The printed record is in *Minutes of the Methodist Conferences Annually Held in America from 1773 to 1813, Inclusive* (New York: Daniel Hitt and Thomas Ware, 1813) and *Minutes of the Annual Conferences of the Methodist Episcopal Church*, vols. 1 and 2 (New York: Mason and Lane, 1840), vol. 3 (New York: Carlton and Porter, 1845), vols. 4, 5, and 6 (New York: Carlton and Phillips, 1852, 1855, 1860).

At the national level, the relevant publications are *Journals of the General Conference of the Methodist Episcopal Church*, vols, 1 and 2 (New York: Carlton and Phillips, 1855), and *The General Conference of the Methodist Episcopal Church from 1792 to 1896* (Cincinnati: Curts and Jennings, 1900).

Finley's Publications

Finley's first book was *History of the Wyandott Mission at Upper Sandusky, Ohio* (Cincinnati: Wright and Swormstedt, 1840). It was his best effort at historical narrative and the most difficult one for him to write. His last book, *Life Among The Indians: Or, Personal Reminiscences and Historical Incidents Illustrative of Indian Life and Character*, ed. Rev. D.W. Clark (Cincinnati: Cranston and Stowe, 1857), repeats some of the earlier material but contains more information on Native American activities in the late eighteenth and early nineteenth centuries. His *Memorials of Prison Life*, ed. Rev. B.F. Tefft (Cincinnati: Swormstedt and Power, 1850) is based on a journal he kept from March 3, 1846 to January 30, 1847. His most widely quoted book was *Autobiography of the Rev. James B. Finley: Or Pioneer Life in the West*, ed. W.P. Strickland (Cincinnati: Cranston and Curts, 1853). *Sketches of Western Methodism: Biographical, Historical, and Miscellaneous, Illustrative of Pioneer Life*, ed. W.P. Strickland (Cincinnati: Methodist Book Concern, 1854) contains brief biographies and anecdotes about many of the early pioneering circuit riders in the Ohio River area.

Most of his many articles are found in *The Methodist Magazine* and the *Western Christian Advocate*. His earliest was a letter about a revival printed in the *Methodist Magazine* 2 (1819): 308-10. His last was in the May 6, 1857 issue of the *Western Christian Advocate*.

The New Market Devil

Most of the information about Finley's youth is gleaned from his *Autobiography*. The details about his father's contact with Nathaniel Massie and their skirmishes with Indians are revealed in David M. Massie, *Nathaniel Massie, a Pioneer of Ohio: A Sketch of his Life and Selections from His Correspondence* (Cincinnati: Robert Clarke, 1896) and William H. Smith, *The St. Clair Papers: The Life and Public Services of Arthur St. Clair*, 2 vols. (Cincinnati: Robert Clarke, 1882).

Of the many Ohio county histories, the most useful in relation to Finley's activities are Elsie Johnson Ayres, *The Hills of Highland* (Springfield, Ohio: H.K. Skinner, 1971), Joseph B. Doyle, *20th Century History of Steubenville and Jefferson County, Ohio, and Representative Citizens* (Chicago: Arnold, 1910), Nelson W. Evans and Emmons B. Stivers, *A History of Adams County, Ohio* (West Union, Ohio: E.B. Stivers, 1900), Charles S. Van Tassell, ed., *Story of the Maumee Valley, Toledo and the Sandusky Region*, 4 vols. (Chicago: S.J. Clarke, 1929), and Mary Gould Brooke, *Historic Eaton and Fort Saint Clair* (Eaton: n.p., 1930).

The most recent major contribution to the extensive literature on the Cane Ridge revival is Paul K. Conkin, *Cane Ridge: America's Pentecost* (Madison: Univ. of Wisconsin Press, 1990). Conkin has traced the camp meeting's origin to seventeenth-century Scottish communion services. He has minimized the environmental influences of the frontier and has focused on sacramental aspects of the famous camp meeting. The most readable scholarly account of the Cane Ridge revival is Bernard A. Weisberger, *They Gathered at the River: The Story of the Great Revivalists and Their Impact upon Religion in America* (Chicago: Quadrangle, 1958). See also John B. Boles, *The Great Revival, 1787-1805* (Lexington: Univ. Press of Kentucky, 1972) and Catharine C. Cleveland, *The Great Revival in the West, 1707-1805* (Chicago: Univ. of Chicago Press, 1916).

A revealing eyewitness account of social and religious life in Ohio in the early nineteenth century is found in William Cooper Howells, *Recollections of Life in Ohio, from 1813 to 1840* (Cincinnati: Robert Clarke, 1895).

There have been two dissertations written in the twentieth century based on the Finley Papers. They are Joseph A. Thacker, Jr., *James B. Finley: A Biography*, Ph.D. dissertation (Lexington: University of Kentucky, 1967) and Paul J. Boase, *The Methodist Circuit-Rider on the Ohio Frontier*, Ph.D. dissertation (Madison: University of Wisconsin, 1952). Boase has also published several scholarly articles on this period. See especially, "The Fortunes of a Circuit Rider," *Ohio History* 72 (1963): 91-115. The most caustic assessment of Finley's views is contained in Arthur K. Moore, *The Frontier Mind: A Cultural Analysis of the Kentucky Frontiersman* (Lexington: Univ. of Kentucky Press, 1957).

For the most illuminating information on the Ohio River Valley history in the early 1800s, see Robert L. Reid, ed., *Always a River: The Ohio River and the American Experience* (Bloomington and Indianapolis: Indiana Univ. Press, 1991) and Andrew R.L. Cayton, *The Frontier Republic: Ideology and Politics in the Ohio Country, 1780-1825* (Kent: Kent State Univ. Press, 1986). The letter attributed to James B. Finley in Cayton's book, however, was probably written by another Finley. The most recent comprehensive history of

Ohio is George W. Knepper, *Ohio and Its People* (Kent: Kent State Univ. Press, 1989). Other good volumes are Beverley W. Bond, Jr., *The Foundations of Ohio*, William T. Utter, *The Frontier State: 1803-1825*, and Francis P. Weisenburger, *The Passing of the Frontier, 1825-1850*, which are volumes 1, 2 and 3 of Carl Wittke, ed., *The History of the State of Ohio* (Columbus: Ohio State Archaeological and Historical Society, 1941).

The Expansion of Methodism in Ohio

The most prolific writer on Methodist history has been William Warren Sweet, and his influence on modern scholars was extensive. See especially, *Revivalism in America* (New York: Methodist Book Concern, 1923) and *Religion on the American Frontier, 1783-1840*, vol. 4, *The Methodists* (Chicago: Univ. of Chicago Press, 1946).

Of the nineteenth-century histories of Methodism, one should start with Jesse Lee, *A Short History of the Methodists in the United States: Beginning in 1766 and Continued till 1809* (Baltimore: Magill and Cline, 1810) and Henry Boehm, *Reminiscences, Historical and Biographical, of Sixty-four Years in the Ministry* (New York: Carlton and Porter, 1865). More objective, later accounts are Nathan Bangs, *A History of the Methodist Episcopal Church*, 4 vols. (New York: Lane and Tippetts, 1838-1853), Abel Stevens *The Centenary of American Methodism* (New York: Carlton and Porter, 1866) and *A Compendious History of Methodism* (New York: Phillips and Hunt, 1867), John M. Barker, *History of Ohio Methodism* (Cincinnati: Curts and Jennings, 1898), and James M. Buckley, *A History of Methodism in the United States*, 2 vols. (New York: Harper, 1898).

The most detailed account of Methodism by twentieth-century scholars is Emory S. Bucke, ed., *The History of American Methodism*, vols. 1 and 2 (New York and Nashville: Abingdon, 1964). One of the more readable accounts is Frederick A. Norwood, *The Story of American Methodism* (Nashville and New York: Abingdon 1974). See also his *Sourcebook of American Methodism* (Nashville: Abingdon, 1982).

A more recent work, Russell E. Richey, *Early American Methodism* (Bloomington and Indianapolis: Indiana Univ. Press, 1991), focuses on the years before 1810 and traces the evolution of Methodism through its different languages. A broader work that includes a scholarly treatment of several denominations is T. Scott Miyakawa, *Protestants and Pioneers: Individualism and Conformity on the American Frontier* (Chicago: Univ. of Chicago Press, 1964).

More specialized accounts are found in Albert H. Redford, *The History of Methodism in Kentucky*, 3 vols. (Nashville: Southern Methodist, 1868-1870), Samuel W. Williams, *Pictures of Early Methodism in Ohio* (Cincinnati: Jennings and Graham, 1909), Elizabeth Nottingham, *Methodism and the Frontier: Indiana Proving Ground* (New York: Columbia Univ. Press, 1944), and Walter

B. Posey, *The Development of Methodism in the Old Southwest, 1783-1824* (Tuscaloosa, Ala.: Weatherford, 1933). John Lewis Smith, *Indiana Methodism* (Valparaiso: n.p., 1892) contains accounts of some of Finley's exploits.

The scholarly works need to be supplemented by individual accounts by Methodist leaders although they tend to be less objective and more optimistic in describing their accomplishments. Of particular value are Elmer T. Clark, ed., *The Journal and Letters of Francis Asbury*, 3 vols. (Nashville: Abingdon, 1958), Peter Cartwright, *Autobiography of Peter Cartwright: The Backwoods Preacher*, ed. W.P. Strickland (New York: Carlton and Porter, 1857), Maxwell P. Gaddis, *Foot-prints of an Itinerant* (Cincinnati: Methodist Book Concern, 1855), Rev. Elnathan C. Gavitt, *Crumbs From My Saddle Bags: Or, Reminiscences of Pioneer Life and Biographical Sketches* (Toledo: Blade, 1884), William H. Milburn, *Ten Years of Preacher-Life: Chapters from an Autobiography* (New York: Derby and Jackson, 1859), Thomas A. Morris, *Miscellany: Consisting of Essays, Biographical Sketches and Notes of Travel* (Cincinnati: L. Swormstedt and A. Poe, 1852), John Stewart, *Highways and Hedges: Or Fifty Years of Western Methodism* (Cincinnati: Hitchcock and Walden, 1870), and Jacob Young, *Autobiography of a Pioneer: Or, the Nativity, Experience, Travels, and Ministerial Labors of Rev. Jacob Young, with Incidents, Observations, and Reflections* (Cincinnati: Swormstedt and Poe, 1857).

Of the many biographies of circuit riders worth reading, the ones by John McLean, *Sketch of Rev. Philip Gatch* (Cincinnati: Swormstedt and Poe, 1854), Robert Paine, *Life and Times of William M'Kendree*, 2 vols. (Nashville: M.E. Church, South, 1868, 1870), and John F. Marlay, *The Life of Rev. Thomas A. Morris* (Cincinnati: Hitchcock and Walden, 1875) have been particularly useful. See also William B. Sprague, *Annals of the American Pulpit*, vol. 7, *The Methodists* (New York: Robert Carter 1873), Matthew Simpson, ed., *Cyclopaedia of Methodism* (Philadelphia: Louis H. Everts, 1878), and Joseph B. Wakeley, *The Heroes of Methodism: Containing Sketches of Eminent Ministers, and Characteristic Anecdotes of their Personal History* (New York: Carlton and Lanahan, 1856).

The role of the circuit riders in enhancing book sales is recounted in James P. Pilkington, *The Methodist Publishing House: A History* 2 vols. (Nashville and New York: Abingdon, 1968), which is more comprehensive than the earlier work by H.C. Jennings, *The Methodist Book Concern: A Romance of History* (New York and Cincinnati: Methodist Book Concern, 1924).

The most effective books on camp meetings and revivals are Charles A. Johnson, *The Frontier Camp Meeting: Religious Harvest Time* (Dallas: Southern Methodist Univ. Press, 1955), Timothy Smith, *Revivalism and Social Reform* (Gloucester, Mass.: Peter Smith, 1976); and William G. McLoughlin, *Revivals, Awakenings, and Reform* (Chicago: Univ of Chicago Press, 1978). Johnson has been criticized for placing too much emphasis upon frontier influences. See, for example, his article, "The Frontier Camp Meeting: Contemporary and Historical Appraials, 1805-1840," *Mississippi Valley Historical Review* 37 (June 1950): 91-110, and "Early Ohio Camp Meetings, 1801-

1816," *Ohio State Archaeological and Historical Quarterly* 61 (1952): 32-50. Smith is especially convincing in showing how revivals inspired reform movements before the Civil War. McLoughlin ignores the work of Finley and draws heavily on the career of Charles G. Finney. I first advanced the "safety valve" theory of revivals in *The Social Ideas of the Northern Evangelists, 1826-1860* (New York: Columbia Univ. Press, 1954). George M. Thomas, *Revivalism and Cultural Change: Christianity, Nation-Building, and the Market in the Nineteenth-Century United States* (Chicago and London: Univ. of Chicago Press, 1989) provides a more sociological perspective and concentrates more on the late nineteenth century. John R. Bodo, *The Protestant Clergy and Public Issues, 1812-1848* (Philadelphia: Porcupine, 1980), which is limited by excluding those clergy who were not graduates of colleges or seminaries, questions whether circuit riders had much apprehension of their role in society. Although Leonard Sweet, ed., *The Evangelical Tradition in America* (Macon, Ga.: Mercer Univ. Press, 1984) ignores James B. Finley and slights frontier Methodism, the first chapter provides an extensive bibliographical survey of modern scholarship on the subject. A recent perceptive article that supplements Sweet is Robert T. Handy, "American Methodism and its Historical Frontier," *Methodist History* 23 (Oct. 1984): 44-53.

For comments on the social and political history of the period, see Daniel Drake, *Pioneer Life in Kentucky, 1785-1800* (Cincinnati: Robert Clarke, 1870), Emilius O. Randall and Daniel J. Ryan, *History of Ohio: The Rise and Progress of an American State*, 5 vols. (New York: Century History, 1912), James McDonald Miller, *The Genesis of Western Culture: The Upper Ohio Valley, 1800-1825* (Columbus: Ohio Archaeological and Historical Society, 1938), Roscoe C. Buley, *The Old Northwest: Pioneer Period, 1815-1840*, vols, 1 and 2 (Indianapolis: Indiana Historical Society, 1950), Jack Larkin, *The Reshaping of Everyday Life, 1790-1840* (New York: Harper and Row, 1988), and Stephen C. Fox, *The Group Bases of Ohio Political Behavior, 1803-1848* (New York: Garland, 1989).

Encounter with the Wyandots

There is no satisfactory, definitive history of the Wyandot Nation. The most informative volumes are Conrad Heidenreich, *Huronia: A History and Geography of the Huron Indians, 1600-1650* (Toronto, Canada: McLelland and Stewart, 1971), Bruce G. Trigger, *The Huron: Farmers of the North* (New York: Holt, Rinehart and Winston, 1969), and John H. Vogel, *Indians of Ohio and Wyandot County* (New York: Vantage, 1975). Vogel's book, however, contains some inaccuracies.

Additional information on Wyandot history is contained in Frederick W. Hodge, ed., *Handbook of American Indians North of Mexico* (Washington, D.C.: Smithsonian Institution, Bureau of American Ethnology, 1910), Helen Hornbeck Tanner, ed., *Atlas of Great Lakes Indian History* (Norman: Univ.

of Oklahoma Press, 1986), John R. Swanton, *The Indian Tribes of North America* (Washington, D.C.: Smithsonian Institution, 1952), Barbara A. Leitch, *A Concise Dictionary of Indian Tribes of North America* (Algonac, Mich.: Reference, 1979), Carl Waldman, *Atlas of the North American Indian* (New York: Facts on File, 1985), and Paul Stuart, *Nations Within A Nation: Historical Statistics of American Indians* (New York: Greenwood, 1987).

Claude A. Nichols's book, *Moral Education Among the North American Indians* (New York: Bureau of Publications, Teachers College, Columbia University, 1930), provides a different focus by describing the dimensions of Native American ethical morality.

Useful nineteenth-century volumes include Henry R. Schoolcraft, *The American Indians: Their History, Condition and Prospects*, rev. ed. (Buffalo: George H. Derby, 1851), George Catlin, *Letters and Notes on the Manners, Customs, and Conditions of the North American Indians*, 2 vols. (Philadelphia: Willis P. Hazard, 1857), John Wesley Powell, *Wyandot Government: A Short Study of Tribal Society* (Salem, Mass.: Salem, 1881), and William E. Connelley, *Wyandot Folk-Lore* (Topeka, Kans.: Crane, 1899). The three volumes of Thomas L. McKenney and James Hall, *The Indian Tribes of North America*, were reprinted (Edinburgh, Scotland: John Grant, 1933-1934).

In respect to the Methodist mission, the most comprehensive account is Finley's own *History of the Wyandott Mission at Upper Sandusky, Ohio* (Cincinnati: Wright and Swormstedt, 1840). Charles Elliott's *Indian Missionary Reminiscences, Principally of the Wyandot Nation* (New York: T. Mason and J. Lane, 1837) contains details not otherwise recorded. Information about John Steward is in Joseph Mitchell, *The Missionary Pioneer: Or, a Brief Memoir of the Life, Labours and Death of John Stewart* (New York: J.C. Totten, 1827) and Thelma R. Marsh, *Moccasin Trails to the Cross: A History of the Mission to the Wyandot Indians On the Sandusky Plains* (Upper Sandusky, Ohio: John Steward United Methodist Church, 1974).

Finley's journey to the Michigan Territory in 1823 is recorded in John H. Reed, *James B. Finley's Trip From Upper Sandusky to Detroit/Saginaw, December 1823* (Delaware, Ohio: West Ohio Conference United Methodist Church Commission on Archives and History, n.d.).

The most comprehensive account of Methodist missionary activity in general is in Wade C. Barclay, *Early American Methodism, 1769-1844*, 2 vols. (New York and Nashville: Board of Missions and Church Extension of the Methodist Church, 1949).

Fight against the Federal Government

Documents that must be consulted in tracing the federal government's Indian policy, especially as it relates to removal, include *American State Papers: Indian Affairs*, 2 vols. (Washington, D.C.: Gales and Seaton, 1832), Thomas C. Cochran, ed., *New American State Papers: Indian Affairs*, vols. 1, 2, and

4 (Wilmington, Del.: Scholarly Resources, 1972), and Charles J. Kappler, ed. *Indian Affairs: Laws and Treaties*, vol. 2 (Washington, D.C.: G.P.O., 1904).

The Wyandot attacks during the American Revolution are documented in Earl P. Olmstead, *Blackcoats among the Delaware: David Zeisberger on the Ohio Frontier* (Kent and London: Kent State Univ. Press, 1991).

An early account of the federal government's actions in respect to Indians is contained in Annie Heloise Able, "History of Events Resulting in Indian Consolidation West of the Mississippi," *Annual Report of the American Historical Association for the Year 1906*, (Washington, D.C.: G.P.O., 1908) 1: 233-450.

The most detailed account of the government's efforts to regulate trade with the Indians is Ora B. Peake, *A History of the United States Indian Factory System, 1785-1822* (Denver: Sage, 1954).

George D. Harmon, *Sixty Years of Indian Affairs* (Chapel Hill: Univ. of North Carolina Press, 1941) provides an overview of the subject, but the book lacks sufficient sensitivity to nineteenth-century racial injustice. The most prolific scholar who wrote on Native Americans and the government is Francis P. Prucha. See especially his *The Great Father: The United States Government and the American Indians*, 2 vols. (Cambridge: Harvard Univ. Press, 1985). His article "Andrew Jackson's Indian Policy: A Reassessment," *Journal of American History* 56, 3 (Dec. 1969): 527-39, however, is probably too generous to Jackson. A more critical view is expressed in Edward Pessen, *Jacksonian America: Society, Personality and Politics* (Homewood, Ill.: Dorsey, 1978).

The best book on the political leaders of this period who were involved in supervision of Indian affairs is Herman Viola, *Thomas L. McKenney: Architect of America's Early Indian Policy, 1816-1830* (Chicago: Swallow, 1974). His book is a good corrective to Thomas L. McKenney, *Memoirs, Official and Personal: With Sketches of Travels among the Northern and Southern Indians* 2 vols. (New York: Paine and Burgess, 1846), part of which was written to justify the author's actions. Also of value is Leonard U. Hill, *John Johnston and the Indians in the Land of the Three Miamis* (Piqua, Ohio: Stoneman, 1957) and Frank B. Woodford, *Lewis Cass: The Last Jeffersonian* (New Brunswick: Rutgers Univ. Press, 1950).

The principal publications which critique the government's role in Indian removal are Wilcomb E. Washburn, *The Indian in America* (New York: Harper and Row, 1975), who asserts that the removal policy was expedient, Ronald N. Satz, *American Indian Policy in the Jacksonian Era* (Lincoln: Univ. of Nebraska Press, 1975), who illustrates how the government sought Indian acculturation rather than assimilation, and two books by Francis P. Prucha, *American Indian Policy in the Formative Years* (Lincoln: Univ. of Nebraska Press, 1962) and *Indian Policy in the United States* (Lincoln and London: Univ. of Nebraska Press, 1981). Another noteworthy volume is Jane

F. Smith and Robert M. Kvasnicka, eds., *Indian-White Relations: A Persistent Paradox* (Washington, D.C.: Howard Univ. Press, 1976). See especially Herman J. Viola's chapter, "From Civilization to Removal: Early American Indian Policy."

Robert F. Berkhofer, Jr., *Salvation and the Savage: An Analysis of Protestant Missions and American Response, 1787-1862* (Lexington: Univ. of Kentucky Press, 1965), examined missionary activity by all the Protestant churches and emphasized its limitations in the face of society's racism. Richard Drinnon, *Facing West: The Metaphysics of Indian-Hating and Empire Building* (Minneapolis: Univ. of Minnesota Press, 1980), which focuses on individuals from the seventeenth century to modern times who were involved in Indian affairs or western expansion, shows how Indian-hating became justified by the pressures to build a continental empire. The book contains strong criticism of nineteenth-century whites and also has an excellent chapter on McKenney's career. It is a forceful restatement of the land-hunger theme. Henry B. Bowden, *American Indians and Christian Missions: Studies in Cultural Conflict* (Chicago: Univ. of Chicago Press, 1981), provides an overview of the subject. Calvin Martin, ed., *The American Indian and the Problem of History* (New York and Oxford: Oxford Univ. Press, 1987), which is marred by the lack of an index, contains essays by nineteen authors who supply evidence on the limitations of white scholars in writing about Indian culture and history. For this study, the most useful chapter was Robert F. Berkhofer, Jr., "Cultural Pluralism Versus Ethnocentrism in the New Indian History." We are indebted to James Axtel for his concept of "cultural suicide," which is one of his themes in *The Invasion Within: The Contest of Cultures in Colonial North America* (New York and Oxford: Oxford Univ. Press, 1985). See also Roy H. Pearce, *The Savages of America: A Study of the Indian and the Idea of Civilization*, rev. ed. (Baltimore: Johns Hopkins Press, 1965).

Two scholarly articles on the Wyandots' last years in Ohio are Dwight L. Smith, ed., "An Unsuccessful Negotiation for Removal of the Wyandot Indians from Ohio, 1834," *Ohio State Archaeological and Historical Quarterly* 58 (July 1949): 305-31 and Carl G. Klopfenstein, "The Removal of the Wyandots from Ohio," *Ohio Historical Quarterly* 66 (Apr. 1957): 119-36.

Power and Struggle

Most of what is known about Finley's career during the years after he left the Wyandot mission can be gleaned from the Finley Papers and his *Autobiography*. Examples of his opinions on religious, moral and political subjects are best seen in his manuscripts and his many articles, most of which were printed in the *Western Christian Advocate* after its establishment in 1834.

Secondary works not yet mentioned which were of use in writing this chapter were R.E. Lowry, *History of Preble County* (Owensboro, Ky.: Cook and McDowell, 1981), Elias D. Whitlock, Nathaniel B.C. Love, and Elwood O. Crist, *History of the Central Ohio Conference of the Methodist Episcopal Church* (Cincinnati: Methodist Book Concern, 1913), and Charlotte Reeve Conover, *Dayton and Montgomery County Resources and People*, 2 vols. (New York: Lewis Historical, 1932).

The description of Finley's treatment of Alfred Brunson is based partly on Brunson's autobiography, *A Western Pioneer*, 2 vols. (Cincinnati: Hitchcock and Walden, 1872).

Crusade for Temperance

Details on Robert Finley's suspension from a Kentucky presbytery are taken from William Warren Sweet, *Religion on the American Frontier, 1783-1840*, vol. 2, *The Presbyterians* (Chicago: Univ. of Chicago Press, 1936), and Paul K. Conkin, *Cane Ridge: America's Pentecost* (Madison: Univ. of Wisconsin Press, 1990). James never referred in writing to his father's drinking.

Information on the popularity of drinking in the early 1800s can be found in Henry Howe, *Historical Collections of Ohio*, 2d ed. 2 vols. (Norwalk, Ohio: Laning, 1896, 1904), Rhea Mansfield Knittle, *Early Ohio Taverns* (Ashland, Ohio: privately printed, 1937), and Jack Larkin, *The Reshaping of Everyday Life, 1790-1840* (New York: Harper and Row, 1988).

The positions taken by the Methodist Episcopal Church in respect to drinking are described in detail in Richard M. Cameron, *Methodism and Society in Historical Perspective* (New York and Nashville: Abingdon, 1961), and Henry Wheeler, *Methodism and the Temperance Reformation* (Cincinnati: Walden and Stowe, 1882).

One of the best standard volumes on the nineteenth-century temperance movement is John A. Krout, *The Origins of Prohibition* (New York: Knopf, 1925). An excellent chapter on the temperance crusade is in Alice Felt Tyler, *Freedom's Ferment: Phases of American Social History from the Colonial Period to the Outbreak of the Civil War* (New York: Harper, 1944).

Most of the publications on the Sons of Temperance are apologia. The most useful are Samuel Ellis, *The History of the Order of the Sons of Temperance* (Boston: Stacy, Richardson, 1848), Abel Fletcher, *The History, Objects and Principles of the Order of the Sons of Temperance* (Philadelphia: Gihon and Porter, 1845), Orlando Lund, *The Order of the Sons of Temperance* (New York: Barns, Smith and Cooper, 1847), and Philip S. White and Ezra Stiles Ely, *Vindication of the Order of the Sons of Temperance* (New York: Oliver, 1848). A later volume is R. Alder Temple, *A Brief History of the Order of the Sons of Temperance* (New York: National Temperance Society, 1886). For the Ohio activities by the Order, see P.R.L. Peirce, *A History of the Order of the Sons of Temperance in the State of Ohio* (Cincinnati: J.A. Collins, 1849).

A Hero in Spite of Himself

The gradual changes in Finley's attitudes toward slavery and abolitionism are best revealed in his manuscripts, letters, and articles. The most comprehensive overall review of the antislavery cause among Methodists is Donald G. Mathews. *Slavery and Methodism: A Chapter in American Morality, 1780-1845* (Princeton: Princeton Univ. Press, 1965).

Particularly forceful interpretations of the subject are contained in John R. McKivigan, *The War Against Proslavery Religion: Abolitionism and the Northern Churches, 1830-1865* (Ithaca: Cornell Univ. Press, 1984), which documents the Southern influence in Methodist Episcopal Church policy prior to 1844. David T. Bailey, *Shadow on the Church: Southwestern Evangelical Religion and the Issue of Slavery, 1783-1860* (Ithaca and London: Cornell Univ. Press, 1985), points to the changes which took place among Southerners in their attitudes toward slavery, and Ernest G. Bormann, *The Force of Fantasy: Restoring the American Dream* (Carbondale and Edwardsville: Southern Illinois Univ. Press, 1985), has a good chapter on the style of evangelical antislavery rhetoric.

John L. Hammond, *The Politics of Benevolence: Revival Religion and American Voting Behavior* (Norwood N.J.: Ablex, 1979), is worth mentioning for its analysis of the influence of revivals on voting behavior, especially in regard to antislavery. Hammond, however, gives more attention to Presbyterian than to Methodist religious activity. Robert W. Fogel, *Without Consent or Contract: The Rise And Fall of American Slavery* (New York: W.W. Norton, 1989), is a recent addition to the literature which includes attention to the British as well as the American antislavery efforts and which contains a good essay on the moral problem of slavery.

The most valuable twentieth-century accounts of the 1844 division in the Methodist Episcopal Church are John N. Norwood, *The Schism in the Methodist Church, 1844: A Study of Slavery and Ecclesiastical Politics* (Alfred, N.Y.: Alfred University, 1923), Richard A. Cameron's and Norman W. Spellman's chapter, "The Church Divides, 1844," in Emory S. Bucke, ed, *The History of American Methodism*, vol 2. (New York and Nashville: Abingdon, 1964), and Thomas B. Neely, *American Methodism: Its Divisions and Unification* (New York: Fleming H. Revell, 1915). A description of the Southern position is well stated in Lewis M. Purifoy, Jr., *The Methodist Episcopal Church, South, and Slavery, 1844-1865* (Ph.D. diss., University of North Carolina at Chapel Hill, 1965).

Nineteenth-century accounts which reflect their authors' bias but which are reasonably balanced are Charles Elliott, *History of the Great Secession from the Methodist Episcopal Church in the Year 1845* (Cincinnati: Swormstedt and Poe, 1855) and *The Sinfulness of American Slavery*, 2 vols. (Cincinnati: Swormstedt and Power, 1850, 1851), and Lucius C. Matlack, *The Antislavery Struggle and Triumph in the Methodist Episcopal Church* (New York:

Phillips and Hunt, 1881), which was originally published in 1849, as well as *The History of American Slavery and Methodism, from 1780 to 1849* (New York: n.p., 1849).

For accounts of some of the Southern participants in the 1844 General Conference see George G. Smith, *The Life and Letters of James Osgood Andrew* (Nashville: Southern Methodist, 1883) and Horace M. DuBose, *Life of Joshua Soule* (Nashville: Smith and Lamar, 1911), which is lacking in objectivity. The article by Joseph Mitchell, "Traveling Preacher and Settled Farmer," *Methodist History* 5 (July 1967): 3-14, documents the economic circumstances of the Southern clergy at the 1844 General Conference.

Details of Associate Justice John McLean's role in helping to resolve the controversy over the division of the Methodist Book Concern assets are best described in Francis P. Weisenburger, *The Life of John McLean: A Politician on the United States Supreme Court* (Columbus: Ohio State Univ. Press, 1937).

The Prison Years

Finley's "The Ohio State Prison journal of the moral instructor, 1846 March 3 - 1847 Jan 30," was the basis for his book, *Memorials of Prison Life*, ed. Rev. B.F. Tefft (Cincinnati: Swormstedt and Power, 1850).

The best histories of the penitentiary system in the United States are Thomas L. Dumm, *Democracy and Punishment: Disciplinary Origins of the United States* (Madison: Univ. of Wisconsin Press, 1987), Orlando F. Lewis, *The Development of American Prisons and Prison Customs, 1776-1845* (Montclair, N.J.: Patterson Smith, 1967), and Blake McKelvey, *American Prisons: A Study in American Social History Prior to 1915* (Chicago: Univ. of Chicago Press, 1936), which was reissued in 1977. A brief account is contained in Alice Felt Tyler, *Freedom's Ferment: Phases of American Social History from the Colonial Period to the Outbreak of the Civil War* (New York: Harper, 1944). McKelvey's book covers a longer period, but the Lewis volume is particularly applicable for the first few decades of the nineteenth century. Dumm raises some provocative questions about the relationship between democratic ideals and the concept of punishment.

For more detailed information on Ohio, see Clara B. Hicks, *The History of Penal Institutions in Ohio to 1850* (Columbus: F.J. Heer, 1924).

A good first-hand evaluation of the Auburn system is contained in the outstanding volume, Gustave de Beaumont and Alexis de Tocqueville, *On the Penitentiary System in the United States and Its Application in France*, trans. Francis Lieber (Philadelphia: Carey, Lee and Blanchard, 1833). Dorothea L. Dix, *Remarks on Prisons and Prison Discipline*, 2d ed. (Philadelphia: Joseph Kite, 1845), was a major work by a remarkable reformer whose visit to the Columbus Penitentiary in 1844 was influential in correcting abuses there. See

Bibliographical Essay 261

also Enoch C. Wines and Theodore W. Dwight, *Report on the Prisons and Reformatories of the United States and Canada* (Albany, N.Y.: Van Benthuysen, 1867), for a nineteenth-century survey of prison conditions.

In the 1840s, the Ohio Penitentiary, *Annual Report of the Directors and Warden of the Ohio Penitentiary* (Columbus: James B. Gardiner, 1846-1848), also contained statements by the physician and chaplain. The record of Clark Guernsey's visit to the penitentiary is printed in Merton L. Dillon, ed., "A Visit to the Ohio State Prison, " *Ohio Historical Quarterly* 69 (Jan. 1960): 69-72.

The devastating cholera epidemic in Columbus, Ohio, in 1849 is described in Jacob J. Studer, *Columbus, Ohio: Its History, Resources, and Progress* (Washington, D.C.: Office of Librarian of Congress, 1873), William T. Martin, *History of Franklin County* (Columbus: Follett, Foster, 1858), and J.H. Matthews, *Historical Reminiscences of the Ohio Penitentiary 1835 to 1884* (Columbus: Chas. M. Cott, 1884).

Finley's role in the "promiscuous seating" controversy is well told in Paul H. Boase, "Let the Men and Women Sit Apart," *Bulletin of the Historical and Philosophical Society of Ohio* 20 (Apr. 1962): 33-48.

Travelers' Accounts

Accounts by foreign travelers reveal interesting information on American social and religious history, but they also frequently display a critical bias which must be taken into account. This characteristic is especially apparent in Frances Trollope, *Domestic Manners of the Americans* (London: Whittaker, Treacher, 1832). Charles Dickens, *American Notes*, 2 vols. (London: Chapman and Hall, 1842), was the last foreigner to visit the Wyandots in Upper Sandusky. Other travelers' accounts worth mentioning are James Dixon, *Personal Narrative of a Tour through a Part of the United States and Canada with Notices of the History and Institutions of Methodism in America* (New York: Lane and Scott, 1849), I. Finch, *Travels in the United States of America and Canada* (London: Longman, Rees, Orme, Brown, Green and Longman, 1833), James Flint, *Letters from America* (Edinburgh: W. and C. Tait, 1822) Adam Hodgson, *Letters from North America* (London: Hurst, Robinson, 1824), Isaac Holmes, *An Account of the United States of America* (London: H. Fisher, 1823), F.A, Michaux, *Travels to the West of the Alleghany Mountains in the States of Ohio, Kentucky, and Tennessee* (London: B. Crosby, 1805), Peter Neilson, *Recollections of a Six Years' Residence in the United States of America* (Glasgow: David Robertson, 1830), and Simon A. O'Ferrall, *A Ramble of Six Thousand Miles through the United States of America* (London: E. Wilson, 1832).

Index

Adams County (Ohio), 2
Adams, John Quincy, 83, 86, 96
Akron Beacon, 166
Algonquin Indians, 41
American Antislavery Society, 132
American Bible Society, 37, 171
American Colonization Society, 133
American Fur Company, 77
American Indians, The: Their History, Condition and Prospects (Schoolcraft), 189
American Society for the Promotion of Temperance, 118
Anderson, James H., 219
Andrew, James O., 139-44, 148
antislavery movement, 130-60
Armstrong, John, 157
Arthur, Timothy Shay, 128
Asbury, Francis, 7-8, 16, 27-29, 30, 52, 198
Astor, John Jacob, 77
Atmore, W.C., 158
Auburn Prison System, 163-64
Augusta College, 55, 60, 110, 146, 157, 206
Autobiography of the Rev. James B. Finley, 3, 5, 17, 25, 37, 56, 94, 109, 193-99
Axley, James, 118, 203
Axtel, James, 97

Badger, Joseph, 42
Baltimore Conference, 62, 139-41

Baltimore (Md.), 53-55, 57, 62-63, 66, 102, 108, 121, 183
Bangor (Maine), 118
Bangs, Nathan, 62, 101, 153
Barbour, James, 96
Barclay, Wade, 98
Barker, John, 219
Barnes, Albert, 128
Barnesville (Ohio), 7-8
Barnesville and West Wheeling circuit, 8, 201
Bascom, Henry B., 107, 110, 118, 150, 154, 205-6
Batavia (Ohio), 30
Bayard, John, 132
Bayard, Mary, 131
Beauchamp, William, 203
Beaumont, Gustave de, 163; *On the Penitentiary System in the United States*, 163
Beecher, Lyman, 37, 114, 123, 128; *Plea for the West*, 114
Bellefontaine (Ohio), 93
Belmont County (Ohio), 28
Benezet, Anthony, 117
Benton, Thomas Hart, 77
Berkhofer, Robert, 98
Between-the-Logs, 49, 53, 61-62, 65, 76, 104, 188
Bigelow, Russell, 205
Billington, Ray, 34
Birney, James, 134
Blackman, Learner, 203
Boardman, Benjamin, 133

Index

Boehm, Henry, 7, 26, 106
Boone, Daniel, 1-2, 208
Bormann, Ernest, 25
Boston (Mass.), 163, 173
Bowman, Elisha, 35
Bracken Academy, 110
Bradford, Samuel, 175, 177, 191
Bradford, William, 162
Bradley, Rebecca, 2
Bradstreet, John M., 217
Brockmier, Samuel, 131
Brooke, Charles F., 111
Brooke, John C., 119, 205, 213
Brown County (Ohio), 30
Brown, Ethan Allen, 95
Brown, Kenneth, 27
Brown, Samuel (Wyandot interpreter), 62
Brown, Samuel (of Charleston), 151
Brown, Thomas, 105
Browning, Wesley, 101
Brunson, Alfred, 105-6
Bryan, John A., 90
Bucks County (Pa.), 2
Buffalo (N.Y.), 56, 62
Burke, William, 7, 19, 106, 200-201
Butler County (Ohio), 126
Butler, Richard, 16

Calhoun, John C., 64-66, 68, 75, 78-80, 187, 210
Callahan, George, 16
Cambridge (Ohio), 7
camp meetings, 4-7, 26-31, 32, 35-37, 49, 70, 102, 196, 203
camp meeting manual, 27-28
Canada, 40, 93
Cane Ridge (Ky.), 1-2, 4-6, 28, 33, 35
Cane Ridge revival, 1, 4-6, 196-97, 201
Canton (Ohio), 7
Capers, William, 140
Carroll, Andrew, 22
Cartier, Jacques, 40
Cartwright, Peter, 5, 20, 25, 28, 118, 139
Cary, Samuel F., 124-25
Cass, Charles L., 69, 85, 197, 210
Cass, Lewis, 42, 50, 59, 61, 66, 69, 75, 81, 87, 89-90

Catlin, George, 212; *Letters and Notes on the Manners, Customs, and Conditions of the North American Indians*, 212
Cayuga Indians, 41
Celina (Ohio), 127
Champlain, Samuel de, 40
Chandler, T.W., 150
Charleston (Va.), 151
Cherokee Indians, 189
Chippewa Indians, 48, 50, 61, 75, 210
Chillicothe district, 102
Chillicothe (Ohio), 3-4, 6, 11, 16, 22, 28, 35-36, 43, 111, 116, 174, 195, 208
Choctaw Indians, 87
cholera epidemic, 102, 176
Christian Advocate, 57, 180
Christian Advocate and Journal, 152, 212
Christie, William B., 186, 198
Chute, James, 165
Cincinnati Academy of Medicine, 101
Cincinnati (Ohio), 7, 12-13, 16, 23, 31, 40, 53-55, 61, 93, 102, 104, 109, 111, 117, 123, 132-33, 179, 183, 198, 201, 203
Cincinnati circuit, 101
Cincinnati Conference, 215
Cincinnati district, 201
circuit riders, 15-26, 39, 77; as book sellers, 11, 22-23, 103-4; poverty of, 9, 11, 18, 21-22, 100, 105; rotation system for, 22; reputation of, 19-21
Civil War, 39, 44, 144-45, 152
Civilization Fund, 69, 73, 78-80, 89
Clark, Davis W., 207
Clark, Francis, 16
Cleveland, Catharine, 25
Cleveland (Ohio), 101
Clinton Street Methodist Church, 198, 214-15, 217
Coke, Thomas, 29, 44
Collins, John, 1, 7, 30, 36, 204
Columbus (Ohio), 36, 41, 47, 55-56, 64, 83, 93, 101, 111-12, 124, 162, 171, 174
Conkin, Paul, 5
Cooper, Ezekial, 183

Cox, Horatio, 162
Crane, John, 204
Crawford County (Ohio), 83, 91
Crawford, T. Hartley, 92, 97
Crawford, William, 209
Cross Creek circuit, 8, 204
Crume, Moses, 52
Cumberland (Md.), 102

Dane, Isaac, 88
Daughters of Temperance, 127
Dayton district, 213
Dayton (Ohio), 38, 54, 105, 114, 177
Deer Creek (Ohio), 28
Deerfield (Ohio), 36, 91
Delaware Indians, 48, 75, 82, 94-95, 155, 205, 208
Delaware (Ohio), 49, 91, 182
Dewey, Lamin, 166, 172-73, 176, 191
Detroit (Mich.), 4, 47, 61, 75, 210
Dickens, Charles, 92-93
Dickerson, Thomas, 155
Dillon's Falls (Ohio), 8
Discipline, Methodist, 7, 20, 22, 104, 108, 130, 178, 180, 210
distilleries, 117
Dix, Dorothea, 165, 173; *Remarks on Prisons and Prison Discipline*, 165-66
Donahoo, J.T., 176
Don-Quot, 42
Drake, Benjamin, 208-9; *Life of Tecumseh*, 209
Drake, Daniel, 7, 31, 117
Dred Scott decision, 216, 219
Dromgoole, Edward, 16
Drummond, Thomas, 206
Dumm, Thomas, 163
Dwight, Louis, 37, 162
Dwight, Timothy, 117

Early, J.M., 132
earthquake, 38, 196
Eaton circuit, 101
Eaton (Ohio), 101, 166, 213
economic conditions, 11-12, 39
Eliot, John, 44
Elliott, Arthur W., 102
Elliott, Charles, 47, 51-52, 55-58, 68, 71, 110, 132, 150, 152, 155, 183, 186-87, 190, 200, 213-14, 217
Elliott, H.S., 127
Ellis, Michael, 201
Emery, Nathan, 56
Emory, John, 77
Erie Canal, 59, 62
Erie Conference, 10
Evansville (Ind.), 216
Evarts, Jeremiah, 189

factory system, 76-77
Fairfield circuit, 8
Fairfield (Ohio), 112
Fallen Timbers, Battle of, 3, 42
Finley Chapel, 105, 180-81
Finley, Eliza, 4, 47
Finley, Hannah, 4, 47, 91, 182, 196, 199, 218
Finley, James B., 2; abolitionism, views of, 114, 132-33, 136-37; activities at Ohio Penitentiary, 105, 111, 162, 166-76; activities at Wyandot mission, 40, 43, 45-72, 79-81, 88, 93, 97, 187-89, 209-11; admitted on trial, 7; appointed presiding elder, 8, 13, 37, 40, 43, 47, 70, 97, 101, 105; appointed sub-agent, 66-69, 97; Book Concern issue, views on, 153-55; books, interest in, 58, 103, 115, 170; boyhood in Kentucky, 2, 111, 129, 194; camp meetings, attitude toward, 28-29, 31; camp meetings conducted, 8, 28-31, 35, 49, 70, 91, 106, 111, 182, 203; cities, attitude toward, 101, 107, 195, 197; contributions to Wyandots, 44-72; early settlers, views of, 189, 194-96, 201; education of, 2, 4; educational ideas of, 48, 51, 65, 107-10; evaluation of, 63, 85, 97, 115, 219; first circuit, 7; first conversion, 1, 4-6, 197; free pews, views on, 178-81; fund raising efforts of, 8, 47, 52, 53-56, 62, 65, 110-11, 127, 170-72, 211, 215; government Indian policy, criticism of, 73-88, 97, 99-100, 211-12; health of, 9, 33, 47, 50, 69-70, 102, 115, 127, 169,

Index

174-76, 183-84, 197, 217-18; history, interest in, 50, 182-83, 200; literary style, 105-7, 187-88, 190-91, 207, 212; marriage, 4; Masons, views of, 113-14; medical studies, 4, 21, 101; meeting with Calhoun, 64-65, 187, 211; ministerial training, 107-8; ministerial training, views of, 25, 107-9, 202; Native Americans, views of, 198, 207-12; nature, idealization of, 106-7, 194-95, 206; Ohio, move to, 3, 129, 195; other circuits, 8-11, 18, 101; other denominations, attitude toward, 37, 104, 112, 114, 152-53; personality, 8, 105-7, 196; physical description of, 8-9; political views of, 111-13; preaching, views of, 24, 202-3, 206; prisons, views of, 168-69, 172-74, 191-93; publications, views on, 23; publishers, contacts with, 23-24, 103-4, 183-87, 190; role in 1844 General Conference, 141-44; salary, 7, 11; second conversion, 1, 6, 35, 196; selling books, 11, 23-24, 103-4; slavery, attitude toward, 130, 135-37, 152-54, 158-61, 191, 216; superannuated, 213-14; temperance, activities for, 119-28; temperance, views of, 48, 114-20; women, views of, 108-9, 170, 207; youth of, 3-4, 129, 196; Works: *Autobiography*, 1, 3, 5, 17, 25, 37, 56, 94, 109, 193-99; *History of the Wyandott Mission at Upper Sandusky*, 99, 104, 183, 187-89; *Life Among The Indians*, 100, 207-12; *Memorials of Prison Life*, 99-100, 189-93; *Sketches of Western Methodism*, 21, 70, 106, 200-7

Finley, James (nephew), 145
Finley, John, 1, 2, 4, 10, 12, 55, 60, 198
Finley, Robert W., 2-4, 115-16, 129, 206
Finley, Robert Jr., 2, 16
Finley, Samuel, 2
Finley, William P., 2, 12, 205
Finney, Charles G., 128
Fisher, William, 131
Flemingsburg (Ky.), 2
Flint, Timothy, 20
Fort Harmar, 75
Fort Industry, 75
Fort Meigs, 80
Fort St. Clair, 213
Fort Washington, 16
Fox Indians, 87
Franklin, Benjamin, 162
Franklinton (Ohio), 114
Fremont, John C., 111
frontier conditions, 2-3, 6-7, 194-95, 200-201

Gabriel, Ralph, 39
Gaddis, Maxwell, 30
Gard, B.F., 162
Gardiner, James B., 89
Gatch, Philip, 35
Georgia (state), 2
Georgian Bay, 40
Germantown Academy, 109
Germantown (Ky.), 152
Germantown (Ohio), 105, 115
Gilruth, James, 69, 72, 108, 132
Goddard, Elliott, 61
Granville (Ohio), 111, 118
Gray Eyes, 93-95, 155, 157
Green, Ashbel, 154
Grenade, John A., 203
Greenville Treaty Line, 75
Groveport (Ohio), 171
Gurley, James, 157

Hamilton County (Ohio), 117
Hamilton, Samuel, 31, 206
Hamline, Leonidas L., 111, 145, 150, 161-62, 186, 214-15
Hammond, John, 33
Hancock County (Ohio), 115
Handy, Robert T., 39
Harlan, L.D., 214-15
Harrison, William Henry, 7, 21, 42, 92-93, 112
Heath, Uriah, 18, 145, 170
Hedding, Elijah, 156
Henkle, Moses, 43
Hicks, Catherine, 95
Hicks, John, 42, 95

Highland County (Ohio), 4, 47
Hillsboro (Ohio), 4, 47, 61, 196, 213
Hinde, Thomas, 5, 7, 34, 85
Hinthorn, James, 110
History of the Wyandott Mission at Upper Sandusky (Finley), 99, 104, 183, 187-89
Hitt, Daniel, 23, 110
Hocking County (Ohio), 41
Holmes, Isaac, 31
Hooper, Jacob, 59
House of Representatives Committee on Indian Affairs, 78, 86-87
Houston, George, 109
Howard, Soloman, 110
Howe, Henry, 174, 190, 193, 219
Howells, William Cooper, 10, 18, 26, 39
Huron Indians, *See* Wyandot
Huron County (Ohio), 106

Indian Biography, 209
Indian Civilization Act, 96
Indian Removal Act, 87, 96
Indiana (state), 115, 208
Indianapolis (Ind.), 159
Indians. *See names of individual Native American nations*
Inquiry in the Effects of Spiritous Liquors on the Human Body and Mind (Rush), 117
Inskip, John S., 177-81, 199
Iroquois Indians, 41
Ithaca (N.Y.), 62
itinerant preachers. *See* circuit riders

Jacques, Henry, 93
Jackson, Andrew, 87, 89, 92, 111
Jefferson County (Ohio), 117
Jefferson, Thomas, 74
Jennings, Obadiah, 44
Johnson, Charles, 25, 29
Johnson, G.W., 111
Johnston, John, 12, 46, 52, 57, 59-61, 64-67, 77, 82-83, 92-93, 95, 111, 210
Jordan, David, 217
Juvenile Wesleyan Missionary Society, 52

Juvenile Finleyan Missionary Mite Society, 54-55, 57

Kansas (river), 94
Kansas (state), 94, 161, 219
Kentucky Conference, 109-10, 148, 151
Kentucky Penitentiary, 170
Kentucky presbytery, 116
Kentucky (state), 2, 14, 27, 42, 66, 107, 111, 129, 131, 146, 194-95, 202, 208
Kickapoo Indians, 95, 155
Knepper, George, 117
Knox circuit, 7
Knox, Henry, 78
Kobler, John, 16

Ladies Repository and Gatherings of the West, 36, 103, 107, 182
Lakin, Benjamin, 202
Lancaster district, 56
Lancaster (Ohio), 9
Lane debates, 132
Larkin, Jack, 87
Latta, Samuel A., 149-51, 154, 157, 217
learned ministry, Finley's attitude toward, 20-21
Lebanon district, 13, 31, 40, 43, 70, 101, 109, 209
Lebanon (Ohio), 147
Lee, Jason, 27
Letters and Notes on the Manners, Customs, and Conditions of the North American Indians (Catlin), 212
Lewisburg (Ohio), 161, 218
Lexington (Ky.), 66, 117
Leib, John L., 85
Liberty (Ind.), 218
Life Among The Indians (Finley), 100, 207-12
Life of Tecumseh (Drake), 209
Lincoln, Abraham, 121
Lindsey, Marcus, 42, 205
"Lion of the Forest," 9
Lockport (Ill.), 216
Logan (Ohio), 41
Logan County (Ky.), 27

Index

Longstreet, Augustus Baldwin, 144
Louisville (Ky.), 111, 216
Louisville Convention, 148-49
Lucas, Robert, 90

McAdow, Dr. Edward, 4
McArthur, Duncan, 42, 75
McDonald, John, 145, 187, 190, 217
McElvain, John, 90
McGee, William, 27
McHenry, Barnabus, 202
McKelvey, Blake, 177
McKendree, William, 7, 10, 27, 44, 46, 49-50, 55, 58-61, 63-64, 71-72, 130, 188-89, 197-98, 210-11
McKenney, Thomas, 49, 58, 66-67, 69, 77-78, 87, 93, 189
McLean, John, 21, 47, 55, 58, 62, 64, 66, 70, 85, 106, 111-12, 156, 160, 177, 199, 204, 219
McLean, Nathaniel, 55, 70, 86, 204
McLoughlin, William, 32
Mad River and Lake Erie Railroad, 92
Madison, James, 7, 65, 74
Maffit, John N., 102
Maine Law, 126, 128
Maley, George W., 132
Manchester (Ohio), 4, 116
Manley, Robert, 29-30
Marietta (Ohio), 2, 7, 11, 35, 42, 49, 171, 205
Marlay, Michael, 149, 151, 168
Maryland (state), 102
Mason, Thomas, 23, 53, 55-57, 60, 62, 104
Massachusetts Society for the Suppression of Intemperance, 118
Massie, Nathaniel, 2-3, 208
Massie's Settlement (Ohio), 208
Mather, Cotton, 44
Mathews, Donald, 33, 144
Matlack, Lucius C., 134
Mead, A.P., 34
Memorials of Prison Life (Finley), 99-100, 189-93
Methodism, 201; contribution to society, 15-16, 22; expansion of, 10, 14-16, 35, 38; message of, 24-25; preaching, 97
Methodist Book Concern, 22-24, 44, 55, 103-5, 110, 143, 150, 153, 155-56
Methodist *Discipline*, 7, 20, 22, 104, 108, 130, 178, 180, 210
Methodist Episcopal Church South, 95, 148, 153, 155-56, 201
Methodist Episcopal Church, 69, 72, 138; bishops of, 7, 16, 19, 63, 104, 108; circuits of, 7-10, 15-18, 35, 40, 77, 101-2; class meetings, 2, 16-17; deacons, 16; districts of, 7, 8, 18; division of, 143-44; elders, 16, 108; missionary activity in, 40, 43-44, 46-70, 97-99, 209-11; organization of, 15-19; presiding elders of, 22-23, 77, 97, 101, 105-6; rotation system of, 32; services of, 26
Methodist Female Missionary Society, 55, 58, 62
Methodist General Conference, 9, 18, 26, 219; in 1820, 19, 24, 178, 197; in 1828, 23; in 1836, 133; in 1844, 139-44; in 1848, 155-56; in 1852, 180; in 1856, 159-60, 215, 217; alcoholic beverages, policy toward, 117-17; rules regarding slavery, 130, 133-35, 139-41
Methodist Magazine, 34, 45-46, 54, 61, 182
Methodist Missionary Society, 43, 53, 56, 58-59
Methodist Protestant Church, 131
Methodist Quarterly Review, 25, 180, 193, 199, 212
Mexican War, 111-12, 191
Miami district, 28-29, 101
Miami Indians, 75
Miami University, 37, 52, 110
Michaux, F.A., 194
Michigan (state), 93, 208
Michigan Territory, 50
Miley, John, 17
Miller, Perry, 39
Mills, Samuel, 166
Mississippi (river), 73-75, 79-80, 85, 87-89, 92, 127, 158, 211
Mississippi (state), 132
Missouri Fur Company, 77
Missouri (river), 94
Missouri (state), 88-89, 93

Mitchell, Joseph, 139, 143
Miyakawa, T. Scott, 34
Mohawk Indians, 41
Mononcue, 43, 49-50, 61-62, 63, 64, 104
Monroe, James, 64, 74, 78, 80, 87, 187, 211
Monroe (Ohio), 126
Montgomery, James, 43, 66, 110-11
Moody, Granville, 162, 179-80
Moore, Arthur K., 199
Moravian Indians (Delaware), 208
Morris, Thomas A., 36, 94, 102, 111, 115, 140, 186, 213
Mound Hill Union Cemetery, Eaton, 218
Mt. Pleasant (Iowa), 160, 216
Muskingum circuit, 17
Muskingum district, 28

Nashville Advocate, 154, 168
Native Americans, 194, 207-12; treaties with U.S., 12, 14, 42, 73-76, 80, 82, 87, 89-92, 95; Algonquin, 41; Cayuga, 41; Cherokee, 189; Chippewa, 48, 50, 61, 75, 210; Choctaw, 87; Delaware, 48, 75, 82, 94-95, 155, 205, 208; Fox, 87, Iroquois, 41; Kickapoo, 95, 155, 157; Miami, 75; Mohawk, 41; Oneida, 41; Onondaga, 41; Ottawa, 61, 75, 89, 210; Pottawatamie, 75; Sauk, 87; Seneca, 41, 47, 61, 75, 208; Seneca-Cayuga, 95; Shawnee, 3, 46, 89, 95, 155, 157, 208; Sioux, 87; Tarway, 47. *See also* Wyandot
New England, 14
New England Antislavery Society, 132
New England Conference, 132
New England Conference Temperance Society, 118
New Hampshire Conference, 132
New Lebanon (Ohio), 28
"New Market Devil," 1
New Market (Ohio), 1, 6, 16, 116
New Orleans (La.), 8, 158
New Philadelphia (Ohio), 7
New Plymouth (Ohio), 111
New York (city), 56, 62-63, 68, 104, 114, 121, 128, 139, 173

New York Tribune, 139
Newton (Ind.), 115
Newark (Ohio), 118
Newburgh (N.Y.), 62
Nolley, Richmond, 197
North American Review, 87
North Bend (Ohio), 93
North Carolina (state), 2, 27
Northwest Ordinance, 6, 14, 131

O'Ferrall, Simon, 29
Oglesby, Joseph, 203
Ohio Anti-Slavery Society, 134
Ohio Conference, 14, 16, 19, 23-24, 31, 43, 45, 47, 49, 51, 54, 57, 72, 77, 95, 103-4, 106, 109-10, 113, 131, 133-34, 146, 148, 150, 157, 174, 178-80, 185, 196-97, 209, 213
Ohio Constitution, 126
Ohio district, 10, 14, 196-97
Ohio legislature, 165
Ohio Penitentiary, 55, 105, 111, 162-77, 190-93; description of, 164, 166; duties of chaplain, 167; duties of guards, 168-69; inmates attending chapel, 167; inmates, descriptions of, 173-74, 176, 192; library, 171-72
Ohio (state), 165, 208, 219
Ohio (river), 2, 3, 8, 12, 14, 42, 93, 127, 194, 196
Ohio Star, 166
Ohio State Journal, 172
Ohio State Temperance Convention, 126
Ohio University, 110
Ohio Wesleyan Female College, 110
Ohio Wesleyan University, 110, 213
Oklahoma (state), 95
Olin, Stephen, 141
On the Penitentiary System in the United States (Beaumont and Tocqueville), 163
Oneida Indians, 41
Onondaga Indians, 41
Ottawa Indians, 61, 75, 89, 210
Oxford (Ohio), 37, 110

Paine, Robert, 15
Paint Creek (Ohio), 2, 208

Index

Parker, Samuel, 203
Patterson, John, 166
Peck, George, 150, 153
Pennsylvania Prison System, 163
Pennsylvania (state), 14
Pettit, Samuel, 137
Philadelphia (Pa.), 63, 134, 143, 162, 173, 215
Philanthropist, 134
Phillips, William, 206
Piqua Gazette, 84
Piqua (Ohio), 12, 64, 77, 84, 137
Pittsburgh (Pa.), 8, 44
Plan of Separation, 143, 153-54, 156
Plea for the West (Beecher), 114
Poe, Daniel, 206
Porter, James, 33, 143
Porter, Peter B., 86
Portsmouth (Ohio), 36, 101
Pottawatamie Indians, 75
Powell, John Wesley, 42
Priest, Loring, 99
Princeton College, 2
Prison Discipline Society of Boston, 37, 163, 165
prison reform, 37, 162-66
"promiscuous seating," 177-81
Prucha, Francis, 74, 76
Putnam, Rufus, 74, 78

Quarterly Review, 199
Quinn, James, 7, 20

Raper Chapel, 180
Raper, William H., 180, 206
Redman, W.W., 139
reform movements, 37, 78, 115, 117-28, 130-60, 162-66
Remarks on Prisons and Prison Discipline (Dix), 165-66
Republican party, 111, 161, 218
revivals, 1, 4-6, 31-38, 89, 95, 102; excesses in, 31-32; results of, 34-35
Rhon-Yan-Ness, 207
Richey, Russell, 26
Richmond Christian Advocate, 150, 152, 155
Riddle, Elizabeth, 151
Ridgeville, Ohio, 57, 72, 102
Roberts, R.R., 55, 72

Roberts, W.C., 55
Roszel, Stephen, 53-54
Rush, Benjamin, 117, 128, 162; *An Inquiry into the Effects of Spiritous Liquors on the Human Body and Mind*, 117
Russelville (Ohio), 30
Ruter, Martin, 48, 50, 55, 111, 204
Ryan, Daniel, 9

St. Clair, Arthur, 3
St. Clairsville (Ohio), 8, 29, 131
St. Lawrence (river), 40
St. Louis (Mo.), 127, 159, 161
Sale, John, 7, 9, 16, 203
Sandusky district, 47
Sandusky (Ohio), 76
Satz, Ronald N., 75, 87, 98-99
Sauk Indians, 87
Savage, James, 152
Schoolcraft, Henry, 41, 73, 87, 96, 189, 208; *American Indians, The: Their History, Condition and Prospects*, 189
Scioto circuit, 7, 16, 35, 58, 196, 203
Scioto (river), 2-3, 41, 91, 111
Scott, Orange, 133-34, 138
Second Great Awakening, 33, 39, 43
Seneca Indians, 41, 47, 61, 75, 208
Seneca-Cayuga Indians, 95
Shalhope, Robert, 96
Shaw, John, 65-67
Shannon, Wilson, 93
Shawnee Indians, 3, 46, 89, 95, 208
Sioux Indians, 87
Sketches of Western Methodism (Finley), 21, 70, 106, 200-207
slavery, 129-31, 133-45, 147, 151-53, 155, 158-61, 191, 205, 218
Smith, Henry, 16
Smith, John L., 111
Smith, R.D., 145
Society for Alleviating the Miseries of Public Prisons, 162
Sons of Temperance, 121-25; Ohio Division, 123-24
Soule, Joshua, 23, 44, 47, 50, 64, 140, 143, 146-49, 154, 156, 185, 211
South Carolina Conference, 44

Southern Christian Advocate, 144
Southwestern Christian Advocate, 149, 152
Springfield (Ohio), 93, 110, 179
Station Prairie (Ohio), 3
Steubenville circuit, 9
Steubenville (Ohio), 10-12, 16
Stevens, Abel, 9, 130, 155, 180
Stevens, Edward, 125
Stewart, John, 9, 42-43, 46, 49, 55, 65, 93, 99, 129, 205, 209
Stewart, John (of Salenes, Va.), 151
Stockton (Ky.), 129
Stone, Barton W., 5
Storrs, George, 134
Strane, Hannah (later Hannah Finley), 4
Strange, John, 205
Strickland, W.P., 123, 171, 193, 200, 207, 214
Stuart, Paul, 96
Stubbs, Harriet, 47
Sunderland, La Roy, 134, 138
Sutherland, William H., 215
Swayze, William, 55
Sweet, William Warren, 31
Swormstedt, Leroy, 147, 183-86, 190

Tarway Indians, 47
Tecumseh, 7, 209
Tefft, B.F., 190
temperance movement, 114-28
Tennessee, (state), 5, 27, 55
Terrill (N.C.), 27
Thatcher, B.B., 209; *Indian Biography*, 209
Thomas, H.S., 121
Tippecanoe (Ind.), 7
Tiffin, Edward, 3, 203
Tocqueville, Alexis de, 163; *On the Penitentiary System in the United States*, 163
Tomlinson, J.S., 146, 157
Treatise on Class Meetings, A (Miley), 17
Treaty of Greenville, 3, 14, 208, 211
Treaty of St. Mary's, 76
Trimble, Allen, 56, 214
Trimble, Joseph, 110-11, 151, 179, 214

Trollope, Frances, 31
Troy, (Ohio), 105
True Presbyterian, 158
Tyler, John, 92

Ulin, John, 206
Union (Ohio), 105
United Methodist Historical Society of Ohio, 183
United States Bank, 12
United States Bureau of Indian Affairs, 96
United States Department of War, 58, 64, 69, 84-87, 90-91, 96
United States Department of Indian Affairs, 61, 90-91, 94-95, 97
United States government Indian policy, 44, 58, 73-100
United States Office of Indian Trade, 77, 96
United States Supreme Court, 156
United States Treasury Department, 58, 70-72
Upper Sandusky (Ohio), 13, 40-42, 46, 50, 55-56, 60, 64-66, 69, 72, 75, 84-85, 89-92, 94, 98, 101, 110, 209, 212
Urbana (Ohio), 50, 93, 145

Vaux, Robert, 162
Vicksburg (Miss.), 145
Vincennes (Ind.), 74
Virginia (state), 14

Walker, George W., 104-5, 150, 178-79
Walker, William, 72, 84, 89, 91, 185
War of 1812, 38, 42, 76, 105
Ware, Thomas, 23
Warrenton (Ohio), 16
Warwick, A.N., 126
Washburn, Wilcomb, 96
Washington County (Ohio), 31, 206
Washington, D.C., 63-65, 112
Washington, George, 76
Washington Union Daughters of Temperance, 127
Washingtonian Temperance Society, 121
Wayne, Anthony, 3, 14, 42, 208
Webster, Daniel, 37
Weisberger, Bernard, 33

Index

Wentz, Richard, 29
Wesley, John, 44, 117
Wesleyan Antislavery Society, 134
Wesleyan Methodist Connection of America, 138
West Union (Ohio), 2
West Wheeling circuit, 8
Western Christian Advocate, 23, 35, 91, 93, 103, 108, 110, 127, 133-34, 146, 148-50, 154-55, 158, 160, 170, 178-79, 182-83, 185, 199, 212, 214-16, 218
Western Conference, 7-8, 14, 16, 22, 28, 131
Western Historical Society, 183
Western Methodist Book Concern, 103-4, 183-84, 204
Whig Party, 111-12, 114
Wheeler, James, 93
Wheeling, Virginia, 102
White Oak Creek, 4
Wiley, A., 139
Williams, Mary, 170
Wills Creek circuit, 7, 196
Wilmington (Ohio), 145
Winchester (Ind.), 218
Woods, John, 85-86
Worthington Female Academy, 109
Worthington (Ohio), 52, 109
Worthington, Thomas, 3-4, 16, 111
Wright, Elizur Jr., 36
Wright, John F., 144, 156, 183-86
Wright, John S., 117
Wyandot Indians, 40-73, 53, 63, 71, 75-76, 155-57, 185, 187-89, 205, 207, 209-12; attitude toward Finley, 45, 49, 64, 89, 97; camp meetings, 49, 70, 91, 182; customs, 40-43, 45; early history, 40-43; preference for Ohio Conference, 157; removal from Ohio, 80-82, 85-86, 89-94, 98, 211; removal policies toward, 74, 80-83, 87, 90, 95-96, 97-99; response to removal policy, 80, 83, 89-93; reservation improvements, 59-60, 81, 84-85, 92; store, 59, 85; treaties with U.S., 42, 73-78, 80, 89-92, 95; trip to Missouri, 89-90; U.S. citizenship, 95; Wyandot mission, 13, 40, 42-72, 77; mission church, 53, 64-65, 67, 69-72, 93, 98, 99; mission school, 46, 50-54, 58, 64-65, 69-70, 72, 79, 85

Xenia (Ohio), 54, 93, 105, 112, 185

Yellow Springs (Ohio), 213
Young, David, 9-10, 17, 38, 57, 59, 64, 70, 88, 113, 118, 155, 178, 198
Young, Jacob, 30, 49, 55-56, 106, 109-10, 148, 160, 179-80
Young Men's Prison Society, 166
Young, William, 204
Youngstown (Ohio), 106

Zanesville (Ohio), 7, 10, 38, 56, 88, 119, 125, 155
Zanesville district, 105, 146
Zion's Herald, 180-81, 212
Zion's Herald and Wesleyan Journal, 152

www.ingramcontent.com/pod-product-compliance
Lightning Source LLC
Chambersburg PA
CBHW022053160426
43198CB00008B/218